ABOVE ALL EARTHLY POW'RS

Above All Earthly Pow'rs

Christic in a Postmodern World

—⦿⦿⦿—

DAVID F. WELLS

WILLIAM B. EERDMANS PUBLISHING COMPANY
GRAND RAPIDS, MICHIGAN / CAMBRIDGE, U.K.

© 2005 Wm. B. Eerdmans Publishing Co.

All rights reserved

Wm. B. Eerdmans Publishing Co.

2140 Oak Industrial Drive N.E., Grand Rapids, Michigan 49505 /

P.O. Box 163, Cambridge CB3 9PU U.K.

Paperback edition 2006

Printed in the United States of America

13 12 11 10 09 08   9 8 7 6 5 4

Library of Congress Cataloging-in-Publication Data

Wells, David F.

Above all earthly pow'rs: Christ in a postmodern world / David F. Wells.

p.   cm.

Includes bibliographical references (p.   ) and index.

ISBN 978-0-8028-2455-4 (pbk.: alk. paper)

1. Postmodernism — Religious aspects — Christianity.

I. Title: Above all earthly powers.   II. Title.

BR115.P74W45   2005

261'.0973 — dc22

2005050063

www.eerdmans.com

To

McKenna, Caitlin, Caleb, Megan, Reagan, and Allison

The Lord bless you and keep you:
The Lord make his face to shine upon you,
and be gracious to you:
The Lord lift up his countenance upon you,
and give you peace.

NUMBERS 6:24-26

Contents

—⟨ℓℓℓℓ⟩—

Preface	xi
Introduction	1
The Front Lines	5
Christ and Context	6
I. Miracles of Modern Splendor	13
Outside In, Inside Out	17
The Heretical Persuasion	25
The Modern Revolution	31
Gone with the Wind	33
Hollow Chests	48
Miracles of (Human) Power	52
II. Postmodern Rebellion	60
The Withering of the Enlightenment Soul	62
Modernity to Postmodernity	62
The Postmodern Outlooks	67
No (Comprehensive) Worldview	74

CONTENTS

	On Having a Worldview	74
	Consumer Culture/Postmodern Culture	75
	The Way Things Were	79
	No Truth	84
	No Purpose	88
III.	**Migrations, the Banquet of Religion, and Pastiche Spirituality**	**91**
	Pizza, Bagels, and Fish on Fridays	96
	Enchiladas, Chow Mein, and Soul Food	104
	The New Spiritual Quest	109
	The Third Stream	109
	The House or the Journey?	119
IV.	**Christ in a Spiritual World**	**125**
	The New Spiritual Yearning	127
	An Ancient Spirituality	136
	A Spirituality of Postmodernity	145
	The Empty Landscape	146
	"My Own Little Voice"	149
	It's About Me	152
	Confrontation, Not Tactics	155
	Fragmented, Not Innocent	164
	Public, Not Private	168
	Personal, Not Impersonal	175
V.	**Christ in a Meaningless World**	**177**
	The Culture of Nothingness	178
	Bewilderment	178
	The Black Hole	181
	Suicide to Snickers	184

Contents

Fear, Anxiety, and Dread   188

When the Future Dies   191

This Side of the Sun   194

God Whispers in the Night   199

God Reaches Down   203

    The Presence of Eternity   203

    Majestic Condescension   212

    Grace Triumphant   218

VI. Christ in a Decentered World   **233**

An Open Future   234

    From Experience to Philosophy   234

    From Freedom to Danger   238

    From Providence to Bad Luck   240

An Open Theology   242

    Libertarian and Autonomous   248

    Autonomous and Decentered   249

Christ the Center   251

    Creation's Center   251

    The Church's Center   258

VII. Megachurches, Paradigm Shifts, and the New Spiritual Quest   **263**

Why Do Church Differently?   268

    The New Seeker   269

    Evangelicalism Falters   269

    The New Marketplace   270

    The New Social Environment   274

    Old Fears   277

Business as Usual   283

Growing the Church   288

CONTENTS

    Gated (Spiritual) Communities   288

No Entry   292

    Birds of a Feather   293

    Selling the Faith   297

VIII. The Day of New Beginnings   **310**

God's Open Door   311

The Call to Authenticity   314

Bibliography   318

Index   335

Preface

———❦❦❦———

I am most appreciative to the Trustees of Gordon-Conwell Theological Seminary for their continued support of the sabbatical program for faculty. Without a sustained period away from everyday responsibilities, it would be quite difficult to do serious research and thinking. So it was that this particular book began with a half-sabbatical.

Before this book saw the light of day, it was my privilege to present some of its substance in other parts of the world. In fact, while it was just in an infant stage I gave two lectures from its material at the Jonathan Edwards Institute in Maryland in 2002 and in 2004. In 2004, I also traveled to Australia and was the guest of the three theological colleges in Sydney: Moore Theological College, Sydney Missionary and Bible College, and the Presbyterian Centre. My subject in each was "Christ in the Postmodern World." During this same visit, I traveled to New Zealand to give three plenary addresses at the World Evangelical Congregational Fellowship. My subject was "The Uniqueness of Christ," and I drew off some of the material in this book. Finally, it was my privilege to give the Kistemaker Academic Lectures at Reformed Theological Seminary, Orlando, in 2005. There I explored some of the themes of current spirituality which are mentioned in this book as well as their consequences for the Church today.

An author's debts are always very large and most of them quite impossible to acknowledge. Sometimes the reading of a book mostly unrelated to one's current focus is what starts a stream of thought that ends up moving the project forward unexpectedly. These are the delightful experiences that one remembers long afterward. They are, of course, sometimes matched by surprises of a different kind, for at other times one can read assiduously in places that seem the most promising only to end up empty-handed! I think it will be clear in the pages which follow which books I have been able to mine most effectively, whose authors have become a fraternity of discourse without whose thought these pages would have been a lot emptier.

Some of one's debts, however, are not as obvious as this, and they come more from the example of others and of how they have done their work. It is to a rich circle of friends whose work I know, from whom I have profited in so many ways, that I do, indeed, owe a great debt of gratitude. It would be impossible to name them all, but some stand out especially: John Stott, whose home I shared for some years and whose doctrinal fidelity and clarity of expression have always been an example to me; Jim Packer, whom I first heard speak when I was a theological student in London many years ago and with whom I subsequently worked on several projects, who exemplifies both theological brilliance and deep piety as part and parcel of each other; Carl Henry, who regularly visited the institution in which I taught and whom I remember for the way in which he put his considerable theological acumen to work in leading the evangelical world to a more authentic expression of its belief; Francis Schaeffer, with whom my wife and I worked for a time at L'Abri, Switzerland, and who, for me at least, was a pioneer in thinking about the Christian engagement with contemporary culture; Martyn Lloyd-Jones, whose extraordinary expositions I heard weekly over a period of years and whose vision of the greatness and grandeur of God have left a lasting impression on me; Os Guinness, with whom I sat in the same courses in preparation for the dreaded final examinations for the University of London B.D. and whose work in applying the insights of sociology to the issues evangelicalism faces has been so helpful; George Marsden and Mark Noll, historians both and historians of a very high order, with whom for a period of time I taught in the same institution and from whose skill in showing the context of ideas I learned a lot; and finally my own faculty colleagues who have provided what I suspect is a rarity in academia, a fraternity of common interests and uncommon stimulation.

Parts of the manuscript were read by Os Guinness, Gary Parrott, and Garth Rosell. I am grateful for their kindness and help in doing this. Needless to say, the responsibility for these pages is mine alone. From those who have heard the small parts of this study which I have delivered, I have received enough encouragement to think that it is, indeed, mining a vein of legitimate concern in the Church, as well as addressing legitimate questions about how to construct a Christian presence in our postmodern world. With this encouragement beneath its wings, this study now takes flight.

Introduction

———⟨ₒₒₒ⟩———

Tuesday, September 11, 2001.

    The weather in Boston was clear, the sky cloudless, the air crisp, the trees showing just the first hint of fall color. That was the day that two jets left Logan International Airport for California but were hijacked and, a short time later, flown into the towers of the World Trade Center in New York. Thousands of people who thought they were beginning another ordinary day were killed in an extraordinary way. Two other jets were also hijacked that day, one ending up in the side of the Pentagon and the other in a field in Pennsylvania, the latter thanks to brave, bare-handed anti-terrorist action on board. On that day the United States suffered its worst act of terrorism, a ghastly moment of cold, callous, calculated mass murder. It left a gaping hole in the nation's heart and images of chaos and wreckage etched forever in its memory.

    In the days that followed, as dazed Americans watched the pictures from the crash scenes, the distractions that make up the noisy surface where we live were stripped away. It is, of course, the rather mundane routines and events of life that give it a sense of daily normalcy. But these were not normal days and much of the surface clutter simply stopped. It suddenly seemed indecent, inappropriate, in light of this stark, unrelieved tragedy.

    Television cleansed itself of its incessant barrage of commercials

1

and, for a few days, offered uninterrupted coverage of the unfolding events. And how could we ponder this appalling loss and, at the same time, sit back to watch the Miss America beauty pageant or the Emmy Awards? They were canceled. The late-night comedians fled the air. Hollywood studios were quick to finger this pulse and revisited their decisions regarding what movies would be released in the fall. While the nation paused, trying to comprehend this tragedy and the reasons behind it, radio stations thought it might be wise to do a little self-censoring, so some songs were dropped from the roster, like Metallica's "Seek and Destroy," Soundgarden's "Blow Up the Outside World," and the Stone Temple Pilots' "Dead and Bloated." Even the usual bickering and destructiveness of the political process, driven by the competition for power and ever feasting on the nation's social divisions, stopped overnight. National purpose now loomed over these squabbles. It suddenly — and unusually — seemed to be a bigger thing than narrow, partisan interest. Indeed, the politicians seemed almost to have been shamed into attending to matters of national concern.

At all the crash scenes, but especially in New York, onlookers gazed in sad awe at the smoking wreckage, buildings and planes twisted into grotesque shapes and hiding within them the crushed bodies of those taken down. The nation's attention was simultaneously riveted on the heroic actions of those who worked with such determination, and amidst such tiredness, to find any who might still be alive. Here, too, was another telling juxtaposition: the terrorists' dark hatred and the remarkable bravery and fortitude of those who continued to dig for the lost. Many years before, President John Adams, after having suffered a number of personal losses in his life, and with a war raging in Russia where his son was at the time, wrote to his friend Benjamin Rush to say that "war necessarily brings with it some virtues, and great and heroic virtues, too," though he added that it would be nice if those virtues did not have to await a tragedy before becoming so obvious.[1] They were certainly obvious in the days and months that followed the September 11 attack.

At the Pentagon, near the jagged hole in the side of the building, rescue workers unfurled a huge American flag and draped it down the

---

1. David McCullough, *John Adams* (New York: Simon and Schuster, 2001), 609.

side of the building, a symbol of the nation's solidarity and of its refusal to yield before the evil which had been visited on it. And throughout America, in a gesture of pride and unity, the flag was likewise hung by front doors, on mailboxes, on car antennae, in shop windows, and from overpasses. As is often the case in America, however, this quickly turned to excess as merchants seized the moment to produce pins and other items with the image of the flag, and television commercials likewise exploited the tragedy and the surge in patriotic fervor which followed it, and even the government produced its budget wrapped in covers of Old Glory. Yet the surge of unashamed patriotism, and the sadness, undergirded America's new business, which was to find and destroy the networks in the world whose business was to terrorize. The country was now put on a war footing.

Something else that was unusual seemed to happen overnight, too. The word *Evil* returned to people's vocabulary. In a culture strongly influenced by postmodern thought, of course, Evil is conceptually absent. Indeed, prior to this event, the moral majority in America was made up of those who do not believe in moral absolutes. In the absence of enduring standards of right and wrong, in all places and times, we are, unfortunately, stripped of our ability to speak of Good and Evil. Good and Evil contract. In the absence of absolutes, these words go no deeper than our feelings about our personal circumstances, be they pleasant or unpleasant, satisfactory or boring. And what is good for one may not be good for another. But how could Americans, or anyone else, speak of this appalling attack without recourse to a language about Evil which goes far beyond saying what they simply disliked? In view of the carnage that had been wrought, there was a deep need to speak of what is enduringly, eternally wrong. This, however, turned out to be no easy matter because the postmodern conceptual cloud cover had not been dispersed. If the word *Evil* peppered talk about these events, it was also the case that the great majority in America had no framework in which Evil had its place.

In fact, one of the casualties of September 11 appears to have been God himself. Before the terrorist attacks, 72% of Americans affirmed their belief that God is omnipotent and in control of the world, but afterwards that figure dropped to 68%. And just before the attacks occurred, 38% affirmed their belief in moral absolutes which are true for all times and places and not determined by circumstance, but in the days immediately following the attack only 22% were willing to affirm that.[2] The language of evil had become a verbal necessity after September 11, but it remained a cultural and conceptual difficulty. That this was the case was all too evident a year later when signs were popping up all over the cultural landscape suggesting that outrage over the attack was out of order. For example, the National Education Association advised teachers to offer no value judgments to their students on the occasion of the anniversary of the attacks, and the bishops of the United Methodist Church declared that all violence fell into the same moral category, thereby making no distinction between those who used violence to attack and those who used it in self-defense. Without moral absolutes, the business of making moral judgments becomes impossible, although few seemed to see the anomaly that was at work: that those who take the position that judgments should not be rendered on behavior are, often unbeknownst to themselves, also taking a moral position.

This event which was so unexpected, so terrible, and so psychologically intrusive brought into clearer focus a number of other issues. Three of them are particularly germane to this study. First of all, there is the fact that for all of the talk about how America changed after this event there remains an uneasy sense that American culture is actually little different after the event from what it was before — that it still is morally and spiritually adrift and in this it is no different from the other Western countries. Second, the global ambitions of radical Islam called attention to the many Muslims in the West and this, in turn, was a reminder of the West's growing ethnic and religious complexity. To this America is no exception for, in a short period of time, it has become the world's most religiously diverse nation. Third, this moment of tragedy and evil shone its own light on the Church and what we came to see was not a happy sight. For what has become conspicuous by its scarcity, and not least in the evangelical corner of it, is a spiritual *gravitas,* one which could match the depth of horrendous evil and address issues of such seriousness. Evangelicalism, now much absorbed by the arts and tricks of marketing, is simply not very serious anymore.

2. George Barna, "How America's Faith Has Changed Since 9-11," http// www.barna.org.

The Front Lines

These three issues do, of course, have their connections. The first two, I believe, are the major defining cultural realities with which the Church must now intentionally engage: first, the disintegration of the Enlightenment world and its replacement by the postmodern ethos and, second, the fact that through the changed immigration law of 1965, America has become a truly multiethnic society and perhaps the most religiously diverse one in the world. The exotic religions from faraway places that once only filled pages of *National Geographic* may now be next door. Mosques, landmarks that once seemed confined to the Middle East, can now be seen side by side with churches in America, though much of the practice of Islam is also invisible to most people. America is now home to more Hispanics than African Americans; Arabs are coming close to drawing even with Jews in number; and there are more Muslims than Episcopalians, or Congregationalists, or Eastern Orthodox, or Mormons. The arrival of old, non-Christian religions in America and the emergence of more recent spiritualities that are not religious, and often not institutionalized, are a new circumstance. This means that the relation of Christ to non-Christian religions, as well as to these personally constructed spiritualities, is no longer a matter of theorizing from a safe distance but rather a matter of daily encounter in neighborhoods, in schools, at work, at the gas station, and at the supermarket. And what will prove to be even more momentous in the evangelical world than its engagement with the other religions, I believe, will be whether it is able to distinguish what it has to offer from the emergence of these forms of spirituality. Therapeutic spiritualities which are non-religious begin to look quite like evangelical spirituality which is therapeutic and non-doctrinal.

These two developments — the emergence of the postmodern ethos and the growing religious and spiritual diversity — are by no means parallel or even complementary but they are unmistakably defining American culture in a significantly new way. And they are defining the context within which the Church must live out its life. Already there are some signs that this engagement with culture is not exactly going the Church's way. It was certainly noticeable that following September 11 the Church was mostly unable to offer any public reading on the tragedy which did anything more than commiserate with those who had lost loved ones. There was virtually no Christian interpretation, no wrestling with the meaning of Evil, little thought about the Cross where Christians contend its back was broken.

Christ and Context

In 1984, I wrote a traditional christology entitled *The Person of Christ: A Biblical and Historical Analysis of the Incarnation.* This volume was part of a series in which each of the authors was asked to follow the same format: about one third was to be devoted to the biblical materials, one third to historical developments, and the remaining third to a discussion of three or four contemporary thinkers. This is the sort of foundational work which needs to be done in developing a christology. The questions which such an account seeks to address are almost always those that are *internal* to the Church or to academia. This is entirely appropriate. These issues, such as how the person of Christ is spoken of by the different authors of the New Testament, how these lines of thought were taken up in the early Church, how they were debated, how the Chalcedonian Definition sought to resolve these discussions and what heresies fell outside the boundaries it prescribed, what happened in the Middle Ages and Reformation, and why it is that many modern christologies begin on the premise that Chalcedon must be rejected, are central and necessary considerations in a christology. However, it has become increasingly clear to me that while these internal issues are of vital importance, they are not the only issues that should be engaging the Church. They are the indispensable, foundational questions but they do not comprise everything that the Church should be thinking about with respect to the person of Christ. There are also issues that are *external* in nature which should accompany this foundational work. These are concerned with how a christology faces off against, how it engages, its own cultural context.

Those most self-consciously biblical in their views have often eschewed this work, and their suspicions about it are not entirely unjustified. There is a long trail of contextualized theologies, written over the last half century, in which the external dimension virtually replaces the

6

internal, cultural interests eclipse biblical norms, and the result has been the kind of compromise, trendiness, and manipulation which ends up promoting worldly agendas, be they political, social, ideological, or personal, in place of biblical truth. This has been a sorry tale. And somewhere in the making of each of its works the fatal step was taken to allow the culture to say what God's story should sound like rather than insisting that theology is not theology if it is not listening to God telling his own story in his own way. Karl Barth was right to assert that theology "is itself a word, a human response; yet what makes it theology is not its own word or response but the Word which it hears and to which it *responds.* Theology stands or falls with the Word of God, for the Word of God precedes all theological words by creating, arousing, and challenging them."[3] And he goes on to say that if theology wants to be something other than a response to the Word — and I would wish to insist gently that we should understand "Word" as being the *biblical* Word — it will rapidly become empty, futile, and without meaning. There is much in the story of contextualization which proves how futile and empty it became precisely because it did not allow the biblical Word of God to summon it to its task and to judge the results.

That being the case, the volume which I wrote earlier, in 1984, remains foundational to this present volume. The conclusions which I reached then are unchanged today. I ended that volume by saying that "Christ's work was work that only God could do, and that he could only do it in union with flesh that was ours." In Christ, "men and women in all ages and cultures have found that for which [the] deepest impulses of their nature cry out." Not only so, but in him "they have found their Creator and Redeemer." Even more than that, in Christ and through him, we see "the exposition of God's character and ways, the declaration of his love and judgment, the fulfillment of his intention for creation."[4] Nothing has changed in these conclusions nor should anything change in them for they echo the biblical testimony. What has changed is a growing concern on my part to be able to say more exactly how Christ, in whom divine majesty and human frailty are joined in one per-

3. Karl Barth, *Evangelical Theology: An Introduction,* trans. Grover Foley (London: Weidenfeld and Nicholson, 1963), 16-17.
4. David F. Wells, *The Person of Christ: A Biblical and Historical Analysis* (Westchester: Crossway Books, 1984), 179.

A mighty fortress is our God,
A bulwark never failing;
Our helper he amid the flood
Of mortal ills prevailing.
For still our ancient foe
Doth seek to work us woe;
His craft and pow'r are great,
And, armed with cruel hate,
On earth is not his equal.

That word above all earthly pow'rs,
No thanks to them, abideth;
The Spirit and the gifts are ours
Thru him who with us sideth.
Let goods and kindred go,
This mortal life also.
The body they may kill;
God's truth abideth still:
His kingdom is forever.

Martin Luther, *ca.* 1529,
trans. 1853

son, is to be heard, and is to be preached, in a postmodern, multiethnic, multireligious society.

If it is the case that contextualized theologies have all too often become a doomed enterprise, the reason, the most self-consciously biblical believe, is that the project itself is unnecessary. And there is something to be said for this argument, too. For it is certainly the case that the Word of God, read or preached, has the power to enter the innermost crevices of a person's being, to shine light in unwanted places, to explode the myths and deceits by which fallen life sustains itself, and to bring that person face to face with the eternal God. It is this biblical Word which God uses to bring repentance, to excite faith, to give new life, to sustain that life once given, to correct, nurture, and guide the

Church (Jer. 23:29; II Tim. 3:16; Heb. 4:12; Jas. 1:18). The biblical Word is self-authenticating under the power of the Holy Spirit. This Word of God is the means by which God accomplishes his saving work in his people, and this is a work that no evangelist and no preacher can do. This is why the dearth of serious, sustained biblical preaching in the Church today is a serious matter. When the Church loses the Word of God it loses the very means by which God does his work. In its absence, therefore, a script is being written, however unwittingly, for the Church's undoing, not in one cataclysmic moment, but in a slow, inexorable slide made up of piece by tiny piece of daily dereliction.

These objections to undertaking this kind of study are not, however, fatal. Indeed, not to proceed would be an unhappy outcome because theology, if it is true to its own nature, must be missiological in its intent.[5] Its task is not only to understand the nature of biblical truth but also to ask how that truth addresses the issues of the day. Churches today, who send out missionaries to other parts of the world, would be considered greatly mistaken if they instructed those missionaries to depend only on the Word of God and not to attempt to understand the people to whom they have been sent to minister. By the same token, evangelical theology should not need to justify any attempt that it makes to understand the context into which it is called to speak. If there is self-justification to be made, it is by those theologians who, as D. M. Baillie observed, "are apt to be deaf to the questionings of the outside world."[6]

---

5. I have developed the missiological nature of theology in several essays which deal with its methodology: "The Nature and Function of Theology," *The Use of the Bible in Theology*, ed. Robert K. Johnston (Atlanta: John Knox Press, 1983), 175-99; "An American Evangelical Theology: The Painful Transition from *Theoria* to *Praxis*," *Evangelicalism and Modern America*, ed. George Marsden (Grand Rapids: William B. Eerdmans, 1984), 83-93; "Word and World: Biblical Authority and the Quandary of Modernity," *Evangelical Affirmations*, ed. Kenneth S. Kantzer and Carl F. Henry (Grand Rapids: Zondervan, 1990), 153-76; "The Theologian's Craft," *Doing Theology in Today's World: Essays in Honor of Kenneth S. Kantzer*, ed. John Woodbridge and Thomas McComiskey (Grand Rapids: Zondervan, 1991), 171-94; and "The Theology of Preaching," *God's Living Word: Essays in Preaching*, ed. Theodore Stylianopoulis (Brookline: Holy Cross Press, 1983), 57-70.

6. D. M. Baillie, *God Was in Christ: An Essay on Incarnation and Atonement* (London: Faber and Faber, 1956), 59.

In an older but telling novel, *The Ugly American,* the reader early on is introduced to Louis Sears. Sears has been a popular U.S. Senator for eighteen years but loses his bid for reelection. His preference, after this loss, is to receive a judgeship but since there are no openings, he finally settles on becoming the United States' ambassador to the fictional Asian country of Sarkhan. However, he neither learns the language nor the customs of this country. Indeed, he forbids his staff from becoming too involved in Sarkhanese society. The problem which arises, of course, is that he does not know what is happening, since he cannot read the papers, and in Sarkhanese society, etiquette does not allow for translators to pass on bad news to the person for whom they are translating. Furthermore, he cannot communicate American interests to most people since he does not speak their language and they do not understand his.

The haplessness of this situation becomes evident early on when a shipment of rice, carried aboard American ships, and driven inland by American trucks, is presented to the people with smiles by American officials. Unbeknownst to them, however, Communists have stenciled onto each sack the words, "This rice is a gift from Russia." Yet the words are written in Sarkhanese, which none of the Americans there can understand. This ignorance is such a boon to the Soviets, who are attempting to penetrate the country, that their Ambassador sends back a dispatch shortly after this event worrying that the English press, which has become quite critical of the American Ambassador, might succeed in having him recalled. The Soviet Ambassador proposes that a biting critique of Sears appear in the Soviet journal, *Pravda,* as a way of building up his importance in American eyes and thereby preserving his place in Sarkhan![7]

Perhaps, then, we might say that on the one end we have those theologies which have learned Sarkhanese, learned the local culture and habits, but have lost touch with the country whose policies and interests they are supposed to represent as ambassadors. Instead, having cut themselves loose, they have come to see their role as simply representing their own agendas and policies and passing these off as if they were those of the country whose ambassadors they supposedly are. On

---

7. William J. Lederer and Eugene Burdick, *The Ugly American* (New York: W. W. Norton, 1958).

the other end, we have those theologies which are self-consciously am-bassadorial but which fail to learn the Sarkhanese language and cus-toms. Thus they are hobbled in their ability to communicate both the content of, and the reasons for, their country's policy decisions.

In attempting to complete the work in christology which I began in 1984, I should make it clear, I am writing from the perspective of his-toric Protestantism. I am also doing so as an observer of and partici-pant in the evangelical world. And I am doing so at the very moment when American culture is undergoing a drastic change in cultural mood, thereby transforming the missionary context in which the Church is living. Modernity itself is in deep crisis, and the postmodern ethos which is sweeping over it is bringing not only some relief to evan-gelical faith which had been abandoned on the margins by modernity, but also a whole new set of challenges. This crisis is creating a world which is quite different from the world evangelicalism inhabited in the early years following World War II.

And yet, the history of the church shows that in every generation there are cultural challenges, in some places hostility against religion, overt persecution, difficulties of every kind, and yet generation after generation the Church has joyfully proclaimed the greatness of Christ and his humility in assuming our flesh, taking upon him our sin as if it were his own, and in conquering that sin also conquering both its con-sequence of death and the devil. The looming threats of aggressive reli-gions, of hostile government powers, of tribes and nations bound in their opposition to Christ, are no match for the power of God made known in the gospel. Even in moments of persecution, from dark pris-ons, this greatness of Christ has still been proclaimed. And so it is here.

The two motifs which are transforming culture — the emergence of the postmodern ethos and the new, growing tidal wave of religious pluralism — are deep and powerful currents that are flowing through the nation. But they are not peculiar to America. In fact, Europe appears to be well ahead of the United States in its experience of postmodernity and it also appears to be caught in more painful perplexity about immi-gration and its consequences. Yet there is nothing in the modern world that is a match for the power of God and nothing in modern culture which diminishes our understanding of the greatness of Christ. It is from this vantage point that we must now begin our journey.

It starts, in the first two chapters, in the postmodern world, where we will consider why it is that such hard times have befallen modernity. We will think about the postmodern mood which has followed the crisis in modernity. In the third chapter, I take up the changing patterns in immigration following the rewriting of the law in 1965 and explore the rearranged spiritual landscape which has accompanied these changes. In the three chapters which follow I have attempted to think about the message of Christ from within this postmodern world which I have spent time describing. In these, I take up the theme of spirituality, which really speaks with the soul of postmodernity, and the two ways in which postmodern unbelief is expressing itself in the language of the meaninglessness and decenteredness of life. In these chapters, I am self-consciously ambassadorial, representing the policies and positions of my country, so to speak, but hoping to do so in a way that connects with the preoccupations and mental habits of the Sarkhanese. I then examine, and weigh, the most important large-scale attempt at the churchly level of engaging postmodern culture. It is the new ways of "doing church" among the "seeker sensitive." I find myself viewing all of this sometimes with a sense of bemusement and sometimes of befuddlement. It has left me wondering if, in these churches, ambassadorial language is being heard or if the practitioners of this new churchly mode have simply decided that they are only going to speak Sarkhanese: Sarkhanese, that is, passing itself off as being ambassadorial.

This is the final volume in a series that began with the publication of *No Place for Truth: or, What Ever Happened to Evangelical Theology?* in 1993. This project was the result of an extremely generous grant from the Pew Foundation for which I am still grateful. It launched me on an undertaking that has lasted a full decade. After *No Place for Truth* came *God in the Wasteland: The Reality of Truth in a World of Fading Dreams* in 1994, and this was followed in 1998 by *Losing Our Virtue: Why the Church Must Recover Its Moral Vision.* In these volumes, I have been exploring the places of intersection between different aspects of the Christian confession and our (post)modern world.

This volume, then, brings this personal literary odyssey to its conclusion. For those kind enough to want to read what I have written, the last leg of the journey begins on the next page.

CHAPTER I

Miracles of Modern Splendor

—◈◈◈—

Her hair was totally 1950s Woolworth perfume clerk. You know — sweet but dumb — she'll marry her way out of the trailer park some day soon. But the dress was early '60s Aeroflot stewardess — you know — that really sad blue the Russians used before they all started wanting to buy Sonys and having Guy Laroche design their Politburo caps. And such makeup! Perfect 70s Mary Quant, with these little PVC floral appliqué earrings that looked like antiskid bathtub stickers from a gay Hollywood tub circa 1956. She really caught the sadness — she was the hippest person there. Totally.

DOUGLAS COUPLAND

We think little about the world. We think about the things that it imposes upon us. We must think about the workplace, about appointments we have made, people we will meet, and jobs that must get done. We must think about car maintenance and train schedules, neighbors and parents, life insurance and taxes, groceries and vacations, dangers and death. We cannot avoid the sudden, painful emptiness left behind by a death, and we would not want to miss the moment when we are allowed to enter a small child's enchanted world. In a thousand ways, every day, we think about the world of which we are a part, the world we experience. We think about what we must give it, do for it, do with it, or do without it, and we think about how we will use it or how we wish we could use it.

We do not, however, often think about the world at a deeper level. We no more wonder about it than we do about the sun or moon. We take it as a given, like the fact that Tuesday has always followed Monday, May has always followed April, summer has always followed winter, and in New England, the Red Sox, as far as memory records, have always faded in fall just as the leaves are coming into their full glory. (It is a funny coincidence: both are dying but only the leaves are worth watching.) There was an interruption in the pattern in 2004, but all Red Sox fans know that normality will soon return!

That the world might have been different from what it is, that it might yet be different, that the West might yet succumb to its own self-induced sicknesses and, like a worn-out old dinosaur, topple over and die, making the species finally extinct, seems inconceivable. Thinking about these things seems as worthless as pondering under what circumstances water might be induced to flow uphill, or time stop its relentless ticking, or ocean tides might be held back from their rhythmic advance toward and retreat from the shore. These things just are. And that is why we do not think more deeply about the world. It just is.

It is as familiar to us as an old pair of shoes. It is true, we live in only one small part of it, we work only one small corner of it, we know only a few of the billions who inhabit the planet, but television and the Internet do much to fill out the picture for us. And, for the most part, it is quite an agreeable circumstance — at least here in the West. It is true that anxiety, loneliness, insecurity, and boredom are our occasional, or even frequent, companions but medical care is at hand, the malls are filled with more goods than even King Midas might have wanted, and ours is a day of manifest liberations from all external authorities except on the boundaries where freedoms cross the line into illegalities. So, we are able to think a lot about ourselves, how we might best beguile away our time, and what will most satisfy our needs. We do not think much about the world or why it is as it is.

The world does not strike us as a particularly dangerous place here in the West. There are pockets of lawlessness, we know, streets that should not be walked at night, and there are new kinds of lawbreakers, like the white-collar thieves who work with computers and who have made our sense of security a little less robust. Yet the West in general and America in particular is to us a place of plenty, of opportunity, and of choices, not a place where we feel greatly endangered. We certainly do not think of it as a place where we can lose our souls. If such thoughts do cross our minds, we would be inclined to suppose that souls are lost by doing large and inhumane acts of evil, not by living in the realm of shallow and empty triviality where so much of our life is moored. We live not out in the depths of what is truly wrong, but on the surfaces where nothing is right or wrong and nothing really matters. Others, however, have not been quite so sanguine about this state of affairs.

Karl Marx had his own (utopian) agenda, of course, but he was re-markably prescient in seeing what was coming in this our Western world where everything solid has melted into air. So, too, was Ma-hatma Gandhi. He feared the West as well. He thought that the Western acids that dissolve all beliefs and morality would be brought to India by the use of technology. He therefore urged Indians to resist it, especially in the fabric industry, and preserve the old ways of spinning, weaving, and cloth making. By that point, however, India had significantly pene-trated the international market and there was no turning back. It was one of the few political setbacks Gandhi suffered which was perma-nent. What these outside eyes saw, however, is lost on us. They feared the West; we do not. We have no fear of it at all. It is, after all, the hand that feeds us with more affluence, more opportunities, more choices, more miracle drugs, more pleasurable distraction than any civilization has ever known. We are now so much a part of its workings, we are now so addicted to its largesse, that life is inconceivable without these blessings of our modernized world. But what does all of this do to us? That is what we do not think about. That is what we simply think *is*, as much a part of life as Chevrolets, *Time* magazine, movies, and pizza are and as unavoidable as the rising sun tomorrow.

In this and the following chapter, I want to try to understand our modernized, Western life. And what I am going to be doing is asking how it affects us internally, what living amidst the fruit of all its bril-liant ingenuity does to us, and how our experience of it makes us prone to look at the world in certain ways. I do so because it is not possible to live with any degree of authenticity as a Christian unless the modern world is understood to be what, in fact, it is: delicious but dangerous, like the Turkish delight that proved so irresistible and so lethal to one small boy in C. S. Lewis's *The Lion, the Witch, and the Wardrobe*.

I am going to try to accomplish this by melding together two kinds of thinking that have often seemed to be antithetical to each other and certainly whose practitioners have usually had little patience with each other. The one kind of analysis has looked only to *ideas* in offering its analyses of how the modern world has emerged. And specifically, it has attempted to root the modern conception of life in the ideas of the Enlightenment. The other kind of analysis has argued that modern life is an enigma if we do not understand its *social processes*, its economic capitalism and the social organization that that demands and the modern state which is one of its results. I happen to think that both approaches are right and both are necessary. More than that, I am inclined to think that the Enlightenment ideas would never have taken root as they did without the modernizing of the world. It was the modernizing of the world which gave to Enlightenment ideas their plausibility because the processes of modernization themselves produced an environment which was remarkably similar to the conclusions for which philosophers of the Enlightenment had argued.

I realize that what I am attempting to do will generate some new complexities. It is no small undertaking to develop a good understanding of what has dominated Western thinking. And it is no small task to be able to show how the processes of modernization — capitalism, urbanization, technology, mass communications, and the state — have produced a psychological environment in which certain beliefs and habits seem normal and others do not. To attempt to show the parallels between the two is an even more daunting task. I fear that it might burden readers with a mass of considerations with which they might choose not to be burdened! And yet, it also holds out the best hope for finding some of the answers to many of the questions which we might like answered.

However, before coming to these parallels, I need to think about something which is preliminary to both. It is how we know things. So, I am going to begin by reflecting on how our experience of the world outside becomes a part of our private, interior world. I shall then elaborate on this by illustrating in some detail how the Enlightenment ideas about life have dovetailed with what happens within us as we enter our technological world, learn the art of endless consumption, and foster delusions about the remaking of human life.

Outside In, Inside Out

When we think of "the outside world," we may be thinking of nature or we may be thinking of the world we have created from, or on top of, nature — quite literally in the case of cities, roads, and communications towers. And when we are thinking about what we have done with, and on, nature, we are necessarily thinking about culture, a notion whose meaning has changed quite a lot.

In nineteenth century Europe and Britain, the word *culture* had an agricultural resonance to it. Cultured people were thought of as men and women who tended the soil of their lives, who worked at self-improvement, especially by immersing themselves in those matters which were thought to improve the human condition: classical music, great literature, high moral discourses, and the pursuit of disinterested goodness through philanthropy or works of mercy.[1] This would produce such an ordering in one's life, it was thought, such refinement in one's manners, that one would become cultured. Thus it was that the words *culture* and *civilization* became interchangeable. A cultured person was a civilized person. There was still a remnant of this understanding in the American theologian H. Richard Niebuhr's classic book *Christ and Culture,* which was published in the 1950s and which bears

---

1. Matthew Arnold, like many other Protestant liberals, accentuated the moral and social dimension in this understanding rather than the personal and aesthetic. Thus he said that culture comprises "the love of our neighbour, the impulses toward action, help and beneficence, the desire for stopping human error, clearing human confusion, and diminishing the sum of human misery, the noble aspiration to leave the world better and happier than we found it — motives eminently such as are called social, — come in as part of the ground of culture, and the main and preeminent part. Culture is then properly described . . . as having its origin in the love of perfection; it is *a study of perfection.*" *Culture and Anarchy,* ed. Samuel Lipman (New Haven: Yale University Press, 1994), 30-31.

the distinction of having given us a way of conceptualizing the ways in which Christianity and culture have been related in the past. For him, though, culture was mostly what we would call "high culture" and it was mostly innocent. Let me pursue this idea a little so that we can see how much the word *culture* has changed in meaning.

The difference between nature and culture, Niebuhr said, is the difference between a river and a canal, between a stone and an arrow, between a moan and words.[2] Culture, he argued, is what human beings make of nature; it is what we impose upon nature by way of cities and transportation systems, or what we make from it by way of artistic artifacts. It is also the social fabric, social organization, and the structure of beliefs in a particular place. At the time when he was writing, America was a more innocent and a far less developed country than it is today. The imposition of our highly technological, densely urbanized way of life on nature is what drastically transforms the meaning of culture. The difference is not simply at its most obvious point — that is, that manual work, in which one is close to nature, is replaced by mechanized and computerized labor in which there may be no direct link to nature. The difference is in what is imposed on nature. It was the coming of our machine age that greatly troubled the German philosopher Oswald Spengler and provoked his 1918 vision of the declining West, and this was something which was not on Niebuhr's mind at all.

What Niebuhr did not ponder is the stunning commercial success that industrialization has brought, and this is what has begun to change the meaning of culture. The avalanche of commercial images and sounds under which we now live was just gathering force in Niebuhr's day. The "commercial," Stuart and Elizabeth Ewen argue, "reaches out to sell more than a service or product; it sells a way of understanding the world."[3] This has infused an altogether different quality into culture.

If, then, culture is still, in Stuart Ewen's words, "the accumulated understanding by which a given people live and maintain themselves

2. H. Richard Niebuhr, *Christ and Culture* (New York: Harper and Row, 1951), 32-39.

3. Stuart and Elizabeth Ewen, *Channels of Desire: Mass Images and the Shaping of American Consciousness* (Minneapolis: University of Minnesota Press, 1992), 24.

in a given society,"[4] we nevertheless need to enlarge our view of it beyond Niebuhr's thought that it is what we make of nature, or build upon it, to include what takes place within those who live within the artificial environment we have made. Culture includes all of those ways of looking at life, the habits of mind, that become typical and normative in a given context. It is what resonates within ourselves with modern societies with their highly sophisticated systems for the production of goods and services, centered around our cities, all made efficient by technology, all tied together by unprecedented lines of communication and information, and all of which are dominated by giant bureaucracies both corporate and governmental. Society is external to us but it is also the world we inhabit mentally and psychologically. We have no way of thinking about life, or about ourselves, except in the context of this external world. It is this world which impinges on us, makes demands of us, sometimes alarms us, sustains us, and occupies us. It is this world that envelops us in a myriad of images in terms of which we think of existence, by which we respond to it, through which we communicate with others. And so many of these images by which we understand ourselves are commercial in nature.[5] This has consequences for everything from fashion to politics to religion.

We can now begin to see where some of the building blocks lie in what we know. This external world becomes the inescapable "other" in

4. Stuart Ewen, *All Consuming Images: The Politics of Style in Contemporary Culture* (New York: Basic Books, 1988), 41.

5. Television has had many effects upon our consciousness but the two most important are that it has expanded our world, annihilating the significance of space; and it has become the principal conduit of commercial images, show business blurring into big business. McKenzie Wark notes, on the first point, that our telecommunications networks crisscross the globe, bringing home images of life and conflicts, tragedy and conquest from faraway places, and that what is not real to the eye is not unreal to our perception. The tragedies on the other side of the world are felt as if they were tragedies known to us directly. See his *Virtual Geography: Living with Global Media Events* (Bloomington: Indiana University Press, 1994). Secondly, the reason so much commercial television is so bland and banal is that it runs on the principle that it should be programming that no one will feel a strong inclination to turn off. That is because while viewers think of themselves as consumers "buying" the program, in actual fact, argues Joshua Meyrowitz, the "products are the viewers who are sold to the advertisers." See his *No Sense of Place: The Impact of Electronic Media on Social Behavior* (New York: Oxford University Press, 1985), 73.

our knowing. Our consciousness is wrought through a complex interaction between our interior and exterior worlds, between the "I" within us and the world by which we are surrounded. In many important respects, this world provides us with the ways in which we think of ourselves. And, to some extent, we provide the ways in which that outside world is ordered and experienced.[6] For example, a materialistic scientist and an animist who believes that trees have souls comparable to his own will look at the same trees rather differently. The difference lies not in the trees, but in the interpretive framework in which they are understood. Similarly, the world as we know it is not simply given to us, and it does not impose itself on all people in the same way, but neither is our knowledge a private, free-floating creation which is merely prompted by this external world — be it the creation or a text — as some postmoderns want to claim. There is, instead, a delicate choreography which takes place in which what is external is grasped and understood by what is internal, and what is internal lives much of its time within the boundaries of what is external. The exact relation between the internal and external, of course, has become an increasingly consternated debate across a number of disciplines today, from philosophy to theology to literature and even into law and science.[7]

6. See Peter L. Berger, *The Sacred Canopy: Elements of a Sociological Theory of Religion* (New York: Doubleday, 1969), 83-85; see also Peter L. Berger and Thomas Luckman, *The Sociological Construction of Reality: A Treatise in the Sociology of Knowledge* (New York: Doubleday, 1966), 19-46; Peter Berger, Brigitte Berger, and Hansfried Kellner, *The Homeless Mind: Modernization and Consciousness* (New York: Random House, 1973). For a brief summary of the main motifs and complexities in Berger's thought, such as his idea of the social construction of reality, everyday reality, symbolic universes, and plausibility structures, see Robert Wuthnow, *Rediscovering the Sacred: Perspectives on Religion in Contemporary Society* (Grand Rapids: William B. Eerdmans, 1992), 9-35.

7. Neil Postman has also spoken about the different habits of mind, the different preoccupations which arise when, as is the case in the West, we are moving from being literate cultures to video cultures through television principally. Once we engaged life with the same habits of lineal thought that a book culture encourages, but now we engage it with the same disjointedness and the same appetite for entertainment that television encourages. His argument is that this medium changes the nature of our public discourse, that it accentuates certain aspects of the mind, and that it favors a particular kind of content which changes the way we tell the truth. The way we think about life and the way we speak about it are thereby changed. See his

And there is a third factor in our knowing which also needs to be considered. In addition to the dance carried on between the internal and external worlds, our consciousness is also wrought by the means we have for engaging the world outside of ourselves. Eileen Powers' classic study *Medieval People* contains a chapter in which we follow Bodo, the peasant, from his home into the fields of the medieval estate on which he lives. The way he sees life could not be more different from the way life is viewed today by someone, say, working in a corporation in a city office building. And that difference has to do not only with a changed worldview, and not only with a drastically changed world to view, but also with the passing of the horse-drawn plow and its replacement by omnipresent technology and our greatly magnified channels of knowledge and perception. The computer, along with other technology, subtly changes how we see the world, what we think we can do with life, and how we go about doing that. The extension of ourselves that is possible through the computer, and even through television, gives us ways of thinking about life that would not have crossed Bodo's mind.[8]

It is true, of course, that within this larger meaning of culture there are the smaller units of, for example, ethnicity, socioeconomic status, and generation: smaller groups that have their own ways of looking at life and their own agendas as to what they want from it. The amount and degree of differentiation here appear to be growing. For example, the census of the United States taken in 1950 offered only two racial categories: "white" and "nonwhite." With each succeeding decade, how-

---

Amusing Ourselves to Death: Public Discourse in the Age of Show Business (New York: Penguin, 1985). "It is a truism to say," wrote Malcolm Muggeridge, "that the media in general, and TV in particular . . . are incomparably the greatest single influence in our society today, exerted at all social, economic and cultural levels." Malcolm Muggeridge, *Christ and the Media* (Grand Rapids: William B. Eerdmans, 1977), 23.

8. Postman has also suggested that cultures might be distinguished as tool-using, technocracies, and technopolies. In the tool-using, the tools are really incidental to the life, customs, social patterns and traditions in the tribe or nation. In technocracies, some of the traditional forms of life still are present, though social custom and religious sanction are much loosened. Invention and technological innovation are at the heart of the development before which all else is moved back. In technopoly — America being the exemplar — we have "the submission of all forms of cultural life to the sovereignty of technique and technology" in the belief that "technique of any kind can do our thinking for us." Neil Postman, *Technopoly: The Surrender of Culture to Technology* (New York: Vintage, 1992), 52.

ever, the number of choices increased until in the 2000 Census the number had grown to twelve in order to accommodate the gathering importance of racial difference. There is also the growing bonding of kin we see in the new expressions of tribalism — nationalistic, ethnic, and generational. It is these smaller units of meaning within which people belong in their minds which has led some to think that they constitute the building blocks for a postmodern understanding of the world in which meaning can never be the same for any two of these groups — or maybe even for two people. That, however, has to assume a level of disengagement from the wider culture that is today simply impossible.

While it is true, then, that there are smaller worlds of meaning and special interest groups, we should not lose sight of the fact that they always exist within a larger, homogenized world. In this world we are increasingly linked together by information and computers, products and e-mails, movies and music. This produces an all-embracing world culture, one in which an American pop star like Michael Jackson can have a more avid following in Japan than in the United States, and Britons can enjoy Oprah Winfrey just as much as Americans can. Coca Cola and pizza, American movies and rock music, are universal. It is this larger umbrella of (pop) culture under which everyone lives in the West.

What this means is that the kind of world in which we live, and the kinds of ways which we have for engaging it and negotiating it, will often mean that our consciousness and our habits will reflect that world which is outside of ourselves, regardless of generational, gender, or ethnic particularities. The habits which have emerged in the productive order of our modernized world tend to become ubiquitous, regardless of how different we may be in some other ways. Consider, for example, the way we view time. In the workplace, every minute counts, regardless of the worker's gender or generation; in many homes, we rarely escape the sense of urgency which the awareness of time brings. Even our moments of recreation are carefully timed. Ways of thinking and organizing in our society often become our ways of thinking about ourselves and organizing our lives.[9] Thus, those who gaze at a computer screen by

9. Gordon McDonald is quite correct to think that there are people who are disorganized and whose gifts are, as a result, squandered. Yet his book *Ordering Your Private World* has the smell of the corporation on almost every page. He divides his

day and a television screen by night may well feel awkwardly obsolete in church if there is not another screen on which to gaze. The demands of efficiency, and the rational, impersonal workings of bureaucracy, are so much a part of who we have become that many of us also want our churches to have the feel of a smoothly run corporation. Our capitalism has been so virile and abundant, filling our lives with goods in quantities unknown in any previous age, that it seems only natural — at least in middle class, white churches — to expect the same range of choice in programs and services as we experience in the commercial world. The norms of the workplace so easily and so unknowingly become our own internalized norms. And this is true of most people.

This certainly connects with what the Bible has told us to expect. It is not only from the "passions" of our fallenness that we need to be redeemed, Paul tells us, but also from "following the course of this world" — our embeddedness in culture at the point of its fallen horizons, false belief structures, and misdirected devotions — all of which are kept in place by the powers of darkness (Eph. 2:1-3). This is what gives to all culture its curiously ambiguous quality for it is an extension both of human life made in the image of God and of human life now fallen. In the Christian scheme, then, we have to be redeemed from sin and uprooted from what is dark in culture, from what in the Bible is called "this world," for Satan's captivity is exercised through the instrumentality of

---

private life into five segments. Time, he insists must be "budgeted." He develops four laws regarding "unseized time" which, if followed, enable one to "command" it. And in his *Rebuilding Your Broken World,* he has eighteen "Bottom Line" principles for rising from the ashes, which include a discussion of the four sources of temptation and the seven ways to guard against it. Not only is this the corporate habit of control, so essential to success, but several of his books exude the sense of American can-do which is also the essence of the business world. *Forging a Real World Faith, Mastering Personal Growth, Renewing Your Spiritual Passion,* as well as the two books already cited ring the changes on this characteristic in their titles: "Ordering," "Rebuilding," "Forging," "Mastering," and "Renewing." There is a provenance to these books in the circumstances of late-twentieth-century, modernized, American culture of which the author appears to be entirely oblivious. A similar proclivity for managing Christian faith is evidenced in some of Lyle Schaller's books such as *21 Bridges to the 21st Century, 44 Questions for Church Planters, 44 Questions for Congregational Self-appraisal, 44 Steps off the Plateau, 44 Ways to Expand the Teaching Ministry of Your Church,* and *44 Ways to Revitalize Women's Organizations.* Christianity, it appears, is all about packaging and managing reality.

sin and that of "the world."[10] It therefore becomes a matter of no small moment to be able to discern what in our culture is good, what is simply innocent, and what is neither.

This relationship between our external world and our internal consciousness is not, however, deterministic. That was what Marx believed, though Lenin and Stalin tried to modify his understanding when they saw that the external economic order was not bringing about a classless society of its own accord. They had thought that through political revolution internal consciousness could be changed and, in effect, they could bring about a utopia. They mistakenly thought that this relationship was one of strict cause and effect. The truth is quite different. This relationship between the external culture and internal consciousness is one only of influence, ranging from the very subtle to the brazenly insistent, but never one of irresistible, deterministic force. Lesslie Newbigin has rightly said that without "opting for either the view that ideas are primary and their political and social consequences are secondary, or the view that ideas are merely a by-product of social change, one can accept the fact that there is a reciprocal relationship between them and that one does not truly account for one without attending to both."[11]

That being the case, we need to think about our world in terms of the parallel I have suggested. On the one hand, we have to think about the modern world in terms of the ideas that arose in the Enlightenment because they have come to dominate the way people think about life in the West. On the other hand, we need to think about the way in which our social fabric has been reshaped through the processes of modernization because this has created a psychological environment which we all inhabit. The additional challenge is, then, to show how these ideas and this reshaping have worked toward the same ends, the one reinforcing and giving plausibility to the other.

10. Craig M. Gay, in his *The Way of the (Modern) World: or, Why It's Tempting to Live As If God Doesn't Exist* (Grand Rapids: William B. Eerdmans, 1998), has woven a biblical understanding of "the world" throughout his analysis of the modern world. See also my own study, *God in the Wasteland: The Reality of Truth in a World of Fading Dreams* (Grand Rapids: William B. Eerdmans, 1994), 35-56.

11. Lesslie Newbigin, *Foolishness to the Greeks: The Gospel and Western Culture* (Grand Rapids: William B. Eerdmans, 1986), 29.

The Heretical Persuasion

The first point of entry into an understanding of our modern life, and of how modern people see their world, is given to us by the ideas generated by the Enlightenment. I want to think briefly about how these ideas worked and then what kind of person was their outcome.

What the Enlightenment ideology did was to provide an interpretive grid, an all-encompassing understanding, that was laid over the whole of life. This understanding was not so much a worldview as an ideology. Ideologies, we might say, are worldviews with an attitude. The intent of every ideology is to *control.* With the passage of time and the desire to be triumphant, ideologies tend to become simplistic. They find acceptance because they tap into our need, the Canadian writer John Saul says, "to believe in single-stroke, cure-all solutions"[12] often presenting us with stark alternatives: "Accept the ideology or perish. Pay the debt or go bankrupt. Nationalize or starve. Privatize or go moribund. Kill inflation or lose all your money."[13] Because they leave only one way out, they become coercive. At the same time, ideologies create a sense of inevitability about themselves. They produce passivity in people because what is inevitable cannot be resisted. And they breed intolerance of those who might be opposed to their understanding of life or might raise questions about it. It is these characteristics which help explain why it is so difficult to challenge an ideology once it has become socially ensconced. And yet this is exactly what has been happening with the Enlightenment ideology since the 1960's.

The Enlightenment spilled out into many fields — art, architecture, philosophy, theology, history, science — and meant different things in different countries, but it was, nevertheless, the intellectual hinge by which the premodern world moved into the modern.[14] This transition, however, involved much more than simply thinking about life in new ways; it included a total social reorganization which, it turned out, worked hand in glove with the new Enlightenment think-

12. John Ralson Saul, *The Unconscious Civilization* (New York: The Free Press, 1997), 22.

13. Saul, *The Unconscious Civilization,* 21.

14. Franklin L. Baumer, *Modern European Thought: Continuity and Change in Ideas, 1600-1950* (New York: Macmillan, 1977), 141.

ing. It is here, in a way, that my attempt to analyze first the Enlightenment ideas and then the modern remaking of our social fabric with all of its consequences for how we see the world becomes a little blurred. It becomes blurred because many in the Enlightenment world believed that its ideas were synonymous with the modern remaking of the world by science, technology and government. To be part of the Enlightenment was to be modern; to be modern was to think in Enlightenment ways. That clearly is being contested today. There are many postmoderns who are thoroughly modern in the sense that they live in a world of high capitalism and wonder drugs but they are, nevertheless, hostile to Enlightenment thinking. Indeed, this has always been true of traditional Christian believers, too. But the confusion did yield some enormous benefits. It enabled proponents of the Enlightenment to pass themselves off as being progressive and modern and make any who disagreed with their ideas suffer under the opprobrium of being obscurantist, dated, backward-looking obstacles to progress. It is worth pondering this a little more because it is this confusion which gave the Enlightenment enormous coercive power.

Premodern societies were typically rural and their populations were not concentrated in cities. They were dominated by tribes or clans in which there were a fixed hierarchy and fixed conventions with significant sanctions for those who broke the rules. The supernatural was a given, one might say a "natural" part of life. Families were the dominant social unit, personal relations were the coin of the realm, and tradition was strong and linked the past to the present.

There were two principal shadows which attended this arrangement. The first was nature, which posed risks by way of diseases which were untreatable as well as droughts and famines which, in the absence of transportation systems and information, were far more damaging than they are today. The other risk was posed by the supernatural, which threatened those who acted ignorantly or unwisely. Medieval Catholicism gave the central expression to this matrix of God and society in Europe. However, the world was changing. By the sixteenth century, nationalisms had reached a new level of activity, the old feudal order was strained to breaking point, capitalism was just beginning, and the printing press was making its debut. In an astonishingly short period of time, the outlines of the modern world began to appear. The Enlightenment occurred as these changes in society were taking root and for a long time it seemed as if they were synonymous.

By contrast, modern society as we now know it is dominated by large urban centers. In the West, 94% of the population lives in cities and in 1999, for the first time, the world became urbanized with more people living in cities than not. Modern society is also shaped by the needs of capitalistic production and consumption, so labor is intensified into forms of work which are more and more specialized for this increasingly complex system. In the premodern world, understanding about life was homogeneous and shared unquestioningly by those in a society; in the modern world it is not. In place of the single, overarching understanding of meaning, which was once religiously derived, are now multiple worldviews in competition with each other and these may not be religious at all. In premodern societies, the sacred was a matter-of-fact part of life; in modern societies, God has been excluded from public life,[15] pushed to the margins of relevance, and made to live out his life, as it were, underground and out of sight. And whereas relations in the premodern world were personal, they are now more functional in society. In society, it is what one does, not the family from which one comes, that is usually important. We ask simply what a person's competence is to do the work we want done; we do not think of that person in terms of who his or her mother or father is. In fact, it is most unlikely that we will even know that person's family. Modern societies are also highly technological. Technology makes innovation possible and economies flourish on innovation. This produces constant revisions, a never-ending flow of new products, and new ways of doing the old jobs. What is past inevitably carries with it the sense of being obsolete, superseded by what is newer and better. The past becomes irrelevant and tradition an encumbrance; the future becomes the constant preoccupation.

The shadows here are somewhat different from those in the premodern world. The dangers in being modern are those that arise from being cut loose from place and community, from clan and family,

15. Richard John Neuhaus develops this case with respect to America in his *The Naked Public Square: Religion and Democracy in America* (Grand Rapids: William B. Eerdmans, 1984). What he described two decades ago has only become more pronounced.

and sent off to drift upon a mighty ocean amidst all of its storms, storms of violence which technology has sometimes made possible and storms of loneliness and meaninglessness, with no shore points in view. If the old social order was held together by the bonds of kin and custom, here social relations are stabilized all too often only by fleeting sexual encounters. In this situation almost anything can happen and often it does. What was once safe and predictable no longer is and therefore the future looms ahead of us full of risk. On the other hand, the danger which the supernatural once posed has passed. The divine has now been rendered harmless or it has become an irrelevance.[16]

The Enlightenment, however, was not what generated all of these changes. They came about for a variety of reasons behind which was no single conception of how the world should be. What is significant, though, is that a number of the important outcomes in this rearranged

16. This transition from a premodern to a modern world was effected over centuries in Europe but it has by no means been effected in the same way outside Europe. Most Asian countries are currently modernizing but a number of Islamic societies are in their structure and function still quite premodern even though they may also have capitalistic interests and may use modern technology. Inasmuch as they remain premodern in their view of the world and in their social structures, it is inevitable that they feel themselves to be at war with the modern Western world with its individualism, its loss of the centrality of God, its irreverence, and its moral vacuity. Hollywood producers who produce many of the images by which America is understood outside its borders are, wittingly or not, a part of American foreign policy as well as a factor in its security. On the different ways in which modernization took hold see C. E. Black, *The Dynamics of Modernization: A Study in Comparative History* (New York: Harper and Row, 1966). Samuel Huntingdon has argued that once the Cold War ended, global politics have been driven less by politics and more by religion, less by ideology and more by civilizational considerations. And in this, Islam has become a major player which is becoming more assertive. Alongside the purely religious differences are clustered the important attitudes in Islamic civilization which grow out of them. These are at many points in conflict with the fruit of modernization such as its secularizing tendencies, its individualism, and the moral perversions which Western freedoms allow. See his *The Clash of Civilizations and the Remaking of World Order* (New York: Simon and Schuster, 1996). For an analysis of Arab society see Halim Isber Barak, *The Arab World: Society, Culture, and State* (Berkeley: University of California Press, 1993). Islam has always been ill at ease with democracy, if not overtly hostile to it, and democracy has been an essential piece in the story of modernization in the West. On the interface with the modernized West see John Cooper, Ronald I. Nettles, and Mohamed Mahmoud, *Islam and Modernity: Muslim Intellectuals Respond* (London: St. Martin's Press, 1998).

world had psychological and cognitive consequences which came to be paralleled in the thought of the Enlightenment and so it became as natural as it was mistaken to think them.

The Enlightenment's centerpiece was freedom. Indeed, its *demand* was freedom: freedom from the past, freedom from God, and freedom from authority. It demanded freedom from every system of thought that would be resistant to its intellectual innovations. It resolutely opposed all ideas rooted in what was eternal, fixed, and unchanging. Immanuel Kant claimed in 1784 that the Enlightenment was really the next stage in human maturity. Immaturity, he said, "is the inability to use one's own understanding without the guidance of another." That, he said, was "the ball and chain" from which humanity needed to be freed.[17] The Enlightenment produced what its thinkers saw as a new era: in *knowledge,* a new, certain way of knowing, exemplified best in science, would produce increasing control over nature; in *application,* technology would use the new knowledge in the production of an abundance of goods which would not only raise the quality of life but also eliminate poverty; in *authority,* the human being for the first time would make decisions about life that would be rational and unencumbered by the pressures and perversions of "superstition" from the past.[18]

Thus the modern person began to take shape: "a newly self-conscious and autonomous being," writes Richard Tarnas, "skeptical of orthodoxies, rebellious against authority . . . responsible for his own beliefs and actions . . . assured of his intellectual capacity to comprehend and control nature . . . and altogether less dependent on an omnipotent God."[19] Human reason became the source of morality, the

17. Immanuel Kant, "An Answer to the Question: What Is Enlightenment?" in *From Modernism to Postmodernism: An Anthology,* ed. Lawrence Cahoone (Cambridge, Mass.: Blackwell, 1996), 51. See the discussion of the modern struggle for autonomy in Colin E. Gunton, *Enlightenment and Alienation: An Essay Toward a Trinitarian Theology* (Grand Rapids: William B. Eerdmans, 1985), 57-70.

18. Langdon Gilkey, *Society and the Sacred* (New York: The Crossroad Publishing Co., 1981), 4. For an account of how the Enlightenment took hold in America, see James Turner, *Without God, Without Creed: The Origins of Unbelief in America* (Baltimore: The Johns Hopkins University Press, 1985).

19. Richard Tarnas, *The Passion of the Western Mind: Understanding the Ideas That Have Shaped Our World View* (New York: Harmony Books, 1991), 282.

only source from which to draw explanations about life. It was from the human being that meaning would be constructed. This was an ideology that initially inspired great optimism. The 1898 *Encyclopaedia Britannica,* for example, was advertised as providing the record of "the wonderful story" of modern progress; the claim was that it would tell "how the light was spread." But, as we now know, the Enlightenment has produced great dismay in its postmodern inheritors, who see its promises of progress as failures and frauds. And the promise of breathless innovation and new realms of discovery in the human spirit has been overtaken by the anonymity of today's mass society, by mindless fads and fashions, by a world emptied out of significance and filled instead with banality. Once the eternal restraints were cast off, we were free to do what we wanted and in the twentieth century that meant spilling more blood than we had ever spilled before. This, of course, is the side to the Enlightenment which its advocates try not to remember or see as a betrayal of its real interests. The fact is, though, that with the rise of commercial power in the eighteenth century, and the matching growth in the power of the state in the nineteenth and twentieth centuries, the possibility of reaching the goals of the Enlightenment by means of forceful social engineering became irresistible. And so were born the horrifically destructive totalitarianisms of the twentieth century.

Clearly the Enlightenment promised far more than it was ever able to deliver; one way of understanding this is to think of it as a Christian heresy. What Christian faith had offered was retained while the Source from which that offer had been made was rejected. The prerogatives that had belonged to God did not simply disappear; now they reappeared in human beings. The revelation he had given now reappeared in the form of natural reason, which would do what revelation had done but without the discomfort of requiring humanity to submit to the God from whom the revelation had come; the idea of salvation was retained but transformed into the drive for human perfectibility, at first achieved by moral striving and then, as we know it today, by psychological technique; grace became effort; the life of faith became the hope of personal growth; and eschatology became progress (what Lord Acton called the religion of those who have none). Thus was the Christian Trinity replaced by a substitute trinity of reason, nature, and progress.[20] The place God had occupied was now occupied by the human being. Meaning and morality, which only God could give, were taken to be purely human accomplishments; but in promising what only God could do, the Enlightenment sowed the seeds of its own downfall. It promised too much. It promised, in fact, that all human problems could be solved by purely natural means — and that, plainly, rested on false assumptions. It both underestimated the magnitude of the problems and overestimated the capacity of human nature to remedy them.

The Modern Revolution

What gave this Enlightenment ideology its staying power and plausibility, I have suggested, was the fact that it came to prominence as the Western world was being reshaped and transformed by modernization. It is because of modernization, and not really because of the Enlightenment, that the West has moved from being premodern to being modern in its organization. It was this process which created a public environment in which commonplace assumptions about life came to parallel what the Enlightenment thought, even though there were few direct links between the Enlightenment thinkers and those who lived in this modernized world. Enlightenment ideas, on the one hand, and experience in the modern world, on the other, thus reinforced each other, the latter giving plausibility to the former. Had modernization never happened, one wonders if the Enlightenment ideology could have sustained itself for very long. As it was, however, the Enlightenment thinking came to dominate how the West has thought about life. Today, however, the growing complexity of the social fabric is probably what has contributed to the crisis in which the Enlightenment world finds itself. Enlightenment ideology is being taken down. As so often happens at junctures like this, we are hearing in the collapsing Enlightenment world "the swan song of a dying epoch," in Stanley Rosen's words, and in the postmodernity which is following it, the "firebird that

20. David Lyon, *Jesus in Disneyland: Religion in Postmodern Times* (Cambridge: Polity Press, 2001), 10.

arises from the ashes of its own corpse."[21] This I will take up in the next chapter.

What is extraordinary about the common, as opposed to elite, revolution which modernization has spawned is that it has been carried out by very ordinary people, and yet it parallels what the Enlightenment thinkers launched. These ordinary, everyday revolutionaries are not Enlightenment philosophers but people who oftentimes think no great thoughts at all, may read very little (half of all Americans, in fact, never read a single book during the year), are content with television's banal sitcoms, and think that the weekend was made for Budweiser and football. Yet in them Enlightenment attitudes have taken form. How have these very ordinary citizens reached such radical ends?

The answer, I believe, is that they are reflecting, sometimes in very unthinking ways, the assumptions that become normal when societies are modernized. These very ordinary revolutionaries are those whose ideas and attitudes, whose wants and horizons, are resonating with this fabulous remaking of the world which modernization has brought about, yet they are in most cases oblivious to what the Enlightenment intellectuals wanted. For this world not only offers unprecedented goods and services, not only has it multiplied opportunities and hopes, not only has it opened doors and understanding but, in that very process, it has ushered us into the psychological atmosphere that is created by the interconnections between these great defining realities of our time: urbanization, technology, capitalism, telecommunications, and the modern state. This is *our* world, the world within which we think about life and its meaning, the place where we fashion out for ourselves what it means to be human and what it takes to be happy. And here we encounter at least three of the fundamental beliefs of the Enlightenment which have come to us by an entirely different route: the disappearance of God, the disappearance of human nature, and the omnicompetence of the human being. The Enlightenment belief, on the one hand, and what modernization does within those who live within its horizons, on the other, become indistinguish-

21. Stanley Rosen, *The Ancients and the Moderns: Rethinking Modernity* (New Haven: Yale University Press, 1989), 1.

able from each other. This happens without those who live in the modernized world encountering a single Enlightenment thinker! I am, therefore, going to take up these three themes and hope to be able to show the extraordinary parallels that have emerged between ideas and social context.

Gone with the Wind

I begin with this first theme from the Enlightenment, the disappearance of God. It is, of course, the case that there was not a single and common understanding of God amongst the Enlightenment thinkers. Some were atheists, some were theists, and still others were deists. The Enlightenment thinkers were, however, united in their opposition to what they saw as "superstition" and they as adamantly favored the powers of reason to pry open the mystery of God's being. The eighteenth-century English Deists led the way with volumes like Matthew Tindall's *Christianity as Old as the Creation* and John Toland's *Christianity Not Mysterious,* which was published as the century dawned. Theirs was, to say the least, an inert God, one who had withdrawn to a great distance and simply observed life without ever interfering with it. Most of the Enlightenment thinkers, however, actually held to some kind of theistic view, rather than deistic, and saw God as somewhat vaguely engaged with life. This was true even of Voltaire, as it was of Hume and perhaps of Kant. But, what was of real significance was that by about mid-century, the discussion about God, in the absence of revelation, had run into a dead end. The issues were unresolvable and the conversation had turned stale. Attention now shifted away from these earlier preoccupations to very this-worldly concerns such as social and political life. This became the pattern. Preoccupation with what was human, with what the human being could do, with the remaking of human life, replaced the older vision of a world over which God presided and in which human ability to reconstruct life was quite limited.

This set of naturalistic perceptions from the Enlightenment was, however, to be replicated, and generated, by an altogether different means as the world became modernized. This same shift away from God, and the same low horizons which lead people to be occupied solely with life as we see it, are also the invariable outcome in societies that are modernizing even in the absence of any knowledge of the Enlightenment.

Indeed, the exact outcomes are reached by these quite different means. The Enlightenment eviscerated society of God but so, too, has modernization. The older secularization thesis argued that the degree to which a society became modernized was the degree to which God vanished into the ether and the society would cease to be religious.[22] This thesis has seemed to hold water in Europe, which has been very considerably stripped of organized religion — assisted, no doubt, by the fact that organized religion has very considerably withered of its own accord — but the situation has been different in America. Here, secularization has not banished religion but it has taken a different route. Here, it simply insists that religion remain a purely private passion which does not intrude itself into the public domain. Thus it is that we now have a country which is heavily modernized but which is also quite religious in a private kind of way. Indeed, if we include the many spiritualities that are being practiced, advocated, and sold, modern America is a very spiritual society — but a deeply secular society, too![23]

From many directions, modernized society has been emptied out of the divine. Max Weber spoke of "the tremendous cosmos of the modern economic order" and of the way it is now bound "to the technical and economic conditions of machine production" and of how, together, these great social realities act on the lives of all within their embrace with "irresistible force."[24] And this force moves us in the di-

22. After completing an extended analysis of the fate of Catholic faith in Europe at the end of the 1970s, S. S. Acquaviva observed that "the sense of the sacred decays for many profound reasons, engendering irreligiosity to an extent previously unknown in human history." See his *The Decline of the Sacred in Industrial Society*, trans. Patricia Lipscomb (Oxford: Blackwell, 1979), 161.

23 It would be a mistake to think, however, that this situation is entirely novel. It has, in fact, been long in the making, and the current expression of its dual nature — secular and religious — is but an intensification of what preceded it. Midway through the last century Reinhold Niebuhr wrote brilliantly about this same dual character in the nation in his *Pious and Secular America* (New York: Charles Scribner's Sons, 1958).

24. Max Weber, *The Protestant Ethic and the Spirit of Capitalism*, trans. Talcott Parsons (London: George Allen and Unwin, 1976), 181.

rection of seeing the world emptied of God and the supernatural order, at least as factors to be considered in the course of everyday life.
Weber spoke of this as the "disenchantment of the world" when
machine-like rationality, for him epitomized in the bureaucrat,[25]
would strip the world both of its past — history and tradition — and of
its meaning, by squeezing it through the gray, orderly, and unvarying
workings of rules, mechanisms, and procedures, along the way ex-
punging human creativity. Weber's vision, though dystopian, has
turned out to be quite accurate.

Capitalism requires the pervasive presence of technology, and
technology is a two-edged sword. On the one hand, it has allowed us to
transcend our world, to achieve what was unimaginable only a short
time ago, to effect an unparalleled degree of efficiency in the production of the goods which fill our malls and showrooms, an elevation in
their quality, a new array of medical procedures, more information,
and more information spread more rapidly. Today, as Zygmunt
Bauman asserts, there "are more — painfully more — possibilities than
any individual life, however long, adventurous and industrious can attempt to explore, let alone to adopt."[26] On the other hand, what began
as the physical conquest of our world by technology, the annihilation of
space and time, the control of some of nature's forces, and the exploitation of its resources, has now become a profoundly *psychological* reality. The benefits of technology all come packaged in values — values
which are naturalistic and materialistic. These fill the air, quite literally, all the time. We find no solitude. We have no escape. The experience of this new culture is intense and intrusive in ways that older cultures never were.

All of this, of course, is quite unintentional and often unnoticed.
There is a matter-of-factness about everyday life, a normality about it,
which inclines us not to ask too many questions of it. We simply accept
it for what it is. And in this case, since technology is so much a part of
our world, so much a part of the workplace, we simply enter into its do-

25. See Max Weber, *Economy and Society: An Outline of Interpretive Sociology*,
ed. Guenther Roth and Claus Wittich, trans. Ephraim Fischoff et al. (2 vols.; Berkeley:
University of California Press, 1978), 956-1305, 223-25, 1394-95. See also Berger, *The
Homeless Mind*, 41-62.

26. Zygmunt Bauman, *Liquid Modernity* (Cambridge: Polity Press, 2000), 61.

main. Its domain, however, is one in which there is a bias to the way in which it works. As Robert Wuthnow notes, it "generates its own culture."[27] It is a bias that leads us to think of the world only through the kind of rationality that is technology-like. Jacques Ellul first made the case effectively that technology has spawned a kind of narrow rationality that by itself greatly impoverishes our understanding of the rest of life. For life should not only be about means, which is the direction in which technology pushes us, but it should include ends as well. This preoccupation with means produces a kind of hard pragmatism that reduces everything to results, an ethics of efficiency, for what is done best and accomplished in the shortest time must be right.[28] Since the focus of technology is always narrow — how to get things done better and faster — everything else in life, if technology is the prism through which we are experiencing it, tends to be marginalized or lost. Life is flattened out, its height and depth surrendered as it is all reduced simply to process. And everything in life is then evaluated by this same standard: what is done better and faster must be right. This leads, for example, to books on spirituality that read like the owner's manual for operating a machine, replete with steps, easy-to-follow directions, and practical "how-to-do-it" formulae. In so reducing the greatness of God and of his truth to formulae and rational steps, this mindset makes of Christian faith a small, this-worldly, manageable formula for success which, in the end, comes to differ very little from all of the other small, manageable formulae for success of the secular therapeutic kind which are also on the market.

In this technological society, a cognitive style has emerged, Berger says, in which the connections between the parts of life are

27. Robert Wuthnow, *The Restructuring of American Religion: Society and Faith Since World War II* (Princeton: Princeton University Press, 1988), 283.

28. Craig Gay has argued that "those who operate under the assumption that all human problems can be converted into technical problems amenable to technical solutions are, in effect, automatically predisposed to accept the nihilistic proposition that reality is itself a kind of human artifact, and that there is no truth or order in the world save that which we have managed to construct for ourselves. After all, both modern technological making and modern philosophical nihilism have as their focus the human *will-to-self-definition* or, as Nietzsche put it, the 'will to power.'" Craig Gay, "The Technological Ethos and the Spirit of (Post) Modern Nihilism," *Christian Scholar's Review*, xxviii, No. 1 (1998), 92.

lost.[29] In life, one does not remark on how good the eggs, flour, and vanilla tasted; one remarks on how good the cake was.[30] But the technological mindset separates and disengages things. It leads us to talk about eggs, flour, and vanilla in isolation from each other.

As reality loses its connectedness, everything drifts apart. It begins to resemble confetti — a myriad of experiences, none of which is related to the other and none of which, in the absence of this relation, can mean anything. The human being becomes "homeless," adrift in a world that is beyond comprehension. This may explain the obsession some people exhibit with technology, for in its own narrow world the technological mindset has everything under control. The constant preoccupation with planning likewise discloses, Craig Gay remarks, "an obsession with control and a kind of religious commitment to the validity of technological rationality."[31]

This kind of mentality is thoroughly anthropocentric in its outlook because it is thoroughly this-worldly in its working. It has no place for what does not fit in with how technology works and what technology accomplishes. Although from one angle technology is but a tool, from another it has inclined us to see our world as only a flat plane without height or depth, the plane where we get things done. Here, one's vision is short-ranged and looks only a few steps down the road and does not look up at all. Its unintended consequence, Gay argues, is "the exclusion of God, grace, and morality from contemporary public discourse."[32] It therefore produces a kind of know-how savvy but what it excludes, among other things, is a place for wisdom in life, that way of knowing which takes its bearings on the character and revelation of God, brings that understanding to life in all of its dignity and wretchedness, and issues in principled, good judgments. Those judgments are irrelevant to the way our technologized world works since they have no apparent place in how the computer works.[33]

29. Berger et al., *The Homeless Mind*, 27.
30. O. B. Hardison, *Disappearing Through the Skylight: Culture and Technology in the Twentieth Century* (New York: Penguin Books, 1989), xiii.
31. Gay, *The Way of the (Modern) World*, 36.
32. Gay, *The Way of the (Modern) World*, 94.
33. Alexis de Tocqueville visited America early on in the nineteenth century and subsequently published his two-volume work *Democracy in America*. In these

We arrive at about the same point as we have with the social consequences of technology when we consider the effects that capitalistic organization and output have upon us. As is so often the case when we think about the modern world, we realize that there are two sides to be considered. There can be no doubt that capitalism is the most efficient, productive, virile, and beneficial system for the manufacture and distribution of goods and services that has ever been devised. Indeed, it is market economies that hold the hope for the impoverished countries of the world. It is the free market economies that have produced employment, that have raised the standard of living, that have filled life with an abundance of goods and opportunities that once were only distant dreams, if they were even dreams at all. But here, as elsewhere, there are costs to be considered along with the benefits, and while the benefits are everywhere present and obvious the costs are often hidden and unnoticed.

It is undoubtedly the case that capitalism, like technology, has a built-in rationality by which it works. Gay, using Weberian categories, has explored this at some length showing how intentional is its orientation to the sole concern of profitability, of devising means that will produce that end. This is the practical, "bottom line" consideration of business.[34] Undoubtedly this is true and the hard, narrowly focused pragmatism which it spawns naturally excludes God from the process because he has no part in what the bottom line looks like. Knowing God, it would seem, has no bearing at all on how profits might be increased.

God's disappearance not only is evident on the one end of the production chain. It is evident all the way along and, not least, in what keeps it all going: unbridled consumer desire. In an older time, desire used to be bridled.

---

books, he repeatedly mused on the fact that the American mind had a practical bent to it, and that even in its religious expression it tended to focus less on what was eternal than on what was temporal, such as immediate prosperity and a this-worldly peace. The particular "cognitive style" that coexists most naturally with technology is simply the latest reincarnation of this bent. On this, see John Crowell and Stanford J. Searl, eds., *The Responsibility of Mind in a Civilization of Machines* (Amherst: The University of Massachusetts Press, 1979), 195-213. See also Richard Hofstadter, *Anti-Intellectualism in American Life* (New York: Vintage Books, 1963).

34. Gay, *The Way of the (Modern) World*, 131-79.

Simon Schama has exquisitely detailed at length the way in which a Christian asceticism played itself out among the Calvinistic Dutch of the sixteenth and seventeenth centuries. His account in part explores the anxieties which accompanied the superabundance of that time. This was a time of remarkable cultural and commercial achievement, but what he shows is how the Dutch mind was "adrift between the fear of the deluge and the hope of moral salvation" and how it was carried back and forth "between worldliness and homeliness, between the gratification of appetite and its denial, between the conditional consecration of wealth and perdition in its surfeit."[35] This seems to be the explanation of the fact that in no other country of the time were so many engravings made of Jonah and the whale. The fact that whales did beach themselves from time to time along the coast made a natural connection with the biblical story, but more important was the symbolism of "the sinking of the soul into the deep and redemption through atonement."[36] The whale was a portent of judgment and it was this understanding that energized the search, in an age of great plenty, for a way between worldly luxury and acceptable comfort. The Dutch of this time inhabited a moral universe, one which, as it were, reached into their homes and customs, their work and pleasure, and was constantly demanding accountability.

Today, however, there is no such sense of unease with our superabundance because this kind of moral understanding has much withered. In a secularized culture, God has ceased to be a player in regulating our desires and, besides, his regulation, such as it is, has ceased to be moral and has become only therapeutic. The restraints, therefore, are gone. Capitalism has no internal logic or morality which will place limits on the abundance or surfeit which it produces. As a result, in the rough-and-tumble scramble for success, our markets are flooded with far more goods, far more choices, than we actually need. If there is to be restraint it has to come from those who are the beneficiaries of such plenty, but we suffer from none of the introspection and doubt the Dutch exhibited in wondering what a moral use of life would look like. America, as a result, has become a paradise of unlimited, endless con-

35. Simon Schama, *The Embarrassment of Riches: An Interpretation of Dutch Culture in the Golden Age* (New York: Alfred P. Knopf, 1987), 609.
36. Schama, *The Embarrassment of Riches*, 141.

> It is possible for multitudes in time of peace and security to exist
> agreeably — somewhat incoherently, perhaps, but without con-
> vulsions — to dream a little and not unpleasantly, to have only
> now and then a nightmare, and only occasionally a rude awak-
> ening. It is possible to drift along somewhat nervously, some-
> what anxiously, somewhat confusedly, hoping for the best, and
> believing in nothing very much. It is possible to be a passable
> citizen. But it is not possible to be wholly at peace. For serenity
> of soul requires some better organization of life than a man can
> attain by pursuing casual ambitions, satisfying his hungers, and
> for the rest accepting destiny as an idiot's tale in which one
> dumb sensation succeeds another to no known end.
>
> Walter Lippmann, *A Preface to Morals*

sumption, where desire now substitutes for the moral norms which
were once there. And desire is never satiated. The mountainous garbage heaps every city creates, the numerous used car lots, the garage
sales, and the storage lockers all tell the story of use but they often tell
the story of desire, too. Desire, today, is the only norm and this is another indication of the way in which our modernized world has
brought us to a place which, at a practical level, is godless.

This godlessness, in turn, works itself out in the way we think of
ourselves. Modern consumption, Colin Campbell has written, is "an activity which involves an apparently endless pursuit of wants," and the
wants themselves are "inexhaustible." As one want is satisfied its place is
taken by one which is not. It is an endless chain, a process that is "ceaseless and unbroken."[37] It was probably in the 1970's that the marriage between this kind of consumption and self-improvement occurred. David
Frum speaks of it as "the greatest rebellion in American history" as millions of Americans sloughed off the rules their parents and grandparents
had recognized and decided they "would live *for themselves*." An adver-

---

37. Colin Campbell, *The Romantic Ethic and the Spirit of Modern Capitalism*
(Oxford: Basil Blackwell, 1987), 37.

tisement for hair dye early in the 1970s "featured a lovely blonde simpering, 'This I do for me.'" The ad, he says, "would have spoken more directly to the times had it only added: 'and this, and this, and this,'"[38] one product after another in a never-ending chain of purchase — and all for *me*.

Years ago, Reinhold Niebuhr wrote that we are "somewhat embarrassed by the fact that we are the first culture which is in danger of being subordinated to its economy. We have to live as luxuriously as possible in order to keep our productive enterprise from stalling."[39] Today, we are not embarrassed at all. It is exactly what we want and what, we have come to think, we *need*. This kind of avid consumerism, Christopher Lasch observes, "promotes an ethic of hedonism . . . and thus undermines the 'traditional values' of thrift and self denial."[40] This never-ending transformation of luxuries into necessities, the experience of comfort only fueling the desire for even more comfort, "appeared to give the Anglo-American idea of progress a solid foundation that could not be shaken by subsequent events," he remarks, "not even by the global wars that broke out in the twentieth century."[41] And even though the wars in fact stimulated economic activity, it now turns out that this sense that life is moving toward pastures ever greener and more lush has collided with a number of painful social realities which have put the idea of progress, once at the heart of the Enlightenment's vision, in considerable disrepute. And yet what has not been shaken is the belief that consuming is essential to the nurture of the self.

This experience of abundance which is the result of both extraordinary ingenuity and untamed desire is a telltale sign that we have moved from a traditional society to one that is modern, from a time when God and the supernatural were "natural" parts of life, to one in which God is now alienated and dislocated from our modernized world. In traditional societies, what one could legitimately have wanted was limited. It was, of course, limited because people lived with only a few choices and little knowledge of life other than the life they

38. David Frum, *How We Got Here: The 70s: The Decade That Brought You Modern Life (for Better or for Worse)* (New York: Basic Books, 2000), 58.

39. Niebuhr, *Christ and Culture*, 3.

40. Christopher Lasch, *Progress and Its Critics* (New York: W. W. Norton, 1991), 514.

41. Lasch, *Progress and Its Critics*, 14.

lived; their vision of life had not been invaded, as ours is, by pictures of beguiling Caribbean shorelines, sleek luxury under the Lexus insignia, time-shares in fabulous places, or exotic perfumes sure to stir hidden passions. Wants then were not stimulated as they are today and they were also limited by tradition. Those who tried to pursue their own goals and ambitions, their own needs and wants, were viewed as being dangerously anti-social. However, what was looked at askance then has become the heartbeat of our modern individualism today and an essential component in how our capitalism works. Our advertising feeds on the fact that in a consumer culture, experience and status, indeed, even a new *persona,* can all be purchased and the only limitation on what we can do or become is our ability to pay for it. Product after product is therefore pitched to us, offering experiences we have never had. Desire in the imagination projects itself onto the product and the bond is sealed by purchase. The very heart of modern consuming, Campbell says, is "autonomous, imaginative pleasure-seeking."[42]

Since the 1960s, to the consumption of goods has been added a growing consumption of services. These are, of course, of all kinds, ranging from lawn services, health clubs, and inspirational lectures, to sporting events, rock concerts, and movies. Those of a recreational kind present themselves as miniature escape routes, taking us out of our own private reality and into another. The duration of each of these moments of consumption is quite brief, but then brief duration is of the essence of our modernized world from our aerosol cans, vacuum sweepers, and cars to our TV advertisements, fashions, and fads. This rapid turnover in production and consumption fuels some of the habits in which we are now caught up. What it does, Harvey argues, is to "accentuate volatility and ephemerality of fashions, products, production techniques, labor processes, ideas and ideologies, values and established practices. The sense that 'all that is solid melts into air' has rarely been more pervasive. . . ."[43] These life patterns accentuate the im-

42. Campbell, *The Romantic Ethic and the Spirit of Modern Capitalism,* 99. The same argument is developed by Grant McCracken, *Culture and Consumption: New Approaches to the Symbolic Character of Consumer Goods and Activities* (Bloomington: Indiana University Press, 1988), 104-17.

43. David Harvey, *The Condition of Postmodernity: An Inquiry into the Origins of Cultural Change* (Oxford: Blackwell, 1992), 285-86.

portance and desirability of what is instantaneous, like fast-food production, and what is disposable, like Styrofoam cups, plastic knives and forks, and diapers. The result is an accelerated transience that greatly fuels both fragmentation and diversity. This is, in Frederick Jameson's narrative of capitalism, the outcome to "late capitalism," a phase which began in the 1950s and is characterized by the dominance of the multinational corporations for whom national boundaries are inconsequential, by ever multiplying choices, by a fascination with such surface-level qualities as style and novelty, and by a fragile, disappearing sense of the self. And here, too, is another wrenching relocation of the self, away from what is eternal, unchanging, and enduring, and into what is shifting, faddish, fleeting, and ephemeral. It is no wonder that as God disappears, the self gets flimsy and thin and often has the sense that it is no more durable than the cans and plastic paraphernalia that are taken in great profusion to our garbage dumps.

And, in the final evolutionary lurch, the service economy has blossomed into the "experience" economy which is as distinct from services as services are from goods. Walt Disney's theme parks, for example, grew out of his dissatisfaction with the amusement parks his children visited, which had swings and rides but no "story," no alternative reality to be experienced, and so he founded the happiest place on earth. In the same way, the indoor environments of our malls may well lead us through a tropical jungle, or we might pass an oasis, or see some remnants of a classical civilization, or intimations of the future. Yet it is not only malls that can be "themed" in this way; almost anything can, from car showrooms to hospitals. And the point of doing this is to engage the customer and change his or her view of reality in some small way, for at least a few short minutes, to smooth the ritual of purchase. In buying, we also buy some reality. Well, maybe it is only fantasy but the internal residue of feeling is good and renewing.[44] The idea is that shopping should not be done out of necessity alone. No, it should also be fun. The mall should beckon.

Much, of course, has been said about this state of affairs. Clearly, the experience of such plenty easily leads people to define life in terms

---

44. B. Joseph Pine II and James H. Gilmore, *The Experience Economy: Work Is Theatre and Every Business Is a Stage* (Boston: Harvard Business School Press, 1999), 45-68.

of the things possessed and consumed. The gospel of our secular, this-worldly age is that to have is to be and to have not is to be damned. For products are sold to us, not merely for our use, but for our improvement, to enhance our sex appeal, to elevate our importance, or to make us feel better about ourselves. As such, and in combination, they do serve as a kind of pseudo-gospel. However, this may not be the most important consequence of our obsessive consuming.

Perhaps more important than this is the habit which, to one degree or another, many indulge, which is to think that they can create, or buy, a new self. Style, for example, is a way of saying who we are or, perhaps more correctly, who we want to be perceived as being. Our consumer paradise offers us a rich palette from which to paint this image of ourselves consisting of stylized goods, name brands, logos, fashions, new looks, retro looks, reshaped noses and breasts, whitened teeth and exotic accessories which are all delivering information. In a world of bureaucracy and rationalized impersonality, style is how we stand out, how we say who we are, how we assert our unique individuality.[45] So, from these purchases we assemble the parts of who we want to be, the parts which can combine in different ways as the whole comes together each day. Zygmunt Bauman has used the metaphor of the liquid to describe our modern situation since liquids do not keep their shape, are often light and flow, assuming the shape of what they are flowing into. This is now our "individualized, privatized version of modernity" for we are "malleable to an extent unexperienced by, and unimaginable for, past generations."[46] Of course! God has done a disappearing act and what are we left with? Only what is shifting and changing, what is superficial and impermanent, only with ourselves and what we can make of ourselves.

Much modern literature has spoken of our *anomie,* the aloneness and sense of drifting which afflicts those who live in our fragmented social world. It is certainly ironic that the capitalism which has somewhat contributed to this situation as it has fueled change and mobility, also thrives on the fragmentation which it has, in part, caused. Those haunted by their own solitude, distracted by their own sense of frag-

45. Ewen, *All Consuming Images,* 148.
46. Bauman, *Liquid Modernity,* 7-8.

mentation, hurt by the absence of enduring friendships, of connections to place and family, their sense of being impotent to change so much that affects them, are often driven to the pursuit of affluence, in the hope that what is consumed might offer some solace for these wounds. In the nineteenth century, the waves of mostly European immigrants which broke on America's shore brought into proximity with each other those from several European nations. Although the language of the melting pot is a little strained, it nevertheless did describe what was coming about as *Americans* emerged from all of these contributing nations. By contrast today, consumer society produces only brief, fleeting connections and no bonding in the melting pot. The more descriptive image of the postmodern experience would be not the melting pot but the cocktail party. This is the place of brief encounter where those who may be strangers perform the ritual of instant, but evaporating community, one that springs into being as the sun sets and is gone before the moon arises. The modern self, as a result, has grown very thin, insubstantial, and distracted. It lives in a world of fleeting experiences and constantly shifting images, images which we create and by which we sometimes even pass ourselves off as something we are not. In this world of images and shadows, the only constant is not the self behind them, or the self consuming them, but the corporations which create and exploit them.

The central character in Don DeLillo's important novel, *White Noise,* is Jack Gladney, the head of the department of Hitler studies at a well-to-do liberal arts college called the College-on-the-Hill. Murray J. Suskind, a former sports writer and now an adjunct professor at the college in the department of popular culture, becomes friendly with Gladney. He is impressed, however, that unlike his own department, whose professors seem to read nothing but cereal boxes, the department of Hitler studies has made the College internationally respected, and whenever Hitler's name is mentioned it is always with a nod to Gladney.

It is, Suskind declares quietly to Gladney, what he wants to do for Elvis. However, Gladney's success had not come without some thought. Some years earlier, the chancellor had told him that if he wanted to be taken seriously as a Hitler innovator he would have to do something about his name and appearance. Jack Gladney therefore became J. A. K.

We are quartered in Centenary Hall, a dark brick structure we share with the popular culture department, known officially as American environments. A curious group. The teaching staff is composed almost solely of New York emigres, smart, thuggish, movie-mad, trivia-crazed. They are here to decipher the natural language of the culture, to make a formal method of the shiny pleasures they'd known in their European-shadowed childhoods — an Aristotelianism of bubble gum wrappers and detergent jingles. The department head is Alfonse (Fast Food) Stompanato, a broad-chested glowering man whose collection of prewar soda pop bottles is on permanent display in an alcove. All his teachers are male, wear rumpled clothes, need haircuts, cough into their armpits. Together they look like teamster officials assembled to identify the body of a mutilated colleague. The impression is one of pervasive bitterness, suspicion and intrigue.

Don DeLillo, *White Noise*

Gladney by the addition of an initial, "a tag I wore like a borrowed suit."[47] And he was advised to gain weight, a more substantial appearance suggesting a more substantial self, and that becoming more ugly might be helpful to his career. So, he added a small touch of menace by way of dark glasses in thick rims. "I am the false character," Gladney confides to the reader, "that follows the name around."[48]

Thus it is that "image management" has become a lucrative business driven by both necessity and by the emptiness of the modern or postmodern self. Whether in commerce, politics, careers, or personal relations, the appearance is, as it were, stage-managed. But the upshot of all of this is, as Ewen argues, that "the powers of appearance have come to overshadow, or to shape, the way we comprehend matters of substance."[49] Indeed, as often as not, matters of appearance threaten to

47. DeLillo, *White Noise* (New York: Penguin Books, 1995), 16.
48. DeLillo, *White Noise*, 17.
49. Ewen, *All Consuming Images*, 259.

take the place of substance. In 2001, for example, CNN touted the advent of its new anchorman, Aaron Brown, with the words, "News delivered in a rare voice. A human voice." What is important here? The news or the person through whom it comes? What has happened on any given day or the rare human voice by which it is heard? Substance or (audible) appearance? In the persistent preoccupation with surfaces and appearances, God and matters of ultimate concern simply disappear. With that, the Enlightenment philosophers would have been delighted. They struggled and fought, sometimes literally, to bring about this end. We have done so with no struggle and no war. We have done it with no tears. We have done it all in the pursuit of making a more pleasurable world.

At America's genesis, we set out to make happiness the end of life and enshrined its pursuit as an inviolable right in our constitution. Along the way, however, we have come to think that happiness is unattainable and unimaginable in the absence of comfort and affluence. The means to reach this end — capitalism and technology — have, in the absence of serious engagement with the truth of God and the God of that truth, become themselves the final ends of life. The means become the end as the affluent live only for their own affluence. This kind of development is what David Lyon calls "Disneyfication," what "diminishes human life through trivializing it, or making involvement within it appear less than fully serious."[50] It is a fearful idolatry and the immediate judgment that is being visited upon us is that our culture has become shallow, cheap, and vulgar. And far from challenging this emptiness and futility, evangelical churches have too often been its exemplars, as I shall argue in a later chapter, pitching their "product" to "consumers" and emptying themselves of every vestige of spiritual *gravitas* as if striving for a serious faith were a failing of great magnitude and one to be avoided at all costs.

By a different and unintended path, then, our modernized world, with its technology and abundance, has brought us, in an unthinking way, to where the Enlightenment intended to take us by deliberate intent. For the Enlightenment thinkers, God and the supernatural order could not be seen as inhibiting human freedom in any way and, further-

50. Lyon, *Jesus in Disneyland*, 4.

more, the human project became their sole preoccupation. It is so within the ethos created by modernization, too. While the reality of God is not assaulted in the same way, the bias of modernized life is overwhelmingly in favor of human preoccupations. It inclines us to think only of style and surfaces and look no deeper, and it entices us with the same fraudulent possibility that human life can be remade humanly, though perhaps we may have to be satisfied with only the appearance of the remake. Never mind. The surface is the substance, is it not?

Hollow Chests

The experience of our modernized world leads us to think of it not only as the absence of God but, as it turns out, the absence of human nature. This is no coincidence. The death of God is always followed by the death of the human being.

In the early 1950s, C. S. Lewis took aim at the evisceration of human nature that some in the field of education had unwittingly accomplished. Their ideas were leaving people without the internal capacity for making moral judgments about the world. If we are stripped of the belief that some things are ultimately true and others ultimately false, Lewis contended, then any statements that make what we call "value judgments" can only be reflections of our own feelings. On this understanding, to say that a mountain is magnificent is simply to say that we experienced feelings of grandeur as we looked at it. By this same logic, to say that a heinous crime is evil is to say merely that we have awkward, uneasy feelings about it. Our world is thus emptied of the possibility of real, objective goodness and real, objective evil. "In a sort of ghastly simplicity," he said, "we remove the organ and demand the function. We make men without chests and expect of them virtue and enterprise. We laugh at honour and are shocked to find traitors in our midst. We castrate and bid the geldings be fruitful."[51]

What Lewis was objecting to, however, had been long in the making. The idea that there is such a thing as human nature which defines

---

51. C. S. Lewis, *The Abolition of Man: or, Reflections on Education with Special Reference to the Teaching of English in the Upper Forms of School* (New York: Macmillan, 1953), 16.

human beings as human and sets them apart from animals was increasingly attacked by those in the train of Enlightenment thinking. For one thing, it depended too much on a distinction between the natural and the supernatural and all too often on the Christian notion of a Creator and a creation made in his image. In the modern period, God either vanished, or was banished, or, in a kind of rear guard action mounted in the frail hope of rescuing some of his reality from the relentless assault that had all but destroyed it, he was relocated within the human psyche. Whatever the outcome, human nature now made no sense. The idea of human nature also seemed to suggest that there was a kind of essence that had been deposited in each body which was the same in all people. This collided with the growing individualism of the West which assumed just the opposite, the uniqueness of every person. But perhaps most important of all, this idea did not seem to be helpful in understanding the meaning of the person; and meaning, it should be remembered, has become the single most elusive and hauntingly unrequited pursuit in the modern period. I will be examining this later on.

In the late nineteenth century, I have noted elsewhere[52] and so can only sketch briefly here, several important shifts occurred, the end result of which was the loss in popular culture of the idea of human nature. This came about along an entirely different route than the one the Enlightenment had taken, but the conclusion reached nevertheless paralleled the ideas of the Enlightenment. This happened in several ways.

The first major shift in this period was the replacement of Virtue[53] by values. It was the practice of the virtues, those aspects of the Good that were the same for all people in all places and were what endured, that gave life its structure and meaning. The belief in Virtue, however, was slowly replaced in the wider culture by that in values, and values could be nothing more than personal preferences which are not normative for all people. Thus it was that values have come to be thought about in an ironically value-free way.

52. David F. Wells, *Losing Our Virtue: Why the Church Must Recover Its Moral Vision* (Grand Rapids: William B. Eerdmans, 1998), 104-45.
53. See the narrative of this transition in Gertrude Himmelfarb, *The De-Moralization of Society: From Victorian Virtues to Modern Values* (New York: Alfred A. Knopf), 1995.

Consonant with this change was a second shift, that from a focus on character to one on personality. Warren Susman noticed how this change was reflected in the language of the popular advice manuals that were published just before the turn of the twentieth century. When it was the virtues which were being pursued, and good character was the desired end, then the words used in these manuals were typically *citizenship, duty, democracy, work, building, golden deeds, outdoor life, conquest, honor, reputation, morals, manners, integrity,* and above all, *manhood.*[54] As the shift to focusing life around personality occurred, the language in these manuals also changed. Now, the words most commonly used were *fascinating, stunning, attractive, magnetic, glowing, masterful, creative, dominant, forceful.*[55] It was a shift away from the older moral concern with personal restraint and sacrifice to the new concern with self-realization and self-expression. It was a shift away from one's inner moral fabric and toward how one felt or how one appeared to others. Now, it was becoming important to express one's uniqueness, to stand out in the crowd, and to know how to use one's personality as one navigated through life's stormy channels or came upon its opportunities. This "shift from character to personality," wrote Philip Cushman, "reflected a profound change in the cultural terrain of the era. The self was in process of being configured into a radically different shape."[56]

These two shifts provided the foundation for the third main change, that of speaking of the self in place of human nature. This has only been accelerated since then by exposure to consumer culture. Human nature used to be thought of as being the same in everyone, whatever other differences adhered to it such as gender, ethnicity, class, and personality type. Self-consciousness, by contrast, is different in everyone. The self became that place within each person that configured his or her own gender, ethnicity, and unique life experiences into a perception of the self and of the world that defined him or her as *different* from everyone else. At its center, wrote Roy Baumeister, are "thoughts, feelings, intentions, personality traits, latent talents and capabilities,

54. Warren I. Susman, *Culture as History: The Transformation of American Society in the Twentieth Century* (New York: Pantheon Books, 1984), 273-74.

55. Susman, *Culture as History,* 277.

56. Philip Cushman, *Constructing the Self, Constructing America: A Cultural History of Psychotherapy* (Reading: Addison-Wesley, 1995), 65.

the wellsprings of creativity, the key ingredients of personal fulfillment, and the solutions to many of life's problems."[57] The self also establishes a boundary for each person: I am not another. This language of the self has seemed to be far more adaptable to the kind of world in which we live with its endless varieties of what we can do, be, and buy than is the fixed concept of human nature. Modern life requires change, malleability, and adaptation because it is fluid and in constant change. When the world was simpler, and ruffled by only a little change, it resembled a fixed abode and in that setting human nature made sense to people. Today, that fixed abode has disappeared and life is more like an uncertain, unpredictable journey. The idea of the self seems to cohere better with the understanding of life as a journey which has no clear destination and where a person will encounter constantly changing circumstances than does human nature. This, in turn, has produced some major revisions in what people imagine spirituality is and how it exhibits itself, a theme to which I will return later as well.

The self sees itself as a sovereign and individual consciousness, liberated by education from the traditional bonds of religion, by democracy from the strictures of class, by technology from the drudgery of poverty, and by self-knowledge from the tyranny of the unconscious — and therefore free to pursue its own destiny without God.

Walker Percy, *Lost in the Cosmos*

In place, therefore, of the older order which imposed moral restraint on people has emerged this new order which does not. What rules here, Philip Rief said, is "the superiority of all that money can buy, technology can make, and science can conceive."[58] The moral axis in life has collapsed and has been replaced by the assumption that each

---

57. Roy F. Baumeister, *Escaping the Self: Alcoholism, Spirituality, Masochism, and Flights from the Burden of Selfhood* (New York: Basic Books, 1991), 3-4.
58. Philip Rief, *The Triumph of the Therapeutic: The Uses of Faith After Freud* (New York: Harper and Row, 1965), 253.

person must be his or her own person, must pursue one's own uniqueness, must realize oneself, must make of oneself what one can, and
must buy whatever will bring her or him to these ends. The single most
important signal that this is what has happened is our shift from talking about human nature to talking about the self. Our whole society is
being reordered around the self understood as autonomous from others, from the past, and from a moral order. This transformation has
gathered momentum since the 1970s and it is now what characterizes
our public discussion. The "public display of one's wrongs, one's piti-
ableness, one's misfortunes, which would have seemed shameful, igno-
ble, even disgusting before World War II, became in the 1970s," Frum argued, "the distinctive American style. Don't bottle it up; you have a
right to tell others how you feel."[59] Thus it is that by an entirely different route the broader culture has reached conclusions whose practical
outcomes parallel what we see in the Enlightenment thinkers whose
progeny eviscerated the internal capacity for moral discrimination.
The Enlightenment idea that there is no such thing as human nature
seems thoroughly plausible in our modernized culture because that is
how we experience ourselves in this consumer paradise. In this paradise, there is no moral restraint or need for moral discrimination. Here,
in this land, heaven and hell have contracted into the small flashes of
pleasure or the daily bumps of pain that become our lot and nothing
more. Here, we experience ourselves as selves who can be remade,
selves whose desire must be satiated, selves whose uniqueness and
whose pleasures, pains or perplexities, are matters to be revealed before any audience, large or small, indeed, anyone willing to hear. God
has receded into the far-off distance; and human nature is now part of
a forgotten language, one we have no interest in recovering.

Miracles of (Human) Power

It is rather ironic that these first two themes — the disappearance of
God and of human nature — should accompany the third, which is the
bloated sense of human capacity. But that is what has happened.
What the Enlightenment believed in this regard we have come to as-

---

59. Frum, *How We Got Here,* 99.

sume is correct, but we have come to this assumption by a different route.

The kind of overweening confidence in human ability which Kant exhibited in his famous essay on the meaning of Enlightenment became a hallmark of this movement. What, in an earlier age, people believed only God could do, the Enlightenment now placed within human reach. There was, therefore, a pervasive sense of a brand new epoch that was opening up, a moment in history which would be quite unlike any that had preceded it. Human beings would remake life and remake it closer to their hearts' desire.

This assumption that we have the power to remake life has had many outworkings, some more pernicious than others. In architecture, LeCorbusier, who designed some of the most brutally stark but aesthetically beautiful buildings of the twentieth century, was one who spoke of the new "epoch" we had entered. Like many other modernist architects he was looking for an architecture that would capitalize on the accomplishments of our machine age. However, in his mind, the architect was not simply designing aesthetically pleasing buildings but was also redesigning life. He believed that a socialistic egalitarianism would be the best outcome to the buildings he created. That kind of ideological framework, and that kind of confidence in the Enlightenment assumptions about remaking life, became quite pervasive among leading architects in the twentieth century.

Charles Jencks, who first used the word *postmodern* in architecture (though not in the sense of being more modern than modern but, rather, of being open to the past and of being more human), has aptly illustrated what was so wrong about much of this modernist architecture. In 1972, the Pruitt-Igoe housing complex in St. Louis, after suffering much verbal abuse from its critics, and after inflicting much degradation on its inhabitants, was dynamited. This public housing project had been a monument to the most progressive (read: Enlightenment) ideals and was a prize-winning realization of LeCorbusier's ideas. Like so much other modernist architecture, it turned its back on the past, and its designer also engaged in a bit of social engineering. It would be the architect's right to remake life so that it would better reflect the ends in which he believed. The traditional pattern of life was, therefore, upended. Streets would not be horizontal but were conceived as being vertical. Now they — the stairways, that is — would be free from cars, though, as it turned out, not from crime. And the more traditional ideas of semi-private space and gardens were banished in favor of *public* spaces for trees, laundries, conversation, and creches, regardless of whether people actually wanted to use these spaces in these ways.

Twenty years later, Michael Jones described a visit he made with a social worker to the high-rise public housing projects on the south side of Chicago. "Miss Hardy had explained on the way to Tawanda's apartment that not all of the public housing projects in Chicago were high-rise buildings of the sort that march off into the horizon south of the ITT campus," Jones explained. He then learned about the alternative. "There are also low-rise buildings, which are virtually never vacant. They are the coveted public housing in Chicago; the high-rise projects are where you go when you have no place else." What, Jones wondered, was the difference? "Miss Hardy," he said, "who is black and has lived in the Projects herself — whose mother, in fact, still lives in the Projects — suggests that a house with a yard gives one a greater sense of possession." She went on to say that "even if you don't own the building, it seems as if you do. With the sense of possession comes a greater sense of responsibility, of control over one's life, and, with that, less likelihood of succumbing to the pathologies associated with the ghetto — promiscuity, despair, drugs, and so on."[60]

This kind of sentiment had been brusquely set aside when the project was built in St. Louis. It was built, Jencks says, on Enlightenment "naivetés too great and awe-inspiring to warrant refutation," namely, that "the intelligent planning of abstract space was to promote healthy behavior." Alas, it did not. The buildings were vandalized, the windows broken, the walls daubed with graffiti, many of the inhabitants were tyrannized by gangs and drug lords. The final *coup de grace* was a merciful end to this episode of Enlightenment arrogance, at least in this corner of St. Louis.[61]

In a parallel but different circumstance, there may also be a case

60. E. Michael Jones, *Living Machines: Bauhaus Architecture as Sexual Ideology* (San Francisco: Ignatius Press, 1995), 17.

61. Charles Jencks, *The Language of Post-Modern Architecture* (New York: Rizzoli, 1984), 9-10.

for saying that it is this same belief in human omnicompetence which has fueled the staggering growth in the size of government, at least in America in the post-War years. The issue is undoubtedly complicated by the fact that the United States, like all of the countries of the industrialized world, has had to move, like it or not, from the kind of laissez-faire, freewheeling, independent capitalism of the nineteenth century, which did not require much state involvement, into the highly competitive globalized markets of today, which do. The state, which is inextricably tied into this development because of its own self-interest as well as its responsibility to provide regulation, has had to make the same kind of adjustment as businesses have and that has required its expansion. Not only so, but some of the state's expansion in other areas, such as regulation in that of civil rights, has been driven by religious or civil demand and was not originally rooted in government's desire to place its mark on all of life.

Nevertheless, it is also the case that after the Depression, the state felt obliged to take a more active role in social relief, now an enormous part of its budget, and this has happened often at the cost of the Church's involvement. Robert Wuthnow notes that in the pre-War period, churches assumed responsibility for the financial upkeep of 15% of all hospitals, 42% of all homes for the elderly, and about one third of the nation's institutions of higher education.[62] In the years after the War, much of this responsibility was assumed by the state, which has felt the obligation not merely to write laws and provide for their enforcement, not only to defend borders and mend roads, but also to regulate life in far-reaching ways. And, from time to time, there are significant crises to which the state has had to respond. Expansion of its reach into life, then, has tended to come in spurts, rather than by incremental enlargement, and this usually after these social crises. Once the crisis has passed, however, the governmental structures and agencies which were erected in order to manage the crisis simply stay on in perpetuity.

The state is our collective statement of how we think we can best secure what we want and best preserve what we have. There was a time when it looked as if it was about to sink beneath its own bureaucratic weight, a victim of its own serried layers, inertia, and inefficiency. But,

---

62. Wuthnow, *The Restructuring of American Religion*, 319.

voila, the computer! While the state's arms and agencies may not rival corporate America in its efficiency, they have been revived enough by this technology to sustain our faith in them. It is true, as Gay says, that from time to time we lose heart in particular politicians and parties but we have a virtually religious faith in what we think the political process can deliver.[63] The Enlightenment proposed a counterfeit faith which is widely believed today. What Christian faith had promised, the state would now deliver on its own secular terms. Both had the same objective in mind, as William Cavanaugh asserts: "salvation of humankind from the divisions which plague us."[64] All of this rests, Gay argues, on a "bloated estimation" of human potential and on "a vastly exaggerated sense of human responsibility in and for the world."[65]

The melancholy fact is, however, that the considerable outlays which are made to rectify social ills have, in the post-War years, proved quite ineffective in many cases. Despite the multi-billion dollar war on poverty in the United States begun under President Lyndon Johnson in the 1960s, for example, poverty levels, sadly, remain unchanged. There are maladies of the human spirit that are simply not responsive to, or will not be solved by, governmental programs, no matter how lavish and generous they may be. That, however, does not stand as a hindrance to our earnest hopefulness that somehow government will be able to change life in deep and transforming ways. It is, in fact, what has given to some politicians a moral calling to assume responsibility for bettering broad swaths of life which are actually well outside the power of government to change. The resistance of human ills to well-intentioned governmental programs is brushed off as if it were an irritating fly. And every attempt to change the level of taxation, by which all of the desired programs are to be funded, is treated as cold-hearted and unfeeling. By a different route, then, the Enlightenment's assumption that human beings would do for life what God had once done is working itself out at a political level, too.

It is this same Enlightenment assumption regarding the human

63. Gay, *The Way of the (Modern) World,* 31.

64. William T. Cavanaugh, "The City: Beyond Secular Parodies," in *Radical Orthodoxy: A New Theology,* ed. John Milbank, Catherine Pickstock, and Graham Ward (London: Routledge, 1999), 182.

65. Gay, *The Way of the (Modern) World,* 31.

ability to resolve all human ills that now drives the self-help industry, which has become both an industry and a cultural phenomenon. Its more popular books sell prodigiously. And here we see rather clearly how what was once a religious quest has been transformed into a very human one. The twelve-step programs, despite the wide variety of addictions and maladies which they are seeking to abate, are quite similar in their techniques. They all profess a belief in a higher, though otherwise undefined, power. But then matters rapidly turn to psychological technique. Here is the attempt, Rief says, to conquer "the last enemy," which is not death as the apostle Paul explained, but our own personalities.[66] As a result, psychologists, and those who pretend they are, have set themselves to "work out ever more affirmative and uplifting therapies that promise not only personal regeneration," says Lasch, but "in many cases, social regeneration as well."[67] And the premise beneath it all, what produces this "liberation psychotherapy" as John Rice calls it,[68] is made up of a set of very simple beliefs: we do have a self; the self can be found; the self is essentially benign; and most importantly, the self carries within itself its own healing powers just as the body does.

Of course, it is also the case that this industry would not exist if people did not believe themselves to be victimized in some way, which is what has led to the expansion in all directions of the original AA formula.[69] These victims are the offspring of mean-spirited parents, they are middle-class men unappreciated by their wives, they are those who struggle with the consequences of what were once called bad habits and bad choices but are now partly sanitized as addictions, addictions to too much shopping, too much food, too much sex, too much drink, and too many of the wrong drugs. The maladies are numerous and, no doubt, genuine, and in the midst of the mindless jargon and foolish-

66. Rief, *The Triumph of the Therapeutic*, 391.

67. Christopher Lasch, *The Minimal Self: Psychic Survival in Troubled Times* (New York: W. W. Norton, 1984), 211.

68. John Steadman Rice, *A Disease of One's Own: Psychotherapy, Addiction, and the Emergence of Co-Dependency* (New Brunswick: Transaction Publishers, 1996), 29.

69. See Charles J. Sykes, *A Nation of Victims: The Decay of the American Character* (New York: St. Martin's Press, 1992); Wendy Kaminer, *I'm Dysfunctional, You're Dysfunctional: The Recovery Movement and Other Self-Help Fashions* (Reading: Addison-Wesley, 1992).

ness of this literature there are occasional insights into why people do things. Yet what stands out most of all are the evasions and the touching trust in the self, the unquestioned naiveté about life, the assumption that it all boils down to tapping into those inner powers, with a glance now and then at the higher power, if we want to find regeneration and redemption. Here is the Christian heresy writ large.

The Enlightenment, then, was an aggressive ideology on the high end of culture. At its heart were the demand for freedom from all external authority and the belief that it was reason which carried in itself the means of unlocking the riddles of life and paving the way to progress, of finding for itself meaning in life and finding a way out of human darkness. It was, of course, an elitist movement, and so it is quite unrealistic to think that where today, in popular culture, we find comparable attitudes these must somehow have trickled down unconsciously from the Enlightenment *philosophes*. Rather, the explanation is to be found in the modernization of our world, which has produced its own psychological environment which parallels the intellectual climate of the Enlightenment. Within this public world, those ideas and attitudes, wants and beliefs, resonate with a modernized world and so they seem normal. Because they seem normal they come to exercise an informal authority of being normative. So it is that by an entirely different route God becomes dislodged from public life and, in fact, becomes weightless. In his absence, life becomes empty and banal but filled with the bright wonders of malls and theme parks. Human nature, assaulted by the Enlightenment, also disappears in modernized culture but for a very different reason as values replace virtues, personality replaces character, and the self takes the place that human nature had once had. And the amazing confidence the Enlightenment rested in unaided human power and ingenuity we see reflected, by a different rationale altogether, in Big Government and our belief in the regenerative powers of the self. What this explains is why Enlightenment ideas endured so long and why they were so hard to dislodge. They appeared inevitable and invincible because modern experience has led people in the wider culture to reach the same conclusions though for entirely different reasons. The Enlightenment was *thought;* modern life has been *experienced.* The experience has supported, reinforced, and given great plausibility to the thought.

This cozy relationship between Enlightenment ideology and modernized social context, each lending weight to the other, has now fallen on hard times. The Enlightenment, which has been the soul of modernity, is dying. This passing of an ideology that once brooked no rivals has precipitated a crisis of gargantuan proportions within modernity. Indeed, it has led those who are heady with triumph to speak of this moment as being *post*modern. It is, to say the least, a galling epithet to those still enamored with Enlightenment beliefs, for, to those who still believe in progress, to be called passé is a thunderclap of judgment more dreadful, it would seem, than anything God could deliver. This is no small development and it is to this that we must now turn.

CHAPTER II

Postmodern Rebellion

—⟨∞⟩—

Let us be honest enough to confront our culture in its entirety and ask: is it merely coincidence that, in the midst of so much technological mastery and economic abundance, our art and thought continue to project a nihilistic image unparalleled in human history? Are we to believe there is not a connection between these facts?

THEODORE ROSZAK

In the 1960s, emerging ideas about postmodernity were trendy, especially in art, architecture, and literature, but today many who rode this initial wave — even some who were on its forefront — have become leery about the word. What does *postmodern* even mean now? Like other cutting-edge fashions, it lost its edge once it spilled out into popular culture. I would not be surprised today to learn that the word *postmodern* had been overheard in a casual beauty parlor conversation, or that the idea was part of a strategy for decorating a flashy boutique, or that it determined what (superficial) fare to serve up in a glossy magazine. It has already popped up in some American newspapers. And publishers have reflected the new interest with books like *Women and Postmodernity, The Postmodern Bible Reader, The Postmod-*

ern God, and *Postmodern Youth Ministry.* As news spreads of our postmodern condition,[1] as the word slips into ever wider and ever more promiscuous usage, as more and more people seem to think they know what it is, definitional clarity becomes the most obvious victim.[2] There is an irony to this, of course, since definitional clarity is something that was prized in modernity, with its Enlightenment rationality, and is not so prized in postmodernity. Indeed, it is often reviled as being simply the tool of those who want to exercise power over others. In a strange way, it is the postmodern ethos which is helping to obscure its own nature.

The widespread misuse of the idea of postmodernity and the multiple uses to which it is put undoubtedly have spread confusion. If we are to use this word to describe this moment of deep transition in the West, we are obviously going to have to purge the word and uncomplicate it a little. Doing this, however, is no mean undertaking. Richard Tarnas has observed how varied the postmodern mind is, that its attitudes are indeterminate, that it bears within itself many diverse currents, that it draws off pragmatism, existentialism, Marxism, psychoanalysis, feminism, language theory, and theories about science.[3] This is all true. But it gets worse. Here again we encounter the same dilemma that is everywhere present in modernized societies. What is the relation between the ideas that the philosophers and artists are exploring which are of a postmodern kind and the attitudes, often incoherent and muddled, that emerge more broadly in culture which can also be said to be postmodern? If the broader postmodern attitudes are not drawn directly from the intellectuals — and they are mostly not — then from whence have they come? If we are to understand postmodernity, do we not have to be able to answer these questions?

1. The language is that of Jean-François Lyotard, *The Postmodern Condition: A Report on Knowledge,* trans. Geoff Bennington and Brian Massurri (Minneapolis: University of Minnesota Press, 1984); cf. David Harvey, *The Condition of Postmodernity: An Inquiry into the Origins of Cultural Change* (Cambridge: Blackwell, 1989).

2. On the history of the idea of postmodernity, see the illuminating discussion in David Lyon, *Postmodernity* (Minneapolis: University of Minnesota Press, 1999), 6-24.

3. Richard Tarnas, *The Passion of the Western Mind: Understanding the Ideas That Have Shaped Our World View* (New York: Harmony Books, 1991), 395.

In this chapter, I want to begin by developing, in a very modest way, a usable understanding of postmodernity, despite the substantial literature and despite the fact that postmodernity is a cultural ethos which presents a moving target. The central argument I want to make is that the rebellion against the Enlightenment project which postmodern thinkers have waged and which they think has produced a clean breach with the modern world — and hence they are *post*modern — is only a small part of the story and, in my judgment, not the most important part. Indeed, what I will argue is that modernity and postmodernity are actually reflecting different aspects of our modernized culture. They are more like siblings in the same family than rival gangs in the same neighborhood. At the same time, postmodernity is also giving us a chance to evaluate modernity from a little enforced distance, to come to terms with deep social change, and it has brought us to a juncture where we are being forced to ask ourselves: which way do we really want to go? It has opened up what was, in a way, a closed secret about modernity. We can now "read the signs of the times as indicators," David Lyon writes, "that modernity itself is unstable, unpredictable, and seems to forsake the foreclosed future that it once seemed to promise."[4]

The Withering of the Enlightenment Soul

Modernity to Postmodernity

There is no question that postmodern thought has been hatched rather self-consciously in opposition to Enlightenment ideology, nor is there any question that that ideology is now disintegrating. There is irony here, too, because this postmodern opposition has achieved what more than two centuries of steady, sometimes brilliant, Christian opposition failed to accomplish. On just about every front Enlightenment ideas have been fought by Christians — whether in the academy, with its pervasive humanism and naturalism, or, more specifically, in the biblical arena which, in developing one sophisticated critical appa-

4. Lyon, *Postmodernity*, 90.

ratus after another, has succeeded in ensconcing unbelief in the very source from which Christian belief arises, or in Western governments which have taken as normative the assumptions of secularism, or in Western societies in which materialism, fueled by a bottomless affluence, has dominated the way people think and behave. In these and in many other ways, Christians have argued for an alternative way of life, have written about it, preached for it, tried to live it, and on occasion demonstrated for it. It would not be correct to say that all of this has been futile, for there are certainly many people who, as a result of these efforts, have come to think about life in ways that defy the oppressive Enlightenment orthodoxies, and many are doing so in specifically Christian ways.

However, what is striking about this effort is that its success has registered at only a *personal* level. Our elites in the entertainment world, in academia, in corporations, and in government, those whose collective power to shape what people think about life and what they want from it is simply unparalleled in history, are completely indifferent to this Christian effort. Indeed, they are frequently hostile to it. The gatekeepers to our culture have not allowed Christian ideas past the threshold. American society, like societies throughout the West, has rumbled on as if the Enlightenment view of life was inevitable and its philosophy of life so patently obvious that only the harebrained or dullwitted would question its veracity and triumph. In Berger's graphic image, America, in that it is a deeply religious country ruled over by a secular elite, is like an India ruled by a Sweden.

However, the Enlightenment view of life is being rejected today. Thomas Oden speaks of its decadence, its decay, its dissolution.[5] Even John Thornhill, who thinks that our best hope for the future lies in a reinvigorated modernity, concedes that the "project of modernity has been overtaken by uncertainty and seems to face the prospect of increasing fragmentation."[6] This is happening not because of religious opposition but because its own progeny have finally found it intolerable and incredible. It is unbelief taking revenge on unbelief which has

5. Thomas C. Oden, *After Modernity . . . What? Agenda for Theology* (Grand Rapids: Zondervan, 1990), 81-82.

6. John Thornhill, *Modernity: Christianity's Estranged Child Reconstructed* (Grand Rapids: William B. Eerdmans, 2000), 4.

brought this about — and all of this has happened since the 1960s. More than two centuries of Christian critique left the Enlightenment world unscathed; during the four decades of postmodern assault from within, the Enlightenment world is coming crashing down. So what are we to conclude from this?

It would not be illogical to think that the Christian critique failed because it was misguided, insipid, unpersuasive, or simply too uninformed to be effective and, conversely, that the postmodern attack has succeeded because it has been so sharp and to the point that Enlightenment ideas have been sent reeling. Logical as it may seem, that is not, in my view, the answer. The answer lies in understanding why ideas in any age gain currency and traction or, at some later point, lose their hold and credibility.

As we try to understand our contemporary world, it is necessary, I believe, to distinguish between postmodernism and postmodernity. The former is the intellectual formulation of postmodern ideas on the high end of culture. It is their expression in architecture, in literary theory, philosophy, and so on. Postmodernity, by contrast, I am taking as the popular, social expression of the same assumptions but in ways that may be unselfconscious and often not intellectual at all, making this a diffuse, unshaped kind of expression. If the one is found in books and art, if it is debated on campuses and in the academy, the other is found in rock music, in the malls, on television, and in the workplace.

As it turns out, it has proved tempting to try to subsume postmodernity under postmodernism and therefore to imagine that the broad cultural phenomenon somehow derives from the postmodern philosophers and artists whose ideas have supposedly trickled down onto the rocks of society and now are splashing over everyone. Intellectuals are naturally prone to this flattering delusion. One of the more laughable instances of this was Allan Bloom's *The Closing of the American Mind*. This book began with a helpful and illuminating discussion of the students he taught at the University of Chicago whose unexamined operating premise was that truth is relative. This attitude, he argued, destroys the educational enterprise because if nothing is ultimately true then it is pointless for students to expend too much energy pondering the meaning of life now. These students saw education as offering nothing more than some knowledge about other cultures and minority groups, and they coupled that with a saccharine moral code about everyone getting along with one another. But then came his remarkable claim that this relativism, dispersed throughout the educational system from our children's earliest age through to the upper echelon of postgraduate study, and now rooted everywhere in society, stems from — German philosophy! "The self-understanding of hippies, yippies, yuppies, panthers, prelates and presidents has unconsciously been formed by German thought of a half-century earlier,"[7] the American lifestyle becoming but a superficial version of the Weimar Republic! His assertion that this has all happened "unconsciously" is certainly incontrovertible. Since it is doubtful that too many hippies, yippies, or yuppies have been immersed in German philosophy, and it may be that quite a few do not even know what the Weimar Republic was, this influence must have been quite unconscious! That we can show the similarity between ideas in one place and those in another place, or those on one end of the culture and those on the other end, does not necessarily mean that any direct influence has occurred. There are explanations other than that of direct causation which Bloom never pondered.

Intellectuals like Foucault and Derrida are undoubtedly contributors to postmodern thinking, but what is often left unexplained is how we get from Foucault to MTV, from Derrida to the centerless young people whose canopy of meaning in life has collapsed, from Fish and Rorty to our movies. Are we really to suppose that this is to be explained by an assiduous reading of these authors? Furthermore, why is the whole far-flung Enlightenment enterprise, which has been deeply entrenched in American society, coming down *now?* Is it credible to think that this massive edifice is being toppled by thinkers whose writing is often elusive, complex, and inaccessible? In an age not given much to reading and thought, this seems unlikely. Furthermore, those who are devoted to Foucault and Derrida, to Fish and Rorty, in the scale of things, are a numerically inconsequential minority, on the face of it quite unlikely to be solely responsible for the destruction of an edifice as large and imposing as the Enlightenment has been.

7. Allan Bloom, *The Closing of the American Mind: How Education Has Failed Democracy and Impoverished the Souls of Today's Students* (New York: Simon and Schuster, 1987), 147.

What has not been taken sufficiently into account, of course, is how we are embedded in our culture, how this acts upon us, and what its shaping forces are. And what is seldom explored is whether this culture might have had a hand in what philosophers, artists, and novelists are thinking even as it has in what our empty, centerless young people are thinking.

Throughout the West, it is now apparent that there is a major shift in mood and outlook taking place. It is doubtful that this shift is deep enough, and decisive enough, to have established a clean breach with modernity and hence to inaugurate a new cultural phase we can call *post*modernity, even though I do use the word. Harvey has concluded, I believe with justification, "that there is much more continuity

---

In modern experience, the possibility of establishing man within knowledge and the mere emergence of this new figure in the field of the *episteme* imply an imperative that haunts thought from within. . . . What is essential is that thought, both for itself and in the density of its workings, should be both knowledge and a modification of what it knows, reflection and the transformation of the mode of being of that on which it reflects. Whatever it touches it immediately causes to move: it cannot discover the unthought, or at least move toward it, without bringing the unthought nearer to itself — or even, perhaps, without pushing it further away, and in any case without causing man's own being to undergo a change by that very fact, since it is deployed in the distance between them. . . . The modern one [ethical stance], on the other hand, formulates no morality, since any imperative is lodged within thought and its movement toward the apprehension of unthought; it is reflection, the act of consciousness, the elucidation of what is silent, language restored to what is mute, the illumination of the element of darkness that cuts man off from himself, the reanimation of the inert — it is all this and this alone that constituted the content and form of the ethical.

Michel Foucault, *The Order of Things*

---

than difference between the broad history of modernism and the movement of postmodernism." He goes on to say that it seems more sensible "to see the latter as a particular crisis within the former, one that emphasizes the fragmentary, the ephemeral and the chaotic . . . while expressing a deep skepticism as to any particular prescriptions as to how the eternal and immutable should be conceived of, represented, or expressed."[8]

The Postmodern Outlooks

This postmodern outlook comes in all kinds of shapes and expressions, which is what probably explains the multiplicity of definitions which have been advanced. Its own ethos almost guarantees that there will be no such thing as *a* postmodern outlook but rather there will be many different postmodern perspectives. Yet what they have in common is that they all believe that meaning has died. This has to be qualified immediately by the assertion that what has most obviously died is the kind of *rational* meaning which the Enlightenment provided — but postmoderns find no grounds for any other kind. If postmoderns do not want to find any objective realm in which what is true and right finds its validation — and they do not — what other avenues are left open to them but that of nihilism? Without some kind of "meta-narrative" to discipline private consciousness, meaning inevitably dies, "the triumph of wild and unregulated interpretation" is assured, "stable meanings" disintegrate, Frederick Bauerschmidt notes, and the strong "assert their will to power without regard to such eternal values as truth, goodness, unity, and beauty." Universal narratives about the meaning of life are "shattered into micro-narratives of race, class, and gender."[9]

However, we should not be too hasty in declaring the complete overthrow of the Enlightenment regime. There are important threads of continuity between modernity and postmodernity and not least among these is the fact that at the center of both is the autonomous

8. Harvey, *The Condition of Postmodernity*, 116.
9. Frederick Christian Bauerschmidt, "Aesthetics: The Theological Sublime," *Christian Orthodoxy*, 201.

self, despite all the postmodern chatter about the importance of community. During the Enlightenment, this was worked out in anti-religious ways, the Enlightenment thinkers refusing to be fettered by any transcendent being or any authority outside of themselves. In postmodernity, the autonomous being refuses to be fettered by any objective reality outside of itself. In the end, the difference is simply that the revolt in the first case took a more religious turn and in the second a more general turn.

This crisis has been brought about in general by a growing disaffection with the Enlightenment's promise of progress and, in the academic world, by a growing sense that some of the Enlightenment's most basic assumptions are awry. These affect how we view science, the function of reason, philosophy, language and literature.

The Enlightenment made much of the greatness of the human being — in fact, too much — but even more fallacious was its blindness to human corruption and the capacity of the human being for misery. What recognition there was of Evil tended to be obscured beneath the bright prospects of progress which were everywhere heralded, a celebrated series of lectures in London late in the nineteenth century even predicting that the human race would soon evolve out of war, leaving behind the elements of the ape and the tiger which have resided in human nature. But what we have seen in the modern period is that the very genius which has remade our world through science and technology is the same genius which has wrought the means of the world's destruction. Ours is now a nuclear world and one in which biological and chemical weapons have been used. It is a world where terror can strike unexpectedly and in massive ways, sending its shock waves through our consciousness — as it did on September 11 in New York and Washington, and as it has done repeatedly in many other parts of the world.

If there has been progress in some aspects of life, there are costs that are being paid in other areas. Even the consumer paradise that the West has become turns out not to be such a paradise after all. It is true that it remains replete with technological marvels and gadgets. It has all of the devices and accoutrements of comfort. Yet it asks that we pay for what we so dearly treasure. And the price we have to pay increasingly qualifies the progress that we once thought we were making and which the Enlightenment led us to believe was inevitable. The modernization of life has heightened everyday tensions, sometimes to fearful levels, because we are confronted at every turn by hard-driving, materialistic pragmatism and by the indifference of anonymous corporations and bureaucracies. Cherished freedoms of choice have, in reality, become severely narrowed by the actual circumstances of work. At best, the idea of progress has lived on only in a privatized, individualized way, but even that is now disintegrating for the simple reason that we cannot make the small improvements that we want given the large, immovable structures of the societies in which we live. We cannot escape the all-invasive character of their modernity.

The modern reconfiguration of life, necessary if *la dolce vita* is to be ours, has in many ways, then, been the story of great and spectacular success but it is also now being trailed by its shadows. It has allowed our streets, and many of our young people, to be filled with illegal drugs. It has sundered apart half of our families by divorce and it has so taken the bloom off the idea of marriage that many are no longer even trying. And it has left us drifting in a world we often do not understand and where it is increasingly hard to make enduring connections to place or people. One of the novelist Douglas Coupland's characters is described as skipping over the surface of life, "like a waterspider" — unconnected, light, and superficial. We are getting close to doubling life expectancy from what it was a century ago, but despite the fact that diseases have been pushed back or are more treatable there is still a brittle fragility to life. Many are living longer, but life is still brief and, at the end, often lonesome and debilitated. We are still stalked by cancer. We face the possibility of viruses more deadly than what we have seen in the past. We have built cities of spectacular accomplishment, but they befoul the air and are haunts of criminality. Progress is about self-confidence, about having the sense that we can rearrange life, overcome what has ailed us. The problem is that there is no agency today that inspires such confidence. Government is too inefficient, too large, too directionless to accomplish this; politicians are too venal and we do not trust them; business is too consumed by the drive for its own success. It easily becomes rapacious.

And so we are left to ponder life, to see its rips and tears, to reflect, sometimes painfully and somberly, on what might have been. It is our greatness to want to live in a world in which life is meaningful, to know why it is so, to know where it is headed, and to know why our guilt is not a simple and nagging neurosis; it is our wretchedness that modern life has not yielded up those answers for us (and cannot). It is for these and similar reasons that our cultural mood has turned sour on this whole notion of progress and in that sourness are the seeds from which the postmodern mood has been sprouting.

It is a mood which is reactive to the intellectual rackets and unrealistic promises of the modern past, but it is also reactive to much which was not fraudulent. If Enlightenment rationality was logical, favored clean categories, and sequential thought, postmoderns, in casual and not so casual ways, like to juxtapose things that do not belong together in a kind of flippant, or maybe ironic, dismissal of logic: in architecture, styles of the past worked into parts of an otherwise very modern building. In movies, a director might splice a black-and-white section into a color film, thereby blurring the distinction between past and present, or juxtapose images so that it is hard to tell what is real and what is not, or use narrative which is separated from any referent so that the viewer is left with a collage of jarring surface images, or use images so that the categories by which we read reality, visually and cognitively, are removed. *Blade Runner* is the gold standard of this genre.[10] In advertising, one does not always see what the connection is

---

10. *Blade Runner* is set in Los Angeles in 2019, though the city is unrecognizable as Los Angeles. It could be any city and, in fact, it almost looks like a city one might encounter on another planet. Neon advertising signs appear frequently, however, suggesting that it is indeed our own Los Angeles set in the midst of our consumer paradise even though the nationalities of many of those in the movie are not recognizable. It is always raining, the scenes are always dark, searchlights ominously cut through the sky at all times, the city is dirty and untidy, and relations between people are edgy, brusque, and uneasy. So much for progress! The story concerns a cell of criminals who have been created out of genetic material by the Tyrell Corporation whose motto is "More Human Than Human." Although these creations possess superhuman powers, they are not fully human. They are less human than human. Here is just another commercial fraud! These humanoids are subject to "accelerated decrepitude" which means that they live for only four years. They are haunted by the prospect of their death but, the movie suggests, so is everyone. These *replicants* have had human memories implanted in them; and in a telling scene, photos of one of the *replicant's* human "family" are used to reinforce memory, false fragments of external "reality" thus confirming her internal being. And is this different from what pertains for humans in our postmodern culture? And yet our categories for reading reality

70

between the product and the story one has just viewed, which suggests that the connection between words and what they signify has been lost; and on MTV, America's rock music channel, which never stops for breath, there are the soft rock videos of the 1960's, the social protest videos of the 1970's, the nihilistic heavy metal bands of the 1980's, and the angry urban rap of the 1990's, all played side by side, in a homogenized orgy of sound and sometimes fury, but the effect is to produce only so many different "looks" rather than a point of view. MTV videos are all images and no narrative.[11]

The sculptor Christo sprang to international attention with the creation, in 1971, of his *Running Fence,* a feat he duplicated with variations in other locales subsequently. This fence of wire and fabric ran for twenty-four miles across two counties in California. It was, in some ways, an absurd creation, for it had no use, could not be purchased, and had no future since a condition of the approval which allowed its construction was that it would shortly thereafter be disassembled. Some searched for a serious purpose in this work of art, that it was an "aesthetic of linear structure," that it was "naming" the shapes of modern structures which are in our consciousness, like pipelines, highways, and telephone lines.[12] The significance of it, I believe, was otherwise. Its significance lay in two related facts. First, it created a minor uproar among the farmers, the authorities from whom permission had to be sought, and the public, which was drawn into an increasingly agitated discussion about whether to approve the piece's construction. It was an act of provocation. Second, shortly after it was put up, it was removed. The fence was a fading, transient moment. The implication was that life is like that: much ado about nothing. It is ephemeral. And how do we respond to what is always fading and empty? "So here we

also break down here because although these humanoids give every appearance of being human they clearly have powers which are not human. And throughout the movie, the broken planes, the bizarre shapes, the juxtaposition of the overwhelming darkness and the pinpoints of light suggest that reality itself has been shattered and fragmented. This is a dystopian view of the future which is on par with Aldous Huxley's *Brave New World.*

11. Steven Connor, *Postmodernist Culture: An Introduction to Theories of the Contemporary* (Oxford: Basil Blackwell, 1989), 160.

12. O. B. Hardison, *Disappearing Through the Skylight: Culture and Technology in the Twentieth Century* (New York: Penguin Books, 1989), 135.

stand at the end of the twentieth century," writes Paul Lakeland, "a century which has seen two world wars, countless holocausts, the end of the myth of progress, and the near-death of hope, playing our computer games and whiling away the time with the toys that material success brings."[13] The games and toys, however, do not conceal what lies behind them, which is a nihilistic outlook. In its more philosophical moments it is dark, but in its popular expression it may even be flippant and certainly it is disengaged, uncommitted, and shallow. And this expresses itself in a fascination with style and image, with surfaces and appearances, with difference and contrast. Here there are no fears about inconsistency in style or thought, there is no truth or meaning, and so there is not much depth, either.

There are, of course, two sides to this rejection of the Enlightenment outlook and the search for an alternative way of thinking to take its place. The collapse of the Enlightenment ideology is long overdue and the disappearance of its coercive humanism is no small boon. In science, for example, the embargo on mentioning God when discussing the origins of the universe has been lifted. The narrow humanistic confines in which Enlightenment reason chose to work have been overthrown and the world has been opened up to what is unpredictable and maybe even miraculous. In the Christian domain, this could well mean that the disintegrating Enlightenment will take down with it much of the critical apparatus that has been developed in biblical studies, which would open the way for more fruitful methodologies. The rejection of the idea of progress means that earlier developments in the Christian story, such as those of the patristic period, take on fresh currency since they can no longer be seen as intrinsically inferior to the present. There are new prospects for Christian thought.

At the same time, postmodern attitudes are part and parcel of our postmodern context which, in its sparest and most unqualified expression, rejects worldviews, absolute truth, and purpose. This, of course, states the matter starkly. It is true that the French thinkers like Derrida and Lyotard, whose views are stark and nihilistic, have been rejected by other postmodern thinkers. Nancey Murphy also argues correctly that

13. Paul Lakeland, *Postmodernity: Christian Identity in a Fragmented Age* (Minneapolis: Fortress Press, 1997), 9.

Anglo-American postmodernism is different from continental European postmodern expression.[14] In fact, what we see is a spectrum of views from the most negative on the one end, such as Derrida, Foucault, and, in theology, Mark C. Taylor and Don Cupitt, to the more constructive proposals on the other end. These assume the end of the Enlightenment era, the impossibility of returning to being premodern in a world as highly modernized as the West is, and so they are in search of a new "paradigm" which they hope will avoid the pitfalls of the more negative postmoderns. In theology, we might include in this category John Milbank and the "radical orthodoxy" project. Thomas Oden has spoken quite exuberantly of the possibility of a "postmodern" theology, but he has in mind its final liberation from the destructive constraints of the Enlightenment and its awakening to the possibility of reconnecting with earliest Christianity. This is a little different from the attempt that Stanley Grenz is making at rewriting evangelical faith in terms that are more compatible, not only with the passing of the Enlightenment, but also with the emerging postmodern ethos. What we are hearing is the dying swan song of the Enlightenment and what we are seeing is the firebird that is arising from its corpse.

What greatly complicates the quest of those who are attempting to walk a more constructive path which is also postmodern, however, is the fact that in the aftermath of the Enlightenment, there is a gravitational pull toward the death of all worldviews. Not every postmodern thinker moves consistently in these directions but every postmodern thinker has to resist this vortex, for those who find no cognitive footholds soon disappear into it. The Enlightenment assumptions may be rejected but the new cultural assumptions that follow its death are just as corrosive and destructive. The postmodern mood beckons us away from the old Enlightenment world, but its call is also a siren song, for we are drawn toward a place in which there are no worldviews, no truth, and no purpose. Let me explore each of these traits briefly.

---

14. Nancey Murphy, *Anglo-American Postmodernism: Philosophical Perspectives on Science, Religion, and Ethics* (Boulder: Westview Press, 1997).

No (Comprehensive) Worldview

On Having a Worldview

It is actually misleading to speak of the disappearance of worldviews in the postmodern world. What have undoubtedly disappeared are the Enlightenment "metanarratives," those overarching structures of meaning, derived by unaided reason, which enabled people to interpret life as a whole and to see the connections of its parts and where it was all heading in its progress away from darkness and ignorance. These metanarratives were what enabled people to have a perspective on life within which questions of meaning were grasped, and typically this perspective rested on a belief in the existence of truth of a universal kind, unrevealed though it was. All of that has now collapsed. And in its place has arisen the view that individuals, as David Naugle notes, should "set themselves up autonomously as the *acknowledged* legislators of the world" and now "they claim an essentially divine prerogative to conceptualize reality and shape the nature of life as they please."[15] Any attempt, therefore, at seeing life in terms of a worldview is dismissed as typical Enlightenment arrogance or as a failure to see that all thought is conditioned by its cultural context and must, accordingly, be acknowledged as being relative.[16] There is no question, then, that the very possibility of having a worldview in this older sense has been rejected. But does it follow that what has replaced it is not also, albeit in a different way, a worldview? I believe that that is the argument which needs to be made.

What has replaced the worldviews that once sought to encompass the whole of existence in their understanding are now privatized worldviews, worldviews that are valid for no one but the person whose world it is and whose view it is. They qualify as worldviews because postmoderns are still addressing questions about what is ultimate (the answer is nothing) about the meaning of the universe (the answer is that it has none) and about human experience. They are no less inter-

15. David K. Naugle, *Worldview: The History of a Concept* (Grand Rapids: William B. Eerdmans, 2002), xvi.
16. See the general discussion of this in Carl F. H. Henry, "Fortunes of the Christian World View," *Trinity Journal,* 19, NS, No. 1 (Spring, 1998), 163-76.

ested at a private level in interpreting the facts and experiences that make up the reality of their lives than were intellectuals in the Enlightenment who did it in a rationalistic way. Postmoderns are just as interested in giving their account of "truth" and "morality" from their own perspective even if it is to say that neither truth nor morality in any ultimate and binding way exists. And they are just as interested in speaking about meaning as were the earlier figures even if their speech is filled with denials of meaning. We are, in fact, bumping up against an old conundrum. To say that there is no metaphysical reality is itself a metaphysical statement. To say, similarly, that worldviews have collapsed and been replaced by privatized interpretations of existence is no less a view of the world which is answering the question as to whether anything is ultimate than were the earlier attempts at grasping such matters. The earlier worldviews were ambitious and sought to grasp the whole of reality, be it on a humanistic or a religious basis; these are miniature and only seek to grasp reality which is private, personal, and evaporating.

There can be no question that this radical turn involves a deeply skeptical view of reason. Indeed, it actually struggles to disengage itself from the functions of reason, which are seen to be imprisoned within their contextual horizons and trapped within political realities, even though this disengagement has to be rationally explained. In the more spiritual aspect of the postmodern world, to which we will return, what this seeks to do is to explicate, for the individual, the relation between the self and the sacred which, in many instances, is found within the self. This, however, is more sensed than explained and so the view of the world which emerges has little drive to conceptualize itself. It has few, if any, "doctrines," and makes no truth claims beside the fact that there is no universal truth. And that is universally true!

Consumer Culture/Postmodern Culture

Why, one wonders, has the canopy of meaning collapsed so completely on so many? It strains credulity, as I have suggested, that this is the consequence of individuals' having read the work of intellectuals like Foucault and Derrida. I am, therefore, much more inclined to look for explanations, partial though they may be, in the experience of living in this highly urbanized and consumption-driven culture. What, in particular, might have pushed people to these positions?

A tantalizing suggestion has been made by several people, though made in different ways, that what we need to understand is how our society is now dominated by consumer appetite. And it is in the set of attitudes that emerge from within the consumer that we find some of the causes for the breakdown in our ability to sustain a worldview larger than our own individual existence. And the key here is the myriad of choices with which consumers are confronted every day.

In a 1987 American television advertisement, Wendy's, the hamburger merchant, looked in on a Soviet fashion show. Here were none of the slim gazelles that sashay down the glittering runways in the West amidst oohs and aahs, their *très chic* outfits sending a buzz through the gawking audience. No, this fashion show appeared to be taking place in a detention center. The sole model was a stout Russian peasant who displayed her fashions under a harsh spotlight. However, as each costume was announced — "evening wear," "swim wear," and so on — she strode down the runway in the same outfit, "a babushka on the head," says Ewen, "and a baggy, prison-gray smock, cut just above the knees to accentuate her flabby inner thighs."[17] It was an advertisement designed to contrast the bright varieties of modern America with the drabness, the lack of choice, in the Soviet Union. In a disparaging way, it did raise an important point. In the West, but perhaps in America in particular, there is *choice*.

In America, this choice actually exists in multiple, parallel markets. There is a market for consumer goods in the malls and supermarkets, which offer a wide variety of styles and qualities, of price and of brand — far more than is actually needed, the power of technology multiplying variation and new options almost exponentially. But this is paralleled by many other markets: that of ideas, for example, where on any given day, through radio and on television, in books and in magazines, in classrooms and public meetings, on billboards and on bumper stickers, people are confronted by a wild array of ideas, political agendas, and causes — far more than anyone can hear, or read, or keep up

17. Stuart Ewen, *All Consuming Images: The Politics of Style in Contemporary Culture* (New York: Basic Books, 1999), 111.

with, and this is the essence of freedom. Colleges and universities know that they are in a market where products (read: degrees) must be pitched to consumers (read: students). Except for those at the very top of the heap who can count on being besieged by the best and brightest, colleges and universities must market themselves and in so doing they give prospective students a wide variety of choices: location, ethos, prestige, focus. In fact, in America anything and everything can be "commodified" and sold, from style to sex, from ideas to religion. In towns and cities are churches, mosques, and synagogues; in the Yellow Pages there are choices for worship on Sunday morning ranging from the Episcopalians to the Baptists to the Assemblies of God; at the local bookstore, shelf after shelf is filled with books on New Age, self-help, witchcraft, holism, and Buddhism. This is Western freedom and Western commercialized culture. Here, we have the ability to hope for what we want, shop where we want, buy what we want, study where we want, think what we want, believe what we want, and treat religion as just another commodity, a product to be consumed.

The reality is that modern consumption is not simply about shopping because what we are buying is not simply goods and services. Modern consumption is about buying *meaning* for ourselves. It is about the way we construct ourselves, the vantage point from which we want to look at the world. It is, therefore, becoming the defining focus of a new kind of civilization. What was once just a matter of producing goods has become a way of producing culture and meaning, for what we consume has merged into what provides us with our meaning. The road to this meaning, however, is reached only by a path that runs through a valley of choice so diverse and so multilayered that it is easy to become lost.

It is quite striking, then, to note the parallels between postmodern habits of mind and the realities which have come to mark our highly formed capitalism: volatility, obsolescence, the rapid passing of fashions and ideas, the disappearance of stability, constant innovation, constant revision, repackaging, the new look, the newer than new product, the future always looming over the present. The postmodern mind is a reflection of this high capitalism, and it is probably this high capitalism, as much as postmodern argument, which is bringing down the Enlightenment belief about stable, fixed, and unchanging metanarratives.

The experience of this kind of choice has the undoubted effect, at a psychological level, of fragmenting life, of presenting it as only one incident of choosing after another, none of which is related to the others. Fragmentation is, in fact, characteristic of our whole society. God is disengaged from society, at least in its public aspect, work from the home, Church from society, the extended family from the nuclear by the mobility the modern economic order requires and, perhaps, by the divorce which modern life so often produces.[18] Within our increasingly specialized work, professions and disciplines develop their own internal ways of knowing, their own canons of knowledge to which members must subscribe, their own intellectual styles, their own professional societies which function like cartels. In traditional societies there was Authority; today, there are authorities, experts who master a small corner of our pluralistic world. Generations are now separating from each other, the habits of the "Boomers" supposedly different from those of the "Xers" and certainly from the "Builders." Communication across generations, across disciplines, across specializations, and even within families has been made more and more difficult. Is there, then, any kind of unity to life that we can discern which can tame this cacophony and bring order in this chaos? And, even more importantly, is it likely that any one religious interpretation of life can be seen as uniquely valid? It is the experience of this kind of fragmentation which appears to have done more to pull down the Enlightenment idea about metanarratives than what any postmodern thinker has achieved.

Given all of the choice in the West today, then, the awareness of difference and of diversity, the pluralism and plasticity of life, it seems highly implausible that there is any such metanarrative, any such central and single meaning, or viable and compelling worldview. All that we have is our own, individual *petite histoire,* our own story, a story no more compelling than anyone else's and no more true.

This is the case in the academy as well. Even in the sciences, with so many disciplines and sub-disciplines, with such extensive fragmentation of the knowledge project, it becomes harder and harder to see that it is all part of the same undertaking. It is modernity, and its overactive knowledge industry, which has destroyed this aspect of the En-

18. Scott Lasch, *Sociology of Postmodernism* (New York: Routledge, 1990), 8-14.

Simplifying to the extreme, I define *postmodern* as incredulity towards metanarratives. . . . Where, after the metanarratives, can legitimacy reside? The operativity criterion is technological; it has no relevance for judging what is true or just. Is legitimacy to be found in consensus obtained through discussion, as Jürgen Habermas thinks? Such consensus does violence to the heterogeneity of language games. And invention is always born of dissension. Postmodern knowledge is not simply a tool of the authorities; it refines our sensitivity to differences and reinforces our ability to tolerate the incommensurable.

Lyotard

lightenment, for all that remains, once the connections between the parts are lost, is a series of "language games," none with overarching significance. It is modernity itself, and the consumer society which arose from its loins, which has finally pulled down its own false universals. That being the case, Harvey is correct to see that what is called postmodern is really a crisis within modernity even if postmodern thinkers want to take credit for this accomplishment. There is now no narrative which connects together the events of life into a single form of meaning. From a world that was once centered, we now have one that is decentered. In this world, Connor says, "there no longer seems to be access to principles which can act as criteria of value for anything else."[19] Reality is fluid, changing, and always "open."

The Way Things Were

All of this stands in rather stark contrast to the way things once were. At least during the long reign of Enlightenment ideology it was assumed that an understanding of reality in its comprehensiveness could be pieced together incrementally. Enlightenment rationalists looked for a starting point, an indubitable foundation, upon which they could build their rational explanations of the universe.

19. Connor, *Postmodernist Culture*, 8.

In Descartes' case, for example, everything else could be doubted but the fact that he was conscious of being a thinker in the midst of his thoughts. Basic beliefs, which form the foundation, are those which are not derived from another belief by inference but, as it were, stand on their own feet. Believing that a pig cannot be an apple is a basic belief; believing that two plus two equals four is a basic belief; believing that on a cloudless day the sky is blue, or knowing what it was that we had for dinner last night, or that evil cannot be good, are all basic beliefs. Inferences from these basic beliefs are not basic beliefs, such as scientific hypotheses which explain the natural world, or theories about human behavior which assume the distinction between good and evil, or the conclusion that the stomach upset we suffered last night must have had something to do with the dinner we ate. Hypotheses, theories, explanations, logical inferences and extrapolations are not foundational beliefs.

Needless to say, there has been vigorous and contentious debate of a philosophical kind as to what can legitimately be considered "basic" and on what grounds such a belief might be held as being basic. Yet the intention of the Enlightenment philosophers and those who came after them is clear. This effort to identify the foundations to one's belief was undertaken to rid human knowledge of its biases, errors, and uncertainties, the assumption being that human reason by itself could erect a structure of knowledge which was unbiased, untainted, objective, and universally applicable if it started at the right point.[20]

---

20. Anthony Giddens has argued that the rejection of foundationalism should not be seen as marking off the postmodern from the modern but as unmasking what has been hidden in the modern. It has always been the case, he argues, that there was uncertainty at the heart of the Enlightenment project because this was a project that had replaced providence and revelation by progress and reason. A commitment to reason, however, was made only in the name of reason, and since Enlightenment thinkers rejected all dogma, they should have rejected their own dogma regarding reason. If "the sphere of reason is wholly unfettered, no knowledge can rest upon an unquestioned foundation, because even the most firmly held notions can only be regarded as valid 'in principle' or 'until further notice'" (*The Consequences of Modernity* [Stanford: Stanford University Press, 1990], 48-49). What is happening today, therefore, is more along the lines of unmasking what has been there all along. This is undoubtedly correct and what it does is to decrease the significance of the prefix *post* in postmodern.

It is this that postmodern thinkers have attacked, rejecting totalizing "stories" and beliefs, insisting that our focus can only be local and perhaps only individual. And they have rightly contested the Enlightenment premise that reason is antiseptic and unbiased, or that by itself it can reach conclusions which are secure from uncertainty. "With the ascendance of the postmodern mind," writes Tarnas, "the human quest for meaning in the cosmos has devolved upon a hermeneutical enterprise that is disorientingly free-floating: The postmodern human exists in a universe whose significance is at once utterly open and without warrantable foundation."[21] The problem which follows from this, of course, is that if there is no clear starting point, no foundation of basic belief, and most importantly of all, no metaphysical authorization of any truth whatsoever that we can know, formulating belief becomes a matter of trial and error to see what works. Yet none of it has any certain relationship with what is "out there."

Richard Rorty, for example, takes the line that since there is no truth in the sense of a correspondence between what we know and what is actually there, the only way forward is to allow the clash of opinions to sort things out. Typically, when people have sought meaning in the world, he says, they have resorted to either finding it objectively through some kind of connection with a nonhuman reality or they have sought it by solidarity, by connecting with some human community.[22] However, he rejects every claim to having meaning or truth which has some particular starting premise at the foundation and a structure built upon it by some method of inference.[23] The mind, he contends, does not reflect the world "out there" as a mirror might and he also rejects the view that language is capable of describing what is there. There is, therefore, no position that one can find that is outside of life from which to make "objective" judgments which represent what is there. In the end, "truth" becomes relative to the person for whom it is true. However, he denies that this leads to relativism. Relativism is the view that one idea is as good as another. While Rorty has no meta-

21. Tarnas, *The Passion of the Western Mind*, 398.
22. Richard Rorty, *Objectivity, Relativism, and Truth* (Cambridge: Cambridge University Press, 1991), 21.
23. Rorty, *Objectivity, Relativism, and Truth*, 76.

physical grounds for holding one position to be true and another false, for he is naturalistic in his outlook, he says that there are the pragmatic necessities of having to choose with which view one will identify and not all ideas are equally viable.[24]

This pragmatism is the natural outcome of the rejection of both Enlightenment foundationalism, which is a good thing, and any religious basis for knowledge, which is not. The Enlightenment view assumed that God could not be properly foundational to one's thought because his existence is not self-evident and therefore it must be proved empirically to be admitted as a basic belief and this is impossible. It was thus that the Enlightenment foreclosed on a religious view of life which could also be philosophically viable. However, Plantinga counters that, on the Enlightenment's own assumptions, foundationalism itself cannot be accepted as a basic belief since it is not empirically provable nor is it self-evident. It is, in fact, the whole theory of foundationalism as the Enlightenment conceived it which is now tumbling down and this is no loss from a Christian point of view. For, as applied to God, it has to operate off a natural theology.[25] It must assume that there is some truth lodged within human experience from which inferences can be made which lead into a saving knowledge of God. This, of course, is a topic which has a long pedigree of debate, but from the time of the Reformation to today the Protestant consensus has been that this seriously vitiates the necessity for and the role of the biblical gospel. The saving knowledge of God is not the result of the human search for him, or of building up logical inferences to him from the natural order, still less of erecting such access to him though experience, but of his self-disclosure to us in his Son and through his Word. However, God can legitimately be basic and foundational to one's view of the whole of life.[26] Plantinga has developed this philosophically but

24. Richard Rorty, *Consequences of Pragmatism* (Minneapolis: University of Minnesota Press, 1982), 166-67.

25. See the detailed discussion of the history of natural theology in Alister McGrath, *A Scientific Theology* (3 vols.; Grand Rapids: William B Eerdmans, 2001), I, 241-305.

26. See Alvin Plantinga, "Reason and Belief in God," in *Faith and Rationality: Reason and Belief in God,* ed. Alvin Plantinga and Nicholas Wolterstorff (Notre Dame: University of Notre Dame Press, 1983), 135-86. In the same volume Wolterstorff has an

it emerges in theological form in the belief that if God's knowledge of life is exhaustive and true, and if he inspired the biblical Word in order to communicate that truth, then the "totalizing" stories which arise from that Word are not themselves the false absolutes of fallen reason.[27]

In this situation, then, several modernist myths are laid to waste. The idea that reason is objective in its workings and not subject to distortion by the private interests of the individual has now been exploded. Postmoderns, sometimes with more relish and radical intent than is appropriate, have pointed to the frequently concealed motivations that speech masks. And, in fact, this has long been a Christian contention, too, that reason is perverted by sin and that perversion takes many paths. It was Freud, one wag said, who had rediscovered the doctrine of original sin, and certainly it is the case that there has

essay entitled "Can Belief in God Be Rational If It Has No Foundation?" (16-93), which arrives at the same conclusion. For a clear discussion of these issues see Kelly James Clark, *Return to Reason: A Critique of Enlightenment Evidentialism and a Defense of Reason and Belief in God* (Grand Rapids: William B. Eerdmans, 1990), 123-58. More recently, Plantinga has published two volumes which revisit the issues of foundationalism. Subsequently, he has made a substantial contribution to the discussion in his two books, *Warrant and Proper Function* (New York: Oxford University Press, 1993) and *Warrant: The Current Debate* (New York: Oxford University Press, 1993).

27. The difficulty entailed in forging a nonfoundationalist theology which follows postmodern contours is (inadvertently) illustrated in Stanley Grenz and John Franke's *Beyond Foundationalism: Shaping Theology in a Postmodern Context* (Louisville: Westminster/John Knox Press, 2001). To escape a foundationalism, religious authority is reconfigured: "the Bible is authoritative in that it is the vehicle through which the Spirit speaks" (65). To escape postmodern charges that hermeneutics is but a cover for private interest, the business of understanding what the Spirit is saying, it is conceded, "cannot be determined by appeal to either the exegesis of Scripture carried out apart from the life of the believer and the believing community" (65) or personal revelation in the interpreter. Authority, then, lies with the Spirit who speaks rather than the biblical Word he inspired; this is the old pietism whose Achilles' heel made it vulnerable to the old Liberalism. On hermeneutics, this is Protestantism leaning toward Catholicism. However, given its postmodern framing, with its more local reference rather than the universal truths of traditional Catholicism, this hermeneutical work may be vulnerable to the relativism of local communities as they define truth for themselves. There can be no doubt that this proposal, which is well argued, is seriously trying to address postmodern concerns, but whether this direction can be sustained without cost to historical orthodoxy is doubtful.

long been a Christian interest in the reality of those presuppositions that people bring to any project, the assumptions they make about the world which are rooted in their being as both created in God's image and fallen, and there has long been a Christian argument that reason, as a result, is not neutral but it is tainted by sinful bias of various kinds. Furthermore, limiting knowledge to what is empirical, gleaned only by approved scientific method, so that what cannot be scientifically proved cannot be held with any certainty, was an Enlightenment disposition which has created much mischief, and its overthrow at the hands of the postmoderns is welcome. There are many realities that are not scientifically provable in the Enlightenment's narrow terms such as the existence of God, the mind, the moral order, and human nature. In the absence of Christian faith, however, these gains get linked to the collapse of any central, unifying principles in life and that leads away in many unhappy directions.

The postmodern call to abandon every kind of foundationalism therefore needs to be treated with caution. We need to understand why the attack is being made, what its intended outcomes will be, and what its actual outcomes are. There is no question that it has proved seductive in theology, not least because now it liberates theology from the oppressive Enlightenment shackles which insisted that theology had no right to be taken seriously if it did not conform to scientific modes of operating. The overthrow of foundationalism, therefore, allows for theology to reassert its right to live and to think on its own terms. However, non-foundationalistic theology, busy living and thinking on its own terms, also surrenders its claims to having any universal significance. Its vision is particular, partial, and sees but a fragment of the whole, and that really leaves it with little to say to a postmodern culture which finds itself in the same boat.

No Truth

Douglas Groothuis has made the observation that it would be very difficult for us today to write the Declaration of Independence, given its premise that there are truths which are "self-evident," such as that "all Men are created equal; that they are endowed by their Creator with certain inalienable Rights; that among these are Life, Liberty, and the pursuit of Happiness." Today we are a nation of relativists, as Allan Bloom lamented, for whom there are no enduring truths, let alone any that are self-evident. The distance that we have traveled in this matter can be seen in many ways, but not least in the fact that Martin Luther King's appeal, which stirred so many Americans, was made on the basis of the existence of a moral reality larger than any private interest and to which the whole nation was to be accountable. Today, the great majority of Americans do not believe in the existence of truth which is absolute and enduring and to which appeal can be made.[28]

When we speak of truth, we are asking whether it is possible to have an understanding of reality which corresponds to what is there. To say that there is a dog on my lawn when there is one there is to make a true statement; to say that there is a dog there when there is not is a false statement. The statement does not correspond, in the false case, to what is there. Can we, then, make statements about reality which are true in the sense that they reflect and correspond to what is there?

For a long time in philosophy, a rear guard action was waged to preserve the idea that reality is a fixed, objective and intelligible thing "out there" which can be known. When Kant made the argument that, in fact, what is out there is processed by and organized within a mind which places its own shape on what is known, he seemed to be shaking the older view to its foundations. However, he argued that his line of thought should not be seen to be too alarming since the categories within the mind, through which sensory information passes, are themselves timeless and therefore not culturally determined. But soon this line of critical thinking moved on and began to see that these internal categories are, in fact, quite conditioned and that they appear to differ from one place to another, one culture to another, and one time to another, leading people to "see" things differently. That could only mean that there is not an external Reality which corrects and nullifies false perceptions. And thus has emerged a radical perspectivalism which is at the heart of the postmodern enterprise, at least in its academic expression.

28. Douglas Groothuis, *Truth Decay: Defending Christianity Against the Challenges of Postmodernism* (Downers Grove: InterVarsity Press, 2000), 17-19.

In this view, there is nothing certain against which to check our thoughts and theories for their veracity. We have no escape from our history, no place to stand outside its flux and flow. And this kind of radical perspectivalism has played itself out in numerous fields, everywhere leaving behind it unresolved disagreements. In literature, as Gertrude Himmelfarb has observed, we hear it in the insistence that the text does not have a finished, determined meaning, and that the authority of the author in saying what the text means is less than that of the interpreter who may "hear" it differently. In law, it takes the form of denying that what the United States' Constitution, for example, declares as fixed and binding is the case because the law is simply the will of those in power. In history, as in literature, the past is seen not to have embodied or exemplified any absolute truths, but only incremental, partial, and relativistic insights. What, in fact, is more real than the past is the historian's mind in the present.[29] "The world," writes Tarnas, "does not exist as a thing-in-itself, independent of interpretation; rather, it comes into being only in and through interpretations."[30] We are not spectators in Reality's theater, disengaged and observing, but, rather, participants in it, and our participation itself transforms the character of that Reality and, in fact, even creates it. Reality is therefore always ambiguous and always demanding new appraisals. This, clearly, is a mood in which the correspondence view of truth perishes, and without this understanding the task of discerning good from bad, truth from lies, becomes fraught with difficulty.

Western culture, following the invention of the printing press, became a literate culture. The question of the reading and interpretation of texts, be they legal, philosophical or literary, has always been important work. And as this work passed through the Enlightenment experience, the attempt was made, as D. A. Carson says, "to ground all knowledge in infallible reason," which is a good way of putting it because reason had assumed the place of infallible, biblical revelation. It therefore came to be assumed that the meaning of the text was always objective to the interpreter, that it was therefore possible to build up a

29. Gertrude Himmelfarb, *On Looking into the Abyss* (New York: Alfred A. Knopf, 1994), 133.
30. Tarnas, *The Passion of the Western Mind*, 397.

body of knowledge from texts and from inferences which was certain and had an "ahistorical universality," and that reason, if it is operating off a viable foundation and with the right method, is unbiased in its work and not perverted by private agendas of class, ethnicity, or personal ambition.[31] It was also assumed that the intention of the author could be ascertained by the reader and that that intent was determinative of what the text meant.

All of this is now under vigorous assault. It is not true, postmoderns like Derrida and Foucault assert, that the interpreter stands outside the text, or that the interpreter is ever without bias and interest in power, or that the intent of the author can be discerned or that this intent is even important, or that words have fixed, determined meanings. The text is, as Kevin Vanhoozer observed, thus "undone."[32] But so, too, is the reader.[33] Texts come to mean different things in different contexts or when different questions are brought to them. In the absence, then, of a final, definitive interpretation, Vanhoozer points out, the only moral stance which postmoderns like Derrida and Foucault believe we can legitimately have is to resist every interpretation which lays claim to being final and true.[34]

All of this appears to be the end result of two useful insights now gone badly to seed. The first is that human reason has its biases, its presuppositions, its self-justifications, its disinclination to want to see some things and its inclination to want to see things that may not be there. The second is that it is fallacious to think that we can successfully erect a rational tower in the midst of the world from whose upper levels we can survey the whole of reality. The rebellion that rejected this naturalistic arrogance from the Enlightenment, however, has marched off, by way of reaction, into different but equally naturalistic extremes in other directions. These only underscore the fact that

31. For a recounting of this development, see D. A. Carson, *The Gagging of God: Christianity Confronts Pluralism* (Grand Rapids: Zondervan, 1996), 57-92.

32. Kevin J. Vanhoozer, *Is There a Meaning in This Text? The Bible, the Reader, and the Morality of Literary Knowledge* (Grand Rapids: Zondervan, 1998), 98-147. Anthony Thiselton's *The Two Horizons* explored some of the same territory covered in Carson's book and Vanhoozer's.

33. Vanhoozer, *Is There a Meaning in This Text?*, 148-96.

34. Vanhoozer, *Is There a Meaning in This Text?*, 183.

without a belief in biblical revelation we are today staring down the barrel of a dark nihilism.

The historic confession of the Church has been that biblical revelation gives us truth in the sense that it gives us an accurate account of what is "out there," whether we are considering the character of God or his purposes, or the nature of created life, or the end to which human history is going. Its correspondence to what is there is secured by the fact that it is God who has given it. Because this is so, it is objective in the sense that its content is not open to revision or change. It must always be interpreted and every interpreter carries within himself or herself the biases which social location, ethnicity, class — and, we must add, sin — generate. Yet even these biases are themselves subject to the correction of God's truth if it is objective and it is knowable. Furthermore, if it is *God* who has revealed it, then in its reach it is both unvarying and universal, the same for all people in all places and all times. And if it is the biblical God of *holiness* who has revealed it, it will set up antitheses with all that is untrue and all that is wrong for that is what God's holiness does.[35]

No Purpose

The Enlightenment had its eschatology, that of inevitable progress, and now that has died. It is not, however, only the belief in progress that died but, along with it, something that is even larger, which is the belief that there is purpose which has been written into the creation. Here, as elsewhere, Enlightenment ideology and the experience of modernity have conspired to bring about the same end. From the Enlightenment came the reduction of all of life to the explanation only of natural cause and effect, thus eliminating from the created order any purpose that could not be explained naturalistically. This, in turn, led to the disjuncture of "facts" from "values," which meant that facts could never be framed by an understanding of purpose and so it has become impossible to move from statements about "what is" to statements about "what ought" to be. Alasdair MacIntyre has shown

35. Groothuis, *Truth Decay,* 60-82.

conclusively[36] that this Enlightenment disjuncture made it impossible for Enlightenment thinkers, or those who follow in their wake, to develop any ethical viewpoint because the intellectual passage from what is to what ought to be cannot be accomplished.

Postmoderns have set about upending the Enlightenment but, along the way, have created their own obstacles to being able to find meaning, and there is much in our consumer culture that militates against such a discovery, too. Where Descartes' skepticism stopped with his own self-consciousness, postmodern doubting has refused to stop anywhere. Human perspectives are now analyzed and compared, sifted and sorted, but there is no vantage point from which to make a judgment about their truth or error. Thus has postmodern self-consciousness become deeply nomadic, ever moving and never stopping, but it is always movement without a destination. It is without purpose.

What is said here about the academy is paralleled in our habits of consumption. We move as nomads from one oasis to another, ever shopping and never stopping, defining ourselves only by what is present and by what can be purchased and experienced. Margaret, another of Coupland's characters, laments that "most of us have only two or three genuinely interesting moments in our lives, the rest is filler, and at the end of our lives, most of us will be lucky if any of these moments connect together to form a story that anyone would find remotely interesting."[37] Margaret speaks for more than her own generation today.

As our world has thus fallen in on us, stripping us of a worldview larger than our own perceptions, denying that we have access to what is true, and leaving us purposeless, so many people in the West are, perhaps surprisingly, now reaching out for what is spiritual. Today, the world in general is as "furiously religious" as ever, Berger asserts, despite the tides of secularization that have swept over it.

What the older explanation about secularization overlooked is the fact, as Berger puts it, that modernization provoked "powerful

36. Alasdair MacIntyre, *After Virtue: A Study in Moral Theory* (Notre Dame: University of Notre Dame Press, 1981).

37. Douglas Coupland, *Generation X: Tales for an Accelerated Culture* (New York: St. Martin's Press, 1991), 23-24.

movements of counter-secularization"[38] which often take one of two forms. Because modernization undermines "the taken-for-granted certainties by which people lived through most of history"[39] a religion which offers certainty has considerable appeal. From another angle, he notes that the secular interpretation of reality is socially rooted in the cultural elite. This provokes resentment among those over whom the secular tide rolls and who have no power to turn it back. Religion which is anti-secular may therefore sometimes appeal to people for reasons which may not be religious at all. Perhaps these dynamics are at work in this resurgence in spirituality, too, but clearly the story is also complex and will be pursued in a later chapter. It is sufficient here simply to note that this spiritual resurgence, this quest for meaning in a meaningless world, is a very important part of the postmodern context with which the Church must reckon.

Here, then, are what we might call the underlying motifs of the postmodern mind. They constitute a gravitational pull toward three simple affirmations: no (comprehensive) worldview, no truth, and no purpose. However, they appear to be provoking currents that are anti-postmodern, too, for the emptying out of the world is driving the quest to fill the world with part, at least, of what it has lost spiritually. What, then, does a christology which is wanting to be biblical look like in our postmodern world, a world in which orthodoxies have no place, in which the idea of truth has been abandoned, in which worldviews have collapsed, in which religions and spiritualities jostle side by side with each other, and in which the religious consumer is in the driver's seat? That is the central question in this book. Before I can begin to answer it, though, another piece in the puzzle of Our Time must be added. What have been the results, religiously speaking, of the considerable immigration which has taken place in America in the last four decades? It is this question which is pursued in the next chapter.

38. Peter L. Berger, "The Desacralization of the World," in *The Desacralization of the World: Resurgent Religion and World Politics* (Washington: Ethics and Public Policy Center, 1999), 3.

39. Berger, "The Desacralization of the World," 11.

CHAPTER III

Migrations, the Banquet of Religion, and Pastiche Spirituality

—⟨∞⟩—

Give me your tired, your poor,
Your huddled masses yearning to breathe free,
The wretched refuse of your teeming shore,
Send these, the homeless, tempest-tossed, to me:
I lift my lamp beside the golden door.

EMMA LAZARUS

The fall of the Berlin Wall in 1989 symbolically marked the end of the Soviet Union. It also became the unsigned treaty that brought the Cold War to a close. This came at the end of a century in which it was the threat of war, and in the second half of that century, of nuclear war, between the West and the Communist world that had hung like a pall over world affairs, even as it had been the fear of revolution that had shaped the prior century in Europe. But today, while war is always a possibility, terrorism is a reality, and revolutions do break out sporadically, it is migration that is coming to be the defining reality for so many countries in the West, not war or terror or revolution.

Migrations, of course, are nothing new. Some migrations in the world are local, the result of war, politics, famine, and unemployment.

In the larger picture, however, it is *opportunity* that is drawing the East to the West and is moving the South toward the North in astounding numbers. And in the absence of superpower rivalry, and following the collapse of the Soviet Union, which subjugated all of its people to one overarching ideology, it is acute ethnic consciousness which is reappearing in this flow of peoples in ways that often harken back to bygone times.

The hostility of one tribe for another is among the most instinctive human reactions. Yet, the history of our planet has been in great part the history of the mixing of peoples. Mass migrations have produced mass antagonisms from the beginning of time. Today, as the twentieth century draws to an end, a number of factors — not just the evaporation of the cold war but, more profoundly, the development of swifter modes of communication and transport, the acceleration of population growth, the breakdown of traditional social structures, the flight from tyranny and want, the dream of a better life somewhere else — converge to drive people as never before across national frontiers and thereby to make the mixing of peoples a major problem for the century that lies darkly ahead.

Arthur M. Schlesinger, *The Disuniting of America*

This migration into the West, from both the East and the South, has become a major force in shaping its culture. Indeed, the increasingly multiethnic societies which are emerging in Europe and in America are helping to create a religious context of unprecedented diversity — unprecedented, that is, as judged by recent centuries.

Let us first look at Europe. Africans alone make up 31% of the population of Marseilles, France, for example, and 15% of Parisians. But it is not only Africans who are on the move. So, too, are the various Middle Eastern peoples whose populations are exploding at the very moment when those of the indigenous European nations are declining in a startling way because the birth rate has fallen well below what simple replacement would require. That means that European populations will contract significantly in the decades ahead if this pattern is not reversed. In London, 40% of the city is made up of ethnic minorities, many from the Commonwealth who, by legal or illegal means, have taken up residence there. Over the last decade, the number of illegal aliens who have slipped into Europe has grown tenfold. They come by plane with forged documents, by night across unguarded borders, by ship in a transfer of human cargo that now seems almost routine but which is producing a situation that is in fact without precedent. The tensions which this immigration has created appear to be even greater than in America because these nations are all so much older, the memories longer, their ethnic sense deeper, and there is no nation in Europe whose genesis lies, as America's does, in *ideas* and which is made up almost entirely of immigrants and their descendants.

The present often exercises a coercive power over the past, often remaking that past in its own image, and so it may be difficult for Americans today who are frequently besieged by what have become cults of ethnicity to understand that it was not always so. It is easy to mock the notion of the melting pot, and some academics have had a field day doing so, and yet this idea was an essential part of the American story. It was a story more ragged than was sometimes allowed, yet there was at its inception a great surging idealism, a dream, which saw in America the creation of a "new race," "one people," a people without its own particular ethnic memory, one with no inherited ideas or beliefs, and one in which immigrants were expected to shed the particularities of their past in order to become *Americans.*[1] It is true, of course, that this dream was not always realized, that the waves of immigrants from Europe in the nineteenth century were sometimes met with bigotry and hostility. Yet it is the preeminence of ethnic identity today which has emerged as a driving force in society in a way that simply was not the case in earlier periods.

In this chapter, however, my focus is on religion, not the many other issues that surround this immigration. All immigrants have to begin the process of adaptation as soon as they arrive in their host

1. Arthur M. Schlesinger, *The Disuniting of America* (Knoxville: Whittle Direct Books, 1991), 23-43.

country, though in the nineteenth century this was demanded and to-day it is merely hoped for. They are typically caught between two competing desires. On the one hand, they try to hold on to as much as they can of their heritage, their old ways, their old associations, their own language, their own music, and their own food. On the other hand, they know they have to begin to adapt to their new country, to become a part of it, and become productive members of their community if they are to succeed. This is not easy. Writing of the great wave of immigrants in the nineteenth century, John Lukacs observed that "grave troubles, sufferings seared in their hearts," and their lot was made up of "branding humiliations, and superficial injustices."[2] The anguish, anxiety, bewilderment, sense of loss, and the tears that these competing desires exact are part and parcel of every immigrant's story. These pains have to be endured because this is the path along which advancement lies.

In time, most of those who have come to America learn to speak English, if this was not their own tongue, begin to dress like Americans, and accommodate themselves to American cultural habits. However, the religion with which they arrived, if indeed they were religious, is typically the most enduring and unchanging element in their lives.[3] In the initial years of an immigrant's life, this religion contributes to self-identity and is often the bond that holds together those in a particular ethnic group.[4] With the passage of time, of course, this may change as immigrants and their children are absorbed more fully into American life and culture.[5]

2. John Lukacs, *Outgrowing Democracy: A History of the United States in the Twentieth Century* (New York: Doubleday, 1984), 136.

3. It should be noted that there are no automatic correlations between ethnicity and religion. As Barry Kosmin and Seymour Lachman observe: "That most Americans who claim Irish or French descent are not Catholic, that most Asian Americans are Christian, and that not only are most Arab Americans not Muslim but most American Muslims are not Arabs appears strange to those not fully aware of the country's religious and immigration history." *One Nation Under God: Religion in Contemporary American Society* (New York: Harmony Books, 1993), 116. This statement is based on the national census of 1990. Over the last decade, immigration might now have changed the pattern slightly, with most American Muslims probably being Arab.

4. On the relation between ethnic consciousness, or peoplehood, and religion see Timothy L. Smith, "Religion and Ethnicity in America," *American Historical Review*, 83, no. 3 (Dec. 1978), 1155-85.

5. Peter Berger has spoken of the two homegrown pathologies that now are working havoc in American society. One is what has emerged in the underclass with

Today's immigration is creating a multiethnic society, and this, in turn, has contributed to the extraordinary religious pluralism which has emerged, because many of the new immigrants are at least formally religious and some of their religions are relatively new to America. This migration of peoples is therefore raising questions for Christian faith that have not been experienced in the same way in America before. Indeed, it would probably be true to say that the context in which Christian faith now finds itself is, from an ethnic and religious angle, more like the century in which the New Testament was written than, say, the nineteenth century in America or, for that matter, Europe. The reverse side of this is that the mass movements of people into the West, and not least America, put missionary work into an entirely new context. Missionaries once went overseas to work among peoples from other cultures and religions. Now, some of those people are making their way into Western cities and universities and some are from places to which missionaries can gain little or no access. Not only so, but missionaries are also beginning to come to America to work among their own people — and they are coming to work among mainstream Americans, too. European and American missionaries went out into the world; part of the world is now coming to the missionaries.

Perhaps the most surprising part of this story, however, is the emergence of a parallel stream of spirituality that began taking shape in the 1960s. It has come about for a number of reasons which I will explore in the next chapter, but at its heart we need to see that this is the postmodern ethos at work. This is the postmodern spirit which has emptied itself of formal religious doctrines and structures. What is most distinctive about this spirituality, therefore, is its anti-institutional bent, its deeply privatized nature, its rampant individual-

---

its "drugs, crime, illegitimacy, and a chaotic breakdown of moral order." The other has emerged in the elite class which has succeeded in debasing the educational system, politics, law, and the media. They are "miseducating one's children [*sic*], imposing intolerable burdens of government interference on the economy, institutionalizing a strange American replica of the Hindu caste system in politics and law, and creating a joyless world in which the most fundamental human relations, those between sexes and generations, are more and more poisoned." The new flow of immigrants is a counterweight to much of this. Many have strong family commitments, a disposition for hard work, a desire to succeed, and they come uncorrupted by affluence. "Immigration: The Solution Is the Problem," *First Things*, 50 (Feb., 1995), 17.

ism, and its therapeutic *modus operandi.* The emergence of this spirituality is striking and novel. What the non-Christian religions were to liberal Protestantism in the nineteenth century, and to a lesser extent Catholicism after Vatican II in the twentieth century, these spiritualities are becoming to evangelicalism today. They are testing the very nature of what it means to be an evangelical Protestant.

Pizza, Bagels, and Fish on Fridays

The story of immigration to America has been repeatedly told and my interest in it here is really only with the big picture. This story really falls into two parts which are divided by four decades during which time immigration was greatly curtailed. The first phase comprises the immigrants who came to America at its founding and who, with their descendants, were later melded into a nation by the Revolution. However, it was really in the nineteenth century that what had been a trickle of immigration became a torrent. This first phase ended after the First World War of 1914-1918. There had been growing sentiment against the steady flow of European immigrants which the War solidified and there had also been a growing bias against Asians — against the Chinese, for example, from the 1880's onwards especially along the west coast, and against the Japanese beginning at the turn of the century. The Immigration Act of 1924, as a consequence, brought this flow of the poor, tired, and those yearning to be free almost to a halt. In that year, 706,896 emigrated to the United States but by 1931, this had become a trickle of only 97,139 and it reached the lowest point in 1945 when only 38,119 arrived.

However, in 1965 the National Origins Act of 1924 was rescinded and the Immigration and Naturalization Act was passed. The former was one of several acts that had been passed which had excluded non-Westerners from gaining American citizenship. The 1965 Act abolished the existing quota system, committed the United States to giving a significant share of immigration slots to Asians, raised the quotas for all nations, with generous family unification provisions being passed later in 1986 and 1995, and thus reopened the immigration spigot. Latinos, Middle Easterners, and Asians are now pouring into America. America changed, Lukacs believes, from having "some of the most stringent immigration regulations" to having "the least stringent," which he judges "cannot and will not remain so for long."[6]

This Act has, nevertheless, begun the second part of this story of immigration and its effects are profoundly shaping the nation. New "golden doors" to the south and to the east have been opened, bringing to America a very different kind of immigrant from the first phase and producing a different kind of ethnic diversity from what had been the case in the nineteenth century. That was overwhelmingly European and this is not. And what we have yet to see is whether the pot will once again melt these immigrants together. It was one thing for Europeans to find their place among people with whom they had once had a shared history in Europe, but it may be more difficult for these new immigrants to blend in the same way. Today, there is also a heightened ethnic consciousness which stands in the way of what Emerson called the "Smelting Pot" doing its work. And there is another difference. The earlier wave of migration brought mostly varieties of Judeo-Christian religion to America. The new immigrants are bringing with them many other kinds of religion. With these new immigrants, Diana Eck writes, have come "the religious traditions of the world — Islamic, Hindu, Buddhist, Jain, Sikh, Zoroastrian, African, and Afro-Caribbean."[7] This Act, says Gordon Melton, "contributed directly to the massive expansion" in America's religious diversity "and is even now completely altering the overall shape and structure of the American religious community."[8]

Prior to 1819, statistics on immigration are a little hazy. Individual states attempted counts, such as New York first in 1689, Rhode Island in 1708, and Massachusetts in 1764, but the aggregate for the nation was more a matter of inference and guess work than hard counts.[9] In-

6. John Lukacs, *The End of the Twentieth Century and the End of the Modern Age* (New York: Ticker and Fields, 1993), 264.

7. Diana L. Eck, *A New Religious America: How a "Christian Country" Has Now Become the World's Most Religiously Diverse Nation* (San Francisco: Harder, 2001), 1.

8. J. Gordon Melton, *Encyclopedia of American Religions* (London: Gale Research, 1999), 15.

9. On the emergence of statistical methods in the Colonial period see James H. Casey, *Demography in Early America: Beginning of the Statistical Mind, 1600-1800* (Cambridge: Harvard University Press, 1969).

deed, even after 1819, though the figures are the result of hard counts, they have nevertheless produced some inaccuracies.[10] However, the pattern of immigration after this time is rather clear. In 1820, of all of those who came to the United States, 92% were from Europe.[11] And this proportion was more or less sustained throughout the century. In 1846, it was 95%; in 1850, 83%; in 1872, 87%; in 1882, 82%. The high water mark in terms of the numbers of immigrants in this first phase happened in 1914 when 1,218,480 arrived of whom 87% were European, and the greatest decade was from 1901 to 1910 when 8,795,386 arrived. Until the 1860s, the immigration was mostly from northern Europe and was predominantly Protestant in nature; after this time, it was increasingly from eastern and southern Europe and predominantly Jewish and Catholic. In 1924, the year of the Immigration Act, 706,896 immigrants arrived, of whom 52% were European.[12] Then began the four-decade hiatus. However, if we include these decades in this first phase of immigration, and look at the period from 1820 to 1964, we find that of the thirty-five million immigrants who came to the United States, 82% were European, 3% were Asian, and 15% were in a category that included Canadians and Latin Americans.[13] An indication of how massive this immigration was is the fact that the 1916 census of religious bodies showed that of the existing 200 denominations in America, no less than 132 reported that in their churches languages other than English were used in part or in whole during worship.

10. For a brief review of this, see Lukacs, *Outgrowing Democracy*, 125-29.

11. The Bureau of the Census considers Europe to be in four sectors: *Northwestern:* Great Britain, Ireland, Scandinavia, Netherlands, Belgium, Luxembourg, Switzerland, and France; *Central:* Germany, Poland, Czechoslovakia (since 1920), Yugoslavia (since 1920), Hungary (since 1861), Austria (since 1861); *Eastern:* Latvia, Estonia, Lithuania, Finland; *Southern:* Italy, Spain, Portugal, and Greece. The designation of "European" is the aggregate in any year of immigrants from all of these countries.

12. These percentages have been calculated from the figures provided in *Historical Statistics of the United States: Colonial Times to 1957, Prepared by the Bureau of the Census with the Cooperation of the Social Science Research Council* (Washington: U.S. Department of Commerce, Bureau of the Census, 1960), 57. The percentages have been rounded off.

13. *Statistical Abstract of the United States: Prepared by the Bureau of the Census with the Cooperation of the Social Research Council* (Washington: US Department of Commerce, Bureau of the Census, 1965), 93.

I am one-half Norwegian, one quarter Swedish, and one-quarter English, although the English portion was diluted way back in the colonial period by a lone French Canadian. I married a woman who is one-half Swiss-German and one-half Anglo-Irish, which makes my children a polyglot of western Europeans. I am not very good at multiplying fractions, so I have not figured out their exact ethnic proportions. My odyssey with American pluralism is the rule rather than the exception.

James S. Olson, *The Ethnic Dimension in American History*

The nineteenth century, then, was the era of the Great Migration, when Europeans by the boatload set sail for America. The Statue of Liberty, erected toward the end of this first phase, in 1886, naturally looked east, gazing across the Atlantic toward the lands from whence these boats had come. For decades, in fact, the only immigrants who were counted in America were those who landed along the eastern seaboard because it appeared that these were the only immigrants who were arriving in America. Those who docked at west coast ports were not to be counted until 1850, and those crossing America's northern and southern land borders were not included in any count until 1904. That is a good indication of how immigration in the nineteenth century was understood. It was European.[14]

In 1955, Will Herberg looked back over this development and concluded that America had, as a result of this immigration, become "one great community divided into three big sub-communities religiously defined, all equal and all equally American in their identification with the 'American way of life.'"[15] He went on to say that it is not possible to

---

14. For an account of this immigration see James S. Olson's *The Ethnic Dimension in American History* (New York: St. Martin's, 1994); E. Allen Richardson, *Strangers in This Land: Pluralism and the Response to Diversity in the United States* (New York: The Pilgrim Press, 1988); and more recently Michael Barone, *The New Americans: How the Melting Pot Can Work Again* (Washington: Regnery Publishing, 2001).

15. Will Herberg, *Protestant-Catholic-Jew: An Essay in American Religious Sociology* (New York: Doubleday, 1955), 51.

locate oneself in American society without identifying oneself as a Protestant, Catholic, or Jew, and he said this with some justification because at that time 94% of the nation identified itself in terms of one of these groups. Buddhists and atheists "are not even remotely signifi-cant in determining the American's understanding of himself,"[16] he as-serted. Widick Schroeder made much the same point. Americans, he said, gradually "came to consider a basic tri-partite faith grouping rooted in the Judeo-Christian tradition to be normal and natural in the United States." Social identity, he said, "is in part defined by one's rela-tion to these three groups." And he drew the same conclusion that Herberg had. "One may be a Muslim, Buddhist, Shintoist, Hindu and be an American, but such a person is marginal to American life."[17] Even this assessment was a softening of what had pertained because in 1923 the Supreme Court had actually ruled on the citizenship of a Sikh, Bhagat Singh Thind. Although a lower court had granted him citizen-ship, this was appealed. The Supreme Court ruled that he could not be an American even though he was married to an American citizen. Its reasoning was that American citizenship was reserved for the white races.[18]

It is, of course, true that the Great Migration of the nineteenth century did bring to America Protestants, Catholics, and Jews in very substantial numbers and did, for that reason, affect American religious life very significantly. However, it is also important to see that these traditions were themselves quite diverse, and once they arrived in America, and as immigrants blended into American society, the forms of faith they brought with them became part of an increasingly ram-bunctious, innovative, inventive, religious experiment which produced variations of, and offshoots from, these inherited traditions, though more so on the Protestant side than the Catholic or Jewish. Some of the arriving immigrants had belonged to state churches. If they had no de-sire to change, they typically lined up with the Catholics, Anglicans, Lu-therans, or Presbyterians. Others had become disaffected with the

16. Herberg, *Protestant-Catholic-Jew*, 53.

17. W. Widick Schroeder et al., *Suburban Religion: Churches and Synagogues in the American Experience* (Chicago: Center for the Scientific Study of Religion, 1974), 28.

18. Eck, *A New Religious America*, 6, 59-60.

state churches in Europe and sought other connections in America, sometimes sectarian. Thus it was that the practice of belief by the immigrants merged into that of settled Americans, and the diversity they had brought became part of the larger picture in America. Denominations over time took paths that began to differentiate them from what they had been in Europe. Charles Finney, for example, who spearheaded the Second Great Awakening in its early stages and pioneered the "New Measures," gave a face to Presbyterianism which it had never had before. Others, in time, wandered further afield, finding what they were looking for in Mormonism, Theosophy, Millerism, Unitarianism, Swedenborgianism, Freemasonry, Mesmerism, Christian Science, and even fortune-telling, spiritualism, and divination. "By the 1850s," Jon Butler wrote, "religious syncretism and creativity extended across ante-bellum society and easily rivaled the American ingenuity and adaptability evident in exploration, politics, and technology." He went on to say that across the entire social spectrum — White and Black, rich and poor, educated and uneducated — Americans of all kinds "brought forth religious movements astonishing in their variety, numbers and vitality."[19]

What stands out about this diversity is the way in which religious traditions began to take on the characteristics of American political and social life. Is this so strange? It is surely what one might expect, but the danger, of course, was that in some ways the Americanizing could become altogether too successful. And in some ways it did. Writing of the period following Edwards and up to the Civil War, Mark Noll has detailed the profound internal transformations which occurred. The idea of justice, for example, which in the works of Jonathan Edwards was one of the divine perfections, became in those of Finney simply a

---

19. Jon Butler, *Awash in a Sea of Faith: Christianizing the American People* (Cambridge: Harvard University Press, 1990), 255-56. Earlier church historians tended to ignore the diversity, focusing on what they considered "mainline," but in the work of more recent historians like Martin Marty, Sydney Ahlstrom, and Jon Butler this situation has been redressed. See the discussion in R. Laurence Moore, *Religious Outsiders and the Making of Americans* (New York: Oxford University Press, 1986), 3-21. See also Henry Warner Bowden, "The Historiography of American Religion," in *Encyclopedia of the American Religious Experience: Studies of Traditions and Movements*, ed. Charles H. Lippy and Peter W. Williams (3 vols.; New York: Charles Scribner's Sons, 1988), I, 3-16.

functional value in human life. As democracy took hold, and as the pragmatic temper became more and more dominant, and as theology mutated within a changing culture, what had been a dominant "contemplative theocentrism" now became a dominant "activistic anthropocentrism."[20] These were not modest changes on the periphery but they went to the very heart of what was believed.

From his vantage point in the mid-twentieth century, however, Herberg looked upon a nation whose religious differences had now lost their sharpness, he thought. Indeed, talk about civil religion became quite common after this. There was, it was said, a core of belief in which all who had started out as Catholic, Protestant, or Jew could now participate, a sort of national faith which had lost its rough edges and pointed disagreements.[21] This mid-century view, though, was misleading if projected back into the nineteenth century, which lacked the civility that Herberg saw in his own time and was, by contrast, religiously disorderly, noisy, fractious, loud in its disagreements, and diverse in what it had to offer. But it was mostly a different kind of religious diversity from that which came about during the second phase in the immigration story which began in 1965. The key, of course, was the fact that what had poured into America earlier had been overwhelmingly European, and

20. Mark A. Noll, *America's God: From Jonathan Edwards to Abraham Lincoln* (New York: Oxford University Press, 2002), 440.

21. John Murray Cuddihy assails this notion that there ever was such a thing as civil religion if by that we mean certain creedal elements which were held in common. What it was, he counters, was simply "the religion of civility." But despite its pretensions, it was often not civil at all. "Sometimes it waits outside the churches and waylays with its niceness their members as they file out. Sometimes it enters without knocking into their minds, and penetrates the core beliefs of their theologies, refining and 'civilizing' them from within. Sometimes, reaping its benefits serendipitously from social mobility — when entire religious bodies are upwardly mobilized — it refines them behind their backs, so to speak, secretly and gradually substituting its civil and civilized ways for the uncouth truths of an earlier time." In other words, it was more a code of social etiquette when dealing with religious differences than a set of cogent beliefs in its own right. John Murray Cuddihy, *No Offense: Civil Religion and Protestant Taste* (New York: The Seabury Press, 1978), 2. It is certainly of interest that when Wuthnow came to address the subject a little later, he spoke of civil religion only in terms of two political agendas in the Church, one from the left and the other from the right. See his *The Restructuring of American Religion: Society and Faith Since World War II* (Princeton: Princeton University Press, 1988), 241-67.

even as it became modified in America and mutated under its conditions of democracy and freedom,[22] it never entirely left behind its European memories. Nor, for the most part, did it bring religion which was outside the Judeo-Christian tradition. That is what changed after 1965.

These earlier immigrants all came lured by the American Dream, a vision of a society in which freedom was its foundation and unity was its end. To many of the Europeans who came this must have seemed like an impossible dream because they had come to believe that freedom typically produces inequalities. People start out in life with different abilities and dispositions. Gifts that are developed fully and freely lead people into different trades and to achieve different levels of education. Different people bring to their work different levels of proficiency and different degrees of desire to succeed. Some, therefore, end up with large fortunes and others with nothing, some become highly educated and others do not. If freedom is thought of as the ability to be different from others and equality as the right to be like others, it was inevitable that Europeans would think that liberty and equality are contradictory.

In America, however, liberty was understood as the freedom to grasp opportunity, whether it led to a simple log cabin in a wilderness or to the White House, and equality has come to mean the ability to grasp opportunity in the same way that anyone else can. Thus it is that liberty and equality converge on the same point. However, in American life, the individualism that tends to spring from the pursuit of liberty, and the conformity that tends to follow a commitment to unity, have often been in conflict with each other.[23] And once again, as a new chapter in immigration opens, this tension has resurfaced with some vigor. Not only is the country now awash in new religions, and not only is the inherent individualism of the American character now being fanned into a fresh blaze by the modernized world, but there are now debates about what it means to be an American. In what does the nation's unity consist if its multicultural character is going to be allowed its place under the sun? If the nation's motto is "From Many, One," how likely is it that the end result will be, "From One, Many"?

22. See the account in Nathan O. Hatch, *The Democratization of American Christianity* (New Haven: Yale University Press, 1989).

23. I have explored these themes in my *No Place for Truth: or, Whatever Happened to Evangelical Theology?* (Grand Rapids: William B. Eerdmans, 1992), 189-98.

Enchiladas, Chow Mein, and Soul Food

It is impossible to know exactly what contribution post-1965 immigration has made to America's growing religious diversity but it does appear to be large. This is so despite the fact that some of this diversity owes nothing to immigration at all. The Nation of Islam, to take one example, is a homegrown response of alienation from an unwelcoming white American culture.[24] It is not an outgrowth of the communities of Lebanese and Syrian immigrants who had been in America for some time prior to the founding of the Nation of Islam.

However, at least some of America's religious diversity has been carried into it by immigrants. And once these beliefs took root, they also became subject to the American knack for innovation. What was true in the nineteenth century is still true in the twenty-first. Religious traditions rarely stand still. New Age, for example, is Hindu in its roots but in America this Hinduism has become contextualized, secularized, sanitized, sometimes psychologized, made undemanding, comfortable, and middle-class, sprouting new varieties in all directions, many of which are probably unrecognizable to devout Indian Hindus outside of America. And, along more conventional paths, Americans, especially in the second half of the last century, often gave full rein to their individualism, adapting beliefs to their own needs and mixing-and-matching as they went along. For these and, no doubt, many other reasons, religious diversity is growing and flourishing in America but immigration is certainly a part of the explanation.[25]

Recent immigration has changed the mix in important ways. In 1964, the year before the immigration law was changed, 37% of those immigrants who arrived were European, 7% were Asian, and 54% fell into a category of Canadian and Latin American.[26] During the next two

24. See Richard Kyle, *The Religious Fringe: A History of Alternative Religions in America* (Downers Grove: InterVarsity Press, 1993), 239-45.

25. See Stephen R. Warner and Judith G. Wittner, eds., *Gatherings in Diaspora: Religious Communities and the New Immigration* (Philadelphia: Temple University Press, 1998). On the forms which Hinduism, Buddhism, and Islam have taken in America see Eck, *New Religious America*, 80-293.

26. These figures have been calculated from the data in *Statistical Abstract of the United States . . . 1965*, 93.

decades there would be significant changes. From 1981 to 1990, for example, of the 1,013,620 who arrived in America only 15% were European, substantially lower than the figures of 80% to 90% that were typical during the nineteenth century. Asians and Latin Americans who barely registered in the statistics of the nineteenth century were respectively 70% and 12% of the newcomers during this period.[27] In the decade of the 1990s, the figures were 43% and 39% of the total number of immigrants. And between 2000 and 2002, the Latino population grew by 9.8% to make it the largest minority group in the nation, Asians grew 9.0%, and Whites 0.7%. Since most Hispanics are at least formally Catholic and a growing number are Pentecostal, and a significant number of the Koreans who came to America are Protestant, the immediate effect of this was an injection of Christian faith into non-European America. Between 1990 and 2000, the percentage of Americans who identified themselves as Protestant fell from 60% to 52% of the population and that of Catholics fell from 26.5% to 24.5%.[28] This drop actually enlarged a little the impact of the contribution which these immigrants made on Christian faith, Protestant or Catholic, for theirs was an outlook which was neither American nor European and often they brought habits that were correspondingly different.[29]

Like the immigrants of the nineteenth century, those of the twentieth also came for different reasons and, of course, brought their different backgrounds to America. The more recent immigrants, however, are dif-

27. These percentages are calculated from the figures provided in the *Statistical Abstract of the United States: Prepared by the Bureau of the Census with the Cooperation of the Social Research Council* (Washington: U.S. Department of Commerce, Bureau of the Census, 1999), 12.

28. Egon Mayer and Barry Kosmin, "The American Religious Identification Survey," http://www.gc.cuny.edu/studies/key_findings.htm. This survey, the American Religious Identification Survey, was conducted by Egon Mayer and Barry Kosmin through the City University of New York in 2000. They surveyed 50,281 people. The first such study was done in 1990.

29. "During the 20th century, in fact, Christianity has become the most extensive and universal religion in history. There are today Christians and organized churches in every inhabited country on earth. The church is therefore now, for the first time in history, ecumenical in the literal meaning of the word: its boundaries are coextensive with the *oikumene*, the whole inhabited world." David D. Barrett, George T. Kurian, and Todd M. Johnson, *World Christian Encyclopedia: A Comparative Survey of Churches and Religions in the Modern World* (2 vols.; Oxford: Oxford University Press, 2001), I, 3.

ferent not only ethnically but in a way that also reflects the difference between the nineteenth and the twenty-first centuries. In the nineteenth century, immigrants leaving Europe made a clean break with their countries. Very few ever returned and mail was slow so the lines of communication were minimal. Virtually no immigrants today "leave" in quite so final a sense. Not only has air travel erased the significance of distance but telephones, faxes, and emails are linking families otherwise separated by oceans. Indeed, some immigrants can even read newspapers from their former country on the Internet. The result is that the move to America has far less psychological finality to it than it once did.

The sight of many Asian cities today, with their glittering highrises, sparkling corporate headquarters, bustling streets, and vigorous commerce seems to belie the fact that during the twentieth century a number of these countries faced traumatic episodes of war and brutality. Japan occupied Taiwan and Korea during the first half of the century and part of China and Vietnam during the Second World War. Korea fought a civil war as did Vietnam. China in the 1960s and 1970s suffered the Cultural Revolution which Chairman Mao unleashed. It was a self-inflicted wound that produced killings and the uprooting and degradation of millions of people. There were no compensating gains in this brutal social experiment, only confusion, oppression, and hopelessness. Looming over all of this, in China, North Korea, and Vietnam, has been the crushing Marxist vision that promised a classless, prosperous utopia. What came, instead, as we know, was destitution, loss, and bondage. Twentieth-century Asia experienced much grinding poverty, and episodes of fearful savagery, painful indignities, and much loss of life. Here there really were the "huddled masses yearning to breathe free." But they were not coming to America, not until the Immigration Act of 1965 was passed. Since then, five million have come, some bringing Christian faith, but others Buddhism, Confucianism, and in those who have come from India, Hinduism, and a multitude of belief systems less well known to most Americans.[30]

Prior to the 1960s, political upheaval, especially in Mexico, forced refugees north periodically, but once quiet returned they tended to make their way back home, crossing an unguarded border. Since the

30. Barrett et al., *World Christian Encyclopedia*, I, 249-62.

1960s, however, the surge into the United States has become more determined, more calculated, driven most of all by economic necessity. From Cuba, three quarters of a million people have fled since Castro seized power in 1959. From the South, ten million have entered the United States legally since the Immigration Act of 1965, and it is estimated that thirteen million people, of many nationalities, were in the United States illegally in 2002. All of these groups have come in jerks and starts, leaving their own rural and urban settings to make their way north to America's thriving, throbbing cities, Latinos settling mainly in the Southwest as well as in Miami where they joined exiled Cubans to make up the 61% of the city's population which is foreign-born.

The religious picture in America, as a result of this immigration, has begun to change. While the number of religiously observant Jews declined in the decade from 1990 to 2000 by almost 10%, the presence of Eastern religions grew considerably. Estimating the number of Muslims, Hindus, and Buddhists is part art and part science and the estimates vary quite widely. However, it appears that between the time that the Immigration Act was passed and the end of the twentieth century, the Muslim population in America grew from 800,000 to a little over four million (though some place it as high as six or even eight million), and in 2000 there were more than 1,200 Islamic centers in America. Buddhists, during this time, grew from 30,000 to two and one-half million, and Hindus from 100,000 to one million.[31] In 1987, the first Buddhist chaplain was appointed to the armed services and in 1993, the first Muslim chaplain.

Perhaps the easiest way to see what has happened is to visit a bookstore although it also appears to be the case that the expanded sections on non-Christian religions are visited less by newly arrived immigrants and more by Americans who have become aware of the new religions and are in pursuit of their own forms of spirituality. Regardless, it was once the case that the Bible was the more or less exclusive source for religion in America, and Christianity, in its various forms, was the preeminent faith. Today, however, in bookstores across the country one finds scriptures like the Bhagavad Gita and the Qurân. There are books on Islamic history, calligraphy, and thought; books on Buddhist belief; books on or by the Dalai Lama (among them the bestselling *The Art of Happi-*

31. Barrett et al., *World Christian Encyclopedia*, I, 772.

ness, co-written with an American psychiatrist); books on Sufi poetry, on the techniques and benefits of meditation, on Voodoo, on Sikhism, and on Chuang Tzi. Indeed, one can even see *The Tao of Pooh* and *The Te of Piglet!* There are also books on the myths and legends of the American Indians and the religions of other indigenous peoples like the Maoris.

What can be seen on the bookshelf is appearing in towns and cities across America as Muslim mosques and Buddhist and Hindu temples are rapidly being built, although it is also the case that much of this religion remains invisible in that defunct church buildings are being used as meeting places, as are office buildings, warehouses, and homes. With the exception of Jewish belief, these each represent religious commitments which, in the nineteenth century, were off the psychological map. Their representatives were, at best, few in number and they lived their life on the very periphery of American life. That has now changed. Western preoccupation with the self and with what is therapeutic leads naturally into a disposition that is amenable to Eastern ideas, and Western moral disorder makes Islam look like a haven of moral sanity (except, of course, on its radical and violent fringe). For these and other reasons, these religions which were once "foreign" and strange are now settling in America. "The United States," writes Gordon Melton, "is currently home to more than 1,500 different religious organizations — churches, sects, cults, temples, societies, missions," each the primary focus of spiritual allegiance for its adherents.[32] Some of the more conservative Christian groups continue to speak of America as a Christian country, or at least that it should be a Christian country, or at the very least that in its origins it once was a Christian country. The reality, however, is that America is the world's most religiously diverse nation now and from a Christian point of view it is as fully a mission field as any to which churches now are sending their missionaries. This is true, not only because of the arrival of these new immigrants with their diverse religions, but also because of the postmodern decay in American culture.

It is not inappropriate to speak of the "traditional" or "established" religions which have taken root in America, but it also needs to be remembered that faiths do not stand still and especially in America they do not. It is freedom which makes all of this religious believing

32. Melton, *Encyclopedia of American Religions,* 15.

possible. That is the condition without which innovation and experimentation become impossible. That is a fountain from which change flows and, in America, it usually gushes. Religious movements rise, flourish, and then some decline. New religions are born — about three every day worldwide — and old ones sometimes fade away or, at least, become inconsequential. They spawn competitors, provoke conflicts, sometimes divide, sometimes regroup, sometimes withdraw from the culture, sometimes lose themselves in it by mimicking what it does, sometimes lose their way, sometimes find it again.

Alongside this religious supermarket, however, has sprung up a parallel culture of spiritual yearning. This more recent permutation on religion, this extraordinary flowering of spiritualities during the last four decades in particular, is fueled by more than simply freedom. Freedom is the necessary condition, but expressive individualism and the "triumph of the therapeutic," to use Philip Rief's words, are what have turned this yearning into a cultural phenomenon which may not be very deep but is very wide. And the pressures of postmodernity have ignited it, and the result is now an explosion of personalized spiritualities. This, I believe, is even more significant than the new pluralistic religious mix which I have briefly described and to which immigration has undoubtedly contributed significantly. And it is, as I have suggested, the issue that looms large over the whole evangelical enterprise, threatening to attack its very authenticity even as the non-Christian religions succeeded in doing to the liberal Protestantism of the nineteenth century. This is a novel and extraordinary development to which we must now give some consideration.

The New Spiritual Quest

The Third Stream

Beginning in the 1960s, and blossoming in the 1970s and 1980s, "spirituality," for a significant number of people, came into its own and became preferable to "religion." The distinction that quickly took root was that religion stood for organized belief in its public form. It stood for participation in worship, support of the church or synagogue, and acceptance of its doctrines. Spirituality, by contrast, has come to stand for what is private and internal. What this typically means is that those who are spiritual accept no truth which is not experientially grounded. In the one, there is doctrine which is part and parcel of the church; in the other, mystical encounter which may often be accompanied by an unorthodox disposition. In the one, faith is lived out within a religious structure; in the other, there is suspicion of, if not hostility toward, religion which is organized.[33]

This is the phenomenon which I will be examining more closely in the following chapter and here I simply need to set the stage for that analysis and theological reflection. It belongs in this chapter because it is part and parcel of our new religious and spiritual pluralism. Indeed, Eugene Taylor[34] describes this development in American society as being a "shadow culture," a parallel to the older configuration of Catholic-Protestant-Jew which had its journals and religious periodicals, its structures and institutions, its schools and places of higher learning, and its thinkers and leaders. All of this is now beginning to be replicated in this alternative path which spirituality is forging outside of conventional channels and the older organized religion. If Christianity in all its permutations was the first stream to flow into America, and the Asian and Middle Eastern religions have become the second, this is now the third but with this important caveat: it is less a stream flowing into America than it is a spring bubbling up from within the American psyche and incorporating into its flow other religious ideas. It is not, therefore, the direct result of immigration but its shape has been affected by some of the religious consequences following recent immigration.

This parting of the ways between religion and spirituality is not entirely new. Mention has already been made of the stream of spirituality in the nineteenth century which flowed outside the churches in movements like Swedenborgianism, Theosophy, and Mesmerism.[35]

33. For a further elaboration on the distinction between religion and spirituality, see Brian Zinnbauer and Kenneth Pargament et al., "Religion and Spirituality: Unfuzzing the Fuzzy," *Journal for the Scientific Study of Religion*, 36 (Dec., 1997), 549-64.

34. Eugene Taylor, *Shadow Culture: Psychology and Spirituality in America* (Washington: Counterpoint, 1999), 290.

35. See the full-scale study of this spiritual disposition in America in Robert C.

However, this current development is both larger than it has ever been before, more obviously indebted to Eastern ideas, and now much more mainstream. It is mainstream not only in the sense that it is now no longer viewed as strange but also because some of the ideas that are common in this spirituality have also entered the churches. In churches, according to one survey, 20% believe in reincarnation, 24% read their horoscopes, and 11% believe in trance channeling.[36]

What may be most startling about this development is how fully it has come out into the open, despite the smothering secularism that once gripped the workplace. Spirituality travels light. It needs no buildings, no rituals, no professionals, or even sacred books. It can be practiced alone. Perhaps, then, it should not be so surprising that in the business world, for example, which is driven by fierce competition, suffused with insecurity, where corporate vitality can turn to corporate death with astonishing speed, spirituality is appearing everywhere. There are discussion groups that talk about it and its role in the workplace and its place in leadership. There are spiritual gurus and inspirational speakers who make the rounds, all attesting to the fact that the breeding ground of hard-driving, pragmatic secular materialism has been invaded by the yearning that people have to get in touch with themselves, with their inner self, with the sacred, with something that breathes meaning into their day-to-day existence. And for so many, these needs are not being met by religion. Religion stands outside the office building. "Today," write Laura Nash and Scotty McLennan, "whether basking in sudden wealth or hurting from new competition, business people actively seek new clues and mental paradigms to solve the frightening quandaries and meaning of the global, cybernetic economy," and in the process many are being drawn to spirituality, "hoping for self-awareness, meaning, moral goodness, and effectiveness in their vocational activities."[37]

There is plenty of evidence which bears out this growing parting of the ways between religion and spirituality. In America, four out of

---

Fuller, *Spiritual But Not Religious: Understanding Unchurched America* (New York: Oxford University Press, 2001).

36. Fuller, *Spiritual But Not Religious*, 69.

37. Laura Nash and Scotty McLennan, *Church on Sunday, Work on Monday: The Challenge of Fusing Christian Values with Business Life* (San Francisco: Jossey-Bass, 2001).

ten who say they are spiritual "don't take their faith filtered through the stained glass of a church, synagogue, temple or mosque."[38] Gallup has found that while 78% see themselves as spiritual people,[39] 56% went on to say that in solving life's problems they were more likely to rely upon themselves than upon an outside power like God.[40] This, of course, is consistent with this religious/spiritual dichotomy. Growing numbers of Americans, Robert Wuthnow reports, "say they are spiritual but not religious, or that many say their spirituality is growing but the impact of religion on their lives is diminishing," and still others insist that because spirituality is "private" it "must develop without the guidance of religious institutions."[41] Even those who choose to be within the structures of organized religion commonly complain that these structures are not facilitating spirituality enough. To Gallup's 1989 question as to how churches and synagogues could best improve, the second largest response came from those who thought that they should nurture the "desire for a deeper sense of spirituality and closeness to God"[42] that people have. A decade later, he asked the question: "Do you think of spirituality more in a personal and individual sense, or more in terms of organized religion and doctrine?" 72% opted for the "personal and individual" while 21% opted for what is institutionalized.[43] This is so clearly a cultural reality that in 2001 *Newsweek* decided to report on the work which has been done in locating the parts of the brain which are active in spiritual moments. The edition was entitled: "God and the Brain: How We're Wired for Spirituality."[44] There is a deep sense of frus-

38. Mayer and Kozmin, ARIS survey. Fuller puts the number at around 20%. However, this is based on a computation from previous studies that probably no longer reflect the actual situation. *Spiritual But Not Religious*, 5.

39. George Gallup, Jr. and Timothy Jones, *The Next American Spirituality: Finding God in the Twenty-first Century* (Colorado Springs: Cook Communications, 2000), 184.

40. Gallup and Jones, *The Next American Spirituality*, 185.

41. Robert Wuthnow, *After Heaven: Spirituality in America Since the 1950s* (Berkeley: University of California Press, 1998), 2. See also his *Experimentation in American Religion: The New Mysticisms and Their Implications for the Church* (Berkeley: University of California Press, 1978).

42. George Gallup, Jr. and Jim Castelli, *The People's Religion: American Faith in the '90s* (New York: Macmillan, 1989), 255.

43. Gallup and Jones, *The Next American Spirituality*, 50.

44. Sharon Begley, "Religion and the Brain," *Newsweek* (May 7, 2001), 50-56. In this same section, Kenneth Woodward counters that what scientists have possibly

Years of Catholic school never taught either of them to "cope"; indeed, they said, it only made them more neurotic. By now, "there isn't a church in all of America I want to go to," said Joanne, setting out dinner plates in her Burke living room.

So sometime in the last 10 years the Liveranis began to build their own church, salvaging bits of their old religion they liked and chucking the rest. The first to go were an angry, vengeful God and hell — "That's just something they say to scare you," Ed said. They kept Jesus, "because Jesus is big on love."

From the local bookstore, in a bulging section called "Private Spirituality," they found wisdom in places they had never before searched, or even heard of: In Zen masters, in New Age chestnuts such as *A Course in Miracles,* in their latest find, *Conversations with God.*

Now they commune with a new God, a gentle twin of the one they grew up with. He is wise but soft-spoken, cheers them up when they're sad, laughs at their quirks. He is, most essentially, validating, like the greatest of friends.

And best of all, he had been there all along. "We discovered the God within," said Joanne. "That's why we need God. Because we are God. God gives me the ability to create my own godliness."

Hanna Rosin, *Beyond 2000: A Self-made Deity*

tration with organized religion today which is merging with a renewed yearning for the sacred, and the result is an explosion in these personalized, customized spiritualities.

This appears to be not only an American phenomenon but one that is found throughout the West. In a study that was done in Britain in 2000, for example, it was discovered that during approximately the final decade of the twentieth century, regular attendance at church

---

shown is only the circuitry the brain uses but its use does not mean that we are thereby in communion with God. Kenneth L. Woodward, "Faith is More Than a Feeling," 58. The fact that this is being discussed at all is what is significant.

dropped from being a practice of 28% of the population down to 8%. During this same time, however, those who described themselves as spiritual, or who had had spiritual experiences, rose from 48% to 76%. The components of this spirituality were an awareness of the presence of God, awareness of the presence of evil, believing in the presence of the sacred in nature, believing that one's personal circumstances in life fall into a meaningful pattern, having experienced answers to prayer, and believing in the presence of the dead among the living.[45] It is not clear from this study itself whether the sharp rise in spiritual experience reflects the fact that people are being more spiritual or that they have become more willing to talk about it, but either way there is a belief that there needs to be a spiritual component to life, and one that the Church is not the place to find it.

They wish and they want, they long and they hanker — these young people. For Experience. For Religious Experience. For Extraordinary Religious Experience. An Extraordinary Religious Experience which will put all of their pieces together into one beautiful holy whole, and they will live in spiritual communion with other holified children of the light. Spontaneous, creative, authentic children, stripped of all the dross of technology and materialism. Simple wants. Simple joys. Free of all the clutter and clichés of institutional religions.

Edna Hong, *The Downward Ascent*

What has passed almost unnoticed is that this parallel culture of spirituality is resolving the issue of religious pluralism without even confronting it. This is no small matter in a time of growing religious diversity and sometimes competition. It sees the various religions, not as competitors, but only as possible sources for ideas or insights. The re-

45. David Hay and Kate Hunt, *Understanding the Spirituality of People Who Don't Go to Church: A Report on the Findings of the Adults' Spirituality Project at the University of Nottingham* (Nottingham: Center for the Study of Human Relations, 2000), 12-13.

lation to the other religions is benign because they are nonthreatening. While these religions offer an interpretation of life and of the cosmos, this spirituality lives within the much smaller world of personal experience. It offers a way of meaning, of healing, for the individual. Private worlds of meaning have no ambitions to project themselves onto the cosmos. They are private, not universal and absolute. And this, of course, means that this spirituality is thoroughly at home in the modernized world which, in so many ways, disengages what is private from what is public. Although Enlightenment assumptions have been frequently rejected and ridiculed by postmoderns, here, at least, there is a line of continuity. The autonomy of the individual that the Enlightenment championed has, in the postmodern spirituality, been retained, but also radicalized. This religious, expressive individualism has found a way of living with religious pluralism that the religions often have not, or cannot. They are shackled by their universal truth claims; this spirituality is free from that kind of limitation. That, however, does not mean that it is shy about raiding ideas from the religions.

It has become quite common, as a result, for these postmodern spiritual seekers to feed off the religions, incorporating and adapting tenets along the way in a burgeoning experiment in homemade belief. "Far from excluding non-Christian religions in the development of these new forms of spirituality, Americans were inspired by Hinduism, Buddhism, Native American religions, and various forms of 'paganism' and drew freely from these alternative traditions," observed Amanda Porterfield.[46] However, it is important to see that those who are spiritual insist on the experiential grounding of their beliefs. That means that they may pick and choose from among the ideas they find in the great religious traditions, but it is not possible to be spiritual in this sense and also accept any kind of revelation which is universal, or absolute truth which transcends reason and human autonomy.

This spiritual quest, then, is quite eclectic. It may well draw insights from the Bible but it may also look to the Qurân, the Bhagavad Gita, to medieval mystics and, of course, to contemporary writers like M. Scott Peck whose book *The Road Less Traveled* stayed aloft the *New*

46. Amanda Porterfield, *The Transformation of American Religion: The Story of a Late-Twentieth-Century Awakening* (New York: Oxford University Press, 2001), 41.

York Times bestseller list for more than five years. Or, more recently, Neale Donald Walsh's astonishingly popular *Conversations with God,* which dismisses all external authorities in favor of internal feelings and intuitions, has become for others an inspirational text.

In five years, from 1971 to 1975, I directly experienced EST, Gestalt therapy, bioenergetics, rolfing, massage, jogging, health foods, tai chi, Esalen, hypnotism, modern dance, meditation, Silva Mind Control, Arica, acupuncture, sex therapy, Reichian therapy, and More House — a smorgasbord course in New Consciousness.... I went into therapy for growth. Not fully in touch with my own feelings and needs, I was closed to myself, and therefore closed to others. I felt nervous and lonely. I felt that if I could *see* myself I would *love* myself.

Jerry Rubin, *Growing (Up) at Thirty-seven*

At the heart of this development is a desire to open up windows of internal perception and to experience the sacred. Since the sacred is so often conceived as being within the self, the means of access are, correspondingly, heavily intuitive and psychological. Psychology, it has become increasingly clear, has often been assuming the role which religion once had. It is, in that sense, a secular alternative which, on purely humanistic grounds, offers what religion once provided. That being so, Eugene Taylor has suggested that perhaps, given the place of psychology in these spiritualities it may be able to provide the bridge between Western and Eastern ways of thought.

The fact that popular magazines like *Time* and *Newsweek* in America and *Der Spiegel* in Germany have run articles on this gathering spiritual interest may leave the impression that this is a cultural phenomenon which, like so many others, is here today but will be gone tomorrow, that it is just a passing fad or fashion. To suppose that, I believe, would be a mistake. It is true that Western societies are constantly roiled by change, that little is static and unchanging, and what catches the eye one moment has often become boring or passé the next. It is important to see, however, that this interest in spirituality is not a matter of taste or fashion — what undoubtedly would have a shelf-life of short duration — but it is rooted in the very nature of modernized society and, I believe, in human nature itself.

"During the hippie era, I began on my own to read a little about Eastern religions," she recalls. "I doubted Christianity, and I still felt very estranged from God, but I believed in reincarnation. My brother was reading a lot about the occult, and that got me interested in numerology and Tarot. I read the Seth books by Jane Roberts. Seth was allegedly a spirit guide. I never just embraced these ideas automatically. I had a lot of questions, but I believed some of the things, like the idea that each person has a spirit guide who is available if you want them. I also started going to a spiritualist. And I thought a lot about the Ten Commandments. I wasn't sure they were from God, but I did feel they were a kind of code imprinted on me and that they were a good way to live."

The main result of these explorations was an enhanced sense of freedom. Nancy recalls, "I somehow felt *freer.* I felt as if I had more control over my own life. I felt released from shackles. I still couldn't quite get a grasp on my life, but I was free of the angry God and hypocritical church experiences of my childhood."

Nancy Nylstrom as reported in
Robert Wuthnow, *After Heaven*

And it clearly is speaking to the perception, at least, of the perilous state of religion. "The age-old function of religion — to provide ultimate certainty amid the exigencies of the human condition — has been severely shaken," writes Berger.[47] One of its chief functions has been to offer a theodicy, an explanation of Good and Evil in God's universe, some understanding of the calamities and tragedies of life, of sickness

---

47. Peter Berger, Brigitte Berger, and Hansfried Kellner, *The Homeless Mind: Modernization and Consciousness* (New York: Vintage Books, 1973), 184-85.

and death, of the fragility and finality of life. It is this function which, in the eyes of many, is faltering and, with it, the human being is becoming more and more homeless, not only in the world, but also in the cosmos. This has happened in part because in the contemporary world, belief systems become acutely aware of each other because of the surfeit of knowledge from the many lines of communication that link people together: books, journals, television, the Internet, movies, travel, music, radio, faxes, and telephones. Once again, we see our experience of pluralism, pluralism of all kinds, working against the thought that there can be one unique religious vision which is absolutely true. Given the awareness of life's diversity and pluralism, and given the freedom to experiment which has produced a multitude of spiritualities, is it not highly implausible that there is any central and single meaning to life, any viable and authoritative interpretation of it? In the absence of an authoritative, and perhaps privileged, interpretation, one that can comprehend all of life, what we are left with is simply our own private perspectives. We are left only with our own story, our own individual *petite histoire,* our own private combination of life experiences and intuitions.

And yet this sense of aloneness, of metaphysical loneliness, is what undoubtedly has mobilized many postmoderns to look inside themselves for answers since there are apparently none outside. But the route inside has employed a little sleight of hand. It rests on our translating human nature into the language of the self. This, as I have suggested, has been under way throughout the twentieth century and it is itself a product of the modernized world. Human nature as made in the image of God is the same in all people; the self, as it has emerged in the modern world, is different in all people. It is that unique center in each person, the meeting place of one's own intuitions, one's own experience, social location, knowledge, and gender which, in combination, is quite unlike anyone else's. Human nature inhabits the *moral world* in which God reigns and is itself moral in its capacity (Rom. 1:18-20; 2:14-15).[48] It is the echo of which he is the Sound. The language of

---

48. I have developed this a little further in my *Losing Our Virtue: Why the Church Must Recover Its Moral Vision* (Grand Rapids: William B. Eerdmans, 1998), 158-78.

right and wrong, Good and Evil, is therefore "natural" to it even in the absence of specific revelation because this is how all people are created. The self, by contrast, inhabits a *psychological world* in which Good and Evil have no real objective status but typically dissolve merely into good and bad feelings. Because human nature is being recast as the self, the search for spirituality today frequently takes a therapeutic direction and moral reality is most commonly only in the far-off distance. And by taking up the conceptual language of the self, this search allows people to develop their own spirituality in their own way. It therefore not only validates each person when, in society, there is very little personal validation, but it also is itself an expression of the amazing cultural diversity which has emerged throughout the West. And this resolution basically keeps intact the dichotomy between the public and private worlds while allowing for the search for a spiritual existence to proceed.

What we shall see later is how seeker churches are brilliantly exploiting this spiritual search. It is producing a seeker's culture. America is tuned in to spiritual matters but not to religious formulations. This makes it very easy to gain a hearing for what is spiritual but hard to maintain a genuinely biblical posture because that becomes a part of "religion." It is very easy to build churches in which seekers congregate; it is very hard to build churches in which biblical faith is maturing into genuine discipleship. It is the difficulty of this task which has been lost in many seeker churches, which are meeting places for those who are searching spiritually but are not looking for that kind of faith which is spiritually tough and countercultural in a biblical way.

The House or the Journey?

At this point, it may be helpful to try to crystallize the differences between the way classical Christian faith thinks about itself and sees the world and the way in which these new spiritual searchers do. I want to begin with the two images of contrasting spiritualities in America that Wuthnow found and then I will need to make a modification in them. The contrast is between those living in a house and those seekers who are on a journey. A home is a fixed place with clear, unmistakable outer boundaries, and established internal routines, roles, and expectations. The spirituality of the home — what has here been called *religion* — is one that includes public worship, a set of doctrines, a fixed worldview in which God is unchanging, and in which truth and morality are unaltered by time or circumstance. Wuthnow saw this as a metaphor of an older kind of spirituality which, he believed, described what Christian faith was in the 1950s. What pertained then was "the clinging to safe, respectable houses of worship in which a domesticated God could be counted on to provide reassurance."[49] Security was purchased at the price of depth. The truth is, of course, that the image of the house also captures some of the ideas essential to biblical faith, even though Wuthnow uses it only of times when that truth was superficially grasped.

It is also the case that the thought of a journey is entirely appropriate to the new spiritual search where this language frequently crops up, but in an entirely different way it is also a part of biblical faith. In the Old Testament, the whole historical narrative is framed in terms of the revelatory journey toward the incarnation of Christ. Even the Old Testament patriarchs, though only having tasted what had been promised "from afar," nevertheless saw themselves, as a result, to be "strangers and exiles on the earth" (Heb. 11:13). It is as "aliens and exiles" that Peter also addressed his readers (I Pet. 2:11) for they, no less than Abraham, were looking "forward to the city which has foundations, whose maker and builder is God" (Heb. 11:10), and they were looking for "a better country, that is, a heavenly one" (Heb. 11:16). In biblical faith, there are the elements of both the house and the journey.

In classical Protestant piety following the Reformation, this was explored and set forth perhaps most memorably in John Bunyan's *Pilgrim's Progress*. There are, however, stark and jarring differences between the way Bunyan understood this spiritual journey and the way that postmoderns are thinking about it. The difference lies in the presence of elements of the "house" in Bunyan's conception and their absence in the postmodern; that is what makes these two journeys so very different.

49. Wuthnow, *After Heaven*, 57.

Who would true Valour see,
Let him come hither;
One here will Constant be,
Come Wind, come Weather.
There's no Discouragement
Shall make him once Relent
His first avow'd Intent
To be a Pilgrim.

Hobgoblin, nor foul Fiend,
Can daunt his Spirit:
He knows, he at the end
Shall Life Inherit.
Then Fancies fly away,
He'll fear not what men say,
He'll labour Night and Day
To be a Pilgrim.

John Bunyan, "The Pilgrim Song"

If Bunyan had presented his Christian pilgrim as wandering through life with his burden of sin still on his back all the way to the end, and if Bunyan had seen the river of death as the means of cleansing Christian's soul, he would, indeed, have been thinking in postmodern terms. In fact, however, the journey does not even begin — and it does not begin for anyone — until the burden of sin has been deposited at the Cross. This happens at the *beginning* of the journey. The story is not only about the struggle to get to the Gate of the Celestial City; it is, most fundamentally, about who has a *right* to enter that Gate, and that is settled, not at the end, but when the journey first begins at the foot of the Cross. And the purpose of the river of death is not to cleanse but to sweep some into unfathomable depths and others into the presence of God. For Christian, the pilgrimage through life is all about its destination, not about the experience of wandering or, in contemporary parlance, of being a spiritual seeker. Christian always knew where he was headed; postmoderns on the spiritual journey do not and their *modus vivendi* is to experiment rather than to imagine they know the destination to which they are headed.

This is what is striking about Christian. Along the way he has many misadventures, falls into confusion and sin, but he is always able to apprise himself of his situation, rectify it, and continue on toward his journey's end. This self-knowledge is not the result of nature — we might say today of psychological insight or therapeutic technique — but of grace. As a result, he is able to see and understand what others, like Ignorance and Pliable, cannot. That is really the difference between Bunyan's notion of spiritual pilgrimage and the postmodern idea of spiritual journey. Given the collapse of all metanarratives, postmoderns have no idea if there is a destination or how to discover if there is one. The point of spirituality is in the *experience* of the journeying, not in the *purpose* of reaching the destination. For Bunyan, the pilgrimage is about the certain knowledge that Christians have of "the better country" to which they travel and of the way in which they must conduct themselves on the journey in preparation for the One to whom they are traveling.

The key to Christian's success as he travels through life, beset by a multitude of conflicts and vexatious temptations, is Interpreter. Early on in the book, while Christian is still only a seeker having just fled the city of Destruction but not as yet arrived at the point where his bundle of sin has fallen off his back, he enters the House of Interpreter. Interpreter asks that a candle be lit. This was a familiar image in classical Protestantism for the Holy Spirit's work of illumination. What is illumined is the text of Scripture. It is the Spirit's role to make the meaning of Scripture plain and to bring the reader to the point where its truth can be embraced. So it is that Christian is led by the hand through seven different scenes, each one depicting the deep fundamental truths of Christian faith. By the end, what he has learned is that his pilgrimage must be under the tutelage of the Word of God, the Spirit being the interpreter, and faith the receptacle. Without the saving knowledge of Christ, both the Bible and the eternal world will be empty realities. Fallen nature is subdued, not by law, but by grace. He learns that for the duration of this pilgrimage, he will be beset by worldliness, that system of values and expressed appetites which have fallen nature as their source and whose horizons are low and whose preoccupations are only with the present. Grace works in an unseen way and will sustain him in the conflict with what is fallen as will God in his patience. However, without due diligence to the things of God, despair will quickly become their substitute. Not only so, but beyond this earthly life is the greatly encouraging prospect of eternal life for those who overcome. And framing this entire journey through life are the moral realities set by God's nature as holy. These will require judgment in that day when what is right and true will be put forever on the throne and what is false, injurious, and dark will rest forever under divine judgment. Thus instructed, Christian is ready to begin his life's journey under the hand of God.

This instruction is what comprises the spirituality of the "house" with its set doctrines, its unchanging God, and its absolute moral expectations. Here there are clear boundaries, rhythms and routines, an internalized sense of what is ultimately right and wrong, the disquieting grace which will not allow sin to become routine. That being said, it is also the case that Christian is on a journey. He is but passing through this world in its fallenness and headed for a sure and certain destination which is a "better country." In all of these points, the postmodern journey is different. The journey is not started by God's gracious work within the soul, there are no boundaries, no internal rules and routines, there is no ultimate sense of right and wrong, no ability to understand when the road is leading in the wrong direction, no sense as to what the destination is, and no ultimate accountability.

What sets these two conceptions apart is the possession of revealed truth in the one case and its absence in the other. That being so, the current evangelical disposition to shuck off its cognitive structures and minimize the practical place of revealed truth in the life of the Church means that it has brought itself to the edge of a precipice. It is a precipice precisely because as evangelical faith has chosen to minimize itself in these ways in order to become attractive to postmodern seekers, it is losing what makes it distinctive from all of the other postmodern spiritualities. Today, it trembles on the edge of becoming just one of many spiritualities in the marketplace even as the liberal Protestants much earlier diminished Christianity by making it out to be just one among many religions, better than the others, perhaps, but not unique.

The Church, then, now finds itself in a rapidly changing cultural context in the West. It is a rapidly changing spiritual climate, too. Gone are many of the old certainties, and many of the old ways. How is it to think about itself and its message in this new context? That is the question which I must now take up in the remaining chapters. I will begin in the next chapter by looking in more depth at this emergent spirituality, to which the end of this chapter has served only as a brief introduction, and I will be asking how the message of the gospel has to engage it.

CHAPTER IV

Christ in a Spiritual World

—⟨∞⟩—

> He has made everything beautiful in its time; also he has put
> eternity into man's mind, yet so that he cannot find out what
> God has done from the beginning to the end.
>
> ECCLESIASTES 3:11

It is the "invisible religion"[1] which is the subject of this chapter, the emergence of a new kind of spiritual person: one who is on a spiritual quest but often pursuing this in opposition to what is religious.

1. The language of invisible religions is that of Thomas Luckmann. Over thirty years ago, he saw a new "sacred cosmos" in the making, itself the consequence of the way that modernized society was evolving. At the center of this cosmos was the autonomous individual, what Bellah would later call the "unencumbered self," one which was obliged only to itself. This autonomy, Luckmann argued, was assuming a kind of sacred status. Increasingly, for a variety of reasons, what was ultimate was becoming relocated in the self, in what was private and internal. But here he noticed an interesting ambiguity. It is that the self which is at the center of this new spirituality is itself murky and elusive. Without its discovery, therefore, there will be no spirituality for this new sacred cosmos which does not reflect the self's own murkiness and elusiveness. Since "the 'inner man' is, in effect, an undefinable entity, its presumed discovery involves a lifelong quest," he said. What that means is that the "individual who is to find a source of 'ultimate' significance in the subjective dimension of biog-

That, however, may be stating the matter a little too starkly for it suggests that religions are being understood in terms of what they actually assert. In reality, religions tend to blur in the postmodern mind and become undifferentiated from each other. That is the almost inevitable outcome of our pluralism. When religions become aware of each other in the postmodern world, they typically either lose their sharp edges or are at least seen as having done so. It is as predictable as it is desultory that 44% of Americans think that "the Bible, the Koran and the Book of Mormon are different expressions of the same spiritual truths."[2] Yet it remains the case that this spirituality sees itself as other than what is religious, be this religion which is insistently doctrinal or religion which has become blurred by its passage through the postmodern spirit.

It is this emergent spirituality which is in focus in this chapter, although I do not want in any way to minimize the religious issues which are at stake.[3] It is this spirituality that threatens to rumble through evangelical faith in a way more detrimental to it than any Christian engagement with non-Christian religions. In this chapter, then, I need to accomplish three things: first, I need to provide some description of this new spiritual search; second, I will explore the parallels that exist between this new quest and what the Church has faced before, espe-

---

raphy embarks upon a process of self-realization and self-expression. . . ." Self-realization and self-expression are the principal forms of autonomy in "the modern sacred cosmos." Thomas Luckmann, *The Invisible Religion: The Transformation of Symbols in Industrial Society* (New York: The Macmillan Co., 1967), 110.

2. George Barna, "Americans Draw Theological Beliefs from Diverse Points of View," October 8, 2002. Available online at http://www.barna.org.

3. The religious issue, of course, is whether biblical truth claims are privileged, whether Christians should think of the gospel of Christ as being uniquely true and, if so, what should be said about truth and salvation in the other religions. Alongside the traditional exclusivist view in the evangelical world has emerged one that is inclusivist. This has been articulated in somewhat different ways but the difficulty of even the more modest proposals is well illustrated in Stanley Grenz's discussion in his *Renewing the Center: Evangelical Theology in a Post-Theological Era* (Grand Rapids: Baker, 2000), 249-86. More recently, Amos Young also reviews this discussion in his *Beyond the Impasse: Toward a Pneumatological Theology of Religions* (Grand Rapids: Baker, 2003), 105-28. He has then struck out in a different direction proposing that it is possible to "discern" the work of the Spirit in the other religions; this succeeds in decoupling the work of the Spirit from the person of Christ, which is not a happy outcome.

cially in the patristic period; and, third, I need to outline what a biblical response to this search looks like.

The New Spiritual Yearning

These new spiritualities are now taking their place alongside some older ones, spiritualities which often define themselves over against religion but nevertheless are not averse to incorporating religious ideas. The reappearance of a spiritual dimension, in one sense, is the reappearance of what was once commonplace. Outside the modernized West, it is hard to find peoples or cultures in which there has not been some sense of another world, some sense of the presence of the sacred in life, and therefore of the obligation to offer worship. Human history is replete with images, rituals, and rites related to this Other and with human striving, searching, and hoping about this spiritual reality. Yet it is also true that this spiritual questing in the past usually expressed itself through religion whereas today its relationship to the religions is more complex, distant, and nuanced. The Enlightenment, in its hard rationalism, cast cold water on all of this and imagined that in the triumph of reason all such superstition would, in time, wither and blow away. That, of course, has not happened and we, today, are seeing this massive return of spiritualities which would have been inconceivable only a few decades ago.

Individuals and groups who have thus turned to things spiritual have, since the 1960s, had assorted goals, some of which also overlap. For some, the aim has been that of finding peace of mind or inner transformation; in its Eastern configuration, the goal has been achieving a different kind of consciousness; in its shallowest and most banal form, it is about self-awareness, self-esteem, and self-actualization, achievements which may come in a purely secular form or as a part of spiritual self-discovery; and for contemporary gnostics, the hope is empowerment — not in the ways we encounter in gender politics, which are frequently fueled by resentment, but in the sense of connecting with a power deep within the self.

In Europe and America, a substantial number of people see themselves as spiritual in these different ways, and many oppose this spirituality to what is religious. As we have seen, in America 78% see themselves as spiritual and 56% say that in addressing life's crises, they are inclined to look within themselves rather than to depend upon an outside power such as the Christian God. That, in a way, is no surprise since 54% also think that the only truth that anyone can find will be found through reason and experience rather than in an external source such as the Bible.[4]

When the Enlightenment mindset dominated American culture, those who said that they looked within themselves for answers were, in all likelihood, secularists and humanists of one kind or another. In the postmodern moment in which we are living, however, those who look within themselves are not necessarily divorcing themselves from the sacred. On the contrary, many are actually believers in the sacred which they are pursuing within themselves. They are not seeking the God of the Christian religion, who is transcendent, who speaks to life from outside of it, whose Son came from "above," as the Apostle John repeatedly tells us,[5] and entered it through the Incarnation, whose Word is absolute and enduring, and whose moral character defines the difference between Good and Evil forever. Rather, it is the god within, the god who is found within the self and in whom the self is rooted. This is, for the most part, a simple perception and as found spread throughout American society it comes with few pretensions to having great intellectual depth. Yet that is not always the case. Mircea Eliade, for example, has spoken of the "irruption of the sacred"[6] within life and of the complex ways in which myths and dreams are rooted in the manifestations of the divine within. It is the same belief, then, which comes sometimes in homely ways and sometimes wrapped in complexity —

4. Barna, "Americans Draw Theological Beliefs from Diverse Points of View."

5. The structure of Johannine christology is built around two contrasts, the glory/flesh paradox and the above/below contrast. On the latter, John tells us that Christ came from above (Jn. 6:33) from whence he left the presence of God (Jn. 6:62; 8:38; 10:36). It was from the realm above that he descended (Jn. 3:13; 6:33, 38; 10:36) and from this realm that he was "sent" by the Father. This language of sending is used forty-two times in the gospel (examples being 3:17; 9:39; 10:36; 12:45; 16:28; and 18:37); it provides the basis for saying that John's christology is one of mission.

6. Mircea Eliade, *Myths, Dreams, and Mysteries: The Encounter Between Contemporary Faiths and Archaic Realities,* trans. Philip Mairet (New York: Harper, 1960), 15.

and yet this inward presence invariably proves to be elusive and so the search is always unfinished. In this searching, it is hoped, there will be found the balm of therapeutic comfort, the suggestion of meaning and of connectedness to something larger.

This search is almost impossible to describe with accuracy because it is as varied as are the searchers. Those who have written about it, therefore, have mostly been drawn to the writers who have made explicit what they are thinking. This, of course, is entirely understandable. It is not hard to see, however, that those who have articulated the nature of this new spirituality represent only a part of it, what we might think of as an inner circle, and around them, either near or far, are many others who may share the same assumptions, may be in the same firmament of ideas, but who lack the clarity and the radical nature of the inner circle.[7]

Some of the beliefs of the new spirituality have found reinforcement among the teachers and adherents of Eastern spirituality who have flooded into America in the new waves of immigration or on the airwaves. They have acquired followers. Courses in Eastern spirituality, as well as in the literature of these religions, are showing up on college campuses and on television in much greater profusion than was the case even a decade ago. However, as Richard Kyle points out, there are ways in which Americans are "turning east" which are vaguer and more difficult to specify than what we see in overt disciples of the East, and this is what we are seeing in this new search. Some Americans practice meditation without being fully aware of its religious underpinnings. Others practice the martial arts without being aware of the Buddhist philosophy that underlies them. It is in these and other ways that some in this new spiritual quest are filling out their stock of ideas and practices from Eastern influences but doing so in ways that make clear categorical distinctions difficult.[8]

As we move away from its center in the radicals, the assumptions of this spirituality become ever hazier, the conclusions lose their sharp-

7. Peter Jones describes this inner circle, which he designates the New Religious Left, in his *Spirit Wars: Pagan Revival in Christian America* (Mukilteo, Wash.: Wine Press Publishing, 1998).

8. Richard Kyle, *The Religious Fringe: A History of Alternative Religions in America* (Downers Grove: InterVarsity Press, 1993), 197-202.

ness, the practice becomes more privatized. Away from this center, we find many of the 56% among Americans who say that in life's crises they look within themselves for answers rather than to an outside power like God (as he has been traditionally understood) but who do not necessarily tie this disposition into some expression of formalized spirituality. They may not be radical feminists, may eschew Eastern gurus, may not adhere to New Age, may not meditate, may be quite uninterested in crystals and channelers, may have no use for mantras, may want to keep their distance from witches and the occult, and yet in ways that are loose, often ill-defined, and unformulated, they are nevertheless still part of this new search for what is spiritual. They are in search of a new *consciousness*. If they speak of transformation, as so many do, it is in terms of their own human potential, the innate sources of personal renewal which lie deep within. If they speak of their own intuitions, as they often do, it is with the sense of having onboard a navigational system which enables them to find their place in reality. Or, perhaps more correctly, it allows them to find a better place in reality. And if they speak of a connectedness for which they yearn, it is in the blurry sense that somehow the human and divine are no longer disengaged from each other but, rather, are implicated in each other.[9]

An outside God, such as we find in biblical faith, is comprehensible because he is self-defined in his revelation; the inside god is not. The inside god is merged into the psychological texture of the seeker and found spread within the vagaries of the self. The outside God stands over against those who would know him; the inside one emerges within their consciousness and is a part of them. Religions have their schools of thought and their interpreters, and always the debate is over who most truly understands the religion. Spirituality, in the

---

9. When encounters with the supernatural have been reported, as they frequently have been in recent decades, there has been no terror and no awe in the reporting. Encounters and bright lights have fascinated postmodern seekers because they offered reassurance that there was something to life beyond the harsh, competitive, secular world, and these encounters made those who reported them feel good. In a perceptive comment, Wuthnow observes that the "emphasis on self-gratification in the culture at large is also evident in the ways the miraculous experiences are interpreted. They cater to the interests of persons reporting them, and they provide spiritual comfort without making demands on people's time or commitments." *After Heaven: Spirituality in America Since the 1950s* (Berkeley: University of California Press, 1998), 130.

contemporary sense, spawns no such debate because it makes no truth claims and seeks no universal significance. It lives out its life within the confines of private experience. "Truth" is private, not public; it is for the individual, not for the universe. Here is American individualism coupled with some new assumptions about God which are being glossed off with infatuations about pop therapy, uniting to produce varieties of spirituality as numerous as those who think of themselves as spiritual.

What is held in common across this broad spectrum of spiritual yearning is the desire to find the Real in the midst of the mundane, to look beyond or beneath the surface of modernized life with its hard-driving commerce, its fatuous slogans, its glossy images, crowded thoroughfares, and relentless pressures, and find a connection to something more meaningful. But beyond this, a thick fog descends on what this spirituality actually entails. Is the Real that is sought wholly immanent within the subject or does it also lie outside the subject? Is what is Real actually experienced or is the search for what is Real the means by which some semblance of meaning is found? And what may be expected to result from this spiritual search? Is it a moment of luminous insight? An experience? Is it a sense of tranquillity? Is it liberation from the oppressive experience of human individuality? Is it a psychological liberation from the rasping, grating experience of living in a modernized world? Or is it just a quiet sense that one actually is connected to a larger reality? And how far out of time does this spirituality lead? Into eternity or simply into other pockets of reality that are often obscured by the frenetic activity that happens in a world that is modernized? Or is this spirituality simply a psychological coping mechanism, a technique, for the stresses and strains of modernized life? It is probably the case that all of these options can be found within the contemporary world of spirituality. Without a common worldview and rituals, and with few commonly articulated beliefs, this cultural phenomenon spills out in all directions.

It is helpful, however, to recall the distinction Wuthnow makes between a spirituality of dwelling and one of journeying. The former is what describes traditional Christian spirituality,[10] one that flourishes

10. As noted earlier, Wuthnow's use of this image was applied to the Christianity of the 1950s in America, and in his mind this image of a house is reflective of the rather conventional, sanitized culture of that time. In using this image, I am not thinking of its use in cultural terms but, rather, in those that are doctrinal.

within doctrinal parameters. It demands that the self live within those parameters. And what anchors this self, amidst the pains, perplexities and changes of life, is the knowledge of the God who does not change. His saving purposes were fixed in eternity and were expressed in Christ in whom "all the promises of God find their Yes" (II Cor. 1:20). In this understanding, God, on account of his holiness and perfection, imposes upon humans standards of belief and behavior. Critics down the centuries have insisted that this means that humans must divest themselves of their freedoms, their independence of thought, or risk defying God. They either make their own decisions or they have to slavishly submit to decisions they themselves have not made. This is the "slave religion" that Nietzsche mocked and rejected. And it is what is rejected in the new spiritual quest.

A spirituality of journey in this contemporary sense, by contrast, does not begin with what has been given by God, or with what does not change. Rather, it begins with the self. It begins in the soil of human autonomy and it gives to the self the authority to decide what to believe, from what sources to draw knowledge and inspiration, and how to test the viability of what is believed. The result is that this kind of spirituality is inevitably experimental and even libertarian. Its validation comes through the psychological or therapeutic benefits which are derived. Mixing and matching, discarding or reappropriating ideas in an endless process of searching and experimenting, is what this spirituality is about.

There is, however, an additional refinement that needs to be placed on this image suggested by Wuthnow. A journey it may be, but in many cases the one taking this very modern journey should actually be thought of as being more of a tourist than a purposeful traveler. That is the telling observation Zygmunt Bauman has made.[11] It is really this metaphor of the tourist that best describes this new spiritual search. Tourists are not rooted in the places they visit. They are just passing through, just looking. They are there only for their pleasure and entertainment. They are unrelated to any of their fellow travelers.

11. Zygmunt Bauman, *Postmodernity and Its Discontents* (New York: New York University Press, 1997), 83-94. See also his *Globalization: The Human Consequences* (New York: Columbia University Press, 1998), 77-102.

In a tour through the many finer and coarser moralities which have hitherto prevailed or still prevail on the earth, I have found certain traits recurring regularly together, and connected with one another, until finally two primary types revealed themselves to me, and a radical distinction was brought to light. There is *master-morality* and *slave-morality*. . . . The noble type of man regards *himself* as a determiner of values; he does not require to be approved of; he passes the judgment: "What is injurious to me is injurious in itself"; he knows that it is he himself only who confers honour on things; he is *creator of values*. He honours whatever he recognises in himself: such morality is self-glorification. . . . It is otherwise with the second type of morality, *slave-morality*. Supposing that the abused, the oppressed, the suffering, the unemancipated, the weary, and those uncertain of themselves should moralise, what will be the common element in their moral estimates? Probably a pessimistic suspicion with regard to the entire situation of man will find expression, perhaps a condemnation of man, together with his situation. The slave has an unfavourable eye for the virtues of the powerful; he has a skepticism and distrust, a *refinement* of distrust of everything "good" that is there honoured — he would fain persuade himself that the very happiness there is not genuine. On the other hand, *those* qualities which serve to alleviate the existence of sufferers are brought into prominence and flooded with light; it is here that sympathy, the kind, helping hand, the warm heart, patience, diligence, humility, and friendliness attain honour; for here these are the most useful qualities, and almost the only means of supporting the burden of existence. Slave-morality is essentially the morality of utility.

Friedrich Nietzsche, *Beyond Good and Evil*

They contribute nothing to the country they are visiting (except their cold cash) because they are only there to look and to take in a fresh set of experiences. Tourists never stay; they are always on the move. It is this image, rather than that of the pilgrim, that appears to describe most aptly this new, privatized, experimental spirituality. Can we now put this search in clearer perspective?

Tourists; that's what we are becoming . . .
Tourists, we move through life, flitting from idea to idea, from
novelty to novelty, from new person to new person,
Never settling, always moving . . .
Selecting the best sights, the highlights, the choice cuts,
avoiding the mess on the edge of town, the slums, all the
uncomfortable things, the struggle of really knowing people,
Never settling, always moving lest we hear the hollow clang
    of our own emptiness . . .
Tourists; that's what we are becoming . . .
Inquisitive, curious, picking up the tidbits of other
    people's depth . . .
Tourists, flicking through our snapshots, the paper thin
trophies of our click and run existence, filing them away,
    loading the next roll of film,
Never settling, always moving,
Tourists; that's what we are becoming,
Tourists; that's what we are becoming. . . .

Mark Greene, "Tourists"

To say, as Bloom does, that this spirituality is "gnosticism," and that gnosticism is the "American religion,"[12] is, from a historical and conceptual point of view, too heavy-handed to be helpful. Nevertheless,

12. This "religion," Harold Bloom argues, resolves itself into a spiritual quest in which the self is both subject and object of the search. His argument is that this quest underlies much overt religion which on the surface expresses itself doctrinally and in very different ways — Roman Catholic, Mormon, Seventh-Day Adventist, and Southern Baptist. See his *The American Religion: The Emergence of the Post-Christian Nation* (New York: Simon and Schuster, 1992). As a part of his argument he claims that America is gnostic without knowing it: *Omens of Millennium: The Gnosis of Angels, Dreams, and Resurrection* (New York: Riverhead Books, 1996), 183.

Bloom's case could be better made along slightly different, and more nuanced, lines.

The point of connection with the past is not so much gnosticism but, rather, a primal spirituality which, in the early period of the Church's life, came into expression as gnosticism. The theories of gnosticism were defeated and soon forgotten. However, the spirituality which they were seeking to explain is the point of connection with the past. It is this spirituality which is rooted in the self, which assumes the liberty either to oppose or appropriate external religious forms but is resolute in its opposition to having to submit to external religious authority. It is in these ways that we are also seeing the convergence between this primal spirituality and a resurgent paganism. Camille Paglia has spoken of "the never-defeated paganism of the West"[13] now resurfacing. She says that there are always contradictory impulses in a culture. On the one side is the urge to cross boundaries, to expand moral limitations, to break taboos, and to do the impermissible. On the other side is the urge to define the boundaries, to forbid the transgressions, and to protect the sacred. Today, she argues, the impulse to expand, to break definitions, rules, and limitations is triumphing — and the most visible sign of this triumph is the widespread prevalence of pornography. That there may be some echoes in today's pornography of the old cult prostitution and the fertility rites that were part and parcel of ancient paganism is quite plausible. Yet it would be a mistake to limit the pagan impulse to its debased sexuality. Paganism was not just about sex. It was, as I shall argue, much more broadly about nature, about nature manifesting the divine, and in this there certainly are some parallels to this contemporary spiritual search. This suggests that the point of connection is not so much gnosticism as it is a spirituality which emerges from within the depths of the self of which gnosticism was but one expression and the contemporary spiritual resurgence is but another.

When Christian faith encountered this spirituality in the early centuries, Anders Nygren declares, it had arrived at "its hour of destiny."[14] This was so because this spirituality was in its outworkings, in

13. Camille Paglia, *Sex, Art, and American Culture* (New York: Vintage Books, 1992), vii.

14. Anders Nygren, *Agape and Eros,* trans. Philip Watson (London: S.P.C.K., 1953), 30.

its beliefs, and its view of life, the polar opposite of what we find in Christian faith. It was an opponent. And the besetting temptation which the Church would encounter, sometimes in fierce ways and at other times in more subtle ways, was to wonder if it could lessen the fierceness of the competition by incorporating in itself elements of this pagan way of looking at the spiritual life. These two spiritualities, Christian and pagan, Nygren contrasts in the language of two very different kinds of love, *Agape* and *Eros.* From this time forth, and coming right down into the contemporary moment, the struggle is going to be how Agape is going to preserve itself from the persistent intrusions of Eros.

The opening salvos were, of course, fired in the conflict in the early church over gnosticism; today, they are being fired by the new spirituality. Although the gnosticism of the patristic period was only one particular expression of Eros, it is, nevertheless, worth revisiting because some of the fundamental issues were, on both sides, hammered out during this conflict and they continue to speak into our own time.

An Ancient Spirituality

Ancient gnosticism, like the contemporary spiritual search, was a very diverse movement and it is hard to provide a succinct definition of it. Irenaeus' survey shows how variegated the gnostic world was,[15] though as a set of movements, as distinct from intellectual influences, none predated the Christian faith despite Bultmann's claim.[16] The diversity of these movements arose from the fact that the influences behind them were different: some had their roots in Eastern theosophy, others Greek philosophical speculation, and still others mystical Judaism. These sources produced some very different outcomes among the competing schools of gnostic thought which took root in Egypt, Syria, and along the eastern coast of the Mediterranean. Over time, af-

15. Irenaeus, *Against Heresies,* I, i, 1–I, vii, 5; I, xi, 1–I, xx, 3; I, xxiii, 1–I, xxxi, 4.

16. See Edwin M. Yamauchi, "Some Alleged Evidences for Pre-Christian Gnosticism," in *New Dimensions in New Testament Study,* ed. Richard N. Longenecker and Merrill C. Tenney (Grand Rapids: Zondervan, 1974), 46-70.

ter gnosticism had become a set of movements that paralleled the Church, it changed shape and in mid-career began to appropriate Christian ideas and attempted to incorporate Christian faith into its larger framework. In its final development it came right into the Church and, in thinkers like Valentinus, Marcion, and Basilides, it passed itself off as being an authentic expression of Christianity, thereby confounding definition even further. The word *gnostic,* which encapsulated the understanding of the mystical insight into the nature of things which the various thinkers and movements offered, therefore, meant something different depending on the school in question, its cultural location, its influences, and its stage of development within the overall movement.

It is not insignificant that these gnostic movements germinated in a time of social flux and of great uncertainty, at a time when the cultural nerve was failing in the Roman world, when the prevailing worldview was collapsing, and when the pursuit of what is spiritual offered itself as a way out, almost as an escape from the gathering cultural meltdown. It would be some time before the Roman world finally imploded, but its own writers were warning of the peril long before the barbarians stormed the gates of Rome in 410 A.D. Writers like Tacitus and Seneca, Nero's tutor, may have exaggerated the moral decline a little — moralists and satirists sometimes do — but in hindsight it appears that they saw the unraveling of the Roman empire with a clarity that many, especially those in power, lacked. Rome, Tacitus said, was a place to which all of the abominations of the world were drawn, a place where they met and multiplied and became popular, and Seneca observed that no amount of force could restrain or provide a remedy for the wickedness that was festering in the empire. The picture they and other writers of the period painted was one of power exercised ruthlessly without the restraints of conscience, of a culture in which the senses were gratified as character disintegrated, and where life had been cheapened and made expendable. It may well be, then, that when Rome finally fell it was less because it was conquered from without than because it had died of its own hand. This is the context in which gnosticism grew up, and it is not hard to see that there are echoes of this situation in contemporary Western societies today with their fallen cognitive ceilings, their loss of truth and moral fabric, their hedonism, and their self-abandonment. It is these ingredients that are the stuff from which cultural meltdowns happen,[17] and they are what impel people to seek ways to protect and cure their souls.

Gnosticism proved to be an especially nettlesome matter in the early church, not because the novelty of its ideas swept people off their feet, but because its ideas, in some important respects, already pervaded that ancient world. They seemed normal, natural, and familiar. There had already been a long history of thought on some of its key elements in the East. It is not clear how Eastern thought reached Greece, but classical Greek philosophy sometimes followed some of the important paths originally blazed in the East and these ideas had already permeated the world in which the Church had been planted.

Here, too, is an echo of our own times. The combination of a modernized social fabric and the Enlightenment ideology which took root in it until relatively recently produced, as we have seen, the autonomous self. This is the self which is not subject to outside authority and into which all reality has contracted itself. The result is a radicalized individualism whose outlook is deeply privatized and whose mood is insistently therapeutic. All of this has produced soil throughout society that positively invites the new spirituality. It seems normal and natural. That is why it is as difficult for the Church to contest today as was gnosticism in the early centuries.

Classical Greek philosophy, like Eastern thought, depreciated the natural world and pondered the soul's alienation from it. And like the philosophies of the East, Greek thought typically came to think of the soul as being not a divine creation but a shard which had fallen away from the All or Absolute and was now found in a human body. Its sense of alienation from the world came from the individuality by which it was now afflicted, individuality which expressed itself in thought and

17. Arnold Toynbee's massive *A Study of History* recounts the rise and fall of all of the major civilizations which have preceded ours. In volumes 3, 4, and 5, he discusses why civilizations break down and then disintegrate. The pattern at their end is very similar in most cases. What he describes as the "schism of the soul," which lies behind the outward breakdown, is strikingly similar to much of what we see in postmodernity. See his discussion in *A Study of History* (12 vols.; New York: Oxford University Press, 1934-61), V, 376-568.

consciousness. The irresistible impulse which arose from this was, on the one hand, "to exalt the self-seeking spirit," as Thomas Molnar says,[18] while thinking that one day all things will rejoin the primal, sacred reality. All paganism, in one way or another, is pantheistic.

Socrates: As the soul is immortal, has been born often and has seen all things here and in the underworld, there is nothing which it has not learned; so it is in no way surprising that it can recollect the things it knew before, both about virtue and other things. As the whole of nature is akin, and the soul has learned everything, nothing prevents a man, after recalling one thing only — a process men call learning — discovering everything else for himself, if he is brave and does not tire of the search, for searching and learning are, as a whole, recollection.

Plato, "Meno"

Greek philosophy struggled with how to relate the divine, which is remote and removed from life, with the soul and its struggles within the body. And that was where the gnostics pushed the argument forward one or two steps. At the heart of their spiritual quest was a search for the answer to evil. Wherever they looked, whether to the firmament above or to the bodies in which their consciousness resided, what they saw was a monumentally failed work, a creation that was awry, corrupt, nefarious, and dark. All gnostic systems of thought, as a result, were philosophically dualistic or semi-dualistic, positing that what had been made had been made by an enemy of human beings. There were differences of opinion as to how to work this all out, but typically it either led to the notion that there were two ultimate principles in the universe, one good and one bad, the latter being responsible for the creation; or that there was only one ultimate principle from whom a series of emanations and spirits had proceeded, one of whom was even-

---

18. Thomas Molnar, *The Pagan Temptation* (Grand Rapids: William B. Eerdmans, 1987), 31.

tually so far from the source of good as to be able to bring about this wretched creation. What the various gnostic teachers sought to do was to bring understanding about the human plight, to inculcate insight about the very nature of things and, most importantly, to get people in touch with their spiritual natures. Only then could there be liberation from the clutches of what was evil. This, of course, is no easy matter, for we are all besieged in life by powers contrary to God. Indeed, *The Dialog of the Savior,* one of the gnostic tracts discovered at Nag Hammadi, even depicts the soul at the end of life as having to pass though heavenly realms which are infested by fearful, hostile powers. As each sphere is left behind in this journey, the bondage contributed by these heavenly beings is sloughed off until in the end the soul, thus emancipated from its assailants, arrives before the Savior.[19]

So what is the nature of this insight which held the key to self-liberation for these ancient gnostics? It is, of course, "knowledge." This was not really intellectual knowledge, though it was often accompanied by complex philosophical speculation. It was more of a private insight, an internal revelation, a spiritual perception, one given from within. Gnostics believed that they had dropped from a spiritual existence into the bodies in which they were trapped.[20] They were in search, Jacques Lecarriere says, of "a true consciousness" that would enable them "to cast off the shackles of this world" which had bound them in false understanding.[21] It was not so much knowledge of God that was sought, for he was perceived to be ineffable, distant, removed, and unattainable. He is, as Valentinus said, "that Incomprehensible, In-

19. "The Dialog of the Savior," in James M. Robinson, ed., *The Nag Hammadi Library,* trans. Members of the Coptic Gnostic Library Project of the Institute for Antiquity and Christianity (New York: Harper and Row, 1977), 120-24.

20. Of the numerous illustrations of this truth is one found in the anonymous Nag Hammadi tract, "The Exegesis on the Soul." This likens the soul to a female who "even has a womb" and was content when she dwelled alone with God the Father. However, she fell away and became trapped in a body through which "she prostituted herself." However, in due time and after experiencing great wretchedness, she repented amidst much sighing and in his mercy the Father "will make her womb turn from the external domain and will turn it again inward, so that the soul will regain her proper character." For the whole tract, see Robinson, 180-87.

21. Jacques Lecarriere, *The Gnostics,* trans. Nina Rootes (London: Peter Owen, 1977), 11.

conceivable (One), who is superior to all thought" and who, in fact, is beyond the range of all human thought.[22] They were far more interested in pursuing what was inside in the self. "Other religions," Robert Grant says, "are in varying measure God-centered," but the gnostic "is self-centered."[23] It is this self-knowledge which is redemptive. To know the self in its spiritual dimension is be drawn into a union "with a reality," Hans Jonas writes, "that in truth is itself the supreme subject in the situation and strictly speaking never an object at all."[24] It was, therefore, knowledge of the divine through the self. More than that, it was about the self losing itself in the divine, being absorbed back into it, losing its own individuality and personhood. It is this monism, with its lost distinctions between the creator and the created self, that paganism and gnosticism have in common. Of course, the two are not identical: in paganism, this monism was also extended to the rest of creation; in gnosticism, the rest of the creation was seen to be alienated from God and as having been abandoned by him. However, when it came to the self, the two systems converged in their understanding.

This pursuit of knowledge of the self rested upon a double assumption. The first was, in modern terms, that theology is nothing other than anthropology. "For gnostics," Elaine Pagels explains, "exploring the *psyche* became explicitly what it is for many people today implicitly — a religious quest," not least because gnostics believed that a fragment of divinity was lodged somewhere in their interior world.[25] What they also assumed, second, is that people stumble, suffer, and make mistakes not because of sin, but because of ignorance. It was, of course, to remedy this ignorance that, in the Christian phase of gnosticism, the Son was seen as bringing "knowledge" of the Father — yet this was a far cry from knowledge as it is construed biblically. Thus

22. Valentinus, *Evangelium Veritatis*, IX, 5. This is the document found near Nag Hammadi in Egypt in 1945 which made its way to Europe and was eventually purchased by George H. Page, a Zurich resident, and given to the Jung Institute in honor of Carl Jung. The connections between Jungian psychoanalysis and early gnosticism were thereby acknowledged.

23. Robert M. Grant, *Gnosticism & Early Christianity* (New York: Harper, 1966), 8.

24. Hans Jonas, *The Gnostic Religion: The Message of the Alien God and the Beginnings of Christianity* (Boston: Beacon Press, 1958), 35.

25. Elaine Pagels, *The Gnostic Gospels* (New York: Random House, 1979), 123.

it is that both ancient gnostics and those postmoderns who place such value on psychotherapeutic techniques do so because above all other things they value "the self-knowledge," Pagels notes, "which is insight."[26] And this self-knowledge functions in a revelatory way which is only possible, we need to note, because of the lost understanding of sin.[27] It is ignorance, ignorance of ourselves and especially of our spiritual nature, gnostics believed, that is the key to our ignorance of the nature of things, and of the grip which evil exercises invisibly on all things created and on ourselves not least. And it is the self which, in this situation, reveals its own connections into what is divine.

Exploring the unconscious, however, is no easy matter. Like the ocean in its depths, it surrenders its secrets only slowly and grudgingly. Gnostics spoke of the turmoil that was involved in coming to the knowledge of themselves, and clearly different levels of success were achieved. It was apparently this observation that led gnostics, according to Irenaeus, to speak of human beings as falling into three different classes: those naturally spiritual who are assured of salvation and of their election; those who are suspended in equilibrium between the forces of good and evil and whose destiny could go either way; and those who are irremediably held captive to what is evil because they are so thoroughly part and parcel of what is material.[28] This classification was used by some, though not by all gnostics, but which groups used the classification is less important than its assumption that psychic or gnostic insight is *natural* to some human beings. Not only so, but many of those who were thus spiritual also believed themselves to be emancipated from religious belief and even ethical practice, thus anticipating the extremes of postmodern individualism. If, then, gnosticism was dualistic, or semi-dualistic, philosophically, it was *naturalistic* soteriologically.

It is, of course, no surprise to discover that when gnostics sought to appropriate New Testament writings — a move that was vigorously contested by both Irenaeus and Tertullian on the grounds that these gnostics were attempting to purloin what did not belong to them — it

26. Pagels, *The Gnostic Gospels,* 124.
27. The gnostic understanding of sin, especially among the Valentinians, is explored in Michel R. Desjardins, *Sin in Valentinianism* (Atlanta: Scholars Press, 1990).
28. Irenaeus, *Against Heresies,* I, vi, 1-4.

was the Gospel of John, in particular, that they favored. And, of course, their central contention was that the Church had misunderstood the person of Christ because it insisted that Christ was God incarnate. This was impossible given the gnostic premise of the evil of the material body.[29] This disposition is nicely illustrated in the apocryphal *Gospel of Peter* which solved the problem of a real incarnation by claiming that on the Cross Jesus called out, "My Power, my Power, why have you forsaken me?"[30] The power which had left Christ was obviously the power that had earlier descended upon him, perhaps at his baptism, had accompanied him through his ministry, but was departing because it was in no way incarnate in his body.

To suppose that divine revelation was tied into actual historical realities involved making a fundamental hermeneutical mistake, gnostics argued. That mistake was to read the gospel story literally, for that assumed the divine revelation and redemption came in and with the facts of Jesus' earthly life, his incarnation, life, death, resurrection, and ascension. That simply could not be. These things, then, are but images. "To recognize their true meaning," Pagels writes, "one must come to see that these events do not in themselves *effect* redemption. Rather, they serve to symbolize the process of redemption that occurs within those who perceive their inner meaning."[31] It was the Gospel of John,

29. It is ironic that the gnostic predilection for the Gospel of John persisted despite the unqualified rebuttal of gnostic views in John's epistles. The authenticity of the Spirit's presence is evidenced in the fact that, having brought about the miraculous conception, he now witnesses to it, John says, confessing "that Jesus Christ has come in the flesh" (I Jn. 4:2). There can be no thought here of an impermanent alliance between the Son and Jesus but, rather, the Son came into permanent union with the flesh of Jesus and this represented a frontal attack on gnostic views. Later John wrote of the "deceivers" who will not acknowledge "the coming of Jesus Christ in the flesh" (II Jn. 7).

30. H. B. Swete, *The Akhmim Fragment of the Apocryphal Gospel of St. Peter* (London: Macmillan, 1893), 10.

31. Elaine Pagels, *The Johannine Gospel in Gnostic Exegesis: Heracleon's Commentary on John* (New York: Abingdon Press, 1973), 14. Heracleon, Clement of Alexandria said, was the most famous exponent of the Valentinian school of thought but little is known of him. On his literary remains, see A. E. Brooke, *The Fragments of Heracleon* (Cambridge: Cambridge University Press, 1891). The importance of this commentary in the formulation of gnostic views is suggested by the fact that Origen cites it no fewer than fifty-two times in his efforts at refuting gnostic thinking.

more than the Synoptics, that lent itself to a "spiritual," or symbolic reading and which more easily could be held up as a mirror in which the self could see itself reflected back. But what was apprehended in this way was not merely the self but, as the Valentinians argued, "depth" and "abyss" in, and with, and through it. Self-knowledge, then, was not merely knowledge of the self but also knowledge of what is ultimate through and in and with the self. This depth is what later psychotherapy would call the unconscious, and some would attribute to it religious reality. This knowledge, Pagels says of the Valentinian gnostics, "is not given to human experience, in their view, *either* in immediate sense-perception, *or* in rational and ethical reflection on such perception."[32] It is apprehended psychically.

One of the chief contentions of the gnostics in their polemic against the Church was that "knowledge," in their understanding of it, is superior to "faith." They might as well have said that they were pursuing spirituality, rather than religion, for that is what they meant. They were opposed to a doctrinally shaped and governed Christianity. They were instead pursuing enlightenment through the self, for this kind of understanding, they believed, was itself revelatory. This did not mean that they always eschewed organized religion, for some gnostics entered the churches and suggested that they were the most authentic realization of Christian faith. However, for them the Church was never more than a means toward the end of their pursuit of psychic knowledge, a circumstance being played out again in church after church in the postmodern world where consumer habits have hooked up with a therapeutic orientation that now is subjugating religion to spirituality and spirituality to private choice.

In one very important respect, however, gnosticism was the antithesis of paganism. Paganism was about nature; gnosticism was in flight from nature. Gnostics saw themselves as caught in a creation that is flawed, dark, ominous, whose rhythms bring no connections with anything divine, and whose God is far away, alienated, aloof, and incommunicative. In this respect, they were far removed from the pantheism which was at the heart of paganism. Speaking for gnostics of all times, Bloom argues that the creator God is a "bungler" who

32. Pagels, *The Johannine Gospel in Gnostic Exegesis*, 119-20.

"botched" the creation and precipitated the Fall.[33] This creation offers no home for the human being because, he argues, originally "the deepest self was not part of creation" but was part of the "fullness of God"[34] to which it yearns to return. This yearning, this homesickness, is what often passes as depression, he suggests. And yet, despite this significant difference, there is also an important point of convergence. "God," Bloom tells us, "is at once deep within the self and also estranged, infinitely far off, beyond our cosmos."[35] Here lies the point of connection with paganism: not in the worship of nature (cf. Rom. 1:18-24), but in the access to the sacred that is sought through the self, this "deepest self," which experiences itself as being adrift from life, as not being able to fit in with life, and as offering an exit from the oppressive complexities and manifold pains of this "botched" creation into what is eternal.

A Spirituality of Postmodernity

It seems rather clear, then, that our contemporary spirituality is in continuity with some of the different aspects of what has preceded it. In some of its expressions it has more in common with paganism; in others it is more like gnosticism. New Age, for example, what Bloom mocks as "an endlessly entertaining saturnalia of ill-defined yearnings . . . suspended about halfway between feeling good and good feeling" and "a vacuity not to be believed,"[36] has affinities that are more obviously pagan, but this wider spirituality has some parallels with what was gnostic. We will explore three such parallels: first, that both gnosticism and the new spirituality have arisen in contexts which were experienced as inhospitable; second, that the two share a comparable understanding of the self; third, that the gnostics anticipated today's postmodern expressive individualism.

33. Bloom, *Omens of Millennium*, 27.
34. Bloom, *Omens of Millennium*, 183.
35. Bloom, *Omens of Millennium*, 30.
36. Bloom, *Omens of Millennium*, 18-19.

The Empty Landscape

First, by an entirely different route from that taken in gnosticism, postmoderns have come to a similar conclusion regarding the alien and inhospitable environment in which we are bound to live. For the gnostics, this sense was rooted in the belief that the human self had been abandoned by God to live out its life in a flawed and unfriendly creation; for postmoderns, this sense of alienation, of not being at home, arises not from a particular view of the creation itself, but from the artificial environment we have built upon it in our soulless cities: the mindless repetition of the modern workplace, the cruelty of the economic tides which flow in and out without regard to human suffering, the numbing effect of bureaucracy, and the impersonal tenor of human relations in a society that values specialized functions over the people themselves. It is true, of course, that the modernization of the Western world has also filled it with abundance and with relief from so many of the ills that once afflicted life. It is offering up new possibilities, new choices, and an astounding array of new opportunities. Yet, at the same time, we live with more anxiety, more loneliness, more meaninglessness, a deeper sense of having been uprooted from family, place, and work. And the technology that has produced miracle drugs and genetically altered foods has also produced a world more dangerous and threatening than ever before with its nuclear bombs, its chemical and biological weapons, and its pollution. What has enabled us to progress in some ways also casts its own long, dark shadow across life in other ways.

Still it may seem paradoxical that in the very moment of this Western triumph, cracks are also appearing in the human spirit. But this realization is what, in fact, distinguishes the postmodern sensibility from an Enlightenment one, and it is what is making the emerging parallel to gnosticism easier to see. Gnosticism grew up in a world whose inner fabric was increasingly frayed and damaged, a world that would be overcome by crises of its own making, and long before it finally collapsed there was foreboding in the air. Gnosticism had an explanation of why life seemed so dark and threatening — and the answer, of course, was that it is dark and threatening because it is the expression of its evil creator — and offered itself as a path away from the chaos. It was, in that sense, an escape. The typical postmodern attitude toward creation is, of course, quite different, but the search for spiritual life is often undertaken in the presence of a foreboding about life which is comparable. And it is often seeking an escape into a larger reality as well.

Modernity, which has so powerfully reduced all of life to a this-worldly reality, has left postmoderns, it seems, with only two choices. Either the self can see itself as being purely immanent in this world, its sum entirely contained within the larger equation of modernized life with no remainder, or it can attempt its own breakout, to transcend itself, to wrench itself loose to seek its own greater reality in its own way. If it is seen as immanent, it typically melds itself into the life and pleasures of a consumer society. The pursuit of happiness becomes the pursuit of consumption and diversion and "in this society," Walker Percy observes, "the possibilities of diversion are endless and as readily available as eight hours of television a day: TV, travel, drugs, games, newspapers, magazines, Vegas."[37] Yet a life of such complete immanence always must contend against patches, if not long stretches, of unrelieved boredom and emptiness. This is an affliction apparently not visited on other animals but it has become a painful part of the modern human condition. It is what may produce, in varying degrees of intensity, a hunger for what is Other, what is outside the realm of nature, something that is other than commerce and distraction, even for what is outside the realm of normality, something — no matter how obscure, abnormal, or irrational — which will illumine the moment and suffuse the soul with a sense of connectedness to something larger. We are not alone in the cosmos, we will be able to surmise: our small, contorted existence is actually part of a larger and more significant picture. We are part of an unseen world. We are coming to glimpse the real meaning of things. And in this contemporary spiritual quest, as was the case in gnosticism, it is often assumed that some people are naturally spiritual whereas others are not. Some have an inborn knack for seeing what others cannot see. In reality, of course, the spiritual realm in which psychological connection is being sought often turns out to be elusive. It is not easily found and so experimentation becomes the

37. Walker Percy, *Lost in the Cosmos: The Last Self-Help Book* (New York: Farrar, Straus and Giroux, 1983), 12.

means of its discovery. Experimentation invariably leads to an eclectic outcome as assorted beliefs and practices are cobbled together pragmatically into what become private spiritualities.

The path that this spiritual yearning has taken in the contemporary world was not unanticipated. The modernization of our world, the transformation of its social fabric, impacts human consciousness in profound ways. And what we have to notice in particular are the ways in which our experience of pluralism rattles through our consciousness. For ours is a world in which options multiply like fruit flies, as we have seen. There is too much to choose between in every area of life. We are bombarded by information and we are constantly having to choose what beliefs we will follow, what styles we will adopt, what kind of people we would like to be. We speak of having "lifestyles" which include matters such as how well we choose to live, with whom we want to live, what kind of beliefs and moral norms we will or will not accept. In all of these ways we choose who we want to be and nothing is allowed to impose itself on us from the outside.

As the objective world loses its hold upon us, as the world we know offers fewer and fewer certainties in life precisely because it churns up more and more choices, as more and more of what we experience appears random and unpredictable, we find ourselves searching for a more stable reality within ourselves. "If answers are not provided objectively by society," Berger writes, then people are compelled to "turn *inward*." The result is that modern "Western culture," he says, "has been marked by an ever-increasing attention to subjectivity."[38] This attention has taken different turns but it seems rather clear that the current spiritual search is one of them. It is the resonance within modern consciousness of a profoundly pluralized world, a world stripped of the old certainties, and in which the human being has been uprooted and now lives a kind of psychologically solitary existence, a cork bobbing upon the ocean surface while the currents below move it one way and then another.

This new spiritual quest, then, seems to be rooted in a sense of homelessness in the modern world, of having been abandoned in a

---

38. Peter L. Berger, *The Heretical Imperative: Contemporary Possibilities of Religious Affirmation* (New York: Anchor Press, 1979), 21.

place where we no longer fit, and in consequence it is reaching out for something more certain, more real, more substantial. And, insofar as it is a quintessentially modern experience, it is light years away from the earlier gnosticism. Yet parallels are not entirely absent for the gnostics, for an entirely different set of reasons, also felt homeless. Philosophically, the new spirituality is not replicating some of the old gnostic *theories* about reality, but at a psychological level the parallels are unmistakable.

"My Own Little Voice"

A second parallel between this contemporary spirituality and ancient gnosticism is that today's approach to the sacred is also through the self and within the self and in this sense it is "self-centered." Perhaps those who imagine that their real self once existed within the "fullness" of God and has fallen out of the heavens to be trapped in a created body where it exists in this uncongenial and uncomfortable realm only as a "divine spark" are few in number. Yet the idiosyncratic nature of this view should not obscure the fact that it has in common with many others the thought that it is in the self, in its depths, that one encounters a Reality which is not material, one that is not of this (modernized) world, and one that provides access into something greater and more authentic than what is merely encountered through the senses. It is thus that the self is both the means of engaging this Reality and the object of the engagement. It is in the self that one finds one's exit from a world of conflict, tension, danger, and boredom, and in the self that one also finds some intimations about how to live. It is upon this assumption about the self that paganism, gnosticism, and this contemporary spirituality all converge.

From this flows a changed moral perspective. For the older paganisms, at least, there was no such thing as objective, universal truth because there was no single God who alone existed and who had uniquely revealed himself. There was instead a multitude of divine presences and therefore all truth was relative to those divine beings. The gods and goddesses have gone in the Western world today but so, too, has the single God who alone exists and who has uniquely revealed himself. In the postmodern world, truth is now relative, not to the mul-

Sheila Larson is a young nurse who has received a good deal of therapy and who describes her faith as "Sheilaism." "I believe in God. I'm not a religious fanatic. I can't remember the last time I went to church. My faith has carried me a long way. It's Sheilaism. Just my own little voice." Sheila's faith has some tenets beyond belief in God, though not many. In defining "my own Sheilaism" she says: "It's just try to love yourself and be gentle with your self. You know, I guess, take care of each other. I think he would want us to take care of each other."

Bellah, *Habits of the Heart*

titude of gods and goddesses, but to the multitude of human knowers. The categories of true and false, right and wrong, therefore fall away and are replaced by a different kind of distinction: religion which is useful as opposed to that which is not. Given our cultural climate, religion which is useful is that which is therapeutically helpful. And the need to discern between what is true and what is false, we have come to think, is a bad habit which needs to be abandoned.

Both then and now, access to what is unfallen and unperverted is to be had through the self. Gnostics believed, as do many of those in this contemporary spiritual quest, that the moment spiritual perceptions are codified into dogma or doctrine, the moment these insights become part and parcel of corporately practiced religious life, with its rules and authorities, its expectations and sanctions, the insight has already become corrupted. It is the reality of the deeper self which is put in jeopardy by religion — which, of course, was Emerson's contention, too. Spirituality, they believe, is threatened by religion.

When Wade Clark Roof analyzed the spirituality of the Baby Boom Generation, he noted the fundamental cleavage which has been tracked in these pages: "*Spirit* is the inner, experiential aspect of religion," he wrote, and "*institution* is the outer, established form of religion."[39] From

39. Wade Clark Roof, *A Generation of Seekers: The Spiritual Journeys of the Baby Boom Generation* (San Francisco: Harper, 1993), 30.

this bifurcation arose the further distinction that Boomers are "believers" in the sense that they give credence to their own interior perceptions and intuitions, but they are not "belongers" in the sense that they give much credence to doctrine formulated by others, to traditions passed along through the Church, or to the corporate practice of faith. It is the "inwardness" of direct experience within the self that is most persuasive. Indeed, 80% of Americans, across the generations, believe that people should arrive at their own beliefs independently of religious institutions such as churches and synagogues. And 60% take this view a step further. On the grounds that people have God "within them," churches and synagogues, they believe, are unnecessary. Clearly what Roof was seeing was a *cultural* habit and not, as his book suggests, a generational one. If there is a generational factor which is present it is found in the fact that those who are younger are more likely than those who are older to have been engulfed by ideas of their own autonomy, to be disenchanted with religious institutions (though this may be reversing itself),[40] and to have been more deeply affected by the massive waves of change that have washed across American life in the last five decades in particular.

What is now strikingly clear is how different this contemporary spiritual quest is from the way in which spirituality has been understood in the life of the Church in the past. Some of these differences have already been noted but one more needs to be touched on. In the long history of the Church, what is spiritual has typically been seen as being mediated by, as being compatible with, and as requiring the rhythms of, churchly life and its doctrines. Where churchly life and spiritual life have no longer fed into each other, irruptions of protest have soon followed. In the late Middle Ages, there were Hus and Wycliffe; still later, there were the Protestant Reformers and Anabaptists; then there were the Puritans; and later still there were the Wesleys and Whitefield. Sometimes the protest was sustained within existing church life. John Wesley, for example, declared that he had lived as an Anglican and that he wished to die as one. Circumstances, in time, did lead to his creating parallel religious forms from which

40. This is the argument advanced by Colleen Carroll, *The New Faithful: Why Young Adults Are Embracing Christian Orthodoxy* (Chicago: Loyola Press, 2002).

arose a new denomination and yet his primary disposition was to work within Anglicanism. The Protestant Reformers earlier on had taken a different tack, one that was, in fact, forced upon them. They left the Catholic Church but they then developed different church forms that were consistent with their doctrines concerning the sole authority of Scripture, the gospel of justification by grace alone through faith alone, and the centrality of Christ. They did not simply slough off the church. In each of these cases, and many more like them, the quest for a more whole, more biblical spirituality went hand in hand with finding better ways of expressing that spirituality ecclesiastically and confessionally. In contemporary terms, spirituality and religion were seen as the necessary aspects of a single whole and as indispensable to each other.

By contrast, this contemporary spiritual search is inclined to oppose itself to religion, to doctrine as a set of unchanging beliefs, to the public and institutional forms in which that spirituality might be expressed. While it is the case that the various religions are sometimes raided for their ideas, today's spirituality remains a deeply privatized matter whose access to reality is through a pristine, uncorrupted self. And all of this happens without any necessary reference to, or connection with, others. With its individualism, its wholly privatized understanding, its therapeutic interest, its mystical bent, its experimental habits, its opposition to truth as something which mediates the nature of an unchanging spiritual realm, its anti-institutional bias, its tilt toward the East, its construction of reality, and its can-do spirit, it is something which is emerging from the very heart of the postmodern world. This is, in fact, the postmodern soul. And its ancient forerunner was seen in gnosticism.

It's About Me

Third, this postmodern individualism has its own unique ways of thinking, ways that reflect both the American experience and the passage it has taken through our modernized world. It is not difficult to see that here, too, that there are some parallels to ancient gnosticism.

One of the distinctive characteristics of American life that has already been noted is its individualism, now transposed into the idea of the autonomous self. In its earlier life, when Alexis de Tocqueville was observing it in the nineteenth century, individualism worked through moral character, producing the "inner-directed" person, to use David Riesmann's language.[41] This was the person whose sense of duty and responsibility was worked out of an inward sense as to what was right and what was wrong. Thinking for oneself, taking care of oneself, being self-dependent, and being able to stand alone became the virtues in which this kind of individualism expressed itself — but these virtues most commonly flowered in communities, not in isolation from others. This was the kind of person who, drawing strength from within, did not live for the approval of others, did not die by their disapproval, and chose, instead, to be his or her own person. This sometimes meant acting alone, being independent, and so in the constellation of virtues in this older kind of individualism prominent were courage, fortitude, and hardiness.

In the 1950s and 1960s, however, this kind of individualism began to undergo a drastic change, the "inner directed" person evolving into an "other-directed" person, not finding the grounding for action in an inner moral core but finding it, instead, in the approval of others. With the passage of time and the growing commercial tempo, compelling surrogates for inner virtue could be found easily in peer groups, fashion fads, and the latest trends. It is acceptance with others which now becomes the preeminent goal, and the most dreaded outcome is to become an outcast. It is fitting in, not standing out. It is thus the transformation of the older moral core into a psychological disposition, character into personality, and human nature into the self.[42] As various as are the forms which this kind of individualism takes, the common element is, as Bellah puts it, that "the self becomes the main form of reality"[43] and the pursuit of its rights and unique intuitions, even in the face of others, is what life is about.

It is not hard to see how the older virtues of thinking for oneself

41. I am here summarizing what I have stated more fully in my *No Place for Truth; or, Whatever Happened to Evangelical Theology?* (Grand Rapids: William B. Eerdmans, 1993), 141-61.

42. See Steven Pinker, *The Blank Slate: The Modern Denial of Human Nature* (New York: Viking, 2002).

43. Robert N. Bellah et al., *Habits of the Heart: Individualism and Commitment in American Life* (New York: Harper and Row, 1985), 143.

and acting for oneself passed into a kind of spirituality in which this same self-reliance was worked out in relation to the divine. It was in the individual, not in dependence on others, or even on outward rituals and doctrines of the past, that God was to be found. In its earlier phase this produced a much sturdier kind of spiritual individualism than its expressive, contemporary counterpart today. Today's spirituality is far more likely to be about self-healing and it is far more likely to see itself in consumer terms.

What is the aboriginal Self, on which universal reliance may be grounded? What is the nature and power of that science-baffling star, without parallel, without calculable elements, which shoots a ray of beauty even into trivial and impure actions, if the least mark of independence appear? The inquiry leads us to that source, at once the essence of genius, of virtue, and of life, which we call Spontaneity or Instinct. We denote this primary wisdom as Intuition, whilst all later teachings are intuitions. In that deep force, the last fact behind which analysis cannot go, all things find common origin. For, the sense of being which in calm hours rises, we know not how, in the soul, is not diverse from things, from space, from light, from time, from man, but one with them, and proceeds obviously from the same source whence their life and being also proceed. . . . The relations of the soul to the divine spirit are so pure that it is profane to interpose helps.

Ralph Waldo Emerson, *Self-Reliance and Other Essays*

Clear contrasts now emerge. Traditional Christian spirituality is self-abnegating. It values self-sacrifice and self-discipline, a sacrifice and a discipline which is required by the moral world it inhabits. Because of the felt obligation to curtail and discipline the self, traditional spirituality lives within doctrine that is true and wants to live with corporately practiced faith, at least if that faith has some authenticity, even when there are the expected jolts that come with human relations. Contemporary spirituality which opposes itself to religion is spirituality which, by contrast, is about the business of self-realization, or self-discovery, and is assuming, as Bloom puts it, that real knowledge is found in "an inward knowledge rather than an outward belief."[44] More than that, it is also refusing to live within parameters and boundaries which are drawn by others, within doctrine which it has not constructed, within a corporately practiced belief since that would do violence to the delicacy and authenticity of its own private sensibility.

This spirituality has clear parallels with paganism, but that is not all that it is. While this pagan impulse parallels what was evident in the early gnosticism, it must also be said that it is thoroughly postmodern. This is the kind of spirituality which goes hand in hand with a flexible biography, with the ability to reinvent one's self, remake one's self, shift and adapt consonant with the constantly shifting demands of a virile economy and workplace and with the changing topography of moral reality. It is the psychological counterpart to the market-driven economy and the collapse of moral absolutes. Settled, unmoving convictions, an inward core of moral belief, easily become impediments to the need to be able to make quick adaptations as changed contexts might require. This, then, is the spirituality of those on the move, those who live in the interstices of the postmodern world, those who know its rhythms, its demands, and the punishments which it inflicts on any who are unwilling to shift as it shifts, those who will not change as it changes, those who look askance at expediency. This is a spirituality, then, that is as contemporary as is contemporary society but, in other ways, as ancient as the world is ancient.

Confrontation, Not Tactics

Seeing how this spiritual search is both contemporary and ancient is really the key to understanding how to think about it from a Christian point of view. To put the matter succinctly: those who see only the contemporaneity of this spirituality — and who, typically, yearn to be seen as being contemporary — usually make tactical maneuvers to win

44. Bloom, *Omens of Millennium*, 235.

a hearing for their Christian views; those who see its underlying world-view will not. Inevitably, those enamored by its contemporaneity will find that with each new tactical repositioning they are drawn irresistibly into the vortex of what they think is merely contemporary but what, in actual fact, also has the power to contaminate their faith. What they should be doing is thinking strategically, not tactically. To do so is to begin to see how ancient this spirituality actually is and to understand that beneath many contemporary styles, tastes, and habits there are also encountered rival *worldviews*. When rival worldviews are in play, it is not adaptation that is called for but confrontation: confrontation not of a behavioral kind which is lacking in love but of a cognitive kind[45] which holds forth "the truth in love" (Eph. 4:15). This is one of the great lessons learned from the early Church. Despite the few who wobbled, most of its leaders maintained with an admirable tenacity the alternative view of life which was rooted in the apostolic teaching. They did not allow love to blur truth or to substitute for it but sought to live by both truth and love.

A worldview is a framework for understanding the world. It is the perspective through which we see what is ultimate, what is real, what our experience means, and what our place is in the cosmos. It is in

---

45. The dominant view among sociologists of religion has been that the circumstances of modernity threaten traditional believing because modern life is so replete with multiple forms of diversity and because the public square has been so stripped of all symbols of religion that it becomes highly implausible that the contents of the faith are true. This theory has been explored relative to evangelicalism, for example, in James Hunter's two books, *American Evangelicalism: Conservative Religion and the Quandary of Modernity* (New Brunswick: Rutgers University Press, 1983) and *Evangelicalism: The Coming Generation* (Chicago: University of Chicago Press, 1989). More recently Christian Smith has challenged this view and argued instead that American evangelicalism is actually strengthened by the diversity and pluralism by which it is surrounded. It is "strong not because it is shielded against, but because it is — or at least perceives itself to be — embattled with forces that seem to oppose or threaten it." He goes on to say that "evangelicalism *thrives* on the tensions this threat creates. Without these, evangelicalism would lose its identity and purpose and grow languid and aimless" (Christian Smith et al., *American Evangelicalism: Embattled and Thriving* [Chicago: University of Chicago Press, 1998], 89). However, it is doubtful that Smith's argument is actually an alternative to Hunter's. Modernity does threaten evangelical faith and evangelical faith is strengthened when it confronts the worldview modernity represents.

For Christians cannot be distinguished from the rest of the human race by county or language or custom. They do not live in cities of their own; they do not use a peculiar form of speech; they do not follow an eccentric manner of life. This doctrine of theirs has not been discovered by the ingenuity and deep thought of inquisitive men, nor do they put forward a merely human teaching, as some people do. . . . They busy themselves on earth, but their citizenship is in heaven. They obey established laws, but in their own lives they go far beyond what the laws require. They love all men, and by all men are persecuted. They are unknown, and still they are condemned; they are put to death, and yet they are brought to life. They are poor, and yet they make many rich; they are completely destitute, and yet they enjoy complete abundance. They are dishonored, and in their very dishonor are glorified; they are defamed, and are vindicated. They are reviled, and yet they bless; when they are affronted, they still pay due respect. When they do good, they are punished as evildoers; undergoing punishment, they rejoice because they are brought to life. They are treated by the Jews as foreigners and enemies, and are hunted down by the Greeks; and all the time those who hate them find it impossible to justify their enmity.

Anonymous, "Letter to Diognetus"

these ways, as I have suggested, that we might speak of postmodernity as having a worldview despite the denials of its advocates and practitioners. What they are denying is having an *Enlightenment* worldview, one which is rationally structured and, from their perspective, one that is pretentious because it is claiming to know much too much. Everyone, however, has a worldview, even if it is one which posits no meaning and even if it is one which is entirely private and true only for the person who holds it.

We must go further, however. It is not just any worldview that we encounter in the postmodern world, but one that increasingly resembles the old paganisms. It is one that is antithetical to that which biblical faith requires. It is this transformation of our world, this emerging worldview, which has passed largely unnoticed. That, at least, is the most charitable conclusion that one can draw. For while the evangelical Church is aware of such things as the fight for gay and lesbian rights, hears about the eco-feminists, knows about pornography, has a sense that moral absolutes are evaporating like the morning mist, knows that truth of an ultimate kind has been dislodged from life, it apparently does not perceive that in these and many other ways a new worldview is becoming ensconced in the culture. If it did, it surely would not be embracing with enthusiasm as many aspects of this postmodern mindset as it is or be so willing to make concessions to postmodern habits of mind.[46]

This casual embrace of what is postmodern has increasingly led to an embrace of its spiritual yearning without noticing that this embrace carries within it the seeds of destruction for evangelical faith. The contrast between biblical faith and this contemporary spirituality is that between two entirely different ways of looking at life and at God. Nygren, some years ago, used the Greek words for two different kinds

---

46. The dichotomy which postmodern epistemology wants to force is one between knowing everything exhaustively or knowing nothing certainly at all. And since it would be arrogant in the extreme to claim to know what God alone knows the only other option, it seems, is to accept the fact that our knowledge is so socially conditioned, so determined by our own inability to escape our own relativity, that we are left with no certain knowledge of reality at all. This is the epistemological position accepted by Richard Middleton and Brian Walsh. All attempts at "getting reality" right, they say, have proved to be failures and Christians should concede as much. See their *Truth Is Stranger Than It Used To Be* (Downers Grove: InterVarsity Press, 1995). From a slightly different angle, Brian McLaren has adopted as a positive, even God-directed development, the disjunction between spirituality and religion. The religion in question for him is still evangelical but the disjuncture he promotes leaves behind a faith that is suspicious of reason, resistant to formulated beliefs, and allergic to structures within which faith is practiced, and, of course, it is dismissive of worldviews. Unless these attitudes are allowed to reshape the way Christianity is lived out, he believes, it is doomed to die. Here, indeed, is the old liberal fear of becoming outdated coupled with the postmodern infatuation with spirituality in its divorce from religion. See his *A New Kind of Christian: A Tale of Two Friends on a Spiritual Journey* (San Francisco: Jossey-Bass, 2001). In the cases of Middleton, Walsh, and McLaren, then, the adoption of a postmodern worldview is not inadvertent at all but knowing and deliberate. The consequences of this for the Church will be explored in a subsequent chapter.

of love, *Eros* and *Agape*, to characterize these worldviews, and his elucidation is still helpful. In the one worldview, which he calls Eros, it is the self which is in the center. In the other, which he calls Agape, it is God who is in the center. Eros, Nygren says, has at its heart a kind of want, longing, or yearning.[47] It is this fact, of course, which has always put the Church in something of a conundrum. Is this yearning a natural preparation for the gospel, human nature crying out in its emptiness, calling out to be filled with something else? It was this thought that led Clement of Alexandria in the early church to speak of the "true Christian gnostic" as if gnosticism's yearning for what was spiritual reached its fulfillment in Christian faith. Yet if this yearning is a preparation, it is one that stands in need of serious purging for it carries within itself an understanding about God and salvation which is diametrically opposed to what we have in biblical faith. In this sense, it is less a preparation and more of a wrong turn. Why is this so?

The movement of Eros spirituality is upward. Its essence, its drive, is the sinner finding God. The movement of Agape, by contrast, is downward. It is all about God finding the sinner. Eros spirituality is the kind of spirituality which arises from human nature and it builds on the presumption that it can forge its own salvation. Agape arises in God, was incarnate in Christ, and reaches us through the work of the Holy Spirit opening lives to receive the gospel of Christ's saving death. In this understanding, salvation is given and never forged or manufactured. Eros is the projection of the human spirit into eternity, the immortalizing of its own impulses. Agape is the intrusion of eternity into the fabric of life coming, not from below, but from above. Eros is human love. Agape is divine love. Human love of this kind, because it has need and want at its center, because it is always wanting to have its needs and wants satisfied, will always seek to control the object of its desires. That is why in these new spiritualities it is the spiritual person who makes up his or her beliefs and practices, mixing and matching and experimenting to see what works best, and assuming the prerogative to discard at will. The sacred is therefore loved for what can be had from loving it. The sacred is pursued because it has value to the pursuer and that value is measured in terms of the therapeutic payoff.

47. Nygren, *Agape and Eros*, 210.

There is, therefore, always a profit-and-loss mentality to these spiritualities.

By contrast, in Agape faith, God is not loved simply for the benefits that flow from that loving such as the forgiveness of sins. He is loved for what he is in himself. If Eros loves the sacred because it is worth doing, Agape, by contrast, loves God without ulterior motives. Agape surrenders; Eros grasps. Agape loves simply and only because it should, because God is most lovable. This Agape faith loves God because it is the consequence of his Agape and in his love there is no calculation. It is a completely free and spontaneous love. He is to be worshipped even if there are no returns. Furthermore, he is sovereign and cannot be controlled or manipulated within the human spirit. Indeed, he is not even found naturally in the human spirit. His salvation is not by mystical technique or psychological understanding but by grace, grace alone, grace coming from the outside, and grace that will not tolerate any human contribution. In Eros spirituality there is always a sense of self-sufficiency, one which is also suffused with pride; in Agape faith, it is precisely the recognition of the self's spiritual insufficiency that is the condition for the coming of grace. The one tries to storm eternity borne up on its own mortal wings; the other receives eternity as the pauper does the help which kindness extends.

Contemporary spiritualities must be recognized as a form of temptation. The question they raise, as Barth rightly suggested, is whether the Church is able to take its own revelation seriously. For what these spiritualities do is to invite the Church, theology, and faith "to abandon their theme and object and become hollow and empty, mere shadows of themselves."[48] They do so in their assumption that Christian faith is simply one member in this vast extended spiritual family and one that is not particularly enlightened. And the historic stance of the Church is that this is false. Christian faith, constituted by the Word of God and the Spirit of God, is not just an outcropping of human beings' internal spirituality but something which, in its supernatural construction, in its uniqueness, stands apart from all other

---

48. Karl Barth, *Church Dogmatics*, trans. G. T. Thomson et al., ed. G. W. Bromiley and T. F. Torrance (5 vols.; Edinburgh: T&T Clark, 1936-77), I, ii, 283. Barth, in this section, is speaking of "religion" but he views the functioning of religion in much the same way as I have been considering spirituality.

My first principle is this. Christ laid down one definite system of truth which the world must believe without qualification, and which we must seek precisely in order to believe it when we find it. Now you cannot search indefinitely for a single definite truth. You must seek until you find, and when you find, you must believe. Then you have simply to keep what you have come to believe, since you also believe that there is nothing else to believe, and therefore nothing else to seek, once you have found and believed what he taught who bids you seek nothing beyond what he taught.

Tertullian, "Prescription Against Heretics"

spiritualities. It is by the Word of God, given to the Church, that all religions and all spiritualities are to be judged. The "faith" of the spiritual seeker and the faith of the Christian believer may, in some ways, look alike but, in fact, they are radically different.[49] The one is the upward questing of the human spirit which speaks of human emptiness and uncertainty; the other is the work of God which speaks of his grace and judgment. As authentic as the human questing may be, it is still in biblical terms, unbelief. For the searching is not a search of the one *locus* in which God has spoken and decisively acted; it is a searching for its own sake, a searching for its own rewards. In religion of a Christian kind, we listen; in spirituality of a contemporary kind, we talk. In religion of a Christian kind, we accept a gift; in spirituality of a contempo-

49. The critique which Budde and Brimlow make of the expression of this spirituality which they describe in the corporate world is that it is marginalizing the Church by assuming many of its prerogatives, concepts, and symbols. It transforms ideas like transcendence, vocation, and covenant, and fills them with meaning that is individualistic and which fits in with the corporation's goals of profit and efficiency. The net result, they suggest, is that something like Gresham's Law has now been set to work: "just as bad and counterfeit money drives down the worth of legitimate currency, so too might the tepid and superficial nature of corporate spirituality diminish the capacity to desire and appreciate more substantive notions of faith, commitment, and vocation." Michael Budde and Robert Brimlow, *Christianity Incorporated: How Big Business Is Buying the Church* (Grand Rapids: Brazos Press, 2002), 53.

rary kind, we try to seize God. In the one, we are justified by the righteousness of Christ; in the other, we strive to justify ourselves through ourselves. It is thus that spirituality is the enemy of faith.

The rebel defies more than he denies. Originally, at least, he does not suppress God; he merely talks to him as an equal. But it is not a polite dialogue. It is a polemic animated by the desire to conquer. The slave begins by demanding justice and ends by wanting to wear a crown. He must dominate in his turn. His insurrection against his condition becomes an unlimited campaign against the heavens for the purpose of bringing back a captive king who will first be dethroned and finally condemned to death. Human rebellion ends in metaphysical revolution. It progresses from appearances to acts, from the dandy to the revolutionary. When the throne of God is overturned, the rebel realizes that it is now his own responsibility to create the justice, order, and unity that he sought in vain within his own condition, and in this way to justify the fall of God.

Albert Camus, *The Rebel*

Many in the new seeker-sensitive experiment in "doing church" have seen only the surface habits of this postmodern world and have not really understood its Eros spirituality. Theirs is an experiment in tactics in which innumerable questions have been asked about the ways the Church can become successful in this culture and they are all prefaced by the word *how*. How do we get the Boomers back into the church? How do we get on the wavelength of Generation Xers? How do we do worship so that the transition from home to church, from mall to church, and from unbelief into a context of belief, is seamless and even unnoticed? How do we speak about Christian faith to those who only want techniques for survival in life? How can we be motivational for those who need a lift without burdening them? How can we say what we want to say in church when the audience will give us only a small slice of their attention, especially if we are not amusing? And what is emerging, as the evangelical Church continues to empty itself of theology, is that it now finds that it is tapping, wittingly or not, into this broad cultural yearning for spirituality, and capitalizing on that disposition's inclination not to be religious. Evangelical spirituality without theology, that even sometimes despises theology, parallels almost exactly the broader cultural spirituality that is without religion. Evangelical faith without theology, without the structure and discipline of truth, is not Agape faith but it is much closer to Eros spirituality.

This, however, is not understood. Church talk about "reaching" the culture turns, almost inevitably, into a discussion about tactics and methodology, not about worldviews. It is only about tactics and not about strategy. It is about seduction and not about truth, about success and not about confrontation. However, without strategy, the tactics inevitably fail; without truth, all of the arts of seduction which the churches are practicing sooner or later are seen to be the empty charade that they are; and because the emerging worldview is not being engaged, the Church has little it can really say. Indeed, one has to ask how much it actually wants to say. Biblical truth contradicts this cultural spirituality, and that contradiction is hard to bear. Biblical truth displaces it, refuses to allow it its operating assumptions, declares to it its bankruptcy. Here, indeed, is an anti-god, dressed up in the garb of authenticity, but whose world is a world of fiction. Is the evangelical Church faithful enough to explode the worldview of this new spiritual search? Is it brave enough to contradict what has wide cultural approval? The verdict may not be finally in but it seems quite apparent that while the culture is burning, the evangelical Church is fiddling precisely because it has decided it must be so like the culture to be successful.

To speak of this engagement with culture in the language of confrontation is, no doubt, an offense to sensitive evangelical ears, especially to those who consider postmodern culture to be neutral and innocent and all of it a matter only of taste and preference, and it will be especially offensive to those who are most comfortable only when they are blending in and using it to achieve their own churchly success. That, unfortunately, has been a besetting sin among God's people going back to the beginning of the Old Testament record. And the prophets found, over and over again, that those who have blended in most successfully are those most intent on not being dislodged.

Yet confrontation is always at the heart of the relation between Christ and culture because that relation is one of light in its relation to darkness, truth to false belief, and holiness to what is fallen. It is a confrontation that can take place only if the Church is engaged with culture. Those who, in Niebuhr's typology, adopt a "Christ against culture" position — such as some of the Anabaptists in the Reformation period or the Amish today — are those who withdraw from culture or who minimize their engagement with it. But this posture merely internalizes the felt confrontation and that is entirely inadequate. There can be no transformation of culture by those who have taken themselves outside of it, either physically or mentally, because transformation comes by engagement. It is not until the culture has been engaged by biblical truth, the biblical truth by which it is judged, that the Church has discharged its responsibility. It is then that the culture is judged by him who is the Truth, by him who is above culture and without whom neither rational life in a culture, nor its best intentions, or even its deepest experiences, can ever blossom into true spiritual life. That being the case, a response to this new spirituality needs to be formulated from three complementary perspectives. First, that the self is fragmented, not innocent; second, that truth is public, not private; third, that reality is personal, not impersonal.

Fragmented, Not Innocent

The premise beneath all of these spiritualities is that sin has not intruded upon the relation between the sacred and human nature, that human nature itself offers access — indeed, we assume unblemished access — to God, that human nature itself mediates the divine. Gone are the days when people understood that an avalanche has fallen between God and human beings, that human nature retains its shape as made in the image of God but has lost its relationship to God and stands in pained alienation from him.

It is no small anomaly that we have arrived at this point. How can we be so knowledgeable about evil in the world and so innocent about sin in ourselves? Is it not strange that we who see so much tragedy through television, who are so knowledgeable of the darkness in our world, who can now mock the pretensions of the Enlightenment with its empty hopes of human progress, who pride ourselves on being able to stare with clear eyes and no denials at what is messy, untidy, ugly, and painful, who know only too well the relentless pressures of the modernized world, the overflow of tension, the unhappiness, and anxiety which are spilling across life, are also those who know so little about sin in ourselves? The manifestations of sin are before our eyes, indeed, in our very experience, and yet we have lost the conceptual language to name it for what it is. We are speechless before our own darkness. And, ironically, this inability to name our sin also means, as Barbara Taylor has said, that the language of grace will be eviscerated "since the full impact of forgiveness cannot be felt apart from the full impact of what has been forgiven."[50]

The reason, of course, is that we have lost the moral world in which sin is alone understood.[51] The religious authorities that once gave us rules for life and who gave us the metaphysical world in which those rules found their grounding have all faded in our moral imagination. Today, we are more alone in this world than any previous generation.[52]

The consequence is that we have come to believe that the self retains its access to the sacred, an access not ruptured by sin. In 2002, a national survey by Barna turned up the astounding discovery that despite all of the difficulties which modernized life has created, despite its rapaciousness, greed, and violence, 74% of those surveyed rejected the idea of original sin and 52% of evangelicals concurred. These were the percentages of respondents who agreed with the statement that

50. Barbara Brown Taylor, *Speaking of Sin: The Lost Language of Salvation* (Cambridge: Cowley Publications, 2000), 6-7.
51. See Andrew Delbanco, *The Death of Satan: How Americans Have Lost the Sense of Evil* (New York: Farrar, Straus and Giroux, 1995). See also David B. Morris' reflections on this theme in his essay, "The Plot of Suffering: AIDS and Evil," in *Evil After Postmodernism: Histories, Narratives, Ethics,* ed. Jennifer L. Geddes (New York: Routledge, 2001), 57-64.
52. James Patterson and Peter Kim, *The Day America Told the Truth: What People Really Believe about Everything That Matters* (New York: Prentice Hall, 1991), 27.

"when people are born they are neither good nor evil — they make a choice between the two as they mature."[53] Here is raw American individualism, the kind that "places the burden of one's own deepest self-definitions on one's own individual choice," to use Bellah's words,[54] and here is the heresy of Pelagianism which asserts that people are born innocent of sin, that sin is a set of bad practices which is caught later on in life rather like a disease.

Sin, however, is not some small aberration, some violation of inconsequential Church rules; it is the clenched fist that is raised against God. It is this rebellion which is now native to all human nature from its inception. In America today, though, only 17% define sin in relation to God. The sense that God stands over against us, that there are any habits, practices, or beliefs of which he disapproves, has left us and so has our understanding of sin. Indeed even some prominent Christians, such as Robert Schuller, have come to think that we ought not to speak of sin because this kind of thinking hurts people's feelings and assaults their self-esteem. It is our lost moral compass that produces this fallacious understanding of human nature and it is this fallacious understanding which fuels and drives Eros spirituality. Our presumed innocence leads us to the assumption that the sacred is naturally, easily, and conveniently available to us, when we want it, and how we want it. The sacred is as available, as accessible, as the artifacts of capitalism which are displayed with such allure in the mall.[55] It is there for the taking and we can have it in an unmediated way.

This presumption is what has produced such miscalculation, such blindness, for it is assuming that moral reality, and God himself,

53. George Barna, "Americans Draw Theological Beliefs from Diverse Points of View."

54. Bellah, *Habits of the Heart*, 65.

55. Mark Ellingsen has argued that what is at work here is the old Enlightenment optimism which was recast into the old liberal Protestant theology. The common presumption was that people are good and they "know what they need, and their instincts about truth are accurate and good. Only sinners need the binding authority of the religious community's authoritative teachings to get them on the right path. The good person already has a vision of the right way to go. Select religious teachings are merely a vehicle for supplementing generally sound life instincts." *Blessed Are the Cynical: How Original Sin Can Make America a Better Place* (Grand Rapids: Brazos Press, 2003), 122.

The apostles were sent to find those who were lost, and to bring sight to those who did not see, and healing to the sick, so they did not speak to them in accordance with their previous opinions but by manifestation of the truth. For no men of any kind would be acting rightly if they told blind men who were already beginning to fall over the precipice to continue in their dangerous way, as if it were a sound one and as if they would come through all right. What doctor, when wishing to cure a sick man, would act in accordance with the desires of the patient, and not in accordance with the requirements of medicine? . . . How, then, are the sick to be made strong? and how are sinners to repent? Is it by persevering as they are? or on the contrary, by undergoing a great change and reversal of their previous behavior, by which they have brought themselves serious illness, and many sins? Ignorance, the mother of these things, is driven out by knowing the truth. Therefore the Lord imparted knowledge of the truth to his disciples, by which he cured those who were suffering, and restrained sinners from sin. So he did not speak to them in accordance with their previous ideas, nor answer in accordance with the presumption of the inquirers, but in accordance with sound teaching, without any pretense or respect of persons.

Irenaeus, "Against Heresies"

are not objective and dangerous to us. God is at our convenience because he is accessible on our own terms. In this understanding, there is evil in the world but no sin. Sin is the breach with the divine order, the fist of rebellion shaken at God. Evil, on this postmodern understanding, is simply something lacking between ourselves and the sacred and it is something which can be overcome. The gap can be closed.

The reality, however, is that God stands over against us. To know him is not the same thing as knowing ourselves. This is the fatal principle of all paganism, that the divine and the human are part and parcel of each other, that there is no absolute barrier between God and the creature, that the sacred is found in the self. It is this presumption which produces skewed sight. For if we think of sin as spiritual rebellion, and if we think of God as being a spirit who is resident within human nature, then sin cannot be comprehended because in its spirituality it is indistinguishable from the spirituality of God who is within. The one is part of the other. That is why the Greek philosophers thought about the corruptions in life as being rooted in the senses, in the body, for that at least is something other than the spirit, something which could be objectified and pondered. That, of course, easily leads on to various forms of asceticism as a means of taming the source of corruption. This was the path followed later in Catholic piety and was especially evident in monasticism. It is a path, however, that would be incomprehensible in a culture as sensate, as hedonistic, and as intolerant of limits and controls as is ours. In fact, all forms of asceticism have become blasphemies. What is therefore preferable by far is not to objectify our corruptions, not to locate them anywhere, but to merge them into everything spiritual and to think that God is simply our constant companion, the quiet, accepting presence within the self, and one who sees no evil and hears no evil and from whom there is no alienation.

Public, Not Private

It is quite apparent that the new spirituality is practicing what has become one of the norms of the postmodern world — that is, the belief that each person must be allowed one's own private space within which one has the freedom to define reality for oneself and set one's own rules. Violating this private space is, socially speaking, intolerable. This habit, of course, is an expression of how our postmodern relativism is working itself out in this highly individualistic culture. But it is also speaking to the matter of truth. Truth in this postmodern and individualistic context becomes entirely private. What is true for one, therefore, may not be true for another; what is preference for one will not be preference for another, and the spirituality that works for this person may not work for that. And while this state of affairs bears all the marks of postmodern behaving and believing, it also makes a connection with the paganism of an earlier time when it was also thought that human nature yielded up intimations of "truth" about the supernatural world. And this habit was confronted by the biblical prophets who, in effect, declared that truth was to be thought of as having been revealed in the public domain rather than emerging from within.

Truth, as I have suggested, is what corresponds to reality. It is the faithful and accurate representation of what is "out there," be this in the character and counsels of God, in the created world that he has made, or in the human heart as it has become.[56] To know the truth is to know what is there, to know it in a way that corresponds to what is there. And biblical truth was given publicly, within the framework of redemptive history, and the consequence was that the revelation thus given was as public, as unchangeable, and as objective as the events to which it was tied and through which it had come. It was truth that, because it was public, unchanging, and revealed by God, was universal in its reach. This kind of understanding allows no place for the locus of truth to be private in a postmodern sense, truth for one person being different from truth for another. This kind of radical, postmodern relativism not only pervades American society but it has also become the majority perception in the evangelical Church. "Truth" thus becomes nothing more than a private perception, and credence is given to this perception because in its believing there is supposedly some therapeutic benefit. This capitulation to a postmodern disposition is, in fact, a capitulation to what is quite close to a pagan habit, one that the Old Testament confronted directly.

G. Ernest Wright, some years ago, made this case quite convincingly although, along the way, he unfortunately also jeopardized the historic understanding of biblical authority by disengaging God's speaking from his acting. He did, however, see that while paganism in its various forms was a religion of *nature,* biblical faith arose in the context of *history,* the redemptive history in which God disclosed his character and saving purposes. This distinction between nature and history is, of course, a distinction between the locus of natural and supernatural revelation. God has disclosed himself in the creation but it is not a

---

56. See the discussion of the postmodern challenge to the correspondence view of truth in Douglas Groothuis, *Truth Decay: Defending Christianity Against the Challenges of Postmodernism* (Downers Grove: InterVarsity Press, 2000), 111-38.

saving disclosure. Because the creation is finite and separate from the Creator, it has to be preserved and sustained in its life by him; otherwise it will collapse back into nothingness. And in this preserving work, God gives us a "witness" (Acts 14:17) and an occasion to "seek" him (Acts 17:27), and he also reveals his beauty (Ps. 19) and moral nature (Rom. 1:18-20). Nature by itself, however, yields only natural revelation, not supernatural.

This distinction between nature and history is not an absolute one in paganism, either. In the nature religions of paganism, the gods and goddesses were believed to intervene in life, sometimes leaving behind calamities, reverses and ravages. Yet in none of the pagan religions of the biblical period was there any interest in, or place for, this kind of history as a means of supernatural disclosure, as a place where the intentions of the gods could be discerned. The gods and goddesses may have acted out their caprices in history but those acts were always uninterpreted and therefore mute. Those events were not at the center of pagan interest. Instead, they worshipped the forces of nature and saw themselves as living in a complex hierarchy in which the rhythms of nature, its seasons of dying and regeneration, were part and parcel of the supernatural world. Theirs was a pantheistic understanding of nature. And the disclosure of the intentions of the gods and goddesses was accessed intuitively, not historically. In consequence, the pagan, Wright said, is "an individualist who uses the elaborate means of worship solely for the purpose of gaining his own security, integration and safety,"[57] a description that also fits postmodern spiritual searchers thousands of years later.

The biblical writers broke decisively with this. Nature is simply nature, even if it is providentially sustained by God and does disclose the beauty of its maker. Nevertheless, it yields no saving revelation. But in history, in its flesh and bone, God has acted and done so in such a way that the facts of this history, prophetically interpreted, became the building stones of his special disclosure of himself.

This has proved to be a vexed matter theologically. By the time that the nineteenth century was dawning, at least, this embeddedness

57. G. Ernest Wright, *God Who Acts: Biblical Theology as Recital* (London: SCM Press, 1964), 25.

of revelation in history had become a widespread problem in academia. If this revelation is to be accessed through conventional means of historical research and literary analysis, then religion seemed to be in danger of being taken captive to a purely human undertaking. God was to be discovered, it seemed, and discovered as we discover even the most ordinary facts about life. This perception appalled the neo-orthodox in the last century, and yet they were unable to preserve a stable consensus over their own alternative. Barth distinguished between the ordinary network of events which take place in the flow of time, what is normally thought of as history *(Historie)*, and the sphere of God's saving "history" *(Geschichte)*, which is not grasped by research but by faith. He did so to preserve the idea that Christianity is not about the sinner finding God but about God finding the sinner. Yet, in making this distinction, Barth insisted that although the one kind of history always took place within the other, saving history was not bonded to, was not accessible from, the actual cause-and-event history. This, he thought, was the roadblock that stood in the way of the sinner invading heaven and, by his or her own efforts, entering the presence of God.

Almost immediately, however, this solution began to fall apart. Bultmann, who had been an early ally of Barth's, moved off in a different direction. He also distinguished between the two types of history but then argued that the one took place apart from the other. The resurrection of Christ, for example, had nothing to do with the raising of Christ's body but everything to do with a raising of the believer's internal consciousness. This distinction between these two kinds of history, whether in the Barthian or Bultmannian forms, proved not to be durable. Both views were fraught with too many insurmountable difficulties. And while Pannenberg was right to reject this kind of distinction between different histories, his own proposal proved to be no more attractive. He abandoned the distinction between general history and that which is saving, thereby sliding into the old Hegelian view.[58]

The way in which Scripture views this whole matter seems to be a little different from these solutions for it affirms that God's redemptive purposes are made known *within* the framework provided by real

58. For a wider discussion of these issues, see Carl F. H. Henry, *God, Revelation, and Authority* (6 vols.; Waco: Word, 1976-83), II, 247-334; V, 21-42.

events, events of a *bona fide* kind, of which he is the cause and the interpreter, within the life of his covenant people. It is these events which are remembered, rehearsed, and recited by the people of God (e.g. Ps. 78, 80, 114; Acts 7:1-53) even as they recognize God's wider providential role in the life of the other nations. These events became paradigmatic of how God would always act and, in this sense, he was always predictable insofar as he would always act in a way which was consistent with the ways that he had acted in the past. This stood in stark contrast to the pagan gods and goddesses who were frequently capricious. This was at the heart of Israel's faith, that God was faithful, not capricious or unreliable, that he was the God of promise whose promises never went unfulfilled. As Moses declared, God "keeps covenant" "to a thousand generations" (Deut. 7:9).

Of these acts, three were of particular importance: first, the call of Abraham, for the promise given to him (Gen. 12:2-3) was the explanation for the existence of the people of God; second, the Exodus, to which the prophets repeatedly pointed for it was this deliverance which had made of them a nation in covenant with God; third, the calling of David through whose victories God's people were established in the land. It was in the light of these events in particular, events in which God had made known truth about himself and his saving intentions, that Israel understood herself in the day-to-day circumstances of life.

Francis Foulkes has pointed out,[59] however, that while it is the case that God's acts in the past were prophetic of his acts in the future in that he always acted in a way that was consistent with what he had done in the past, in the prophets the hope also began to grow that in the future God would act in a way that was even more grand than had been the case in the past. As long as the people of God were surrounded by pagan nations and harassed, or were defeated, the promises made to Abraham and to David were not being fully realized. It was to an even more glorious future that the prophets therefore looked. And when we come to the New Testament, it is these acts of God which are seen as being reenacted through Christ in that even more glorious

---

59. Francis Foulkes, *The Acts of God: A Study of the Basis of Typology in the Old Testament* (London: Tyndale Press, 1958).

way. Moses, for example, had spoken of "a prophet," a new Moses, who was yet to come. It was this hope that was alive in Jesus' day (Jn. 1:21; 6:14; 7:40). And Hebrews speaks of Christ (Heb. 3:1-6) as being that new Moses, though one greater than he. Not only so, but in Christ the Exodus motif is also reenacted yet on an even greater scale, his people being liberated from the "Egypt" of sin (Hos. 7:16; 9:3; 11:5) for Christ the "Passover Lamb" has been slain (I Cor. 5:7). Likewise, God promised to David that his throne would be established forever (II Sam. 7:12). In the kings that followed, few came even close to being like David, few enjoyed such victories or blessings as had attended his reign, and so the hope began to grow, a hope nurtured by failure and disappointment, that God would yet act in the future in an even more glorious way (Jer. 23:5; Mic. 5:2; Is. 9:6-7). It is this hope which is seen as being realized in Christ (Matt. 2:6), David's son, whose reign will, indeed, not only be blessed but will also be eternal. It is this kind of pattern of the repetition of God's acts, yet on an even grander scale in the future, that is carried through in a number of additional themes such as the temple, covenant, and new creation.

It is sufficient here to note, however, that this framework of understanding the purposes of God was a framework rooted in the history in which he worked out his purposes. And these purposes were defined objectively by, and revealed unchangeably through, that history. It was thus that the prophets spoke of who God was by what he had done. Theirs was, therefore, a theology of remembrance, recitation, and hope built upon a revelation which God had given in which he disclosed truth about himself. It was this truth that always stood over against the people of God in the sense that it was not subject to change by their desires, perceptions, or inclinations.

This has large ramifications for us in the postmodern world. These acts, interpreted by God the Holy Spirit through the writers of Scripture, have a meaning which is objective to the contemporary interpreter for the acts of which the interpretation speaks are not subject to revision or change. They do not depend for their reality upon the response of the reader. Their meaning cannot be overridden by any postmodern, subjective disposition. They simply have to be understood in their own terms.

Here there can be no Eros spirituality, as if grace is reached as nature extends its arms upward toward it! Not at all. Grace is known only as God acts to make himself known through his Word and Spirit.[60] It is only as the self-revealing God speaks again his ancient Word into the contemporary world that it is heard, only as the illuminating work of the Holy Spirit enters the recesses of a hearer's being that God's address as address is heard. Yet this hearing does not happen, as Barth thought, in a saving realm that parallels but is disconnected from the redemptive acts of Israel's history but, rather, it happens through and in connection with the acts within this narrative. Thus do we have, as Kevin Vanhoozer argues, God's "speech acts" in which are joined at a conceptual level God's acting, his acting in real history, and God's speaking, speaking through the words of Scripture in which the record of those acts is embedded.[61]

Revelation, then, is public, not private. It is public in the sense that God's primary locus of communication is not within the self nor are his intentions accessed by intuition. He has spoken, and he continues to speak, through the words of Scripture which constitute the Word of God. This revelation, however, is anchored by events within the redemptive narrative by which God called out to himself a people, led them, preserved them, judged them, and finally brought the promises he had made to them into final and full realization in Christ. This is a history which took place apart from human consciousness, and not within the human psyche, and though it has to be understood and interpreted, its meaning is always objective to the interpreter. It has to be understood solely on its own terms; Scripture, the Reformers said, is *sui ipsius interpres.* The Holy Spirit who inspired the Scripture is also its privileged interpreter, which means that the content of Scripture is not subject to being overridden by the interests of the interpreter, or those of a later culture, or those of an ecclesiastical tradition.

60. The Protestant principle has always been to see the biblical Word as the external form of authority which is respoken by the internal principle of the Holy Spirit. "In the matter of religious authority," Ramm wrote, "the Spirit and the Word are insolubly conjoined. The Scriptures function in the ministry of the Spirit, and the Spirit functions in the instrument of the Word. In this vital relationship of Spirit and Scripture the Reformers grounded their doctrine of religious authority." Bernard Ramm, *The Pattern of Authority* (Grand Rapids: William B. Eerdmans, 1957), 29.

61. Kevin J. Vanhoozer, *First Theology: God, Scripture & Hermeneutics* (Downers Grove: InterVarsity Press, 2002), 127-203.

To the Church, therefore, God has given his Word, his Word of truth. When God the Holy Spirit acts in his illuminating role, he enters the sacrosanct spaces in which postmoderns hide themselves and in which they define their own reality. God respects no sacred spaces other than the ones he is filling, for what we have been considering in this discussion of postmodern individualism and relativism, this postmodern construction of a sacred reality that reflects postmodern sensibilities, is nothing less than the contemporary version of a very ancient idolatry. Since God brooks no rivals, he respects no self-constructed sacred spaces. These are spaces in which the sinner declares his or her own sovereignty and, in projecting human want and need into eternity, is, in that very act, seeking to control eternity, to have it on his or her own terms. Eros spirituality, however, dies in the presence of God's Word because biblical truth destroys the sinner's sovereignty which is at the heart of this kind of spirituality.

Agape spirituality and Eros spirituality, therefore, are not variations upon a common theme but stark alternatives. In the one, God reaches down in his grace; in the other, the sinner reaches up in self-sufficiency. Not only are they entirely different in their structures and motivations but God's reaching down into someone's life actually excludes the possibility of that person reaching up. There is no possibility of a synergism here, of God's grace in Agape cooperating with the human desire of Eros. These spiritualities belong in two entirely different worlds. God's sovereignty exercised in the one excludes the humanly seized sovereignty exercised in the other. His grace is grace only when it does what no human effort or desire can do.

Personal, Not Impersonal

Christian faith, then, is about listening, listening to the Word of God. Eros spirituality is about speaking. It speaks because there is no one to whom it can listen. There is no address from outside the human situation because there is no one who is speaking or who has spoken into it. However, the truth is that it is impossible to speak *from* the human situation to God. If God has not first spoken of himself, there can be no authentic human speaking of him because that speaking reveals only human longing and intuition. There is, then, no actual speaking about God and the only listening in Eros spirituality is the one in which all that is heard is its own yearnings reverberating around the self.

The difference, then, between an Agape faith and an Eros spirituality, between the God who reaches down in grace and the human creature who reaches up in self-sufficiency, is that in the one case there is address and in the other case only yearning, in the one a summons and in the other only a sigh. In the end, these are two different worlds, for the one is personal and the other is not; in the one God, who cannot be less personal than the human beings he has made, is encountered and in the other he is not. In the other, there is only a seemingly infinite ocean, an ocean in which human personality becomes lost in all of that ocean's immensity. And in the absence of a divine and personal summons through the Word of God there is only the impersonal vortex that threatens to absorb everything into one undifferentiated mass.

To the Church, then, has been given the charge of proclaiming the Word of God. This revelatory Word is not a concatenation of human opinions and ideas but rather is God's own proclamation, the very means by which he speaks, even into postmodern society. It is, therefore, the making possible of what would be entirely impossible without the grace of God and the powerful working of the Spirit through whose work, and despite the stammering and faltering lips of the preacher, is heard once again the divine summons to stand before God and hear his Word. Here is hope. We have not been cast adrift upon that infinite ocean but, rather, we find ourselves in a universe not of our own making where all of our best thoughts of God are swept away as upon a ferocious current only to be replaced by the eternally simple speech of the triune God. He draws near through his Word, he lifts the fallen, he feeds the hungry, he corrects the wandering, he rebukes the self-sufficient, and everywhere there is found the sweet fragrance of his grace where he has spoken through his Word and ministered by his Spirit.

CHAPTER V

Christis in a Meaningless World

—◦◦◦—

> We desire truth and find in ourselves nothing but uncer-
> tainty. We seek happiness and find only wretchedness and
> death. We are incapable of not desiring truth and happiness
> and incapable of either certainty or happiness.
>
> BLAISE PASCAL

Postmoderns are remarkably nonchalant about the meaninglessness which they experience in life. Reading the works of an earlier generation of writers, existentialist authors like Jean-Paul
Sartre and Albert Camus, one almost developed a sense of vertigo, the
kind of apprehension that one gets when standing too near the edge of
a terrifying precipice, so bleak, empty, and life-threatening was their vision. That sense, however, has now completely gone. Postmoderns live
on the surface, not in the depths, and theirs is a despair to be tossed off
lightly and which might even be alleviated by nothing more serious
than a sitcom. There are today few of the convulsions that once happened in the depths of the human spirit. These are different responses
to the same sense of meaninglessness which is one of the threads that
weaves its way from the modern past into the postmodern present.
What changes is simply how those afflicted with the drift and empti-

ness of postmodern life cope with it. In this chapter, then, I first need to explore this theme; second, I want to frame this meaninglessness theologically; and third, I need to think about how life's meaninglessness is addressed by Christ's gospel.

The Culture of Nothingness

Bewilderment

"The first half of the twentieth century," writes Daniel Boorstin, was a time of "triumphal and accelerating science" and yet it "produced a literature of bewilderment without precedent in our history."[1] At the time, this development in the modern world may have seemed strange. In the very moment of social conquest, when science and technology were promising to rewrite the script of life, to eliminate more and more diseases, to make life more bearable, to fill it with more goods, at that very moment the human spirit was sagging beneath the burden of emptiness, apparently ungrateful for all of this modern bounty.

In retrospect, however, it is not so strange. This was the moment when the Enlightenment world, which had promised so much, was showing the first symptoms of the postmodern ethos in the West, of that curdling of the soul that would leave the human being replete with goods, smothered in plenty, but totally alone in the cosmos, isolated, alienated, enclosed within itself, and bewildered. The conquest of the world, the triumph of technology, and the omnipresence of shopping malls — our temples to consumption — are not the tools by which the human spirit can be repaired. Of that there should be no doubt now, for if affluence, and the bright, shiny world in which it arises, could be the solvent of all the human maladies that lie submerged beneath the surface of life, then this *anomie*, this bewilderment of soul, would long since have been banished. The truth, in fact, is that the conquest of our external world seems to be in inverse relation to the conquest of our in-

---

1. Daniel J. Boorstin, *The Seekers: The Story of Man's Continuing Quest to Understand His World* (New York: Random House, 1998), 228.

These are, perhaps, merely the rationalizations of the modern man's discontent. At the heart of it there are likely to be moments of blank misgiving in which he finds that the civilization of which he is a part leaves a dusty taste in his mouth. He may be very busy with many things, but he discovers one day that he is no longer sure they are worth doing. He has been much preoccupied; but he is no longer sure he knows why. He has become involved in an elaborate routine of pleasures; and they do not seem to amuse him very much. He finds it hard to believe that doing any one thing is better than doing any other thing, or, in fact, that it is better than doing nothing at all. It occurs to him that it is a great deal of trouble to live, and that even in the best of lives the thrills are few and far between. He begins more or less consciously to seek satisfactions, because he is no longer satisfied, and all the while he realizes that the pursuit of happiness was always a most unhappy quest.

Walter Lippmann, *A Preface to Morals*

ner world. The more we triumph in the one the less we seem able to hold together in the other.[2]

The appearance of this despairing mood earlier on is, of course, associated with a wide swath of writers but at mid-century it came to the fore not only in Sartre and Camus, but also in writers such as Eugene Ionesco, Samuel Beckett, Harold Pinter, Martin Heidegger, and others, not all of whom were existentialists. In their different ways

---

2. This is the "American Paradox." The paradox, says David Myers, is that we "are better paid, better fed, better housed, better educated, and healthier than ever before, and with more human rights, faster communication, and more convenient transportation than we have ever known." Alongside all of this largesse, however, are the signs of life in pain and travail. Since 1960, the divorce rate has doubled, teen suicide has tripled, violent crime quadrupled, the number in prison has quintupled, illegitimate children sextupled, and the number of those cohabiting has increased sevenfold. David G. Myers, *The American Paradox: Spiritual Hunger in an Age of Plenty* (New Haven: Yale University Press, 2000), 5.

they were all reflecting the empty world they inhabited. It was empty because on the intellectual side in the West, finding any ultimate grounding for things has become an increasingly precarious undertaking. And on the surface, where modernization has brought forth its abundant fruit, it has also produced a secularism which, as Milbank and the other framers of "radical orthodoxy" have seen, proclaims, sometimes uneasily and sometimes unashamedly, "its own lack of values and lack of meaning. In its cyberspaces and themeparks it promotes a materialism which is soulless, aggressive, nonchalant and nihilistic."[3]

That Man is the product of causes which had no prevision of the end they were achieving; that his origin, his growth, his hopes and fears, his loves and his beliefs, are but the outcome of accidental collocations of atoms; that no fire, no heroism, no intensity of thought and feeling, can preserve an individual life beyond the grave; that all the labours of the ages, all the devotion, all the inspiration, all the noonday brightness of human genius, are destined to extinction in the vast death of the solar system, and that the whole temple of Man's achievement must inevitably be buried beneath the debris of a universe in ruins — all these things, if not quite beyond dispute, are yet so nearly certain, that no philosophy which rejects them can hope to stand. Only within the scaffolding of these truths, only on this firm foundation of unyielding despair, can the soul's habitation henceforth be safely built.

Bertrand Russell, *The Basic Writings*
of Bertrand Russell, 1903-1959

This nihilism, whether philosophically conceived or merely assumed amidst the trappings and doings of Western affluence, has moved out along different avenues depending upon which of several

---

3. John Milbank, Catherine Pickstock, and Gordon Ward, eds., *Radical Orthodoxy: A New Theology* (London: Routledge, 1999), 1.

aspects is emphasized. At root, however, it operates by denying that objective ground exists for believing that anything is true or right — or simply by assuming none does. It denies that anything can be ultimate because ultimately nothing is there. There is no hub to hold the spokes or, if there is, we are unable to get our cognitive sights on it. This sometimes takes the form that one can know nothing certainly, that what is true and what is not cannot be distinguished, and that all knowledge is merely an internal construct whose outcomes are, as a result, always provisional; still others press the attack on reality itself, arguing that in the end nothing is, in fact, real. (This last kind of nihilism disintegrates into solipsism.[4]) And in the absence of any reality in which truth can be grounded, all that remains in life is power, as Nietzsche saw so clearly. If there is no ultimate reality before which we are accountable for what we think, say, and do, then there are no restraints upon the exercise of power, upon the imposition of our will on others, either at a personal level, by corporations, ethnic groups, or by the state.

The Black Hole

That there is a black hole, a Void, in the center of reality is really the common theme that links writers whose works have reverberated with a sense that nothing ultimately means anything, though they speak of it in different ways and draw different conclusions.

The French writer Albert Camus was part of this earlier literature of "bewilderment" and his response to this emptiness was expressed in the language of absurdity. A world that can be explained in some measure, even though the explanation is bad, has a certain familiarity to it, he said. However, when there is no explanation, when all illusions have been stripped away, the human being "feels an alien, a stranger," abandoned in a world without any familiarity. There is no memory of the place from which he or she has come, nor yet any hope of a destination. This "exile is without remedy," Camus said. There is here a divorce between the human being who seeks meaning and the universe which

---

4. See the brief discussion in Karen L. Carr, *The Banalization of Evil: Twentieth-Century Responses to Meaninglessness* (Albany: State University of New York Press, 1992), 17-22.

does not reply. Indeed, it is mute. In this situation, "the feeling of absurdity" is inescapable, and the most serious, the most fundamental, philosophical problem to be considered, as a result, is suicide.[5] Camus talked himself out of suicide and, alongside despairing reflections like this, there also lies his belief that in revolting against what is absurd one will find the morality that lies hidden within that revolt and from which a new order might arise.[6] But it is an anomaly that Camus grasped for a morality which could have no ultimate grounding and therefore, in the end, could at best only be provisional and ultimately meaningless.

Although the playwright Samuel Beckett's language was a little different, his sparse style was peculiarly adapted to conveying this postmodern sense of meaninglessness. He accomplished this most poignantly in his much-discussed brief play *Waiting for Godot.* The play, which was first performed in Paris in 1953, opens with a pair of vagabond buffoons, Vladimir and Estragon, in conversation. They are alone on the stage except for a solitary dead tree. The opening line is, "Nothing to be done."[7] That, in a way, is a byline for the whole play, for theirs is an entirely empty world, a point reinforced in the various interchanges that take place with the other two characters who appear, Pozzo and Lucky, who are master and servant. If there is a glimmer of hope in the play, it is that someone called Mr. Godot will appear. It is not at all clear how this arrangement with Mr. Godot was made, or if it really has been made, for at the end of the play Vladimir asks the boy who brings a message what Mr. Godot looks like. There is no plot to the play, no movement, nothing happens, no one goes anywhere, no conclusions are reached, and nothing is resolved. There is only a thin veil of tension that lies over the sparse, almost monosyllabic conversation. That tension has to do with whether Mr. Godot will come.

So, who is Godot? Beckett himself emphatically denied that he knew who this character was. That, however, has only spurred on literary critics to formulate their own theories. Is Godot God (albeit in di-

5. Albert Camus, *The Myth of Sisyphus and Other Essays,* trans. Justin O'Brien (New York: Vintage Books, 1955), 5.

6. Knud Logstrup, "Man in the Perspective of Nihilism," *Lutheran World,* 12, no. 1 (1965), 6-10.

7. Samuel Beckett, *Waiting for Godot: Tragicomedy in 2 Acts* (New York: Grove Press, 1954), 7.

minutive form)? Are the uncertainties about who he is and whether he will come actually reflections of our own deep despair about life given the elusiveness of this Being? Others have even argued that what the tramps were actually waiting for was themselves, for a breakthrough in self-understanding, the illumination that accompanies the "transmigration of the self."[8]

The identity of Godot is a mystery, but what is clear is that in this play all purpose has collapsed. "Nothing to be done." There is an air of unrelieved emptiness because meaning in life has simply gone. If there is any ambivalence at all, it is connected to this perhaps groundless expectation that Mr. Godot will appear. But he never does. At the very end of the play, a boy runs onto the stage and Vladimir says to him, "You have a message from Mr. Godot?" The boy says that he has. Vladimir guesses what it is: "He won't come this evening."[9] The boy confirms that this is the message but then informs him that Mr. Godot says that he will come the next day, "without fail." But, who knows? There is, of course, much else in the play but the overall effect is the sense of human lostness, of being homeless within the cosmos. Beckett's choice of two tramps to make that point is by no means accidental.

More recently, Milan Kundera, the Czech writer, has explored the ambiguities that are inherent in living in an empty universe. His novel, *The Unbearable Lightness of Being,* is a sad tale of random sexual liaisons, of meaningless passion. The novel weaves its way in and out of the overlapping relationships of five people: Tomas, an unrepentant and chronic womanizer, who is married to Tereza but is fascinated by Sabina; Sabina is sexually enthralled with Tomas but also has Franz; Franz has Sabina but also Marie-Claude. The relationships in this novel are used to illuminate a paradox conveyed in this contrast between what is weighty and what is light. It is the passing, transient nature of life that transfixes the author. The passage of life's events, its torments, its passions, its laughter, all that happens, takes place within a blank universe. That means that verdicts about its meaning, about right and wrong, cannot be reached for everything is always "in the sunset of dis-

8. Frederick Busi, *Transformations of Godot* (Lexington: University Press of Kentucky, 1980), 28-64.

9. Beckett, *Waiting for Godot,* 59.

solution," and nothing ever returns. All passes, all is lost. Nothing is re-trievable. And if, in the moment, in the hour, by the end of the day, it has gone, it has evaporated, what is the point in passing judgment upon it, even upon its horrors? There is nothing there.

It is this ephemeral quality to life that empties it of significance, making it "light," for we become without responsibility for anything that happens: "the absolute absence of a burden causes man to be lighter than air, to soar into the heights, take leave of the earth and his earthly being, and become only half real, his movements as free as they are insignificant."[10] What is the alternative to this? The alternative is that each passing moment actually is significant, in which case "we are nailed to eternity as Jesus Christ was nailed to the cross," which is a "terrifying prospect."[11] So, is this terrible burden of ultimate account-ability in a world of meaning worse than the alternative, a terrible emp-tiness in a world devoid of accountability? Does the libertine not carry around the terrifying burden that nothing matters, that all is random, all a matter of chance? And is this burden of knowing that things do not matter worse than the burden of knowing that they do? This is life's most mysterious, most intractable, and most puzzling problem.

Suicide to Snickers

This kind of unflinching, unqualified nihilism has, for the last half-century, been a thread that has run through European culture though it is, of course, by no means representative of everyone. In fact, its con-clusions are so unsparing of the human condition that for many of those who have been drawn into this intellectual world it has become unbearable. There is now a backlash that has been building against this kind of perspective.

However, this acute sense of the emptiness of the world has been far more at home among brooding Europeans than it has been in America and far more apparent among moderns than postmoderns. America is the land of opportunity, of conquest, where frontiers have

10. Milan Kundera, *The Unbearable Lightness of Being*, trans. Michael Henry Heim (New York: Harper and Row, 1984), 5.
11. Kundera, *The Unbearable Lightness of Being*, 5.

been crossed, and where political and economic power is projected globally. If there are traits that are typical of the American personality, they are more likely to be optimistic than melancholic, confident rather than despairing, and they will have far more to do with the pragmatic outlook that drives those busy making things better than with the pessimism of a thinker alone with dark, torturous thoughts. Indeed, this is even exemplified in an intellectual like Richard Rorty, whose universe is as empty as Beckett's but who appears to suffer few pangs of anxiety as he goes about the pragmatic business of allowing the clash of opinions to forge the way ahead in the absence of any ultimate known reality.

This typically cheerful, upbeat disposition reflects America at its surface. This is a country that still pulsates with the "can do" spirit. It is vigorous, energetic, innovative, and entrepreneurial. As a whole it is prosperous, even though not everyone participates equally in its largesse. And behind the hedges of suburbia, on these islands of privacy, much of what is raw and what makes war on the thought that life has meaning never appears, except by way of the evening's news. There, perhaps, one sees the senseless killings, the withered bodies of those devoured by famine, the devastating earthquake, those with insidious, irreversible diseases. Perhaps these images raise, in a fleeting way, the question as to whether life, after all, isn't senseless if these things happen. And, of course, some of these things happen in America, too, and even in the plushest of suburbs. But they are not *all* that happens and that is the difference. In America, there are also options and prospects, choices and opportunities. It is rich with promise and potential. Life is not lived on the bone as it is in the Third World where, too often, existence is tenuous, where strife is common and brutal, where antibiotics cannot always be had, and retirement accounts and insurance policies are all but nonexistent. No, life in America, by comparison, is very sweet.

Beneath this abundance, this surfeit of affluence, however, things are a little different. Today, Thomas Hibbs notes, "there are no frontiers left to conquer, just fleeting appetites and residual desire for fulfillment."[12] And these appetites, and this need for fulfillment, are pursued

12. Thomas S. Hibbs, *Shows About Nothing: Nihilism in Popular Culture from* The Exorcist *to* Seinfeld (Dallas: Spence Publishing Co., 1999), 169.

in a world that is drastically changed from the time when the frontier was the dominant psychological image in America. Much modern literature, in fact, has spoken, not of great national purpose, but of our *anomie,* the aloneness and sense of drifting which afflicts those who live in the modern fragmented social world. Those haunted by their own solitude, distracted by their own sense of disintegration, hurt by the absence of enduring friendships, of connections to place and family, frustrated by their sense of impotence in the face of impersonal bureaucracies and the swirling currents beneath the social surface, often look to affluence in the hope that what is consumed might offer some solace for these wounds.

This produces no deep brooding over the Void in life. One hears instead the belief expressed in different ways that each must create one's own meaning or that it is morally permissible for everyone to do one's "own thing" provided no one gets hurt — a strange proviso which has no moral legs upon which to stand in an empty universe! This moral and metaphysical vacuity, relentlessly suppressed and dressed up in bright, upbeat optimism, is our nihilism. It is also our barbarism. And, beyond that, it is also our failure. The modern self receives little balm amidst the buying, little peace amidst the frantic search to hold off the sense of emptiness. Indeed, it is the self which, it turns out, is unable to bear the expectations that now rest upon it. Helmut Thielicke could have been speaking of America when he said, apparently of Europeans, that because "the 'I' has lost itself, it necessarily loses its world. Loss of the world then reflects back into the ruined landscape of the self in a kind of demonic reciprocation which is completely destructive."[13] And how does this happen? It happens when the self loses its place before what is ultimate, when it turns in on itself, turns itself into a mere function, itself adapting to the culture around it, adapting to its commerce, all within a thoroughly this-worldly perspective. Thus it is that without ultimates to restrain the self, the world takes on an ominous aspect and the human being becomes especially vulnerable to anxiety and fear.

That, at least, is one way of looking at this connection between

---

13. Helmut Thielicke, *Nihilism: Its Origin and Nature — with a Christian Answer,* trans. John W. Doberstein (New York: Schocken Books, 1969), 105.

the postmodern self and the world it inhabits. I believe it is the right way. It is, however, more European in its perception than typically American because it is more stark, more relentless, more unflinching. By contrast, James Edwards, writing from the American context, ends at the same point but does so in an unrepentantly upbeat way. There is no doubt, he says, that the "secret logic of Western culture" is nihilism, that "the worm was in the bud all along."[14] "Nihilism," he goes on, "is now the way the world comes to us, the way it sounds itself out in us: it is the way we comport ourselves to what we are given. We are all now nihilists."[15] Nihilist we may be but that for him does not imply the dark denial of meaning in the world, or any kind of debilitating pessimism, or the absence of conscience. No, it is simply the newly acquired postmodern sensibility that life passes through our own self-constructed filters and therefore no one's philosophy or religion can claim to be more ultimate than anyone else's. The "I" which reads texts is socially conditioned so it can claim no certainty about its "read" on those texts or, for that matter, on reality. Edwards ends up by speaking of religion as "something that exacts an absolute discipline of truthfulness and yet refuses the consolation of an absolute achievement of truth."[16] Of course we need to be modest about ourselves as knowers, realistic about ourselves as rationalizers, but how, one wonders, can we have a discipline of truthfulness if absolute truth eludes us? Would it not be better to say that the tree of Truth was blown away in a tornado and therefore any perception that it still casts a shadow is an illusion? Few, of course, can actually live as if the world had been divested of every single shred of meaning. It is too painful and bewildering to be in such a predicament. So, what we see here at an intellectual level is the kind of psychological maneuvering which is also being acted out in the mall every day as the Void left behind by the departure of meaning is filled with surrogates and fleeting palliatives.

In America, then, the disintegration of the self and the disintegration of its world do not commonly express themselves in the dark lan-

14. James C. Edwards, *The Plain Sense of Things: The Fate of Religion in an Age of Normal Nihilism* (University Park: The Pennsylvania State University Press, 1997), 43.
15. Edwards, *The Plain Sense of Things*, 46.
16. Edwards, *The Plain Sense of Things*, 238.

guage of this earlier literature, though there are exceptions to this in some of the rock music from the 1970s onwards which is full not only of obscenities but of violence, hatred, and fear in a world turned empty. More typically, though, when this bewilderment spilled out into the wider culture in America, it lost its edge. In this earlier literature, there were a sharpness, a painful aching loss, an unbearable emptiness, a disorientation of being, but when this sense of dislocation from life became domesticated in the wider culture it also became much tamer. It lost its acuteness. By the 1990s, when we encounter the television series *Seinfeld,* for example, this sense of internal loss and disorientation had been turned into a brilliantly acted but completely banal sitcom. *Seinfeld,* Thomas Hibbs writes, was "a show about the comical consequences of life in a world void of ultimate significance or fundamental meaning." This show, he adds, was "by its own account, a show about nothing."[17] The darkness of soul had lifted, though not its emptiness. Now we were no longer serious enough to do anything but smirk. The journey into the postmodern world, from the writers of this literature of bewilderment into television shows like this, is one from darkness in the depths to mockery on the surface, from suicide to shallow snickers. The Void is the constant; how we live with it is where the differences arise.

Fear, Anxiety, and Dread

There is often a difference, therefore, between the earlier more self-conscious European nihilism and nihilism as a cultural ethos in postmodern America. The difference is less in the conclusion at which people arrive than in how they experience their world. Cultural nihilism, which is what is growing as the postmodern ethos takes hold, registers more psychologically than philosophically. And yet, whatever the primary experience of the outside world is, that world itself is seen to be empty and the human being is seen as having been disconnected from meaning, as adrift, as ultimately directionless.

At a popular level, this is rarely expressed overtly. Thus it is that there is a physician who plies his healing arts, but he does so only for the recompense which will buy a home in the Bahamas and then, per-

17. Hibbs, *Shows About Nothing,* 22.

haps, another in Aspen, Colorado. Nothing is said to the patient about the empty, useless world to which he or she is being restored. And thus the corporate executive navigates her way through the jungle of office politics, sacrifices family and social life for the next rung up, gouges and destroys to get ahead, and yet, at the end of the day, realizes that it is only a game. It is because there is nothing else that it can only be a game, intense though it may be. However, to reveal any sense of detachment from the daily contest would be lethal to upward mobility because that mobility takes itself with the utmost seriousness. It has a degree of seriousness about it that would, actually, be more appropriate in a worship setting. It therefore creates its own psychological world in which its own enterprise assumes overwhelming importance and creates its own self-enclosed meaning which is at best paper-thin because it has to be maintained in a world which has no indelible, fixed, enduring reality. Other philosophies have had agendas, goals, and objectives; this has none because at the heart of reality, it is believed, there is Nothing. There is just experience, just accumulation, just passing fun, just private perceptions and preferences.

This description, however, may suggest that there is more clarity in this nihilistic outlook than is warranted, for assumptions often are not recognized and often are murky. Thielicke has said of this cultural nihilism that it has "an attitude in which the question of meaning is no longer negated but it is simply not allowed to appear. It is a matter of unquestioning surrender to the moment, to the immediate activity, the immediate duty, the immediate pleasure."[18] There is, in other words, no final purpose, no ultimate meaning that is considered in the pursuit of life but, in fact, the empty Void within is pushed from view by substituting in its place a multitude of activities and much consumption because solitude is a threat, an intolerable affliction.

This, of course, is one of the main differences between this cultural nihilism and that of the earlier writers who have been mentioned. Especially in existentialism, the inner void and the anxiety it exudes were not concealed, still less stifled by activity or stuffed with affluence. Rather, it was exposed, stared at, and unflinchingly owned. To do otherwise was considered a fraud, the essence of inauthenticity.

18. Thielicke, *Nihilism,* 148.

How this was understood is well illustrated in the distinction which both Sartre and Heidegger made between fear and anxiety. Fear has to do with specific events. People may fear that the stock market is going to collapse, or that their job will be lost, or that they are being followed by an unknown person on a darkened street, or that they are getting cancer. In each case the fear is focused in something specific and known. Once the object of the fear is removed or disappears, the fear subsides. By contrast, anxiety has to do with the dread we have of ourselves, and it is always with us. A soldier going into battle may fear the impact of the bullet ripping through his flesh, but he may be filled with anxiety about himself because he does not know how he will comport himself in the thick of battle. Will he fight courageously or will he bolt from the battle and be found later, far from the front line, cowering under a bush? He does not know. That is the source of his anxiety. And this anxiety, this dread about ourselves, projects itself onto the world around us. Fear is of specific threats or calamities, but this dread becomes the lens through which life is seen, and it constantly looks sinister, ominous, forboding. This dread, however, must not be masked or muffled in the quest for an untroubled existence. To do so is to surrender, to consign oneself to superficiality, banality, and inauthenticity.

This anxiety, then, begins with what is unknown within but it inevitably extends to the Unknown within others and, wider still, to the Unknown within the whole cosmos. In the context of the Unknown, of the meaningless, the world is stripped of moral borders. Once that has happened, there can be no transgressors because there is nothing left to transgress.[19] In a world without meaning, there are no restraints. Once God has died and the world has become empty, humans assume a terrifying freedom. It is the freedom to slip off every moral command and every remnant of belief. The 1991 movie *Cape Fear,* Martin Scorsese's remake of a much earlier *noir* film, provides a rather graphic illustration of this. An ex-con, Cady, returns to tyrannize the lawyer who he believed had let him down and to find pleasure in spreading some fear. In the midst of this spree of violence, Cady sidles off to the library to read Nietzsche's *Thus Spake Zarathustra.* Thus is the connection

19. See Wolfhart Pannenberg, *Christianity in a Secularized World,* trans. John Bowden (New York: Crossroad, 1989), 47-49.

made directly between nihilism and the dread of what lies in the darkness outside.[20]

We rightly fear those who are so free, for their actions become unpredictable and unrestrained. This was why all Communist regimes, with their atheistic frameworks, had to become police states. However, this same dynamic is at work outside of the totalitarian states. It has been quite evident in America in the rash of senseless murders in high schools, murders committed by empty teenagers who have been inhabiting their own vacant worlds, worlds in which there are no grounds for restraint. In less grotesque ways, it is also evident in the way in which litigation has expanded exponentially. Where self-restraint declines because there are no grounds for that restraint, the only safety that remains, such as it is, is in the police and in the recourse to the law. When the world becomes meaningless, it also becomes dangerous. Minorities and the weak have much cause for concern when the world becomes empty.

When the Future Dies

It is the loss of any grounding for meaning that also eats away at hope. Viktor Frankl, a psychiatrist who was taken off to the Nazi death-camps during the Second World War, has written with poignant clarity about those who survived and those who did not and in so doing illustrates this point. In the camps, the prisoners were stripped of every semblance of dignity and identity and were under constant threat of death. He wrote about the deadening of emotion that happened as a result, the apathy that so often took hold, and the protective shell of insensitivity in which they took refuge because they had to see so many unspeakable horrors. He also noted that under threat of constant beatings, insults and degradation, prisoners had only their inner lives left and here they could "find a refuge from the emptiness, desolation and spiritual poverty" of their existence.[21] Every strategy was used to stay alive. One of these was to rob the present of its power of destruction by

20. Hibbs, *Shows About Nothing,* 66-75.
21. Viktor E. Frankl, *Man's Search for Meaning: An Introduction to Logotherapy,* trans. Ilse Lasch (New York: Simon and Schuster, 1959), 38.

dwelling in the past, by letting the imagination return to past events, to revisit other people, and by doing so to enter a different world. However, although the past offered some fleeting respite, it was the future that held out the hope for survival. Those who could see no future for themselves simply gave up. They were doomed. "With this loss of belief in the future," he wrote, such a person "also lost his spiritual hold." The prisoner would typically refuse one day to get dressed. Blows, curses, threats, and whippings were to no avail. The prisoner had given up. "There he remained, lying in his own excreta, and nothing bothered him any more."[22] For such a prisoner, meaning had died because there was nothing left for which to survive.

What is so striking is the comparison which naturally arises between these prisoners who had been stripped of every remnant of dignity and reduced to disposable refuse, and those in the postmodern West who likewise have lost their hold on meaning but for precisely the opposite reason. They have not been deprived of everything, nor have they been treated brutally. On the contrary, they have everything, live with unprecedented convenience and freedom, but the future in a world without meaning is as impotent to summon up hope and direction as was that of the prisoners who gave up in the camps. The difference, however, is that these postmoderns, unlike the prisoners, have ways of offsetting this inner corrosion. Luxury and plenty, entertainment and recreation, sex and drugs, become the ways of creating surrogate meaning or momentary distraction, or at least some numbness. It is surrogate meaning and distraction to conceal the inner blankness, the depletion of self, so that its aches can be forgotten. In the "literature of bewilderment," nothing filled this aching Void, for that would be false and inauthentic. In America, things are different.

Modern consumption, as I have suggested, is not simply about shopping, because what we are buying is not simply goods and services. Modern consumption is often about finding substitutes for an ultimate meaning and in this sense it serves a philosophical function. It is for many about the way they construct themselves, their way of looking at the world in the absence of meaning. It is, therefore, becoming the defining focus of a new kind of civilization. What was once just

22. Frankl, *Man's Search for Meaning*, 74.

about buying goods has become a way of producing private, fleeting moments of meaning which compensate for the many other losses in postmodern life. Postmoderns find themselves always moving and never stopping, going from one temporary oasis to another in search of palliatives for what is bleak within, but it is always movement without a destination. Self-definition is constructed only through what is present, by what can be purchased, and by what can be experienced.

This alternative to having to think about any ultimate meaning is, however, a self-defeating strategy. This kind of consuming takes us along a path where choice is so diverse that we experience life only as one incident of choosing after another, none of which has any necessary relation to the others. Indeed, this itself is but a metaphor for what has happened throughout life. It has all fragmented: God has apparently drifted off from society, the Church has taken refuge from the outside world and finds sanctuary in its inner self, the extended family has splintered off from the nuclear, and generations are divided against each other. Once our world was centered; now it is not. Once there were ultimate principles of criteria; now there are not. Once there was Authority; now there are only authorities, specialists who have mastered a small corner of life's complexity. We have been left to drift in the flow of melting reality. This is our nihilism. However, it is not frontal nihilism. It is, instead, sly, evasive, superficial, and furtive in its strategies for avoiding the question of ultimate meaning, hopeful in its ability to surmount the Void. It assumes the complete emptiness of life, but it does not want to linger over that emptiness. Rather than be tortured with dark thoughts, it is better just to make a joke, move on, and buy something.

So pervasive has this sense of inner disorientation and emptiness become, that it is tempting to think that this is a uniquely postmodern phenomenon, that it is what defines people living in this time in the Western world. There is, in fact, a strong argument that can be made to justify this reading of matters. It is in the modern period that the heavens have been shaken, the person has been uprooted from place and family, and what was sure has yielded to what is uncertain, what was permanent to what is transient, what was enduring to what is fading. This is the context in which human restlessness, drifting, and the pains of *anomie* arise and the dissolution of the self is so often the outcome.

These postmodern afflictions should be quite out of place, it would seem, in a traditional society in which the unchanging supernatural order has an unchallenged matter-of-factness about it, social customs are enduring, human relations are settled, families are intact, the rhythms of life are predictable, and beliefs are stable. Yet, such turns out not to be the case. Strange as it may be, the experience of meaninglessness is also an ancient phenomenon. This gives us an important insight into its nature, for while there are abundant reasons for thinking that modern social organization is powerfully able to unhinge the soul and tip it into a seemingly empty, nihilistic world, this clearly cannot be the sole factor in play. I therefore now need to explore this other factor, and to do so I must try to place this cultural meaninglessness within a theological framework.

This Side of the Sun

The question of contemporary meanininglessness, then, is one that has two sides to it, I would argue, and these two sides are sociological and soteriological. However, they have played out a little differently in relation to each other in different times. Biblically speaking, meaninglessness is primarily *soteriological* in nature and only secondarily sociological; as it is experienced by people, its soteriological nature is often not comprehended. If anything is comprehended at all, it is only what is sociological and that might well be misconstrued.

Today, postmodern culture inclines people to see the world as if it had been stripped of its structures of meaning, of its morality, of any viable worldview which is universal, and it collapses all of reality into the self. It eats away at every vestige of meaning for which people grasp. In these ways, it is one of the forms in which the biblical understanding of "the world" takes shape in the West. It therefore adds weight, or gives further reality to, what is soteriological, to that emptiness of human experience which is the outcome to alienation from God and which is the present consequence of his wrath. It is the consequence of being relationally severed from him. And that is registered in the twilight knowledge of God which still persists in human consciousness, leaving people "without excuse," but the relational disjuncture is so substantial and so complete as to leave them always disoriented, always caught in the coils of painful futility.

Nowhere is this better illumined than in the book of Ecclesiastes. Its opening salvo is the author's refrain, "vanity of vanities" (1:2), which recurs some thirty-one times in the book. How utterly transitory, empty, and meaningless is life! It is nothing but the pursuit of the wind. That is the word of the Preacher, considered by many to have been Israel's King Solomon. And what he recounts is his tortured search for some contentment, some respite from, even some escape from, the relentlessly empty world he came to inhabit "under the sun." This phrase is repeated twenty-three times and this appears to be the author's way of speaking of what, in the modern world, has come to be seen in the secularization of the public square whereby life is dislocated from the divine order and all that is ultimate and absolute pushed away to an outer periphery where it becomes irrelevant. His was a traditional society from which the divine had not been banished, but within his own private world things were different. Within his own consciousness, he had become disjoined from what was true, enduring, permanent, and ultimate. In his private world, nothing had significance.

It is useless, Solomon said, to seek for wisdom that unlocks the meaning of life, for in his search he had found only futility (Eccl. 1:17). The human being is afflicted by the longing for knowledge but thwarted in its pursuit. What we see is but the passing, fading surface, and what lies behind it is lost in obscurity. Not only so, but the world is filled with unrequited desire and with vexatious experience. Indeed, everything appears to be random. There is no moral pattern, no reason as to why misfortune strikes this or that person. It strikes the good and bad indiscriminately (9:2). This initial search for wisdom, then, brought Solomon no peace, no inner quietude, but rather restlessness and sorrow. Nor did he find any relief in party-making, revelry, and pleasure-seeking. All of this turned out to be hollow and empty as well (2:1-2). The emptiness within could not be assuaged by ceaseless activity, or by work, or wealth (2:4-11; 4:7-12). Work brings no unmitigated pleasure but only care and carping (4:4-6). "So I turned about and gave my heart up to despair over all the toil of my labors under the sun" — the rewards of which would, in any case, be inherited by another (2:20). He came to loathe life (2:17).

Wealth, too, is a powerful seducer. However, as E. J. Dillon noted, experience shows that the pains endured in its accumulation, "and the anxiety suffered in preserving it, effectually destroy our capacity for enjoying the bliss which it is supposed to insure, long before misfortune or death snatches it from our grasp."[23] There is perhaps no more telling picture of the emptiness in even the world's greatness than Solomon provides in Ecclesiastes 2:1-11. Not great works, great houses, not the trappings of power and prestige, not great cultural achievements in themselves suffice to yield up any enduring meaning. And what we find in others, even in their best moments when they are pursuing the virtues, is the taint of self-serving and the rancid odor of moral corruption which obscures any view of what might be ultimately meaningful. Thus did the Preacher demolish every attempt at finding meaning "under the sun" in a fallen world. For him, it was not possible for *Eros* to reach into the infinite and find meaning

This is not, of course, all that is said in Ecclesiastes about the meaning of life. Yet it is striking to hear sentiments being expressed which, with small linguistic adjustments, could be placed quite comfortably amidst the "literature of bewilderment" written in the last century or in the postmodern context today. And this is so despite the absence then of all that modernization has done to so discomfort life today.

Nor was Solomon alone in expressing this outlook. A number of the sentiments heard in Ecclesiastes are echoed in the book of Job. Further, in one telling sentence Paul directly links the meaninglessness of the world and the resurrection of Christ. This is important because what it tells us is that this sense of life's emptiness, the Void which is at its center, is not simply a postmodern experience; its deepest connection is not sociological but, in fact, *soteriological.* This gives us an entirely different way of thinking about this postmodern disposition.

Without the resurrection of Christ, Paul argued, his own work as an apostle would be futile, his struggles pointless, and not only would this meaninglessness engulf him but it would blanket everyone, for if "the dead are not raised," he concludes, "'Let us eat and drink, for to-

23. E. J. Dillon, *The Sceptics of the Old Testament* (London: Isbister and Co., 1895), 101.

morrow we die'" (I Cor. 15:32). His argument is rooted in the general order of resurrection, of which Christ's is the first fruit. It is the fact of this
resurrection which makes the good life worth pursuing and which
judges the alternative, which is a life of license, revelry, and emptiness.
The words he quoted come from a time in Israel's life when Jerusalem
was being besieged. That was a time, the prophet Isaiah declared,
when the nation should have taken to sackcloth to mourn for its sins
and disobedience. Instead, the streets were filled with mirth and party-
making. "Let us eat and drink," they said to one another, "for tomorrow
we die" (Is. 22:13). Here were people either oblivious to the divine warning or, at least, careless about it, steeling themselves in the face of calamity and in a last orgy of self-abandonment, laughing when they
should have been crying. This was life lived "under the sun," life not
framed by ultimate meaning. Life had become superficial. Life was not
being lived before another order but was being lived simply for its own
sake, on its own terms, for its own pleasures, for its own moment. For
Paul, it is this other order, entered finally through resurrection but
which now penetrates this life, which gives it its purpose. It is this
which explained why he was willing to have his life put "in peril every
hour" (I Cor. 15:30). It explains what energized him (15:10).

Paul's argument is not that life draws meaning simply from immortality — and loses it in the absence of immortality — but, rather, its
meaning derives from the fact of *resurrection*.[24] In this chapter, he

---

24. I do not intend to oppose resurrection to immortality but simply to distinguish between them. In an earlier debate, Oscar Cullmann, for example, opposed immortality to resurrection because the former, he thought, was really a Greek idea. See
his essay "Immortality of the Soul or the Resurrection of the Dead," in *Immortality
and Resurrection: Death in the Western World: Two Conflicting Currents of Thought*, ed.
Krister Stendahl (New York: Macmillan, 1965), 9-53, and C. K. Barrett's reply in his essay "Immortality and Resurrection," in *Resurrection and Immortality: Aspects of
Twentieth-Century Belief*, ed. Charles S. Duthie (London: Samuel Bagster and Sons,
1979), 68-88. Immortality and resurrection, however, are complementary ideas. Immortality is achieved through bodily resurrection in Scripture. Hence, to deny the
one is to deny the other. (See Murray J. Harris, *Raised Immortal: Resurrection and Immortality in the New Testament* [Grand Rapids: William B. Eerdmans, 1983], 229-33).
The idea of immortality "guarantees that resurrection is seen as a state rather than
simply as an event; as permanent rather than a temporary condition; and as a transformed state sustained by the life and power of God" (236). Resurrection, however,
guarantees that the idea of immortality is seen as "personal rather than ideal, racial,

speaks of the resurrection of believers in Christ. And this resurrection is itself evidence of the eternal life secured by and granted through the death of Christ. Without this resurrection, faith is void and preaching useless (I Cor. 15:14), and "you are still in your sins" (15:17); because of this resurrection, new life has been secured (15:22), death has been vanquished (15:55-57) and a fatal blow has been delivered to "every rule and every authority and power" (15:24) which has reared itself against the rule of God in the universe. At the Cross, Christ triumphed over his enemies. In that triumph lie human freedom and meaning. It is, then, the disturbed moral order that Christ has rectified in his death and it is from this righted moral order that meaning in life derives. Paul's teaching is not that life loses its emptiness because there is life beyond the grave but that what has made life empty is destroyed by Christ's death and resurrection. Those in Ephesus to whom he wrote he described as "having no hope and without God in the world" (Eph. 2: 12). They were hopeless and godless, that is, until Christ's death brought reconciliation with the Father and, as a result, entrance into the wealth of meaning that God's acceptance brought.

It is the fact of the resurrection, therefore, that connects us to a moral and spiritual order that lies beyond the grave. And it is this order that sends its clarifying light back into this life today. Its intrusion into life is what, in fact, gives to life its meaning because, in the end, nothing is insignificant. On the day of judgment, it will be discovered that as transient and fading as life seems, apparently ever in "the sunset of dissolution," nothing, in fact, has been obliterated. Nothing is ever lost. All is remembered, and all is subject to the divine reversal of human values and expectations which God's judgment entails. In that day, what seemed like a most insignificant act, such as the gift of a cup of water, an act that was forgotten, is remembered by God and accorded real, virtuous significance (Matt. 25:31-40). The wicked, the psalmist says, speak arrogantly and act oppressively because, they say, "The Lord does not see; the God of Jacob does not perceive" (Ps. 94:7). How mistaken they are! We are, in Kundera's words, "nailed to eternity as Jesus

or pantheistic; as corporate, rather than individualistic; and as somatic rather than spiritual" (234). However, what resurrection in biblical terms also does is to put immortality into a soteriological framework, which is the point being made here.

Christ was nailed to the Cross" but this need not be a terrifying burden. It can, in fact, be a liberating gift.

God Whispers in the Night

It is perhaps ironic that the most foundational and profound causes of the sense of meaninglessness are themselves delivered in the experience itself. Why are we tormented by the sense of life's emptiness and randomness? From one angle, as I have just suggested, the reason is one of spiritual dislocation, of living "under the sun." From another angle, however, the reason is that that sense is itself a judgment, an expression of the wrath of God, and a harbinger of much worse to come. This is the inescapable conclusion to be drawn from what Paul wrote about natural revelation.

That there is a twilight knowledge of God that pervades human consciousness is indisputable from a biblical angle and it is developed in two directions which actually also intersect. And their point of intersection lies in the conscience. From one angle, the dependability, orderliness, and beauty of creation all bespeak a Creator who is in covenantal relation with the creation (Gen. 8:21-22; 9:16). In his evangelistic address in Lystra, Paul spoke of this creation, as a result, as being a "witness" to God in that "he did good and gave you from heaven rains and fruitful seasons, satisfying your hearts with food and gladness" (Acts 14:17). This is really a particular application of what the psalmist says more generally, that the heavens "speak," "they are telling the glory of God" (Ps. 19:1), and even though there are no audible words there is still communication (Ps. 19:3).

The other angle from which this is seen is the fact that the human being remains a *moral* being even in the midst of great moral disorder and confusion and, not least, even as a perpetrator of moral disorder. Indeed, that is what is at the heart of the sense of human futility and confusion. By creation, we are made for a moral world that we cannot honor but from which we cannot disengage. Paul argues that this fact is illumined both externally from the creation and internally from our own moral fabric. From the creation, "from the things that have been made" (Rom. 1:20), are revealed "God's eternal power and deity." As a result, we "know God" (1:21), Paul declares. Yet this knowledge, which clearly is not saving, is no match for the willful disobedience of fallen human nature. The result is that God's existence and character are not allowed to order human life. The consequence of this is that his "wrath" (1:18) is disclosed against every failure in the religious ("ungodliness") and moral ("wickedness") spheres, every failure to acknowledge God for who he is and to live life in a way that reflects his moral character.

All stand under divine judgment. God thunders out his rejection of human pride, arrogance and its fraudulent sense of self-confidence in his presence.[25] This divine No can be heard in the wind, apprehended in the world around us, and it stands as the unyielding barrier, not only into the saving knowledge of God, but to every attempt to forge meaning on our own terms and in the absence of submission to God's Word. "Even the unbeliever encounters God," writes Barth, "but he does not penetrate through to the truth of God that is hidden from him, and so he is broken to pieces on God, as Pharaoh was."[26] Despite its appearances of success, this is what is surely happening in the new spiritual quest examined in the last chapter.

This wrath of which Paul speaks, then, cannot be a disclosure

25. Karl Barth, *The Epistle to the Romans*, trans. Edwyn C. Hoskyns (New York: Oxford University Press, 1968), 42. While there is truth in what Barth held, he also developed his own kind of nihilism which is not helpful. His position was, of course, built around the Kantian distinction between the noumenal and phenomenal. That is, the mind knows what is grasped within sense experience only and cannot know ultimate causations or meanings behind or beyond sense experience. It cannot take hold of God. True faith requires as a condition of its existence the destruction of all human possibility, the recognition that all thought is ambiguous and fraught with uncertainty, and that the world is empty and stripped of all meaning. Only if God breaks through into this situation, breaks through to us, are we able to know of his existence and presence. The traditional doctrine of election is limited to soteriology; this transforms that doctrine into an all-encompassing epistemological standpoint. There is a sense, then, in which the faithful person in Barth's thought stands cheek by jowl with the atheist. And with the nihilist. "For Barth," writes Carr, "nihilism was not the end result of theological inquiry, but, in an important sense, its point of departure; nor is nihilism presented as an alternative to Christian faith, but as an essential part of its makeup" (Carr, 76). It was, of course, this nihilism which Emil Brunner rightly challenged.

26. Barth, *The Epistle to the Romans*, 43.

made only at the end of time, for he speaks of it as a present reality.[27] And in three parallel statements (Rom. 1:24, 26, 28) he explains the present outworking of this judgment. Fallen human beings have dishonored God; God now acts so that they will dishonor themselves. There is more at stake in this divine giving-up than simply bare permission for people to sin. And there is more at stake than simple cause and effect in the moral realm. God, in fact, is *active* in this judgment. He no longer restrains human beings in their expressions of sin and so sin becomes, in the short run, its own judgment. As God's restraints are lifted, and moral and sexual disorder follow (Rom. 1:24-32), the jarring and painful confusions which are part and parcel of the human experience become somber prophecies of a yet greater judgment to come.

This is not all. The additional consequence of this willful disregard of God is the fact that life becomes empty and meaningless. Paul's actual language is that "they became futile in their thinking and their senseless minds were darkened" (Rom. 1:21). Fallen human reason is much given to fallacious ideas and fraudulent judgments because God has given it up to a "reprobate mind" (1:28). Indeed, it is not only fallen minds that are subject to the curse of emptiness but the whole universe suffers under this affliction (8:20-21).

In a fallen world, Fate, Chance, Material, and Emptiness then assume God's place in life.[28] They become the organizing forces in the creation. The outworking of this inner hollowness nevertheless appears to be the essence of wisdom (I Cor. 3:20)! However, the "more the unbroken man marches along his road secure of himself," wrote Barth, "the more surely does he make a fool of himself, the more certainly do that morality and that manner of life which are built up upon forgetting the abyss, upon a forgetting of men's true home, turn out to be a lie."[29] The vanity, emptiness, and futility of fallen reason are the affliction vis-

---

27. Because this is future wrath reaching into the present but by no means exhausting itself now, Markus Barth is correct to speak of its nature as eschatological. Markus Barth, *Justification: Pauline Texts Interpreted in the Light of the Old and New Testaments,* trans. A. M. Woodruff (Grand Rapids: William B. Eerdmans, 1971), 26. Cf. Wolfhart Pannenberg, *Jesus — God and Man,* trans. Lewis L. Wilkins and Duane A. Priebe (Philadelphia: The Westminster Press, 1977), 265.

28. Barth, *The Epistle to the Romans,* 43.

29. Barth, *The Epistle to the Romans,* 49.

ited upon sinners by God's judgment. In every age, this has followed different directions. In the postmodern world today, whose center lies in the autonomous self, all of which is yielding a bountiful harvest of intellectual emptiness and moral disorder, this is not good news. What the postmodern world celebrates in its rejection of all absolutes and in its assumed right to define all reality privately is a sign of God's wrath (cf. Rom. 1:22).

People may plead ignorance in this situation but Paul says they are "without excuse" (Rom. 1:20). Later, he develops this in terms of internal consciousness. Even the Gentiles who are without the written moral law still show that what it requires "is written on their hearts" because their conscience is actively at work within them (Rom. 2:14-15; cf. I Cor. 9:21).[30] This fact is really an anomaly, at least today, because death, some might think, is the purest expression of nihilism inasmuch as the person who dies will no longer be burdened with the internal necessity of having to make moral judgments in a world which, in its emptiness, undercuts all such judging. But in the absence of death, the living have to endure this tangle of contradictions within themselves: they make moral judgments all the time because by nature they are moral beings, but there is no universe of meaning in their minds that allows for any moral judgments to be made.

It is no small scandal what Paul has to say here. What is revealed to all people everywhere? It is not that God is loving, though he is. It is not that he is accepting, though sinners may find acceptance with him. It is not that we have natural access to him through the self, though the Greek poet was not wrong to say that "In him we live and move and have our being" so "he is not far from each of us" (Acts 17:27-28). It is not that we can find him on our own terms, though he should be sought (Acts 17:27). No, what is revealed is the fact that he is *wrathful*. It is true that this disclosure comes alongside the fact that the creation also bespeaks his glory and the greatness of his power. Yet the greatness of his power and his glory do not obscure the fact that God is alienated from human beings. Indeed, his glory is precisely the reason that he is alienated!

---

30. James Q. Wilson has gathered considerable empirical evidence which points to the reality of this natural revelation. See his *The Moral Sense* (New York: Free Press, 1993).

There is, as a result, already a faint foretaste of final judgment as the consequences of sin visit their retribution upon the sinner. This is scandalous to a postmodern ear, but locked in that scandal is the key to meaning in the world and in that meaning there is hope.

God Reaches Down

The Presence of Eternity

Given the collapse of Enlightenment rationality after the 1960s, what alternatives do we have for engaging what is ultimate and how can we find the grounding for beliefs about truth and error, right and wrong? Or are we, like the postmodern nihilists and the earlier existentialist, obliged to live with the fact that there is no such grounding, that there is no objective truth "out there"? If natural reason cannot gain entrance to this world of what is ultimate — and postmoderns now see this to be a doomed and arrogant undertaking — then there remain only two other alternatives: the self and revelation.

Today, throughout America, as we have seen, the option that is being exercised is for the self, for Eros spirituality, for an assumed access which is unmediated into the sacred. In this new spiritual quest, it is the self which is the conduit into the spiritual world. It is through the self that seekers imagine themselves to be peering into, and experiencing, the eternal and by doing so hoping to find some meaning. It is supposed that in the self we receive intuitions about the eternal. And though its language was a little different, this was really the way the earlier Liberal Protestantism traveled until it sank beneath the human debris of war in Europe and the Depression of the 1930s in America, incapable of addressing evil and suffering. It had no place to stand outside the culture. It could offer no judgment on human depravity. It had to assume the innocence of its own means of access into the divine and that assumption simply blew apart.

The alternative connection to what is ultimate is, of course, revelation. In this view, it is not the human being reaching up to seize the meaning of life, or gazing into itself for that meaning, but God reaching down to explain life's meaning. In this understanding, there can be no speaking of

God, no speaking of meaning, before his speaking to us is heard. This way was treated rudely by the Enlightenment luminaries because it both limited human freedom in shaping the meaning of reality and it resorted to what was miraculous in the way revelation has been given. And it has not been treated any more kindly by the postmoderns for whom its grand, overarching Story is anathema and who do not believe that they can escape their own subjectivity. But this is the Christian confession.

This confession is rooted in the fact, as Martin Luther strikingly noted, that the basis of our fellowship with God is not holiness but sin. In the *Eros* spirituality of our day, not to mention the many earlier expressions which bear a family resemblance to it, the assumption which is made is that natural spirituality itself forms the basis of acceptance, itself provides the *entree* to God's presence, and itself offers no impediment to that entry. The biblical perspective, however, is not only that this spirituality of the "natural" human being is flawed and offensive to God but that no amount of moral effort, self-discipline, or self-restraint can ever form a basis of acceptance. The upward reach of *Eros* is always and forever blocked by the God who makes himself inaccessible to it. Biblical faith is about *Agape*, about God reaching down to disclose himself to those who could not otherwise know him, and about grace reaching those who otherwise could not be restored to him.

To speak of these contrasting loves, *Agape* and *Eros*, the one reaching down and the other trying to reach up, is simply to state that there is a boundary between God and human beings. This boundary is not self-evident at all. If it were, there would be no shadow culture of spirituality in America today. In fact, as Barth says, revelation "is needed for knowing that God is hidden and man blind."[31] It is in the light of biblical revelation that the boundary becomes really visible.

31. Karl Barth, *Church Dogmatics,* trans. G. T. Thomson (5 vols.; Edinburgh: T&T Clark, 1936-77), I, ii, 29. The necessity of revelation for which Barth argued was, unfortunately, hitched up to a matching concern which was to reject every attempt at apologetics. This clearly is not a biblical position. Before the Areopagus, for example, Paul thoroughly engaged, and destroyed, the worldviews of the day before speaking about Christ. See D. A. Carson, "Athens Revisited," in *Telling the Truth: Evangelizing Postmoderns,* ed. D. A. Carson (Grand Rapids: Zondervan, 2000), 393-94. See also William Barclay, "A Comparison of Paul's Missionary Preaching and the Preaching to the Church," in *Apostolic History and the Gospel,* ed. W. Ward Gasque and Ralph P. Martin (Grand Rapids: William B. Eerdmans, 1970), 165-75.

Rock of Ages, cleft for me,
Let me hide myself in Thee;
Let the water and the blood,
From thy wounded side which flowed,
Be of sin the double cure,
Save from wrath and make me pure.

Could my tears forever flow,
Could my zeal no languor know,
These for sin could not atone;
Thou must save, and Thou alone:
In my hand no price I bring,
Simply to thy cross I cling.

Augustus Toplady

The importance of this, of course, is that it also declares that meaning is given in *Agape* and is never siezed through *Eros.* It comes in and with the revelation which reaches across that boundary from God to sinners. It is this which then destroys illusions, misconceptions and the assorted frauds that are perpetrated about the meaning of the cosmos. This downward movement of *Agape,* this majestic condescension of God as he graciously makes himself known to us and in that knowledge gives to us an understanding of life's meaning which corresponds to objective reality, is developed in several ways in the New Testament. What I need to do now, then, is to try to compress this material as much as I can, thereby painting with broad strokes or, to change the image, looking more for the forest than the individual trees.

It is impossible to understand how the Bible treats the matter of meaning unless we are able to put ourselves, as it were, within the eyes and hearts and minds of God's ancient people. For it is within the history of his people that all of the foundations are laid for the way in which God brings into life hope and meaning.

The Jewish hope, which slowly swelled in its passage through time, became quite simple. It was the hope that one day the world order would be set right, that what was wrong would be banished and what was right would be rewarded and God's people would be given rest from their enemies. The meaning of the present for those in the post-exilic period hinged to a significant degree on a belief in this future in which what they had lost would be restored, what they longed for would be recovered. It was toward this future that they were oriented and toward which they were journeying.

The Christian confession, as we have seen, is that this future has already arrived, that it has been realized in ways more grand than could have been imagined, that it was divinely ushered in through Christ's death, and that it can be experienced and tasted now, thereby transforming human life. For those in Christ, "the old has passed away, behold, the new has come" (II Cor. 5:17). This is not simply a personal statement, that at a certain time their conversion happened. It is even more profound than that. It is Paul's affirmation that those in Christ have already entered the age to come and have been extracted from the world of darkness in which they once were at ease and at home.

Christian hope is not about wishing that things will get better, that somehow emptiness will go away, meaning will return, and life will be stripped of its uncertainties, its psychological aches and anxieties. Nor does it have anything to do with techniques for improving fallen human life, be those therapeutic or even religious. Hope, instead, has to do, biblically speaking, with the knowledge that "the age to come" is already penetrating "this age," that the sin, death, and meaninglessness of the one is being transformed by the righteousness, life, and meaning of the other, that what has emptied out life, what has scarred and blackened it, is being displaced by what is rejuvenating and transforming it. More than that, hope is hope because it knows it has become part of a realm, a kingdom, which endures, where evil is doomed and will be banished, that it has left behind it the ship of "this age" which is sinking. And if this realm did not exist, Christians would be "of all men most to be pitied" (I Cor. 15:19), because their hope would be groundless and they would have lived out an illusion (cf. Ps. 73:4-14). This I now need to sketch out and will do so in three steps that have to do with eschatology, christology, and the doctrine of justification.

These three doctrines, on first glance, may not seem to relate naturally to the theme of meaninglessness in postmodern culture. However, the point of connection is the inbreaking of "the age to come" and what I will show is how this motif connects the person of Christ and his work, which I will view selectively through the doctrine of justification. It is in the inbreaking of this redemptive age through Christ that meaning and hope are found.

For a long time in traditional systematic theologies, eschatology occupied the final section of the work and was concerned with "the last things" or "the end times," with matters like the return of Christ, the millennium, judgment, and the destruction of Evil.[32] These volumes were, in a way, replicating a view encountered in Judaism. It was the exile that had formed the soil in which hope began to grow. It was the hope that one day God would act in a decisive way both to reestablish Israel and judge the earth. This hope had to do with restoration to Israel's land, the place of the Torah in its life, and with justice. "When Israel's god acted," says Wright, "Jews would be restored to their ancestral rights and would practice their ancestral religion, with the rest of the world looking on in awe and/or making pilgrimages to Zion, and/or being ground to powder under Jewish feet."[33] And this came to be associated with the arrival of Messiah, although there were differing expectations about the Messiah. Thus it was that time came to be bisected into two: the age before Messiah came and the age after he had arrived. The first age ended as the new age began. And these two ages were as different as night is from day. In the one, God seemed to be hidden; in the other, his presence would be plain. In the one, wickedness abounded, but in the other it would be punished. What was hoped for, therefore, was a great reversal of the world order as Israel knew it, one that would set it back on its feet again.

However, one of the great gains in biblical study in the last cen-

---

32. Pannenberg has correctly observed that because "God and his lordship form the central content of eschatological salvation, eschatology is not just the subject of a single chapter in dogmatics; it determines the perspective of Christian doctrine as a whole. With the eschatological future God's eternity comes into time and it is thus creatively present to all the temporal things that precede this future." Wolfhart Pannenberg, *Systematic Theology,* trans. Geoffrey W. Bromiley (3 vols.; Grand Rapids: William B. Eerdmans, 1991-98), III, 531.

33. N. T. Wright, *The New Testament and the People of God* (Minneapolis: Fortress Press, 1992), 285.

tury was the realization that eschatology is not some final adjunct to the body of theological knowledge but more like a thread which is woven throughout its many themes. And it was the coming of Christ that radically transformed it. The conquest of sin, death, and the devil and the establishment of the Rule of God do not await some future, cataclysmic realization. It has, in fact, already been inaugurated although its presence is quite unobtrusive. As Oscar Cullmann notes, "that event on the cross, together with the resurrection which followed, was the already concluded decisive battle."[34] Thus it is that, in the period between Christ's two comings, "this age" and "the age to come" coexist. As a result, eschatology, or the penetration of God's future into the current time of sin and death, is light that floods across a number of New Testament doctrines. Certainly in soteriology, everywhere there is the "already/not yet" tension that the presence of eternity in time creates[35] — or, more accurately, that the presence of Christ's victory that is already present amidst fallen human life creates.

It is important to understand that this is a line of thought that is quite foreign to our typically individualistic patterns of thought that are so common in the Church today. If there is a division in time which we recognize it is that which lies behind, and that which comes after, our own personal conversions. Before this time, there may have been confusion, sadness, and drug use; after this time, sight began to be restored, life began to become more ordered, and things began to look more hopeful. Without in any way diminishing the reality of God's work in people's lives, we should nevertheless note that this is not the most fundamental division that the Bible recognizes.

Paul says that God sent his Son "when the time had fully come" (Gal. 4:4) and that he made known his plan in Christ "in the fullness of time" (Eph. 1:10). It would be quite mistaken to suppose that all he meant was that this had happened at a propitious moment. In Ephesians, his thought is that the redemptive-historical work which God had been doing reached its end in Christ and this coincides with the

---

34. Oscar Cullmann, *Christ and Time: The Primitive Christian Conception of Time and History,* trans. Floyd V. Filson (Philadelphia: The Westminster Press, 1950), 84.

35. This language is borrowed from Rudolf Bultmann, *The Presence of Eternity: History and Eschatology* (New York: Harper and Brothers, 1957).

fact of which he says in Galatians that world time ended, not in the sense that clocks suddenly stopped, but that with Christ "this present age" died.[36] There is not a self-help program on the market today which is not, in some way, utilizing the knowledge, resources, techniques, products, and tools of this "age" which, in biblical terms, is dead. It is filled with offers of help and of hope, of meaning and of fulfillment, and even of surrogate regeneration, but they all come from a world that is spiritually dead and therefore of dubious worth. That is an extraordinary, a breath-takingly radical position to take. The New Testament takes it unapologetically.

There is certainly anticipation in the New Testament that the period in which they were living was coming to a close and the "last days" were beginning. Thus it was at Pentecost that Joel's vision of "the last days" was signaled as having arrived in the miracle of the tongues. In Hebrews, the incarnation of the Son in the "last days" was understood as inaugurating God's judgment of evil and the coming of his presence of blessing (Heb. 1:2-5). In the consummation of the ages, the Son put away sin (Heb. 9:26). And the deception, false teaching and rebellion characteristic of the last days or the "end days" were already present in Paul's time (I Tim. 4:1; II Tim. 3:1). As Paul put it, upon us "the end of the ages has come" (I Cor. 10:11).[37]

It is especially in the language of the two ages, however, that we see the reorganized understanding of eschatology taking shape. It is true that there is no systematic treatment of it, so some questions do not get resolved explicitly. The most important of these is the relation between the language of the Kingdom of God in the Synoptic Gospels and the "this age"/"the age to come" in the epistles. The language of the Kingdom more or less disappears in the epistles. If we are to assume the essential unity of the revelation we have in the New Testament, as I believe we should, then it is not unreasonable to suppose that the equivalent of the Gospels' Kingdom language is that of the two ages in the epistles, that this is simply a different way of speaking

36. Herman Ridderbos, *Paul: An Outline of His Theology*, trans. John Richard de Witt (Grand Rapids: William B. Eerdmans, 1975), 45.

37. See G. K. Beale, "The Eschatological Conception of New Testament Theology," in *Eschatology in Bible and Theology*, ed. Kent E. Brower and Mark W. Elliott (Downers Grove: InterVarsity Press, 1997), 11-52.

of the same reality, perhaps as an adaptation to Gentile audiences unfamiliar with the long Jewish history in which Kingdom language was understood. However, what we also see is how this idea of the two ages is given a treatment even more varied than what we find in the Synoptic Gospels.

In John's Gospel, for example, the intrusion of the "age to come," this inbreaking of God's sovereign, saving, and judging rule through Jesus, is expressed in the language of "eternal life." Jesus is this "life" (Jn. 11:25; 14:6) which was eternally with the Father but has now been historically manifested (I Jn. 1:1-3). Jesus' words are the very words of God (Jn. 3:34; 8:14; 14:10) and so they bring "life" (Jn. 5:24; 6:68; 8:51). And eternal life is something that has already been given to believers (10:28; 17:2-3); it is not something that awaits the final unfolding of events at the end of time. This eternal life is a present reality, received by believing in Jesus (Jn. 3:36; 6:47, 54). And judgment, even though it is a future reality, nevertheless, for believers, was brought into time. For the believer, the judgment has already passed (Jn. 3:18)[38] and already he or she has been resurrected (Jn. 5:24; cf. 11:23-26) even though there will be a bodily resurrection later. The one is an anticipation, a down payment, of the other.

In Paul, the present age is the age characterized by sinful rebellion against God, and the age to come is that in which Christ reigns. However, this Reign has already begun redemptively in the regenerate Church of which Christ is the head. The linguistic contrast between these ages is most explicit in Paul's prayer that Christ might be seen in his exaltation "far above all rule and authority and power and dominion, and above every name that is named, not only in this age but also in that which is to come" (Eph. 1:21). But, as Geerhardus Vos suggests, it is implied in a number of other passages: Rom. 12:2; I Cor. 1:20, 2:6, 8, 3:18; II Cor. 4:4; Gal. 1:4; Eph. 2:2; I Tim. 6:17; Tit. 2:12.[39] This present age belongs to Satan, "the god of this world" (II Cor. 4:4), but for the believer, this age or world has passed, its so-called wisdom has been exposed by Christ (I Cor. 1:20). Paul is not always precise as to where the line lies between these ages. He can speak of the age to come as being

38. On this theme see Rudolf Bultmann, *Theology of the New Testament*, trans. Kendrick Grobel (2 vols.; New York: Charles Scribner's Sons, 1955), II, 37-40.

39. Geerhardus Vos, *Pauline Eschatology* (Grand Rapids: Baker Book House, 1979), 12.

in the future (Eph. 1:21; cf. 2:7) but he can also speak of it as being present (I Cor. 10:11; I Tim. 4:1). It seems clear that for him it is not so much the language that matters but the *fact* that an inbreaking of divine power and grace has happened through Christ which is sending its clarifying, revealing light into life (Rom. 16:25; Gal. 1:12; Eph. 3:3), as it brings eternity into time. The language of the Kingdom of God, then, is collapsed into Paul's christology. To believe on Christ is to enter the Kingdom and is to become a part of the age to come. Paul, however, expands this thought far beyond the personal and ecclesiastical. If Christ is the Lord whom every believer serves, the Head to whom the whole churchly body is responsive, he is also the creator from whom everything derives its existence, the center without which there is no reality. Whether above in the starlit firmament or below within human consciousness, Jesus has "supremacy." So Paul reasons in one of the most exalted christological passages, Colossians 1:15-20.

This is what produces the "already/not yet" tension. It is the delicate balance which has to be maintained between the certainty of what was accomplished and the expectation of its final outworking which is yet to be completed. We are redeemed in full, in that nothing more need or can be added to what Christ has done (Rom. 3:24; Col. 1:14), yet we are not fully redeemed because the life of sin has not yet been destroyed and will not be destroyed until the resurrection body is received (Rom. 8:23; Gal. 2:4). What is said of redemption also cuts though the other motifs in Paul's teaching on salvation, and not least on that of justification. As James Dunn puts it, "something decisive has *already* happened in the event of coming to faith, but . . . the work of God in reclaiming the individual for himself is *not yet* complete."[40] It is the "already" that is decisively present in the truth, power, and reality of God today. What the "already" points toward and anticipates of the "not yet" is what frames the meaning of life. And this is the cradle in which we find hope. John Polkinghorne observes that hope "is essentially moral in its character, for it is for a good future for which we

---

40. James D. G. Dunn, *The Theology of Paul the Apostle* (Grand Rapids: William B. Eerdmans, 1998), 466.

41. John Polkinghorne, *The God of Hope and the End of the World* (New Haven: Yale University Press, 2002), 30.

may dare to hope."[41] It is about this good future that Jesus and the apostles were preoccupied in their language about the age to come.

The language of the Kingdom of God is predominantly that of Jesus but the idea which it describes, the arrival of the "age to come," is central to the thought of his apostolic interpreters. The language is different but the conception is the same. This, says Herman Ridderbos, is what provides "the conceptual connection between Jesus' and Paul's preaching."[42] And it is true of the writer to the Hebrews, too. "The common pattern of New Testament eschatology," writes C. K. Barrett, "is in Hebrews made uncommonly clear. God has begun to fulfill his ancient promises; the dawn of the new age has broken, though the full day has not yet come."[43] The "age to come" is already being tasted and experienced (Heb. 6:4-5) because "the world to come" has already been subjected to Christ's rule (2:5). There is, of course, opposition to his rule (2:8-9; 10:13-14) but there is no doubt as to what the outcome will be (9:26). Thus it is that the author speaks of a salvation being experienced in the present, a redemption, an inheritance, and a covenant each of which is also "eternal" (5:9; 9;12; 9:15; 13:20). In terms that are vivid, the author argues that only the divine Son, coming from above and being incarnate in flesh identical to our own, and acting in our place as a sacrifice, could secure this salvation by destroying sin, death and the devil (2:14; 10:27; 12:18-24).

Majestic Condescension

If the age to come is being tasted and experienced already, the reason is that that future has been made present through Christ. The way that this understanding is shaped in the Synoptic Gospels is, of course, in the language of the Kingdom of God or its reverent equivalent, the Kingdom of Heaven. Exactly what this language means has been an extremely vexed question in gospel criticism and it is not possible here to follow all of the twists and turns in this debate.

42. Herman Ridderbos, *Paul and Jesus: Origin and General Character of Paul's Preaching of Christ*, trans. David H. Freeman (Grand Rapids: Baker, 1958), 22.
43. C. K. Barrett, "The Eschatology of the Epistle to the Hebrews," in *The Background of the New Testament and Its Eschatology*, ed. W. D. Davies and D. Daube (Cambridge: Cambridge University Press, 1956), 391.

There is no question, however, as Wright has contended, that these terms were placed within the context of the Jewish storyline.[44] That story consisted in the conviction that Israel was bound to Yahweh by covenant and so week after week the nation rehearsed how Yahweh, in the past, had protected and delivered her. The first Temple had been the place where Yahweh had dwelled and revealed his glory, so when the Temple was destroyed, Israel suffered a calamity of enormous magnitude. The glory of God had departed and the monarchy had been undone. Thus were the seeds sown from which the hope would arise that God would not only restore the Temple, but also the monarchy and his own people in the future and do all of these things on an even grander scale than before. This narrative of hope included, of course, the destruction of Israel's enemies in an act of judgment. It was this hope that connected immediately with the use of language such as the Kingdom of God. Though the language itself was not familiar in rabbinical teaching or in Philo and is scarce in the Dead Sea Scrolls, nevertheless the thought that God is King did become quite familiar in the prophets. So when Jesus proclaimed the Reign of God he touched the deepest of Jewish hopes and expectations about the end of the world. For this Reign, as Bultmann correctly observed, "would destroy the present course of the world, wipe out all the contra-divine, Satanic power under which the present world groans — and thereby, terminating all pain and sorrow, bring in salvation for the People of God which awaits the fulfillment of the prophets' promises."[45] Yet it is also clear that this hope that God would come and seize control was redirected by Jesus, to the considerable disappointment and confusion of many of those who heard him.

The Kingdom of God in the Gospels is never simply a kingdom. It is the Kingdom of *God.* The primary idea in this language is that God himself has begun to rule. And this, as George Ladd noted, is the key to the puzzle of how the Kingdom is used in the Synoptic Gospels. It assumes different meanings in terms of its realization. "God *is* now the King, but he must *become* King."[46] It thus assumes both a present real-

44. N. T. Wright, *Jesus and the Victory of God* (Minneapolis: Fortress Press, 1996), 202-210.

45. Rudolf Bultmann, *Theology of the New Testament,* trans. Kendrick Grobel (2 vols.; London: SCM Press, 1952), I, 4.

46. George Eldon Ladd, *A Theology of the New Testament* (Grand Rapids: Wil-

ization while also carrying the idea of a fuller and final consummation in the future.

The arrival of this Reign of God was not nationalistically but spiritually focused, which was what caused the consternation among many of Jesus' hearers. Nevertheless, the prophetic vision began to be realized, albeit in an entirely unexpected way, that God would scatter his enemies (Mic. 4:11-13; Is. 13:19; cf. Joel 3:1-17; Zech. 12:1-9), for Satan's forces were being thrown into disarray (Matt. 12:28-29) and they recognized with fear who Jesus was (Mk. 1:24; 5:7-8). The note of judgment which fell on the cities (Lk. 21:20-24; 23:27-31; Matt. 11:20-24) fell decisively on the powers of darkness and Satan's household was plundered (Mk. 3:27).

All of this happened under God's sovereign hand. We can search for the Kingdom of God, pray for it, and look for it, but only God can bring it about (Lk. 23:51; Matt. 6:10, 33; Lk. 12:31).[47] The Kingdom is God's to give and to take away; it is only ours to enter and accept (Matt. 21:43; Lk. 12:32). We can inherit it, possess it, or refuse to enter it, but it is not ours to build and we can never destroy it (Matt. 25:34; Lk. 10:11). We can work for the Kingdom, but we can never act upon it; we can preach it, but it is God's to establish (Matt. 10:7; Lk. 10:9; 12:32). All of this is an expression of the eschatological framework present throughout the New Testament. It has profound ramifications for its doctrines of salvation and the way in which it speaks of hope. God's inbreaking, saving, vanquishing Rule is his from first to last. It has no human analogs, no duplicates, no surrogates, allows of no human synergism. The inbreaking of the "age to come" into the present is accomplished by God *alone*. This is all about *Agape* and not about *Eros* at all. It is about God reaching down in grace and doing for sinners what they cannot do for themselves. For if this is *God's* Kingdom, his Rule, the sphere of his sovereignty, then it is not for us to take or to establish. We receive, we do not take; we enter, but we do not seize; we come as subjects in his Kingdom, not as monarchs in our own.

---

liam B. Eerdmans, 174), 63. Cf. Ben Witherington III, "Transcending Imminence: The Gordian Knot of Pauline Eschatology," in *Eschatology in Bible and Theology: Evangelical Essays at the Dawn of a New Millennium,* ed. Kent E. Brower and Mark W. Elliott (Downers Grove: InterVarsity Press, 1997), 171-186.

47. George Eldon Ladd, *Jesus and the Kingdom: The Eschatology of Biblical Realism* (Waco: Word, 1964), 189.

The Kingdom is his presence in human life and this devolves into two foci in the Gospels: judgment and salvation. The powers of darkness have been overthrown at the Cross and that conquest will be made public throughout the cosmos at the time of the second coming of Christ. To that extent, the coming of the King in human birth marked the beginning of the end of history. It produced Satan's fall (Lk. 10:18; cf. Jn. 12:31; 14:30; 16:11) and the emergence of a people formed to manifest the forgiveness, grace, and victory of this Rule. All of these themes find their place in Jesus' teaching about the Kingdom of God and this is the context in which he defined himself and his work.

In the Johannine literature, it is impossible to disengage the person of Christ from the eschatological framework in which he is presented. Jesus said he was from "above" (Jn. 6:33), where he had pre-existed (Jn. 8:42, 58; 17:8). It is difficult to see how this could mean anything other than the assertion that he existed prior to the creation, he existed outside of the world, and that what was eternal had, in himself, come into time. He left God's presence (Jn. 6:62; 8:38; 10:36) and he descended (Jn. 3:31; 6:33, 38; 10:36). Forty-two times in the Gospel we read that he was "sent" from this realm, that he had come into the world from God (Jn. 3:31; 8:42; 13:3; 16:27-28; 17:8). Thus it was that the Son, who came to reveal the Father, was the same Son as the one from whom the creation itself had arisen (Jn. 1:3). It is true that his human flesh veiled the brightness of his divine glory but it would be a grave mistake to imagine that the Son enfleshed was other than the fully divine Son he had been. To see the Son is to see the Father (Jn. 14:9) for the Father is in the Son and the Son is in the Father (Jn. 10:38; 14:10) and they are one (10:30). He therefore naturally assumed the divine functions of judging, giving eternal life, giving commandments, and answering prayer (Jn. 5:22; 5:24, 40; 14:14; 15:17).

Interpreters of Paul in the modern period have sometimes been tempted to see him in the same mold as what has typically epitomized scholarship in the Enlightenment period: individualistic thinkers who defy tradition, question boundaries, and put all of their inventiveness in the service of new formulations. This temptation has been especially hard to resist because Paul's epistles all emerged out of pastoral contexts in which his brilliance shone brightly as he adapted and applied to those contexts Christian truth. The fact is, however, that Paul made his innovations *within* the framework of the primitive apostolic teaching. He did feel obliged to discuss his teaching with the leaders in Jerusalem, but they were satisfied with what he said to them (Gal. 2:2). When he was later called upon to defend his teaching, it was not against conservatives who were arguing that he had departed from the primitive Christian consensus but, rather, against others, such as those unhappily influenced by Gnosticism or Judaism, who were departing from it. Between Paul and his predecessors there simply was no daylight. "The Christ he preaches," sums up A. M. Hunter, "is the same Christ as his predecessors preached. He simply expanded and interpreted what was implicit in the affirmations of pre-Pauline Christians about Christ."[48]

For our purposes here, then, it is sufficient to see that Paul in no way departs from this fundamental thought that the inbreaking of the age to come, this inbreaking through Christ, is what has brought into life a reality which simply is not natural to it. It is from "above." It is *Agape*, not *Eros*. It is about God, in his majesty, reaching down in grace. What Paul does is to reinforce this thought and add some new angles to it. And he does so by underscoring over and over again that the Son, though personally distinct from the Father, is ontologically and functionally the same.[49]

<hr />

48. Archibald M. Hunter, *Paul and His Predecessors* (Philadelphia: Westminster, 1961), 79. On the relationship between Paul and Jesus, see David Wenham, *Paul: Follower of Jesus or Founder of Christianity?* (Grand Rapids: William B. Eerdmans, 1995).

49. Walter Elwell has assembled the kind of linguistic identification which makes this point. If Yahweh is our sanctifier (Ex. 31:13), is omnipresent (Ps. 139:7-10), is our peace (Jud. 6:24), is our righteousness (Jer. 23:6), is our victory (Ex. 17:8-16), and is our healer (Ex. 15:26), then so is Christ all of these things too (I Cor. 1:30; Col. 1:27; Eph. 2:14). If the gospel is God's (I Thess. 2:2, 6-9; Gal. 3:8), then that same gospel is also Christ's (I Thess. 3:2; Gal. 1:7). If the Church is God's (Gal. 1:13; I Cor. 15:9), then that same Church is also Christ's (Rom. 16:16). God's kingdom (I Thess. 2:12) is Christ's (Eph. 5:5); God's love (Eph. 1:3-5) is Christ's (Rom. 8:35); God's Word (Col. 1:25; I Thess 2:13) is Christ's (I Thess. 1:8; 4:15); God's Spirit (I Thess. 4:8) is Christ's (Phil. 1:19); God's peace (Gal. 5:22; Phil. 4:9) is Christ's (Col. 3:15; cf. Col. 1:2); God's "Day" of judgment (Is. 13:6) is Christ's "Day" of judgment (Phil. 1:6, 10; 2:16; I Cor. 1:8); God's grace (Eph. 2:8-9; Col. 1:6; Gal. 1:15) is Christ's grace (I Thess. 5:28; Gal. 1:6; 6:18); God's salvation (Col. 1:13) is Christ's salvation (I Thess. 1:10); and God's will (Eph. 1:11; I Thess. 4:3; Gal. 1:4) is Christ's will (Eph. 5:17; cf. I Thess. 5:18). Because of this kind of

In what may be Paul's most poignant, but perhaps his most controversial christological statement, Phil. 2:5-11, he comes close to reiterating John's above/below language. The force of his statement, unfortunately, has been obscured by much controversy. Does this passage replicate an early Christian hymn? If so, what is its background (Aramaic, Hellenistic, or Jewish)? And what is its christology? Most obviously, there is the question as to how exactly we should understand the Son's self-emptying and what the consequences of it were.

Despite some inventive new exegesis, it is probably still best to see Paul's language of "form" — "though he was in the form of God" (Phil. 2:6) — as meaning the essential characteristics of a thing, its very essence. In this passage, Paul asserts that he who was of the very essence and nature of God took on the very nature and essence of a servant. This transition required that he "emptied" himself. In the nineteenth century in particular, there was a great deal of reflection on the question of what it was which the Son left behind. Of what did he empty himself? Which attributes? Did he empty himself of his consciousness of being the divine Son? It was a question that was asked in terms of what had preceded this assertion in Paul's argument. What aspects of his essential divinity had to be abandoned for the purposes of incarnation? It is quite conceivable, however, to ask the question in terms of what follows this statement rather than what precedes it, because the context of the passage as a whole is really ethical rather than metaphysical. What this would then mean is that when Christ assumed the role of a servant, to be true to that role, he limited and qualified the ways in which his godness could show. Far from reducing or minimizing the Son's deity, Paul brings us to a deeper understanding of it. Christ was not only God in human flesh but what we see is the God of self-effacing, self-giving, self-sacrificing love. Here is *Agape* love incarnate. Christ in his person thus gives us the unique exegesis of the character of God within the limits of a full and authentic humanity and does so in such a way that to see him is to see the Father. Once and for

---

identification, Paul could say that he was both God's slave (Rom. 1:9) and Christ's (Rom. 1:1; Gal. 1:10), that he lived for both the glory of God (Rom. 5:2; Gal. 1:24) and for the glory of Christ (II Cor. 8:19, 23; cf. II Cor. 4:6). Walter Elwell, "The Deity of Christ in the Writings of Paul," in *Current Issues in Biblical and Patristic Interpretation,* ed. Gerald F. Hawthorne (Grand Rapids: William B. Eerdmans, 1975), 297-308.

all, Christ, by whom all reality was made and in whom all things subsist, stripped away the insignia of his majesty and allowed his glory to be muted by our flesh. In him, the triumphant Messianic age arrived, in him the age to come dawned. This age was one that only God could establish and only in Christ was it established. In him, we are face to face with God and before him we are in the presence of eternity.

Grace Triumphant

From the time of the Reformation, justification *sola gratia, sola fide,* has been considered the central, defining motif in this New Testament gospel. It was upon this doctrine, Luther declared, that the church either stood or fell. Without in any way diminishing the importance of this teaching, it should be noted, however, that justification is also interwoven with other motifs which together express the gospel. This is evident in the interlacing of language that we find. Paul, for example, associates reconciliation with justification when he says that "God was in Christ reconciling the world to himself, not counting their trespasses against them . . ." (II Cor. 5:19). He associates redemption with justification when he says that we "are justified by his grace as a gift, through the redemption which is in Christ Jesus" (Rom. 3:24). Propitiation belongs alongside justification (Rom. 3:24-25). And justification is also the way in which the forces of Evil have been routed, for God not only "canceled the bond which stood against us with its legal demands" but, in so doing, "disarmed the principalities and powers and made a public example of them, triumphing over them in him" (Col. 2:14-15). It is important to see that for Paul, these doctrines were not simply doctrines; they are each ways of understanding the eternal act of God in Christ, whose significance and consequences endure forever.

Justification is the indispensable center to the gospel but the New Testament authors also ransacked their vocabulary to find other metaphors and images which capture the enormity, and even complexity, of what happened at the Cross. It is, therefore, quite fallacious to suppose, as Joel Green and Mark Baker do, that because of the presence of these other metaphors of salvation, justification can be marginalized[50] and

---

50. It is true, of course, that there is not always a direct correlation between the

penal substitution which is at its heart should be rejected.[51] The truth is
that these images — justification, reconciliation, redemption, conquest,
and sacrifice — are not to be seen as unrelated, disparate ways of interpreting the Cross but are the several sides of a fully compatible whole.
And it is a whole which is fully compatible with justification. In selecting justification, with its framework of the law court, as a way of seeing
how God's future has broken into our space-time world, therefore, I am
not arguing that it is the only interpretive metaphor of the Cross. It is,
however, the indispensable center to what we must understand.

In the New Testament, there are three accounts of Paul's conversion (Acts 9:1-9; 22:3-21; 26:4-20) and three elaborations on it in the

---

number of times a word is used and the importance that it has in the thought of the
New Testament. Yet it is difficult to avoid the conclusion that the language of justification is the principal idiom in which Paul casts the gospel. The language of redemption is used ten times, reconciliation five times, propitiation four times, but that of
justification (in its verbal form, noun, adverb, and adjective) no less than two hundred and twenty-nine. That being so, Leon Morris concludes that for Paul, "it was a
dominant idea" (Leon Morris, *The Apostolic Preaching of the Cross* [Grand Rapids:
William B. Eerdmans, 1965], 251). And justification language, which dominates the
way Paul framed the gospel, metaphorically employs the ideas of the law court. It is
very difficult to see, then, how we can think, as Clark Pinnock and Robert Brow want
us to, "about the atonement in personal, not legalistic, terms" (Clark H. Pinnock and
Robert Brow, *Unbounded Love: A Good News Theology for the 21st Century* [Downers
Grove: InterVarsity Press, 1994], 103) without forcing on the text a false dichotomy
and distorting what Paul actually said.

51. Joel B. Green and Mark D. Baker, *Recovering the Scandal of the Cross: Atonement in New Testament & Contemporary Contexts* (Downers Grove: InterVarsity Press,
2000). The authors reject any notion of divine wrath besides that of allowing people
to go their own way: "and this 'letting us go our own way' constitutes God's wrath."
God does not need to be appeased because he "is not estranged from 'the world'"
(59). Paul, they declare, "has nothing to do with an emotion-laden God who strikes
out in frustration or vengeance against [us] who are implicated in sin" (55). "The
Scriptures as a whole," they say, "provide no ground for a portrait of an angry God
needing to be appeased in atoning sacrifice" (51). Penal substitution, therefore, is rejected as ridiculous, and they cite a boy in Sunday School who said, "Jesus I like, but
the Father seems pretty mean. . . . Why is God always so angry?" (30). The caricatur-
ing of this understanding of Christ's substitution is nothing new. During the Reformation period, Faustus Socinus made the same points. His work was subsequently
taken up into the Racovian Catechism and in 1605 adopted by the Polish Unitarians.
It is certainly the case, too, that this type of argument was present in the Liberal Protestantism of the nineteenth and twentieth centuries.

epistles (I Cor. 15:8-10; Gal. 1:13-17; Phil. 3:4-14). It is true that the New Testament does see the Damascus road experience in terms of Paul's calling to be an apostle but the Philippians passage is important because, contrary to what proponents of the "new perspective" claim, it is speaking about his conversion and not simply of his calling to be an apostle.[52] In this passage, Paul says that before the law he was "blameless," that is, as Hagner puts it, "by the standards of practicing Pharisees he had an exceptionally good performance record,"[53] or that like

52. In an earlier and much discussed essay, Krister Stendahl complained that Paul and his doctrine of justification had, unfortunately, been read through the eyes of Luther who had discovered Paul in the midst of his deep struggles with sin. Unlike Luther, however, we find in Paul no stricken conscience and no crushing introspection. On the contrary, he says of his Jewish experience that "as to righteousness under the law [I was] blameless" (Phil. 3:6). Paul did believe in sin but he did not come to his view of the law "by testing and pondering its effects upon his conscience" (Krister Stendahl, "The Apostle Paul and the Introspective Conscience of the West," *Harvard Theological Review*, 56, no. 3 [1956], 204). And what Paul was recounting, Stendahl claims, was his call to be an apostle, not his own conversion. This essay received a sharp rejoinder from Ernst Käsemann. The issues in this debate were helpfully reviewed by C. K. Barrett, "Paul and the Introspective Conscience," in *The Bible, the Reformation and the Church: Essays in Honour of James Atkinson*, ed. W. P. Stephens (Sheffield: Sheffield Academic Press, 1995), 36-48. Dunn and Suggate follow Stendahl in all of this and say that this "Protestant reading of Paul was a reading *back* of Luther's own experience *into* Paul. It was a retrojection back into Paul's first-century self-testimony of what Krister Stendahl has called 'the introspective conscience of the West'" (James D. G. Dunn and Alan M. Suggate, *The Justice of God: A Fresh Look at the Old Doctrine of Justification by Faith* [Grand Rapids: William B. Eerdmans, 1993], 14). Also involved in this discussion is whether Luther was correct to equate the medieval Scholastic belief in the possibility of works righteousness, against which he protested, with the first-century Judaism which Paul confronted. Frank Theilman accepts this reading of the matter and summarizes the discussion in his *Paul and the Law: A Contextual Approach* (Downers Grove: InterVarsity Press, 1994), 14-47. For a review of the issues at stake, see Simon J. Gathercole, *Where Is Boasting? Early Jewish Soteriology and Paul's Response in Romans 1-5* (Grand Rapids: William B. Eerdmans, 2002).

Mark Seifrid has rejected this kind of argument and has shown rather carefully that this justifying encounter with Christ was developed and applied in two main ways subsequent to this encounter. Paul's understanding was solidified in his debates with his Judaizing opponents as seen in Galatians and then was extended to resolve the issue of Gentiles as seen especially in Romans. See *Justification by Faith: The Origin & Development of a Central Pauline Theme* (New York: E. J. Brill, 1992).

53. Donald A. Hagner, "Paul & Paulinism: Testing the New Perspective," in Peter Stuhlmacher, *Revisiting Paul's Doctrine of Justification* (Downers Grove: InterVarsity Press, 2001), 91.

Job (Job 1:1, 8; 2:3) he "held faithful to God, one who stood out from the surrounding wickedness, one who kept company with the faithful," as Dunn puts it.[54]

But that is not all he said. Without the law he would not have known what it was to covet. Once he heard the law, his sinful nature rose up against it (Rom. 7:7). As a consequence, "sin revived and I died" (Rom. 7:9). All of his hopes for himself fell apart. The righteousness which, as a Pharisee, he had gained came to be seen as worthless before Christ (Phil. 3:7). Had he been as confident in his own standing before God as some have imagined, he would not have looked for a righteousness "which is through faith in Christ, the righteousness from God that depends on faith" (Phil. 3:9) in place of what he had himself achieved. When he was confronted by the risen Christ, he was also confronted by his own unrighteousness, and so it was that the outward manifestation of the glory of Christ was matched by an inward experience in which God revealed his Son "in" Paul (Gal. 1:16). Paul does not elaborate on what all of this meant to him emotionally and psychologically, and it is quite mistaken to conclude from this that because he speaks of no internal convulsions there must not have been any. His is a *theological* account. And what is normative for all ages is not how Paul felt before, during, and after this confrontation. The experience of conversion varies from person to person depending on their age, life experience, self-understanding, and personality. What happened to Paul theologically in this divine, justifying encounter is what is normative and that is why he speaks of it in this passage in Philippians.

So what was the significance of Paul's conversion? I believe Wright is correct to say that when Paul saw the risen, glorified Christ, in an instant he understood that the "one true God had done for Jesus of Nazareth in the middle of time, what Saul had thought he was going to do at the end of time."[55] What Wright calls the "great reversal" which was to happen at the end of time, when the pagans who had brought suffering to Israel were going to be defeated, had happened in time, not

---

54. James D. G. Dunn, *The Theology of Paul the Apostle* (Grand Rapids: William B. Eerdmans, 1998), 349-50.

55. N. T. Wright, *What Saint Paul Really Said: Was Paul of Tarsus the Real Founder of Christianity?* (Grand Rapids: William B. Eerdmans, 1997), 36.

to Israel itself but to Jesus by the hand of pagans. But it had also happened to him by the hand of God (cf. Acts 2:23). In Jesus, God the Father had acted uniquely and decisively to accomplish his purpose. Thus it was that the "Age to Come had already begun, had already been inaugurated, even though the Present Age, the time of sin, rebellion and wickedness, was still proceeding apace."[56]

This eschatological age to come, then, was established in Christ and by him, not by defeating pagan powers, but by defeating sin, death, and the devil. The substitutionary language used in the New Testament can only lead us to think that he died, not merely for the sake of others, but more specifically in their place and for their benefit.[57] That is how the age to come has broken into this present age.

---

56. Wright, *What Saint Paul Really Said*, 37. Unfortunately, Wright then links up this understanding of Paul with the work of E. P. Sanders. In two important volumes, *Paul and Palestinian Judaism*, and *Paul, the Law and Jewish People*, Sanders advanced the argument that the Judaism Paul confronted, which was rooted in the Second Temple era, had a doctrine of salvation by grace. This means that it was not a works doctrine that Paul was contesting in his epistles, principally Romans and Galatians, though Sanders himself does not pursue this. He does argue that the issue was one of the covenant, not how a person could get into it (which would correlate with the way Paul's doctrine of justification has been traditionally understood) but how, through obedience, that person could stay in it. This, of course, would put an entirely different light on Paul's' own experience and what his doctrine of justification was. But it rests, I believe, on shaky foundations. This Second Temple Judaism was far more diverse than Sanders, Wright, and Dunn allow; and though there was undoubtedly a doctrine of salvation by grace that was known, it is also the case that by Paul's time this had been much displaced by legalism and works righteousness. I am therefore inclined to think that Luther had far more that was right in his understanding of Paul than does the "new perspective." On the various issues raised by this approach, see D. A. Carson, Peter T. O'Brien, and Mark A. Siefrid, eds., *Justification and Variegated Nomism* (Grand Rapids: Baker, 2001).

57. R. E. Davies has examined the prepositions used in the New Testament with respect to Christ's substitutionary role found in passages such as Mk. 14:24; Lk. 22:19-20; Jn. 6:51, 10:11, 15, 15:13, 17:19, 18:14; Rom. 5:6, 8:32, 14:15; I Cor. 1:13, 11:24, 15:3; II Cor. 5:14, 15, 21; Gal. 1:4, 2:20, 3:13; Eph. 5:2; I Thess. 5:10; I Tim. 2:6; Tit. 2:14; Heb. 2:9, 7:27, 10:12; I Pet. 2:21, 3:18, 4:1; I Jn. 3:16. With respect to one of these passages, Mk. 10:45, his conclusion is that "the preposition *anti always* has the idea of equivalence, substitution or exchange present; it never has the more general meaning 'on behalf of, for the sake of.' Therefore Mark 10:45 can *only* mean that the life of Christ given up in death was given *in exchange for* the forfeited lives of the many." "Christ in Our Place: The Contribution of the Prepositions," *Tyndale Bulletin*, 21 (1970), 90.

Thus it is that alongside statements of his death which are of a more general nature are also found those that are quite specific. It was "for many" that Christ gave his life (Mk. 10:45), it was "for the sheep" (Jn. 10:15), "for the ungodly" (Rom. 5:6-8), "for us" (I Thess. 5:10), "for the unrighteous" (I Pet. 3:18), and it was "for his friends" (Jn. 15:13-14). These general statements are, however, interpreted by those that are more specific. He gave himself "for our sins" (Gal. 1:4; I Cor. 15:3), he "bore our sins" (I Pet. 2:24), and because of his death we have "the forgiveness of sins" (Eph. 1:7). He was "put to death for our trespasses" (Rom. 4:25), he "bore our sins in his body" (I Pet. 2:24), he is the propitiation "for our sins" (I Jn. 2:2; 4:10), and we are "now justified by his blood" (Rom. 5:9). The logic is simple but inescapable. God forgives us because Christ died for us. God forgives us our sins because Christ bore their penalty in our place. His death in our place must, then, be counted as a death that was really ours; otherwise God in his holiness would not be satisfied.

These simple affirmations regarding Christ's penal substitution, which are at the heart of the doctrine of justification, are easy to ridicule because they are not tidy at a rational level. Rationalists from the time of Socinus onwards have, with some glee, exposed what seem to be contradictions and impossibilities in this position. And, on the other side of the aisle, the exponents of Protestant orthodoxy, but especially the scholastics, worked over time to produce explanations and illustrations of a legal kind which showed how it was possible for a person convicted of a crime to have that sentence borne by another. This transference of guilt from one person to another, which justification requires and the legal system typically does not allow, is only one of the issues in play in this doctrine. Alongside of that is the fact that God's character includes aspects that, at a rational level, seem to be incompatible, such as the fact that he is simultaneously holy and loving, just and merciful, the God of salvation and the God of judgment. Also left unexplained by the apostles is what exactly the relation is between the punishment Christ bore in place of sinners and the suffering which he endured. Was his suffering itself the punishment or was it the indication of the punishment? If the suffering was itself the punishment, then the door is open, as Horace Bushnell saw, to thinking that any kind of suffering can dissolve the consequences of sin, that in every human tear there is the hint of a Calvary. It is this raggedness which has been exploited by those hostile to penal substitution. How can God be simultaneously loving and angry with the same person? How can he declare a sinner righteousness when he knows perfectly well that he is not? How can he clear the guilty, and do what no human judge should do, which is to let the guilty off scot-free? How can one person bear someone else's penalty when under every system of law people remain responsible for themselves? If the penalty for sin is eternal separation from God, how could Christ have been resurrected after only three days?

Paul, of course, was not unaware of the dilemma at the heart of justification, which is how God can remain just while justifying sinners (Rom. 3:26), but his doctrine does not require the kind of literal parallels to the human courtroom for which defenders have looked and which attackers have exploited. It, like the other language used in explicating the gospel, is what J. I. Packer calls a "model" in which there are elements of continuity and of discontinuity.[58] These work as do metaphors and similes. To say that a senator fought like a lion for the passage of some legislation, or was a lion in the fight for that legislation, only suggests parallels. There are many differences between lions and senators but in some particular ways they can act similarly. We should not imagine, therefore, that there is a literal courtroom, with a literal prosecutor, judge, verdict and sentence. And the way that human courts work have some parallels in the Pauline doctrine of justification but they are not literal and exact. The parallels do hold at the point that this is a moral universe in which God's wrath is already known and in which he is morally bound to uphold what is right as it is reflected in the law; rejecting the authority of God and his law has unavoidable consequences; punishment is inescapable; and once this punishment has been rendered the law has been satisfied.

It is impossible to understand Paul's doctrine of penal substitution without placing it in the center of the matrix of God's character. God is simultaneously the God of love and of wrath — the one side cannot be surrendered to the other — and in his wrath he judges justly and in his love he himself bears the penalty of his judgment. Paul picks up

58. J. I. Packer, "What Did the Cross Achieve? The Logic of Penal Substitution," *Tyndale Bulletin*, 25 (1974), 3-45.

Hence the Cross, conceived as the expiatory penal sacrifice of the Son of God, is the fulfillment of the scriptural revelation of God, in its most paradoxical incomprehensible guise. It is precisely in His revelation that the God of the Bible is incomprehensible, because in His nearness He reveals His distance, in His mercy His holiness, in His grace His judgment, in His personality His absoluteness; because in His revelation His glory and the salvation of man, His own will and His love for men, His majesty and His "homeliness" cannot be separated from one another. It is thus that He is God, the One who comes, the One who comes to us in reality: who comes in the likeness of sinful flesh, the One who himself pays the price, Himself bears the penalty, Himself overcomes all that separates us from Him — *really* overcomes it, does not merely declare that it does not exist. The real event is His real coming, and therefore it is both the revelation of that which *we* are and that which *He* is.

Emil Brunner, *The Mediator*

this theme early on in Romans where the reader is introduced to the "righteousness of God" (Rom. 1:17; 3:21-26). This much-debated phrase, which opened up the gospel for Luther, speaks of a righteousness as God's saving intervention made known in "the gospel" and "apart from law," as therefore constituting a person's standing before God and thereby revealing God as being right in condemning sinners and in fulfilling his promises to provide salvation. The primary reference is not to his righteous character although his righteous character is revealed in his actions of both judging and saving. This phrase arises out of the Old Testament, Peter Stuhlmacher argues.[59] It connects with the many

---

59. Peter Stuhlmacher, *Revisiting Paul's Doctrine of Justification: A Challenge to the New Perspective* (Downers Grove: InterVarsity Press, 2001), 19. Cf. Beker's statement that "the *dikaiosynē theou* — now manifested in Christ — points backwards to God's promises to Israel and forward to God's full realization of his promises in the apocalyptic hour when Israel, along with the Gentiles and the whole created order, shall 'live' in the *gloria Dei,* when God will triumph over everything that resists his

references to "the righteous acts of the Lord" (e.g. Jud. 5:11; I Sam. 12:7; Ps. 103:6; Dan. 9:16). These acts bring Israel salvation and they bring her enemies judgment (Is. 45:8, 23-24; 51:6, 8; Ps. 71:19; 89:17; 96:13; 98:9; 111:3). When Paul adapts this language it is in the interests of declaring that outside of Christ, God is really angry with sinners, alienated from them by their sin, irreconcilably opposed to them in their sin; inside of Christ, the love of God is seen and known in all of the richness of its splendor, and believers are covered in that righteousness in which alone they can stand before him. God is the God of wrath and love, judgment and mercy, and each of these is simply another facet of his holiness.

However, I believe that it would be more felicitous to say that Christ took upon himself the penalty of our sin than to say that he was punished for sin. His work on the Cross was one in which Father and Son were united in the common task of saving lost sinners, and what Christ bore he bore without any sense of personal desert (cf. II Cor. 5:21). He willingly bowed under the weight of a judgment whose justness only the understanding of one who was sinless could grasp fully, and he bowed under it because from eternity he had purposed so to do. And thus it is that at the Cross, God's triumphant and changeless grace is exhibited in space and time, his holiness is revealed through the necessity of the Cross, and in that revelation is also seen the sinfulness of sin. What is also revealed is a kind of humanity in Christ which is perfectly in tune with the moral character and will of God the Father.[60] What Christ did was not simply to establish the possibility or the hope of redemption from the righteous wrath of God; what he accomplished was that redemption.

Thus it is that God takes action in Christ against sin, death and the devil. The doctrine of justification is not about the workings of impersonal law in the universe, or about manipulating its outcomes,

---

will — the moment in which the promise of 'life' according to Hab. 2:4 (Rom. 1:17) will be fully realized and the *dikaiosynē theou* will be synonymous with the order of cosmic peace *(shalom)*, salvation *(sōtēria)* and life *(zōē)* that has been proleptically manifested in Christ." J. C. Beker, "The Faithfulness of God and the Priority of Israel in Paul's Letter to the Romans," in *The Romans Debate*, ed. Karl Donfried (Peabody: Hendrickson, 1977), 331.

60. P. T. Forsyth, *The Work of Christ* (London: Independent Press, 19190), 180-81.

but it is about God. The moral law is simply the reflection of the character of God, and when God acts to address the outcomes to the broken moral law, he addresses these *himself,* himself taking the burden of his own wrath, himself absorbing in the person of Christ the judgment his righteous character cannot but demand, himself providing what no sinner can give, himself absorbing the punishment which no sinner could bear and remain in his presence. Christ gave himself "for our sins" (Gal. 1:4; I Cor. 15:3), he "bore our sins" (I Pet. 2:24). He was "put to death for our trespasses" (Rom. 4:25), he "bore our sins in his body" (I Pet. 2:24), he is the propitiation "for our sins" (I Jn. 2:2; 4:10) as God's wrath is turned away from its proper objects and directed upon Christ so we are "now justified by his blood" (Rom. 5:9). It was a divine action taken in Christ, in the flesh and bone of history, and yet its meaning, though rooted in that history, also transcends it. It took place in history but its reality is not bounded by that history. The crucifixion was the historical circumstance but in the Cross was the atonement wrought, in the person of Christ was the Kingdom established, and in the Cross did the age to come break into space and time.

Thus with the sweetest names Christ is called my Law, my sin, and my death, in opposition to the Law, sin, and death, even though in fact He is nothing but sheer liberty, righteousness, life, and eternal salvation. Therefore, He became Law to the Law, sin to sin, and death to death, in order that He might redeem me from the curse of the Law, justify me, and make me alive. And so Christ is both: While He is the Law, He is liberty; while He is sin, He is righteousness; and while He is death, He is life. For by the very fact that He permitted the Law to accuse Him, sin to damn Him, and death to devour Him He abrogated the Law, damned sin, destroyed death, and justified and saved me. Thus Christ is a poison against the Law, sin, and death, and simultaneously a remedy to regain liberty, righteousness, and eternal life.

Martin Luther, *Luther's Works*

The mechanism of this in Paul is the imputation of sin to Christ and of his righteousness to the believer. Thus it is that Paul argued that Abraham was not accepted by God on the grounds of what he had done, for then that acceptance would have been earned and expected. The situation was quite the reverse. His acceptance was not earned but "credited" to him (Gen. 15:6; Rom. 4:3). This crediting or counting does have the feel of the accountant's ledger. It is in this sense that Paul wrote to Philemon to say that if his runaway slave "has wronged you at all, or owes you anything, *charge that to my account*" (Philemon 18; italics mine; cf. Rom. 5:13). It is the penalty of sin which is charged to Christ's account and so God "reckons righteousness apart from works" (Rom. 4:6; cf. Phil. 3:8-9) to those who receive it by faith. The righteousness we cannot provide for ourselves is provided by God through Christ on the basis of which we are declared to be free of the law's penalty and free to stand in his presence without condemnation.

This is not, however, a matter of impersonal bookkeeping; it is a matter of great earth-shaking eschatological reality penetrating the routine circumstances of everyday life. Its consequences reach far beyond the parameters of individual experience and into the wounded cosmos, and into the dark reaches of the universe where evil continues to live out its doomed existence. The reach of evil, in its most vital aspect, is now severed. Its domain, this age, is under sentence of death and has no future. The future, the age to come, is already known and is even now reaching back into the present. In Christ, eternity has been brought into time. In time, hope which is the result of *Agape* reaches out into eternity.

So much has been made of the fact that in a video generation such as ours is, it is images that dominate the way people process reality, rather than words. This, in fact, is part of the postmodern attack on modernity, that the centrality of words in our processes of knowing needs to be demolished and the deck thus cleared of the kind of rationalism that dominated the period of modernity. Stanley Grenz even takes a few steps down this road,[61] forgetting that reason was

61. Stanley Grenz, *A Primer on Postmodernism* (Grand Rapids: William B. Eerdmans, 1996), 169-71. In his *Renewing the Center: Evangelical Theology in a Post-Theological Era* (Grand Rapids: Baker, 2000), it is rather apparent that Grenz takes postmodern epistemology to be normative and something to which theology simply must adjust itself. This has led to the justifiable charge that he has domesticated the gospel.

not the invention of the Enlightenment. What characterized the Enlightenment was not its heavy reliance on reason but its insistence on accepting only *naturalistic* reasoning, only empirical evidence when understanding reality. What could not be tested, analyzed, weighed, or handled was rejected as unbelievable. The use of reason *per se* was not itself the distinguishing mark of the Enlightenment. After all, we encounter the use of reason in remarkably developed and sophisticated ways in the early fathers, in Augustine, in medieval scholastics like Duns Scotus and Thomas Aquinas, and even in the Protestant Reformers, all long before it was taken captive to the narrow humanistic agenda of the Enlightenment. And whatever merit there is in stressing that postmoderns place great premium on images, on imagination, on relationships, on being part of a community, none of these things can substitute for the fact that the Church has to *proclaim* the truth about Christ, that it cannot do so without using words, and that words are the tools for expressing our thoughts, and our thoughts must correspond to the reality of what God has done in Christ.

The complexities of the many angles to biblical truth — the eschatological Reign of God, its inauguration, how Christ is seen in this context, how this explains what he said and did, his work on the Cross, its relationship to the character of God, justification and penal substitution — should not be allowed to conceal the central and simple message of the New Testament. It is that the promised age to come has dawned, the promised victory over what has emptied life of meaning and filled it with confusion and dismay is now to be declared. Postmoderns who have, in one way or another, pointed to the emptiness of life, the absence of meaning, of enduring, stable value structures, are astonishingly close to the truth — far closer, in fact, than many in the Enlightenment period who lived off fraudulent meaning. Were it not for the resurrection, Paul suggests, abandoning ourselves to a life of empty party-making and a fatalistic sense of doom would be quite logical. There is no hope in "this age." In this age, Paul says, we are without God and without hope. This way of life which, in the West, seems so full of bright prospects, magnificent technology, robust business, a life awash in affluence, for all of its ingenious achievements lies under the judgment of God. It is all, despite its brilliance, now dying and it has no future. It can offer many pleasurable experiences, many momentary distractions, but it is doomed. It has no long-term future and it can offer no meaning besides what it manufactures for the moment, which is as fleeting as the morning mist.

Meaning comes from God alone. In the person of Christ, the age to come, which alone is what will endure for all eternity, has arrived. It arrived in his person and is made redemptively present through his work on the Cross. In that work, not only is what is eternal present in time in Christ but so is the judgment of the end of time now exhausted within time. For the people of God, the "end time" judgment has already happened. Not only so, but the resurrection which the Old Testament saw as coming when time had run its course is now the way in which the New Testament speaks of the "new creation." The resurrection of Christ, G. K. Beale argues, "is not merely spiritually the inauguration of the new cosmos, but he is literally its beginning, since he was resurrected with a physically resurrected, newly created body."[62] Thus it is, he says, that "Christ's life, and especially death and resurrection through the Spirit, launched the glorious end-time new creation of God."[63] This present age is in "the sunset of dissolution"; the age to come is the dawn whose light bathes life, banishes its shadows, and illumines its meaning because this age is moving the people of God to that time when everything has become subject to Christ and he has rendered it all up to the Father (I Cor. 15:20-28).

Vast, mysterious, and mostly unknown as the universe is, we are neither aliens nor strangers in it. It is our alienation from God that makes us see the world as if we were aliens. It is our estrangement from him which leaves us with this haunting sense that we are alone, strangers in a cold and indifferent universe. So it is that life comes to seem as if it is only a chance collocation of atoms destined to disappear beneath the rubble of a universe in ruins. It can all seem so meaningless, so ephemeral, so pointless. And it is meaningless, a vanity of vanities, until we see that fallen life yields up no meaning higher or deeper than

---

62. Beale, "The Eschatological Conception of New Testament Theology," 19.
63. Beale, "The Eschatological Conception of New Testament Theology," 20.

its own fallenness. In a fallen world God is replaced as its center by Chance, Void, or Material but the only replacement which has actually taken place is in fallen minds. God is hidden to sinners but not replaced. And in their fallen life they are a part of this age which is now passing. It has no future and there are intimations of that in the depths of human consciousness where a tangle of contradictions lie, for we are made for meaning but find only emptiness, made as moral beings but are estranged from what is holy, made to understand but are thwarted in so many of our quests to know. These are the sure signs of a reality out of joint with itself. This is what, in fact, points to something else. These contradictions are unresolved in the absence of that age to come which is rooted in the triune God of whom Scripture speaks. He it is who not only sustains all of life, directing it all to its appointed end, but who also is the measure of what is enduringly true and right and this measure is objective to our minds.

This is why those churches which have banished pulpits or are "getting beyond" the truth question are, however inadvertently, going beyond Christianity itself. The proclamation of the New Testament was about *truth,* about the truth that Christ who was with the Father from all eternity had entered our own time. As such he lived within it, his life like ours marked by days, and weeks, and years. He lived in virtue of his unity with the Father, living for him, living as the Representative of his own before the Father, his very words becoming the means of divine judgment and of divine grace. But in the Cross and resurrection, the entire spiritual order was upended, his victory reached into and across the universe, and saving grace is now personalized in him.[64] The world with all of its pleasures, power and comforts, is fading away, the pall of divine judgment hangs over it, a new order has arisen in Christ, and only in this new order can be found meaning, hope, and acceptance with God. It is truth, not private spirituality that apostolic Christianity was about. It was Christ, not the self as means of access into the sacred. It was Christ, with all of his painful demands of obedience, not comfortable country clubs that early Christianity was about. It was what God had done in space and time when the world was stood on its head that was its preoccupation, not the multiplication of programs, strobe

---

64. Barth, *Church Dogmatics,* III, 2, 439-41.

lights, and slick drama. Images we may want, entertainment we may desire, but it is the proclamation of Christ crucified and risen that is the Church's truth to tell.

CHAPTER VI

Christic in a Decentered World

—◦◦◦—

> At the name of Jesus
> Ev'ry knee shall bow,
> Ev'ry tongue confess him
> King of glory now;
> 'Tis the Father's pleasure
> We should call him Lord,
> Who from the beginning
> Was the mighty Word.

CAROLINE M. NOEL

That there is no longer any center to reality is the central principle, if one may be permitted to use such a word, in the postmodern mind. There is no center which is the norm for all of the human centers, centers of private interest, of ethnicity, of gender, of sexuality, and of perspective. This, of course, correlates with the widespread belief that there are no absolutes in life and it also is a further explication of the meaninglessness of the world. It is, then, a slightly different angle on that meaninglessness which was considered in the prior chapter which is in view in this chapter. Here, I will first describe the loss of coherence to life a little more and I will then follow out the echoes of this in one particular evangelical theology. I will also take up the theme of Christ as the center of the created order and head of the Church as this is developed in Scripture.

An Open Future

From Experience to Philosophy

Two decades ago, William Donnelly wrote about the effects of the electronic media, and although he did not speak of the emergence of the postmodern world from within the modern, he clearly saw what was coming. At that time, he said, people were living amidst the Autonomy Generation. By this he meant that those who belonged in this outlook saw themselves as being at the center of life, as being responsible only to themselves, as having the sole hand in deciding what beliefs to hold and what behaviors to follow. They lived neither for the past nor for the future, not for predecessors and not for posterity. They lived for *themselves,* in the moment, spontaneously shaping their responses to people, ideas, and opportunities without regard to others' perceptions or expectations. They were free and uninhibited. What he was describing in his own language was, of course, the autonomous self.

What he saw coming was the emergence of a new kind of cultural personality out of the Autonomous Generation which was peculiarly adapted to the new cultural environment. He called it the Confetti Generation, but we know it as the postmodern mind. It is what our centerless world has brought forth. Donnelly was focused only on the media images and the way that they helped shape the worldview of this emerging generation but there are, of course, many other potent cultural factors in this equation, as I have suggested in previous chapters.

What is striking about the media images themselves is that although they have produced a quantum leap in information and entertainment, they are often little more than a blizzard of rootless, context-free thoughts and pictures. These images succeed each other at great speed. They are fleeting and ephemeral. Their sole purpose is simply to connect with momentary tastes and passions. At breakneck speed the various images succeed each other, images of soap and perfume being replaced almost instantaneously by those of street fighting in Afghanistan or whales in the Arctic, which in turn are replaced by other snippets of news and then by an advertisement for baking soda and one for a remedy for constipation. The psychological impression which is made by all of this is that everything is in flux and everything is unstable. These images, which blow around in our minds like leaves in a windstorm, are each discrete, all unconnected, all random, all unrelated, and all uncentered. This is the visual counterpart to the postmodern mentality. Here are decentered beings in their decentered world.

In a decentered culture, eclecticism is the coin of the realm. This is what excessive choice has done to us. There is simply too much to choose between, ranging from products, to beliefs, to lifestyles, so choice becomes almost random. And the sheer weight of all of the information — the knowledge of other religions, belief systems, products, and services — blurs everything so that one idea seems no truer than another. In this video-commercial context, and in this personal mindset, everything begins to seem similar and equal. Judgments become not only offensive but, for so many, virtually impossible.

Having been nurtured in an Autonomy Generation, the Confetti citizen consumer will be inundated by experience and ungrounded in any cultural discipline for arriving at any reality but the self. We will witness an aggravated version of today when all ideas are equal, when all religions, life-styles, and perceptions are equally valid, equally indifferent, and equally undifferentiated in every way until given value by the choice of a specific individual. This will be the Confetti Era, when all events, ideas, and values are the same size and weight — just pale pink and green, punched-out, die-cut wafers without distinction.

William J. Donnelly, *The Confetti Generation*

All of this may strike us as being quite novel but, in actual fact, our experience of a decentered world is leading us to encounter a philosophical question which is as ancient as philosophy itself, often thought of as that of "the One and the many."

Is there some unity behind all of life's diversity, something in which all of the difference in life, not to mention the differences in our perceptions, inheres? Are there universals behind the particulars? This was the issue that was raised at the beginning of Colin Gunton's Bampton Lectures for 1992, which are a prolonged Christian reflection on modernity.[1]

In the Presocratics, the two opposing views that were to be passed down to later ages were those of Heraclitus and Parmenides. Heraclitus saw movement, change, and difference, most famously saying that one cannot step into the same river twice (for the water into which one first stepped has moved on); Parmenides saw beneath and behind all of the apparent changes the One which does not change and he thought that perceptions of change were, in fact, illusionary. This One was not God, for Parmenides thought of it as being material but everywhere present. What he seemed to be reaching for was the notion of substance, something that is unchanging and which underlies everything, something which remains even when the surface circumstances or characteristics seem to change.[2] Thus were the lines drawn.

This debate has rumbled on down the centuries coming into our own time, though in quite different language and in a different context. Ours, quite clearly, is a Heraclitian time though this fact reaches us, not through philosophy, but through our experience of a modernized world. It is a time when everything seems roiled by change, when permanence has evaporated, where nothing remains unchanged, and there is no center in which anything inheres. Nothing hangs together, but events, products, and experiences simply succeed each other without having connections. This is a perception which seems to be beyond dispute.

1. Colin E. Gunton, *The One, the Three and the Many: God, Creation and the Culture of Modernity* (Cambridge: Cambridge University Press, 1993).

2. See Bertrand Russell, *A History of Western Philosophy* (New York: Simon and Schuster, 1945), 48-52.

From a philosophical angle we might say that the One has disappeared or, from our experience, we might say that the universe has no Center. This Heraclitian sense has many outcomes.

The immediate result of this, of course, is that, as Gunton puts it, we "do not seek in the world for what is true and good and beautiful, but create our truth and values for ourselves."[3] The reason for this is that the many have taken the place of the One, so the many seek in themselves what was once sought in the One. This, inevitably, produces a shattering and a fragmentation of reality, at least in our understanding.

The disappearance of life's Center is not, of course, without severe costs, as I have already suggested. The tilt of modernity has been away from any form of belief in God which would have the power to abridge human "freedom"; at the same time, alienation from one another has become a staple in modern literature. This sense of aloneness, of disjointedness, of disconnectedness, of *anomie,* is most immediately related to the loss of human community in the modern period. Indeed, Wuthnow has developed the thesis that the reason that small groups are playing so large a role in America today — twelve-step groups, Bible study groups, recovery groups, and so on — is that they are attempting to provide substitutes for this lost community.[4] And yet this sense of aloneness is deeper and more profound than that. At its root is a sense of being alone in the *universe,* not merely our geographical location, of not being able to connect up the fragments of our experience to anything larger than ourselves. It is the sense of emptiness which comes from thinking that nothing that we do ever has any cosmic significance. This yearning for a significance which does not change is what Russell thinks produced the belief in God and immortality, but the Christian confession is that it was God who so made us that we yearn for what is eternal and unchanging, for the One against whom life's diversity and difference can be understood and disciplined. It is in christology that these connections are most obviously developed.

3. Gunton, *The One, the Three and the Many,* 14.
4. Robert Wuthnow, *Sharing the Journey: Support Groups and America's New Quest for Community* (New York: The Free Press, 1994).

From Freedom to Danger

If God did not exist, Dostoevsky ventured, all things would be possible. And that, in fact, is our freedom today, even for those who are spiritual because the sacred rarely intrudes upon their private choices. All things are possible. In our own private universes, we are free of external constraints, free of social custom, free of the past, free of values we ourselves have not selected and in that selection authenticated, and free of all beliefs which are incompatible with our internally constructed world of meaning. We have all become free in a most radical way, and in that radical posture we have become as light as a feather.[5]

Berger has suggested that one of the marks of modern experience is that "the future becomes a primary orientation for both imagination and activity."[6] This is not, of course, a desired outcome. The problem is that living in our modernized world transforms the way that time is experienced because the consequences of modernization intrude upon our minds. In a traditional society, people are oriented to the past. They value tradition and they venerate the elderly. In a modernized society, we are powerfully oriented to the future, we despise tradition, and we idolize the young who symbolize new beginnings and fresh potential. This preoccupation with the future, however, is really about control. Why is control so important?

It is important because modern societies are laden with threat because now, all of a sudden, anything can happen. Unlike traditional, non-modernized societies, Anthony Giddens observes, those that are modern are seen "as a directionless swirl of events, in which the only ordering agents are natural laws and human beings."[7] But can human beings actually succeed in ordering this dangerous swirl of events? By what standards are they to be ordered? By what power? In accordance with whose will? The problem, of course, is that in modern societies there is nothing in them which serves as a means of giving any cosmic

5. This is the argument developed in Christopher Lasch, *The Minimal Self: Psychic Survival in Troubled Times* (New York: W. W. Norton, 1984).

6. Peter L. Berger, *Facing Up to Modernity: Excursions in Society, Politics, and Religion* (New York: Basic Books, 1977), 73.

7. Anthony Giddens, *Modernity and Self-Identity: Self and Society in the Late Modern Age* (Stanford: Stanford University Press, 1991), 109.

significance to anything that is done or which provides any means of restraint. The world is now self-enclosed, empty of any overarching significance, and therefore utterly unpredictable. Indeed, it is open in a way that no traditional society ever is. In traditional societies, there is a common belief at least in fate or fortune, if not in deities, which both determine and limit the future, and it is also what gives to everyday events some cosmic meaning. It is what connects everyday events to some larger meaning in the universe. Although fortune lingers on in our language today in the words *fortunate* and *unfortunate,* the idea itself has long since perished. And though the sacred is now making a return in the modernized West, it is in a form which is wholly domesticated, wholly therapeutic, and completely non-interventional. There are, therefore, no longer any forces that limit the possibilities of the future and none which close off options in advance, none which determine one set of circumstances for this person and another set for someone else. The future, in its unpredictability, looms ominously ahead of us.

A world thus completely "open" is a world which is both hospitable to change and one in which risk is greatly heightened. Indeed, the calculation of risk as people position themselves before the future is an inescapable part of both business and private life. It has become a part of the calculation that goes on in the supermarket at the meat counter, in the insurance company office, and in the politics at the water cooler where one's own imaginary projections of career, five years into the future, and then ten, may well affect what is said and how it is said, for there are risks that lie latent in many a conversation.

This preoccupation with the future really is about control. At least, it is about our attempts at controlling the future as it crests into the present by being able to position ourselves to avoid what is disagreeable and to capitalize on what is advantageous. Indeed, we go even further. We imagine that the future begins in our minds and that we can actually create it. We see this in a whole array of fatuous slogans that fill our magazines and billboards: "The future is now!" "Make your own future!" "You can have a brand new future!" This kind of positioning and posturing is a form of secularized providence, one in which it is we who try to control the oncoming events for our own benefit — and this is exercised in place of God's control which was for his glory. It is

an expression of the world turned upside down by the Fall. This preoccupation with the future is, therefore, not harmless.

It not only brings mounting anxiety — for what is anxiety except
living out the future over and over again before it actually reaches us?
— but also as Berger notes, it brings "endless striving, restlessness, and
a mounting incapacity for repose."[8] This is no small anomaly because
Western cultures all sustain large, flourishing industries whose sole
purpose is to produce leisure and recreation. The more anxiously we
seek ways to relax, the less we seem to be able to do so. Yet this is by no
means its most pernicious consequence. What it also does is to wrench
everyday life free of any cosmic significance, for in a universe which is
decentered and "open," nothing is ever caught up in any kind of significance larger than itself. In one way, the world gets larger and larger as
our imaginations enter the future and conjure up so many of its possibilities but, in another way, the world gets smaller and smaller because
none of these mean anything.

These are the afflictions that we who are living in a decentered
world have come to associate with the postmodern experience, but like
so many other things in the postmodern understanding of life this perception about its decenteredness is only a half truth. What is true is
that these discordant elements are undoubtedly part and parcel of the
postmodern experience; what is not true is to think of this as *uniquely*
postmodern. It is, in fact, part of a much larger story.

From Providence to Bad Luck

It was already clear midway through the nineteenth century that the
world was losing its center. The idea that life was driven by a conscious
purpose larger than what was merely human was being surrendered
slowly. It is now difficult to realize the shock which Charles Darwin's
work produced, for example, when he replaced divine design and providence with natural selection and adaptation. Andrew Delbanco has
pointed out that many of the younger writers who came along later
capitalized on this transformation in outlook and turned "the vertigi-
nous emptiness of sea and plains and scrubland into a universal sym-

8. Berger, *Facing Up to Modernity,* 74.

bol."[9] These were the frequent images which symbolized the disappearance of God and of divine purpose in life, leaving behind, it seemed, only a Void. Today, the idea of providence survives for many only in the word *goodbye,* the contracted form of an old benediction, "God be with you," but, needless to say, it has no providential overtones any more.

What has replaced the idea of providence, of God's exercise of his rule in life, is chance and luck, and evil has simply devolved into bad luck. Perhaps Delbanco is correct that the six hundred thousand who died in the American Civil War contributed much to the demise of the idea of providence, for the events of the conflict seemed so random that it became awkward to attribute even one death to the express will of the one who had made that life. These bloody events seemed so contrary to any possible divine purpose, so unplanned, that it seemed to be more a matter of luck than of some divine intention as to who survived and who did not. However, it was not just war that contributed to this sense of the decentering of the world. Everything in the modern age seemed to point in this direction: why one person was unemployed and another was not; why one woman got pregnant and another did not; why some got fatal diseases in the prime of life and others did not; and why some struck it rich and others remained paupers. Life, it seemed, is just a large, complex, and unpredictable accident. This was the context in which insurance companies began to thrive in the nineteenth century. They developed actuarial charts in an attempt to handicap chance. But was the buying of insurance, this making of bets against the future, really different from gambling? It was hard to know.

So it was that America, under the impulse of modernization with all of its attendant social reorganization and change, began to think differently about life. Before, it had been the land where individualism had flourished, where people took responsibility for themselves. They did so out of a sense of accountability, if not to God, then at least to a sense of abiding moral principles written into life. But now this canopy of meaning began to cave in. Now it became the land where its individualism, as it were, turned inwards and felt little sense of accountability to anything outside the self, and in the world people simply hoped for

9. Andrew Delbanco, *The Death of Satan: How Americans Have Lost the Sense of Evil* (New York: Farrar, Straus and Giroux, 1995), 147.

luck. Now, people played their chances because the connection between moral probity and the circumstances of their lives seemed to have been broken. "In such a country," Delbanco writes, "to pray for grace instead of to wish for luck was faintly embarrassing, like murmuring a rosary in a Protestant crowd." Purpose now came to be seen as non-existent, and in what amounted to "a new kind of paganism," he continues, "the concept of evil developed into bad luck, and 'good luck' became the American benediction."[10]

The decentering of the world, then, is actually quite a long and complex story and one much larger than what many postmoderns imagine. It is, of course, closely related to the loss of meaning discussed in the previous chapter and it is undoubtedly shaping the ways in which the various spiritualities discussed earlier have emerged. Yet this theme does give us its own distinctive angle of vision on our postmodern world and a distinctive point of connection with the gospel. However, before coming to that connection, I need to explore a variant on evangelical theology which, in almost every way, illustrates how this connection should not be made. I refer to open theism.

An Open Theology

It is not possible here to give a full exposition of the various views that have been brought together under the banner of open theism, and which are now being enveloped by a growing cloud of controversy, so I will necessarily have to focus on one of its principal proponents, Clark Pinnock. Indeed, the larger development still has the appearance of a work in progress. However, in the work of Pinnock one finds set forth with candor and forthrightness a way of looking at the world which is strikingly unconventional in historical Christian terms though Pinnock seems to be in no doubt that what he believes has widespread support in the evangelical world.[11] He may, indeed, be correct.

10. Delbanco, *The Death of Satan*, 153.

11. Pinnock's target in particular is Reformed theology and in historical terms it is Augustine who is seen as the chief enemy. He asserts that today "Augustinian thinking is losing its hold on present-day Christians," that "all the evangelists" take God's universal salvific will for granted, that "the believing masses" take for granted a

Pinnock has provided a helpful autobiographical essay in which he shows how he came to his current views.[12] The story begins with the disintegration of the Calvinism which he had believed. This began around 1970. First to go in his old position was the perseverance of the saints. As a part of this belief, however, was an underlying question. As a Calvinist, Pinnock had always believed that human actions could be divinely determined without excluding the exercise of human freedom in those actions. Humans, he had thought, could make decisions for reasons which to them seemed fully persuasive while, unknowingly, they were fulfilling the sovereign will of God. He says, however, that he had always fumbled over this when trying to explain it, sometimes calling it a mystery and at other times calling it an antinomy. Now he came to call it false. Inherent in our dignity as made in God's image is the capacity to make decisions, and these decisions lose their reality if we are encumbered by God's intrusions or affected by his manipulations.

From here, Pinnock began a full-scale revision of all that he had believed. He came to reject election and, instead, to think that God's sovereignty in life is exercised in such a way that he voluntarily limits his power and invites people to "share in the divine creativity." He then says that "God invites humans to share in deciding what the future will be. God does not take it all onto his own shoulders,"[13] which, one has to say, is quite an astonishing thought. He went on to reject the doctrine of total depravity and to endorse a view of universal atonement.

---

belief in human free will, and that it is "hard to find a Calvinistic theologian willing to defend Reformed theology" in its full rigor (Clark H. Pinnock, "From Augustine to Arminius: A Pilgrimage in Theology," in *The Grace of God and the Will of Man*, ed. Clark H. Pinnock [Minneapolis: Bethany House, 1989], 27). At the same time, he also says that the type of theology he is opposing, which is supposedly on the run, actually is "both highly influential and exceedingly harmful" (xi) today. It is hard to know which judgment is the preferred one in Pinnock's mind. However, Richard Rice, who has contributed significantly to the formation of open theism, laments the fact that the Reformed view of God's sovereign control over all of life and his exhaustive knowledge of what is going to happen "has dominated the church's perspective, among thinkers and general believers alike, and it prevails in the attitudes of most believers today." Richard Rice, "Biblical Support for a New Perspective," in *The Openness of God: A Biblical Challenge to the Traditional Understanding of God* (Downers Grove: InterVarsity Press, 1994), 11.

12. Pinnock, "From Augustine to Arminius," 15-30.
13. Pinnock, "From Augustine to Arminius," 21.

Much of this is really no more than what Arminians have always believed. For, as Packer has pointed out, evangelical Arminianism has typically sought to maintain the necessity of "universal redemption, universal sufficient grace, man's ability to respond to God, man's independence in responding, and the conditional character of election."[14] This is the way Arminians think that justice can be done to the love of God, to the work of Christ, to human freedom, and to the necessity of personal holiness. The debate, historically speaking, has been over whether the doctrinal means Arminianism has chosen to protect its concerns actually carry it to the ends which it desires. On the Arminian understanding, Christ's death brings only the possibility of salvation which may, or may not, be realized. The difference, then, is that "Calvinism recognizes a dimension of the saving love of God which Arminianism misses," Packer argues, "namely God's sovereignty in bringing to faith and keeping in faith all who are actually saved."[15] This gives an entirely different perspective on the meaning of God's love, on the complete helplessness of sinners to respond unaided to that love, on the exact nature of Christ's death, and on the role which gratitude plays in a salvation to which sinners contribute nothing but their own sin.

This, of course, is a debate which has gone on in the Church for three hundred years, and Pinnock has cast little new light on these points. What really came to set him apart from this older Arminianism, however, and what can justify calling his position a version of Arminianism which is so extreme that it really has no historical precedent, is his view of God. In this, he stands shoulder to shoulder with the other advocates of open theism.[16]

At the center of Pinnock's new model is a threefold consideration. First, he believes that it is now *impossible* for God to know much of the

---

14. J. I. Packer, "Arminianisms," in *Through Christ's Word: A Festschrift for Dr. Philip E. Hughes,* ed. W. Robert Godfrey and Jesse L. Boyd III (Phillipsburg: Presbyterian and Reformed Publishing Co., 1985), 147.

15. Packer, "Arminianisms," 124.

16. Pinnock acknowledges that historic Arminianism has held to traditional views on God's "unchangeability, eternity, and omniscience" which open theists do not because these beliefs, in their view, jeopardize the divine/human relationship. Clark H. Pinnock, *Most Moved Mover: A Theology of God's Openness* (Grand Rapids: Baker, 2001), 106.

future since the future is made up of choices, both human and divine, which will be made only when the elements in the decision are known. God is unable to know because of the voluntary contraction of his own power and attributes. In this, Pinnock is a little less radical than some of the other open theists who argue this point on the grounds of ontological insufficiency.[17]

Second, it is *imperative* that God not know the future since that knowledge would exclude the exercise of human freedom. By his own assessment, Pinnock has a libertarian view of freedom. This makes the demand that human choice must be uncoerced by God. It must be unencumbered by, must be entirely independent of, God. This demand rests upon the notion that we are not free if God has prior knowledge of what we are about to do or decide. If God were knowledgeable from all eternity of a decision that someone would make on a particular day, that person, Pinnock thinks, would not be free to change his or her mind at the last minute because then, since God had not foreseen this, he would have been mistaken and in possession of false knowledge. To suppose that God might unknowingly be believing something that is false is not felicitous, but neither is it felicitous to think that humans have no freedom because God has boxed in their choices by his knowledge of what they will do.[18] The world "has been given relative independence and derived autonomy,"[19] he says. The future of the world at creation "was not yet completely settled," in order "to make room for

17. Richard Rice suggests that it is incorrect to speak of God's limited foreknowledge. Rather, he argues that "perfect knowledge involves knowing everything there is to know" so the issue is what is possible for God to know. Rice's answer is that much always remains unknown to God and necessarily so. Richard Rice, "Divine Foreknowledge and Free-Will Theism," in *The Grace of God and the Will of Man,* ed. Clark H. Pinnock (Minneapolis: Bethany House Publishers, 1989), 130.

18. John Sanders argues that "the cross was not planned prior to creation" and that when Peter said that Jesus was "delivered up according to the definite plan and foreknowledge of God" (Acts 2:23) all that was intended was simply the thought that God would deliver him to those with a long record of having resisted God's overtures. In this way, when Jesus went to the Cross, it was not because of some eternal decision that this would happen, which would have violated Jesus' own freedom, but simply because the Father and Son ran out of other options. See Sanders' discussion on this and related passages in his *God Who Risks: A Theology of Providence* (Downers Grove: InterVarsity Press, 1998), 101-104.

19. Pinnock, *Most Moved Mover,* 92.

the input of significant creatures."[20] This involves a voluntary limitation of God's knowledge — so he is not omniscient and does not see all of the future even though he could if he wanted to — and, in fact, it also involves a limitation of his sovereignty.[21]

Finally, it is *necessary* that God not know the future if, in fact, he is to be involved in its ongoing unfolding as it arrives in the present. This is what Pinnock has in mind when he speaks of God's having dynamic involvement with the world rather than a static relationship to it. God improvises. As each new situation arises, he assesses the options and possibilities, the pros and cons, and like the conductor of an extended orchestra tries to get all of the players to play together and harmoniously. This analogy, however, is only partially accurate because in an orchestra the players all have the music before them. In the world, the sheets of music, as it were, do not exist. Blueprints are absent. Providence is about divine improvisation. And since there are so many unknowns to God in this undertaking, there is much risk which is involved, a thought which John Sanders has aptly captured in the title of his book on providence called *The God Who Risks*.

This dynamic relation to the world also means that God is open to the impact of his creatures upon himself and, as Pinnock suggests, "some kinds of change even belong to the divine perfection,"[22] which, it is fair to say, is sailing perilously close to process thought. The thought is that God is constantly rethinking his actions, reassessing life as he sees it unfold, and repositioning himself in order to become more deeply involved with his people. The divine/human relationship is a two-way street, and God's will itself is evolving in concert with his creatures, for this is what the divine love means. Here is a God who could override his creatures but chooses not to, who could see all of the future but does not want to, and who could be entirely unchanging in his being but wants to change consonant with his relationship with his creatures.

This, in turn, has produced a new tilt to Pinnock's thought. It is a

20. Pinnock, *Most Moved Mover*, 3.
21. Clark H. Pinnock, "Introduction," in *Searching for an Adequate God: A Dialogue Between Process and Free Will Theists,* ed. John B. Cobb and Clark H. Pinnock (Grand Rapids: William B. Eerdmans, 2000), xi.
22. Pinnock, "Introduction," x.

tilt away from a classically Protestant view of God and toward one that leans closer to the nineteenth-century Liberal Protestant ideas. Here is a God in whose nature love is made primary in such a way that his nature as holy, especially as this comes to focus in the law, is much diminished. This in turn leads to a new definition of sin. Sin is not seen primarily in terms of "a legal infraction or in terms of transgressions that require punishment" but, rather, sin is now simply a "mysterious refusal to accept God's love."[23] This then leads to a different emphasis in understanding salvation. The understanding of salvation moves away "from legal concepts" and more toward "God's sufferings for all of those under the power of death,"[24] which, of course, leaves the doctrine of justification somewhat beached and abandoned because, in the New Testament, the context of this doctrine is that of a court room, the law, the prosecutor, the judge, and a sentence.

What has been undertaken by Pinnock is a full and far-reaching reworking of the body of Christian knowledge. Clearly, he was pushed down this road because of the disintegration of the Calvinistic beliefs he had formerly held. However, beside this theological driving force there is another which he mentions and which partially explains what has happened. It is the factor of culture. He observes that every generation reads the Bible with its own issues in view and that it also brings to bear on that reading its own culturally accepted presuppositions. This is so in his case, too. His new direction, he acknowledges, is the outcome to this process. We are, he says, "making peace with the culture of modernity."[25] Indeed he is!

23. Clark H. Pinnock and Robert C. Brow, *Unbounded Love: A Good News Theology for the 21st Century* (Downers Grove: InterVarsity Press, 1994), 55.

24. Pinnock and Brow, *Unbounded Love*, 96.

25. Pinnock, *The Grace of God and the Will of Man*, 27. See also his *Most Moved Mover*, 153-78. In a remarkable, albeit offhand observation, William Hasker notes that whereas much of philosophy has focused more on what does not change rather than on what does, our experience of modernity reverses this. Now, he says, if anything at all remains constant for a while our response is one of boredom and impatience. This is a correct observation. The conclusion he draws from this surely does illustrate the fact that peace has been made with postmodernity. The "preference for immutability has little hold on our thinking, and the appeal of theological doctrines based on this valuation is weakened accordingly" (William Hasker, "A Philosophical Perspective," in *The Openness of God: A Biblical Challenge to the Traditional Understanding of God*

It is not my purpose here to respond theologically to the arguments advanced by open theists. That has been done by others.[26] My purpose, rather, is to highlight briefly the conjunction between the outlook of open theism and the postmodern disposition. The argument I have been developing in this book is that we should not make peace with postmodernity and that to do so carries the liability of losing Christian authenticity. When open theists made their peace, they lost their ability to speak into the culture effectively as a result. They are losing an alternative understanding of reality because theirs is a way of thought that is deeply enculturated. In fact, what they are doing is flirting with the old, discredited Christ-of-culture position which brought the Liberal Protestants to such a sorry end. This is true at two points. First, the open theists' libertarian freedom is indistinguishable, it seems to me, from the postmodern's autonomous self; second, the open theist's vision of a world in which creatures are autonomous is not easy to distinguish from the postmodern's view of the world as being decentered.

Libertarian and Autonomous

The autonomous self, I have suggested, is a thread that comes into the postmodern era from the modern. It is one of those cultural realities which belies the thought that the postmodern is completely *postmodern*. It is true that postmoderns yearn for community and despise the lonely, walk-alone, rationalistic individualism which they see was part of the Enlightenment world which they have rejected. It is a complete fallacy to think, however, that the yearning for community is a sign that the autonomy of the self has been jettisoned. It is, rather, the

---

[Downers Grove: InterVarsity Press, 1994], 129). The impact of modernity as Hasker has described it is simply accepted as one of the "givens" of life!

26. See, for example, John Piper, Justin Taylor, and Paul Kjoss Helseth, eds., *Beyond the Bounds: Open Theism and the Undermining of Biblical Christianity* (Wheaton: Crossway Books, 2003), Bruce A. Ware, *God's Lesser Glory: The Diminished God of Open Theism* (Wheaton: Crossway, 2000), John M. Frame, *No Other God: A Response to Open Theism* (Phillipsburg: Presbyterian and Reformed, 2001) and R. K. McGregor Wright, *No Place for Sovereignty: What's Wrong with Freewill Theism* (Downers Grove: InterVarsity Press, 1996). The philosophical issues at stake are dealt with deftly in Paul Helm, *The Providence of God* (Downers Grove: InterVarsity Press, 1994).

outcome to that autonomy, because loneliness is an inescapable part of such autonomy.

The autonomous self is autonomous because it has liberated itself from an outside world of meaning, of obligation, of rules, rites, customs, and practices. Or, to be more accurate, what has happened is that the outside world seems to have evaporated and all reality has contracted into the self. It is in the self that the business of life is all settled.

It is true that this contraction often has resulted in a therapeutic preoccupation with the self, with its uncertainties, wounds, and loneliness, and this may or may not coincide with the outlook of all open theists. There does seem to be a point of connection, though, in the fact that for open theists, no less than for postmoderns, in the day-to-day decisions of life, God has absconded. He has effectively excluded himself in important ways from the universe inhabited by open theists. He has done this in order to secure the reality of their choices. The key point here is that they are freed from his intrusions into their decision-making. In this respect, they stand alone in their universe though God is ready to work with the consequences of those choices once they become known to him. This is their liberty. And is it really *that* different from the autonomy of postmoderns for whom reality has also left them alone with themselves?

Autonomous and Decentered

In the postmodern world, there is no Authority which is outside and above each person, no center in which the whole holds together, no way to assess this unhinged world from outside of itself. Life's events, therefore, have to be endured but they cannot really be evaluated because meaning has disintegrated. In another time, these events could have been more easily endured, even those that were painful and disconcerting, because they were seen to have come from a wise and all-knowing providence. There is consolation in that. Now there is no such providence, no such wisdom, no such omniscience, and no such consolation. Now, the divine imperative — "your will be done" — has gone and all that remains is the cacophony of opinions, the coercion of fashion, and the confusions of a broken world. The once grand, majestic purposes of God have slipped from our sight. Now, what we see are only the blind workings of nature with their tragedies, the impersonal forces of the economy which often seem so callous, the malice of evil people, and the peculiar anxieties of those adrift on a sea of affluence. Postmoderns are no longer actors in a vast and unfolding drama. They are actors only in their own *petit* dramas. We are but the pieces of confetti that flutter down, each on its own erratic course, none joined to the others, none connected, but each making its own solitary way through the air.

The grand Narrative in open theism has not entirely disappeared but it is far more uncertain than it used to be. There is no antecedent blueprint, no objective will of God, but it has all become a matter to be worked out in the present. God is the great improviser who maneuvers this way and that as the human story unfolds itself. However, since he does not see the end from the beginning, and cannot see much of the future because almost all of the future is made of the accumulating total of human decisions which are unknown to him until they have happened, there is a great deal of risk entailed. We really do not know, neither does God, if this is going to have a good ending. Is the open theist's sense of risk, then, really *that* different from the postmodern's? For the open theist, God has significantly abdicated from his position as the Center of reality, the one in whom the whole of life holds together, in order to partner with human beings. The cost of that partnership, however, is the practical loss of life's Center.

It seems rather clear, then, that there has taken place a convergence between open theism and the postmodern outlook at these two points. What has driven the open theist to this place are primarily *theological* reasons; what has brought postmoderns to this place is their belief that the Enlightenment explanations did not hold together. It was a rejection of Calvinism, in the one case, and of the rationalism of modernity, on the other, that explains this convergence. At the same time, we should remember that however theological Pinnock's motives were he also sees that the place to which he has now arrived is one in which he is content to have made "peace" with postmodernity. This convergence and this accord explain why open theism of the Pinnockian kind is left with very little to say to the postmodern world since, by a different route, it has fallen into the same morass as that in which postmoderns find themselves. In the one case, the world is now seen to be devoid of a center because it never had one, and in the other the Center has abdicated from being the Center. And if Pinnock is correct that there is much support for these views within the evangelical world, then fresh light has been cast on why evangelicals have been so ineffective in offering a vision which is a real alternative to that which comes through our corporate and entertainment worlds which the Church now appears to be aping. This will be pursued in the next chapter.

Christ the Center

Creation's Center

It is important for us to recall a fundamental distinction here. It is that there is a revelational continuity between the Creator and the creation, between the One and the many, but that this is not *soteriological* in its outcome. There is a soteriological *discontinuity*. This is the difference between revelation which is natural and revelation which is supernatural. If there is a tension resulting from the fact that side by side are laid a revelational continuity and a soteriological discontinuity, it is a tension whose preservation is essential to the preservation of Christianity itself. We have to distinguish creation from salvation though we cannot separate them. The writers in the early church, in their struggle with gnosticism, saw very clearly what the biblical teaching was and made the point, again and again, that in Christian faith the Creator and the Redeemer are one and the same. The creation is not in opposition to redemption but redemption is not to be had through the creation. Christ is the center in which all created reality inheres and Christ is the center and head of his Church. He is the one in whom our culture's displacement of God is reversed and the one in whom the consequent alienation between people begins to be healed.

These two themes are, in fact, central to the way in which Yahweh in the Old Testament disclosed himself. On the one hand, he is the creator and sovereign ruler of the universe, the one in whom all of reality is sustained. On the other hand, he is the one who has acted in Israel's life to disclose his saving purposes and in that disclosure to reveal his own nature. It is these two themes which were at the heart of Old Testament monotheism and they were at the center of Second Temple Judaism. This is important not only because this Judaism provided the background against which we have to understand Christ's own identity in the New Testament, but also because his identity is expressed in precisely these two ways, Richard Bauckham has helpfully argued.[27]

In the Second Temple Judaism which forms the immediate backdrop to the New Testament, Yahweh's unique role in bringing forth the creation and his sovereign rule over it were defining and differentiating beliefs. In his act of creation, a line of demarcation is established between the Maker and what he made, between the sacred and human life. This set off biblical faith from what was pagan, which always blurred this distinction. And in his sovereignty, a sovereignty which is universal, he showed himself to be unlike any of the so-called gods and goddesses, none of whom was sovereign in this way and none of whom exercised their will universally. It is this understanding of God that was expressed in the later chapters of Isaiah. Here, too, we find the teaching on the Servant emerging as well as the hope being expressed of a new Exodus. These chapters, then, were not only central to Second Temple Judaism and its literature but also become central to the New Testament understanding of Christ and his work.[28]

In Isaiah's vision, especially the part of it described in Chapter 40, it is God's power that is in focus. "Behold, the Lord God comes with might, and his arm rules for him" (Is. 40:10). At first sight, it seems entirely unnecessary for the prophet to attempt to persuade his readers on this point. After all, God is the one who has created everything and who sustains what he has made (40:26). He is the "everlasting God, the Creator of the ends of the earth. He does not faint or grow weary," says the prophet, and his understanding is "unsearchable" (40:28). And yet this truth was apparently disconnected from the circumstances of their lives, these who had lost everything (40:27). They had lost their land, their freedom, Jerusalem, and, indeed, everything that had been precious to them. It is to them that God, through the prophet, speaks of

---

27. Richard Bauckham, *God Crucified: Monotheism & Christology in the New Testament* (Grand Rapids: William B. Eerdmans, 1998), 25-42.

28. Bauckham, *God Crucified*, 11.

Who has measured the waters in the hollow of his hand
and marked off the heavens with a span,
enclosed the dust of the earth in a measure
and weighed the mountains in the scales
and the hills in a balance? . . .

It is he who sits above the circle of the earth,
and its inhabitants are like grasshoppers;
who stretches out the heavens like a curtain,
and spreads them like a tent to dwell in;
who brings princes to nought,
and makes the rulers of the earth as nothing. . . .

Lift up your eyes on high and see: who created these?
He who brings out their host by number,
calling them all by name; by the greatness of his might,
and because he is strong in power not one is missing.

Isaiah 40:12, 22-23, 26

comfort (40:1) about which they would have been incredulous without a fresh appropriation of this truth about the greatness of God's power. His power, seen in creation and in his rule over the nations (40:22-26), is not bare and abstract power but power that he uses for the good of his people. They might have been surrounded by hostile nations bent on their destruction, by ominous combinations of ruthless ambition and military might awesome in that day, but to God the people of the earth are but "grasshoppers" and he brings their rulers to "nought." They are withered by the breath of God "and the tempest carries them off like stubble" (40:24). Relative to his sovereign will, these rulers are "as nothing." They are irrelevant in the sense that they are impotent to obstruct the will of God (40:15). "All the nations are as nothing before him, they are accounted by him as less than nothing and emptiness" (40:17).

This does not mean, of course, that God does not use human agency in executing his plans. Indeed he does! He raised up Cyrus "to subdue nations before him and ungird the loins of kings" (Is. 45:1). He works in the lives of nations which do not know him for the sake of his people (43:3) and this could only happen as he guided the counsels of those in power to effect his ends. Many years later, Paul would take up this same point saying of all the nations that God has "determined allotted periods and the boundaries of their habitation" (Acts 17:26). As for Isaiah, so for Paul: the whole sweep of human history is guided by God's sovereign hand.

This sovereignty, then, is expressed over the nature which Yahweh has brought forth and sustains (Is. 49:11) and over people (43:6). And Isaiah warns people of the futility of contesting the will of God. How ridiculous is the person "who strives with his Maker, an earthen vessel with the potter! Does the clay say to him who fashions it, 'What are you making?'" (Is. 45:9; cf. Rom. 9:21-24). This vision of the greatness of God in his power and rule is summed up in the lofty declaration God makes to Isaiah that "I am the first and I am the last; besides me there is no God" (Is. 44:6). This is reiterated much later to John, "I am the Alpha and the Omega, says the Lord God, who is and who was and who is to come, the Almighty" (Rev. 1:8). This language of Alpha and Omega and first and last are merisms which express the two ends of a comparison with the intention of including everything in between (cf. Rev. 21:6; 22:13). This statement, then, expresses the understanding that the God who transcends time, Beale says, "guides the entire course of history because he stands as sovereign over its beginning and its end."[29]

This is the vision that is then carried through into the New Testament where, as Bauckham notes, early Christian theology was careful to contain its understanding within the Old Testament texts.[30] The text which is most widely used to express Jesus' participation in this same divine sovereignty is Psalm 110:1 which is cited some twenty-one times:[31] "The Lord says to my lord: 'Sit at my right hand, till I make your

---

29. G. K. Beale, *The Book of Revelation: A Commentary on the Greek Text* (Grand Rapids: William B. Eerdmans, 1999), 199.

30. Bauckham, *God Crucified*, 28.

31. Bauckham, *God Crucified*, 29. These citations are: Matt. 22:44; Mk. 12:36; 14:62; Lk. 20:42-43; 22:69; Acts 2:33-35; 5:31; 7:55-56; Rom. 8:34; I Cor. 15:25; Eph. 1:20; 2:6; Col. 3:1; Heb. 1:3, 13; 12:2; I Pet. 3:22; Rev. 21.

enemies your footstool'." This was read by the apostles as saying that Jesus shared the sovereign throne of Yahweh, and where this text was linked to Psalm 8:6 it also reasserted some of the themes we have seen in Isaiah 40, that "all things" have been put under Jesus' feet. The joining of Psalms 110:1 and 8:6 clearly combine an assertion of Jesus divinity, his resurrection (cf. Rom. 8:34; I Cor. 15:25), and the fact that in him God's purpose in creating Adam was fulfilled.[32]

Christ, then, has been elevated, Paul tells us, "far above all rule and authority and power and dominion, and above every name which is named, not only in this age but also in that which is to come" (Eph. 1:21). He is at God's right hand now "with angels, authorities, and powers subject to him" (I Pet. 3:22), Peter writes. There is, in fact, a rich vocabulary which Paul uses in describing the sweep of this conquest. Sometimes it is angels who are the conquered, sometimes powers, or rulers, or authorities, or creatures, or spiritual forces, or height, or depth, or things to come, or death (Rom. 8:38-39; 13:1; I Cor. 2:6).

The authority over "all things" that he had at the beginning when he acted in creation (Col. 1:15-16) has been reasserted over this fallen world (Eph. 1:9-10). Because of all of this, he who "descended is he who ascended far above all the heavens, that he might fill all things" (Eph. 4:10).[33] It is hard to understand how open theists who predicate their work on the Bible's authority could have missed all of this.

It has been said that in the Bible we have not so much a doctrine of creation as that of the Creator; and, within limits, this is true, for no part of the creation is ever finally or fully meaningful until it is understood in relation to its Creator. From this flow the many distinctive ways in which Christian faith thinks about life. If everything is made by God, then everything belongs to him and is used rightly only when it is used in accordance with his will. Not only so, but if God is the source of all life then all meaning derives from him in much the same way as it is the artist who can say definitively what the work of art means. The purpose of God's redemption, then, is that, on the one

32. James D. G. Dunn, *The Theology of Paul the Apostle* (Grand Rapids: William B. Eerdmans, 1998), 248.
33. See H. N. Ridderbos, *Paul: An Outline of His Theology,* trans. John Richard De Witt (Grand Rapids: William B. Eerdmans, 1975), 388.

hand, we should take our place in his world, through Christ, and own him as our Maker and, on the other hand, live in his world by his ethical will. Then it is that we see with new eyes God's power in creation (Is. 40:26-28; Amos 4:13), his greatness (Ps. 90:2; Acts 17:24), his wisdom (Is. 40:12-14), and from our experiences as frail, fading creatures we are also constantly reminded of his eternality (Ps. 103:14-8). Thus it is that creation is connected both with redemption and ethics, with worship and service.

When the New Testament comes to speak of Christ, it speaks of him, as we have already seen, in ways that exactly replicate what had been said of Yahweh. If Yahweh "made the world and everything in it" (Acts 17:24) then so, too, did Christ. There is but one God, Paul says, from whom are all things, and one Christ "through whom are all things and through whom we exist" (I Cor. 8:6; cf. Col. 1:16; Heb. 1:3). Here Paul was not only taking up the foundational truth of the Old Testament that "the Lord our God is one Lord" (Deut. 6:4) but now placing that truth into a christological formulation. There clearly is being carried forward here, Bauckham argues, the monotheism of the Old Testament which not only declares that there is only one God but that the God who thus exists is both the creator of all other existence and sovereignly upholds its life and directs its course. That is the kind of God who had called out Israel and to whom Israel owed its exclusive loyalty. The inclusion of Christ in this divine work of creating, upholding, and directing in no way imperils the monotheism. What it does is to exalt the Christ who is so included without diminishing the Father. It places Christ at the center of reality with the Father and, of course, with the Holy Spirit. It places him within the whole godhead.

What is said of Yahweh therefore can be said of Christ. No part of the creation is ever finally or fully meaningful until it is understood in relation to Christ. Everything belongs to him and it is used rightly only when it is used in accordance with his will. And if he is the source of life, it is he who can say definitively what it all means. The purpose of God's redemption, then, is that, on the one hand, we should take our place in his world, through Christ, and own him as our Maker and, on the other hand, live in his world by his ethical will.

What is new in this picture is the understanding as to how Christ is working out his sovereign rule because there is an eschatological dimension to it. While it is the case that "all things" have been delivered to him by the Father (Matt. 11:27; Jn. 3:35), that "all things" have been put under his feet (Eph. 1:22; Heb. 1:8), that such is his power that he is able "to subject all things to himself" (Phil. 3:21) so that we can say unequivocally that Christ "is Lord of all" (Acts 10:36), yet this is a contested reign.

Here again we find the "already but not yet." While it is true that God has disarmed the "powers" (Col. 2:15) and while it is the case that all things have been subjected to Christ, his rule is nevertheless contested. It is contested in the sense that while evil is even now under the sovereign rule of Christ, and even though its doom has been declared, and even though its back has already been broken at the Cross, it has not yet been taken to the scaffold. The Church, therefore, has to be wary as long as it is in this world and must seek the protection of God's armor (Eph. 6:10-18), grace, and power. We have not yet come to the final moment of conquest when he "delivers the kingdom to God the Father after destroying every rule and every authority and power" (I Cor. 15:24-25). Then all of created reality which has been fractured and broken by the intrusions of satanic disorder will be eternally cleansed.

Let us open our eyes and look at the present position of Christ and of his people in the world. *This is not his rest; and it is not theirs.* There is a warfare to be waged, and they must wage it. There is ignorance to be enlightened, and they must enlighten it; error to be corrected, and they must correct it; sorrow to be healed, and they must heal it; all that is holy and full of blessedness for man to be introduced, and they must introduce it. The very power of death has to be destroyed, and they must destroy it, till the world is penetrated by the heavenly life they proclaim. . . . But now, let us observe, all this warfare is to be carried on by Christ through and in that Body of His which lives on from age to age in the world.

William Milligan, *The Resurrection of the Dead*

The Church's Center

What we see in Isaiah is not power in God which is bare and abstract but power which is holy, compassionate, and pastoral. It is God who "will feed his flock like a shepherd" (Is. 40:11). He takes the most vulnerable, the "lambs," in his arms and places them near his heart. He takes those who are most at risk, "those that are with young," and gently leads them. This is what the prophet had in mind when he said that God brought a "reward" with him (Is. 40:10), the reward of his gracious, powerful presence. In this juxtaposition of divine grace and human vulnerability a principle emerges about how God works. The proud, Mary said much later in the *Magnificat,* are scattered "in the imaginations of their hearts," the rich are "sent empty away" (Lk. 1:51, 53), but it is the "low" who are exalted. That is the principle.

Indeed, we find it illustrated in ways both rich and numerous in the New Testament. And it is not simply that a condition for receiving the grace of God is the ability to recognize and confess our own bankruptcy. That is a part of it, but there is more at stake. Marva Dawn has argued for what she calls a theology of weakness. Her argument is that God's power finds its desired habitat, so to speak, when it comes to realization in the context of human weakness. This is *his* neighborhood. This is what Paul learned in a moment of great weakness when God told him, "My grace is sufficient for you, for my power is made perfect [i.e. reaches its final objective] in weakness" (II Cor. 12:9). In life, the powerful usually have neither affinity for, nor interest in, those on the other end of the social scale, those who are impoverished, insignificant, and are far removed from the places where the great policies and decisions of the day are made. But God's power, which is the way by which his character is asserted, is different. This is what explains what seems so odd about many of the stories and comparisons which appear in Jesus' teaching. It seems odd that a despised tax collector ends up righteous rather than a punctiliously religious man (Lk. 18:9-14), that mere birds and lilies are more glorious than the greatest cultural achievements in history to that day (Matt. 6:26-34), that a wealthy man would ever entrust his property to a slave who, almost certainly, would have been judged too lowly and unreliable for such trust (Matt. 25:14-30), or that a shepherd would actually die for a sheep for the value of the shepherd's life far outweighs that of the sheep (Jn. 10:1-18).[34] And, again, we find the same thing in the epistles. To whom did the gospel come? Did it seek out the well-born and well-connected, the *savants* and intellectuals, the powerful or the well-to-do? No. God chose the foolish, the weak, and the low and despised (I Cor. 1:26-29).

The world seems upside down when we ponder these matters but the explanation lies in the upside-down character of the Incarnation itself. Christ, who existed from all eternity, did not exploit his relationship of equality with God for his own benefit but did the unthinkable. He set aside every expression of his innate glory which was incompatible with his mission of seeking, serving, and saving the lost (Phil. 2:5-12). It is this fact, this profound self-concealment, which qualified him on his ascension "to exercise the unique divine sovereignty over all things."[35] It is in this way, this way of humility, that God's power is revealed and his character is sovereignly made known through the created order.

The biblical confession is that this sovereignty is already being realized in the life of the Church. Christ, who is at the center of creation, and who subdues "all things," is also at the center of the Church in whom this triumphant reign is already being savingly realized. The preexistent Christ in whom "all things were created" (Col. 1:16), and in whom "all things hold together" (Col. 1:17), is the very same Christ who is "the head of the body, the church" (Col. 1:18; cf. Eph. 4:15, 5:23). The conclusion, then, is that "in everything he might be preeminent" (Col. 1:18). He is the Church's center, its life, its focus, its glory, and its hope.

There is, then, an analogous relationship between his place in creation and his place in the Church. In both he is central. However, he is Lord over creation in a way that is different from the way that he is head over the Church, and that difference emerges in the fact that he is never said to be head over "all things." In Col. 1:15, where Christ is spoken of as the "image of God," we appear to have a reference that takes us back to the creation of the first Adam from which Paul constructs a parallel. "The new creation that has broken through with Christ's res-

---

34. Marva J. Dawn, *Powers, Weakness, and the Tabernacling of God* (Grand Rapids: William B. Eerdmans, 2001), 35-71.

35. Bauckham, *God Crucified*, 58.

To this end the Son of God sympathetically renounces the glory of his Heavenly state. He does it for God's sake more than for man's, for love of the Holy more even than of the sinner, to glorify the Holy through the sinner, and to hallow his name. And nothing can hallow Holiness but Holiness, nothing else can satisfy it, nothing else can save. . . . To appear and act as Redeemer, to be born, suffer, and die, was a mightier act of Godhead than lay in all the creation, preservation, and blessing of the world. It was only in the exercise of a perfect divine fullness (and therefore power) that Christ could empty and humble himself to the servant he became. As the humiliation grew so grew the exaltation of the power and person who achieved it. It was an act of such might that it was bound to break through the servant form, and take at least for all men's worship the lordly name.

P. T. Forsyth, *The Person and Place of Jesus Christ*

urrection," writes Ridderbos, "takes the place of the first creation of which Adam was the representative"[36] and is more glorious in proportion as the Last Adam is to the first. While the creation awaits its liberation, the Church awaits its final redemption in a rather different way.

And yet this sovereign reign is, in important ways, concealed[37] just as Christ's preexistent glory was during his earthly days. Of the fact of this rule there should be no doubt, but exactly how Christ is exercising it is most often lost on us. There are none of the visible trappings of regal power that are being displayed, for this is a reign that we apprehend by faith and not by sight. We see the tangible results of the hidden work of the Holy Spirit. We know that it is his work to apply what Christ secured on Calvary but exactly how this happens we are never told. The Holy Spirit is like a wind which "blows where it wills, and you hear the sound of it, but you do not know whence it comes or whither it goes" (Jn. 3:8).

36. Ridderbos, *Paul*, 85.
37. Karl Barth, *Church Dogmatics,* trans. G. T. Thomson (5 vols.; Edinburgh: T&T Clark, 1936-77), II, i, 179-204.

Christ's sovereign rule is hidden in this interim period between the "already" and the "not yet" until that time when "every knee should bow, in heaven and on earth and under the earth, and every tongue confess that Jesus Christ is Lord, to the glory of God the Father" (Phil. 2:11). The mystery of iniquity is at work in the world now during this interim time and it is not always clear how its malignant work is being checked, overridden, or woven into the glorious purposes of God. It needs to be remembered, though, that while it was Judas who betrayed Christ, and woe to him for doing so, it was by God's plan that he was thus betrayed.

How modest we need to be in using a word like *theodicy!* For the judgment that has befallen those of us who live east of Eden, is that we have been exiled. Our reconciliation has overcome our broken relationship with the Father but it has not conferred on us vast powers of understanding into his governance of the world. From us as sinners, God has hidden himself and his ways are ultimately known only by himself. God alone knows himself in the depths of his being. What we know is only what he has chosen to make known to us, and he has not chosen to make known much of his dealing with evil in the world or exactly how his purposes are ripening in the Church, which now seems so battered.

What we can say is that as perplexing as the presence of evil is, we nevertheless have the key elements for our understanding. They are that evil is an alien intruder, that that intrusion took place within the sovereign will of God, that its overthrow has happened already at the Cross, and that what we are seeing today is but its final writhings under God's judgment. And already in the Church, despite its manifold weaknesses and sins, we see the dawn of a new order of things in which the displacement of God from life is being overturned and in which the alienation of people one from another is beginning to be healed. In place of sin, we see the Kingdom of God, now planted, now growing, now awaiting its culmination in eternity. "Only it is to be acknowledged," James Orr wisely concluded one of his books, that "our lights on these vast matters are in this life 'broken,' refracted, partial; that it is but the 'outskirts' of God's ways we can discern." We now have only glimpses into the wise, omnipotent rule of God but those glimpses are enough to "steady our thoughts, and guide our feet amidst the shad-

The Church's one foundation
Is Jesus Christ her Lord;
She is his new creation
By water and the word.
From heav'n he came and sought her
To be his holy bride;
With his own blood he bought her,
And for her life he died.

'Mid toil and tribulation,
And tumult of her war,
She waits the consummation
Of peace for evermore;
Till with the vision glorious,
Her longing eyes are blest,
And the great Church victorious
Shall be the Church at rest.

Samuel J. Stone

ows"[38] until that time when we no longer peer into a mirror dimly "but then face to face." Now, says Paul, "I know in part; then I shall understand fully, even as I have been fully understood" (I Cor. 13:12).

Thus it is that we have two diametrically opposed visions of life. In the one, there is no center; in the other, there is and it is Christ. In the one, life is but a succession of random events; in the other, life is lived out under the sovereign rule of Christ. In the one, we are alone in the cosmos; in the other, we are not. In the one, salvation is humanly managed; in the other, it is divinely given. Christianity best flourishes when the sharpness of these opposing visions is preserved, and it becomes sickened when it is not. In the next chapter, I shall explore this question in relation to the evangelical Church.

38. James Orr, *Sin as a Problem* (London: Hodder and Stoughton, 1910), 311-12.

CHAPTER VII

Megachurches, Paradigm Shifts, and the New Spiritual Quest

—⟡—

Cheap grace is the deadly enemy of our Church. We are fighting today for costly grace.

Cheap grace means grace sold on the market like cheapjacks' wares. The sacraments, the forgiveness of sin, and the consolations of religion are thrown away at cut prices. . . . Cheap grace is the preaching of forgiveness without requiring repentance, baptism without church discipline, Communion without confession, absolution without personal confession. Cheap grace is grace without discipleship, grace without the cross, grace without Jesus Christ, living and incarnate.

DIETRICH BONHOEFFER

The last half century has seen an astounding boom in evangelical believing and, in America, at least, a shift in the center of gravity in the ecclesiastical world from liberal to conservative. This shift continues to reverberate through the denominations. Life, however, was not always so good for those whose disposition has been conservative and evangelical.

When the Second World War ended, evangelical faith in both Europe and America was weak and marginalized, its learning was not impressive, and its institutions and organizations were few and far between. Then began an improbable journey, on both sides of the Atlantic and, indeed, in many other parts of the world, from weakness to strength, from the periphery to the center. Academic life flourished and, in the 1970s and 1980s in America in particular, evangelical organizations proliferated like rabbits in a warren. Evangelical denominations began to expand at the very moment when mainline denominations began to contract. In America, evangelicals became a force with which even the politicians began to reckon. No one could have seen that from the small beginnings half a century ago would arise this mighty behemoth. And, if we were able to see ahead another half century, what, one wonders, would we see?

We can, of course, make projections only from what we can see today and these glances ahead are never anything more than speculations, speculations that are frequently confounded, in due course, by reality. Wars, economic crises, the renewing work of the Holy Spirit, and even the judgment of God, all change what happens and none of this can be seen from the present. It is, nevertheless, worth pondering a discomforting thought. Is it possible that some evangelicals are now beginning to walk a road similar to the one that has brought down the mainline denominations in America and many of their counterparts in Europe? In America, we can certainly see what happened to the theological liberalism that has flourished in the university divinity schools and found a happy home in the mainline denominations for decades. What is clear from this is that the church life which it has infected has weakened and declined and we now have before our very eyes a model of how disintegration can happen. If this same model is reappearing in the evangelical world, it is a matter of simple deduction that the same deleterious effects might be anticipated there, too. Is it possible, then, that this vast expansion in evangelical believing in the West, whose effects have been felt all over the world, is now beginning to reverse the gains of the last fifty years and go into a contraction? And what signs might there be that this is, indeed, happening?

The indicators of decline and weakness, I believe, are already beginning to appear, though, as so often happens to those who see themselves as still in the flush of success, these indicators seem not to be there. I can now only attempt to illustrate my judgment in one particular area, that of the new ways of "doing church," though my concern here is obviously selective. What I shall argue is that in this area, the lure of success is the very means by which success is actually disappearing and, in the next generation, we will see the bitter fruit appearing more evidently than we can see it now. And the irony which today is almost completely lost on evangelicals is that in this new quest, this new way of "doing church," those who once stood aloof from the older liberalism are now unwittingly producing a close cousin to it. By the time this becomes so evident that it will be incontrovertible, it will be too late.

We need to begin, however, by observing that this new experiment in reinventing and reengineering the Church is the most important evangelical effort to date at thinking about how to engage the postmodern world which I have tried to describe in this book. It is the most important, at least, if this effort is judged by numbers and the magnitude of the possible outcomes. For that reason, I am revisiting this subject.[1] Here, however, the question is different. Here I am asking if this is really the way the Church should be engaging the postmodern world. I will be arguing that it clearly is not.

This new approach was, of course, pioneered by Willow Creek Community Church. It is undoubtedly the case that in many ways Willow Creek remains somewhat unique even for those who believe that its astounding success can be replicated in other contexts and places. There is, however, a common thread that ties Willow Creek not only to its copycat followers, but also to those who were inspired initially by its success but have gone on to develop their own mutations. That common element lies in the fact that they are all operating off methodologies for succeeding in which that success requires little or no theology.[2]

1. I have addressed this subject previously in *God in the Wasteland: The Reality of Truth in a World of Fading Dreams* (Grand Rapids: William B. Eerdmans, 1994), 72-87.

2. It is not only evangelicals who have been fascinated by this new methodology. Some liberal Protestant mainliners and even Catholics have taken note, too. Indeed, the appeal is even further afield yet. In Los Angeles, the seven thousand members who worship at Agape International Spiritual Center belong to a "church" which makes no claim to being Christian but it has, nevertheless, come about through using the Willow Creek method. Writing of this Spiritual Center, Gene Veith says that

It is an attempt to respond to the spiritual yearnings of Boomers and Xers while creating an experience of the church which is compatible with their habits, likes, dislikes, wants, expectations, and sounds.[3] It produces an evangelism which is modest in its attempts at persuasion about *truth,* but energetic in its retailing of spiritual and psychological benefits. So successful, so alluring, has this experiment become that it would not be an exaggeration to say that it is transforming what evangelicalism looks like.[4]

It may be that a case can be made that even so recent an innovation as this has already become *passé* and that younger evangelicals have already judged it to be inadequate and are looking for another model. This, in fact, is the argument that Robert Webber has made.[5] He sees the era of the "pragmatic evangelicals," which ran from 1970 to 2000, as now being superseded by a new era, that of the "younger evangelicals." This is bringing a different mentality: not megachurches, but small churches, not suburban but urban, not free-floating but connect-

---

intermixed "with the Christian praise songs are the 'Oms' of Eastern meditation. In the obligatory bookstore, the Bible shares space with books by gurus, self-proclaimed goddesses, and mystical pop-psychologists" (Gene Edward Veith, "The New Multi-faith Religion," *World* [December 15, 2001], 16).

3. In 1992 the Willow Creek Association was formed to link "like-minded, action-oriented churches" worldwide. The Association in 2001 had swelled to over 5,000 churches and 65,000 leaders were attending "how to" conferences annually. It is not, however, a denomination. It is an Association. A first-person account of how this came about is offered in Bill and Lynne Hybels, *Rediscovering Church: The Story and Vision of Willow Creek Community Church* (Grand Rapids: Zondervan, 1995). G. A. Pritchard's study *Willow Creek Seeker Services: Evaluating a New Way of Doing Church* (Grand Rapids: Baker Book House, 1996) is useful in giving a well-ordered, accurate account of the programs and operation of Willow Creek but it is, unfortunately, bereft of sociological insight as to why Willow Creek is as it is. Far more useful is Kimon Howland Sargeant, *Seeker Churches: Promoting Traditional Religion in a Nontraditional Way* (New Brunswick: Rutgers University Press, 2000). However telling this analysis is — and it is telling — it faces the daunting reality that at one level at least, Willow Creek is highly successful. In the year 2001, 865,000 people attended Willow Creek services and that was just one of many indicators of its remarkable growth.

4. Even the intellectually serious *Atlantic Monthly* gave a rather breathless review of all of this. See Charles Trueheart, "Welcome to the Next Church," *Atlantic Monthly* (August, 1996), 37-58.

5. Robert E. Webber, *The Younger Evangelicals: Facing the Challenges of the New World* (Grand Rapids: Baker, 2002).

ing with tradition, not generationally limited but intergenerational, and not merely interdenominational but intentionally ecumenical, thereby reaching across older boundaries that once divided Protestants from Catholics and Eastern Orthodox.

This, of course, is always the fate that awaits those who have surfed cultural waves because sooner or later — and in our Western cultures it is usually sooner — a devastating riptide is encountered. When people are not embedded in a confessional tradition, drift loose from a defining structure of thought, are no longer rooted in communities which have moral and intellectual expectations, almost anything can happen — and it usually does. Webber's is, then, a plausible hypothesis. However, his typology is also an argument for a different kind of evangelicalism. What is description and what is advocacy in his book have become a little blurry. A deeply flawed traditional evangelicalism was, he argues, superseded by a deeply flawed pragmatic evangelicalism which, mercifully, is now being superseded by this new kind of evangelicalism in which everything appears to have been made right!

If we are in the throes of such a transition, one has to say that we are at its very threshold. Indeed, Webber dates the moment as probably being the year 2000. If that is so, then we are altogether too close to this transition to have any real assurance that we know that it is taking place or that we know what its outcomes will be. I, therefore, want to cast back a little further in time and think about the way in which Webber's "pragmatic evangelicals" thought — and many still think — about doing church.

Barna reports that 58% of Protestant churches describe themselves as being "seeker-sensitive" which, I am assuming, is the soft version of which "seeker-driven" or "seeker-oriented" is the hard. Yet the very language of seeker sensitivity is definitionally hazy and perhaps deliberately so. Being sensitive to seekers in the church could arise simply from old-fashioned virtues such as courtesy and thoughtfulness, in which case it is hardly unique to this time. That, obviously, is not what is in mind. It is, rather, an attempt to exploit one side of a Pauline paradox. The paradox is that Paul could say at the Areopagus in Athens that God rules in history so that people "should seek" him in the hope that they might "find him" (Acts 17:27) while also saying to the Romans that, as a result of the pervasiveness of sin, "no one understands, no one seeks for God" (Rom. 3:11). Here is the two-sided truth: we should seek God and yet no one seeks God. This paradox reflects our condition as those who, made in the image of God, are made to know him but who, nevertheless, are fallen and will not "honor him as God, or give thanks to him" (Rom. 1:21).

The seeker-sensitive approach typically emphasizes the one side of this paradox while significantly discounting the other, seeing sinners as more or less neutral in their disposition toward God and the gospel and therefore amenable to marketing techniques. It typically does not see sinners as those who are unable to submit to God, despite all the marketing techniques, without his intervention. It is the degree to which these techniques are used, the degree to which the church arranges its life around the seeker impulse, that creates a scale of seeker sensitivity in these churches, from modest on the one end to "seeker-oriented" on the other. This, of course, makes generalizations difficult, but without them understanding is impossible.

In order to explore this development, I will first be asking why this new approach is being taken. Second, I will examine the emerging relationship between commerce and religion. Third, I will look at the origins of this development in the evangelical world. Finally, I examine the assumptions beneath seeker church methodology and I will offer some reasons for thinking that the evangelical world has taken a turn which, if it is not corrected, will have some painful consequences in the years ahead.

Why Do Church Differently?

There is now a widespread sense that the churches simply cannot go on about their business oblivious to what has been happening outside their doors. Churches, after all, are in a new cultural context throughout the West and, not least, in America. American culture, from its universities to much of its television programming, is in a postmodern mood. These churches have understood the fact that the ground is moving beneath their feet, culturally speaking. In five important ways, this experiment is responding to changes in our world which, it is felt, can no longer be ignored.

The New Seeker

First, this changed cultural context is producing spiritual seekers. It is to this "shadow culture," this parallel market of spiritual desire, that seeker churches have been intuitively drawn. Their methodology is peculiarly adapted to this moment because to those who seek spirituality without religion, as so many in the postmodern world do, these churches are offering spirituality without theology. It is, most often, spirituality of a therapeutic kind, which assumes that the most pressing issues that should be addressed in church are those with which most people are preoccupied: how to sustain relationships, how to handle stress, what to do about recurring financial problems, how to handle conflicts in the workplace, and how to raise children. It is these issues, and a multitude like them, which prescribe where Christian faith must offer some answers if it is to remain relevant. While biblical truth is not itself denied, and while the importance of being doctrinally orthodox is not questioned, neither is seen to be central to the *practice* of meeting seekers who are looking for answers to other issues in their lives. They are looking for answers, perhaps to find ways of constructing a spirituality which works for them, but they really have not come into church to find the kind of truth by which the Church has historically been defined, and by which it has lived, across the generations and centuries.

Evangelicalism Falters

Second, this movement is attempting to address what is a genuine problem in the evangelical world. It is that evangelicalism in America — and this is even more evident in Europe — appears not to be growing. The percentage of those claiming to be reborn has remained stagnant since Gallup made it a matter of national conversation in 1976. In fact, Leith Anderson goes so far as to say that "85% of America's Protestant Churches are either stagnating or dying" though this no doubt includes the mainline churches which, for their own reasons, have been declining for decades, but it also appears to be a notable exaggeration.[6] Nevertheless, the health of the evangelical world has become a

6. Leith Anderson, *Dying for Change: An Arresting Look at the New Realities Con-*

Stronger *family* relationships . . . Greater *satisfaction* at work . . .
And even *better* sex . . . and *you* can get *all* these things through
Church. . . . Hey, we're not making this stuff up. It's happening every day, every week, all across America. Don't get us wrong —
you don't walk through the doors of a church and suddenly your
family likes you better and your allergies clear up. There are no
magic potions to happiness. But a good church gives you a place
to explore what God has to say about the kinds of everyday problems we all face: family relationships, stress, sex, ethics, work,
health, romance, kids . . . well, you're human — you know the list.
Church should make a difference in your life Monday through
Saturday, too . . . not just for an hour on Sunday.

> Advertisement for Canyon Creek
> Community Church, Chandler, Arizona

troubling issue and it is to the credit of the seeker churches that they
have raised it. The evangelical ship is, to use a nautical term, "be-
calmed." Its sails are limp. It is not moving in its waters.

The New Marketplace

Third, the seeker churches have recognized that, for good or ill, they
are operating in a marketplace. Just as there is choice in the mall so
there is choice in religion. And what we find there is that it is increasingly a buyer's, not a seller's, market. This has brought into the Church

---

fronting Churches and Para-Church Ministries (Minneapolis: Bethany House, 1990), 10.
This figure apparently comes from George Barna, *User Friendly Churches: What Christians Need to Know About the Churches People Love to Go to* (Ventura: Regal Books,
1991), 15. A major survey done on churches in forty-one denominations in 2001 found
that 51% reported growth over the last five years, so 49% did not, rather than the 85%
Anderson claims. This growth was registered quite evenly between rural, town, city,
and older suburb. The major exception was the newer suburb which showed a 67%
growth. See Carl S. Dudley and David A. Roozen, eds., *Faith Communities Today: A Report on Religion in the United States Today* (Hartford: Hartford Institute for Religious
Research, 2001), 26.

much hopping, shopping, and switching. In 2001, for example, while 8% switched to Catholicism, 17% switched out of it; 19% of those in Methodist churches were new but 25% left; 24% came into Presbyterianism but 25% disappeared; 30% were drawn into Pentecostalism but 19% departed. This, however, appears to be more of a cultural phenomenon than a purely Christian affliction because in this same year, 33% switched into Buddhism and 23% switched out.[7]

This creates an entirely different context for ministry from what prevailed only a few decades ago.[8] This market today is competitive. And increasingly what pastors are up against are churchgoers' *preferences*. This is a buyer's market and what the buyer wants has become as large a consideration as what the church wants to give. And what churches have discovered is that these preferences are significantly affected by deep therapeutic longings, by fallacious assumptions about human potential, by a sense of entitlement to wholeness, by an almost sacrosanct assumption about consumer sovereignty, by the entertainment industry, and perhaps even by a desire to be cocooned from society as much as possible.

This has changed many things in this new experiment in how to "do church." Among them is the fact that concerted attention is now being given to the way in which a newcomer "feels" about the church. That is why Disney World is considered a model that some churches have tried to follow for it has been so successful in creating for its "guests" (as its customers are called) an atmosphere which is clean, bright, optimistic, and fun. It also has demonstrated that it has the know-how to keep its customers satisfied so that they want to return. That is also a key factor in any church's success today. One of the less welcome byproducts of the new consumer mentality is that brand loyalty is a thing of the past

---

7. Egon Mayer and Barry Kosmin, "The American Religious Identification Survey," http://www.gc.cuny.edu/studies/key_findings.htm. This study was conducted by the Graduate Center of the City University of New York.

8. See Craig Van Gelder, "A Great New Fact of Our Day: America as Mission Field," in *The Church Between Gospel and Culture*, ed. George R. Hunsberger and Craig Van Gelder (Grand Rapids: William B. Eerdmans, 1996), 57-68; Richard J. Mouw, "The Missionary Location of the North American Churches," in *Confident Witness — Changing World: Rediscovering the Gospel in North America*, ed. Craig Van Gelder (Grand Rapids: William B. Eerdmans, 1999), 3-15.

Back in the early 1960s, when cars were big and hair was short and families that prayed together stayed together, the Walceks said grace before meals and went to Mass every single morning. Emil and Kathleen sent their eight children to the parochial schools in Placentia, California, and on Sunday mornings at St. Joseph's the family took up two pews.

Then one by one, the children set off on their spiritual travels, and in the process perfectly charted the journey of their generation. Emil Jr., 45, dropped out of church and stayed out. John, 43, was married on a cliff overlooking Laguna Beach, divorced — and returned to the Catholic Church, saying "Maybe the traditional way of doing things isn't so bad." Joe, 41, also returned to the fold after marrying a Ukrainian Catholic. Mary, 40, married a lapsed Methodist and worships "God's creation" in her own unstructured fashion. Rosie, 38, drifted into the Hindu-influenced Self-Realization Fellowship. Chris, 34, picked Unitarianism, which offered some of Christianity's morality without its dogma. Theresa, 36, spent five years exploring the "Higher Power" in 12-step self-help programs. Ann, 30, called off her wedding when her nonpracticing Jewish fiancé embraced Orthodoxy, a crisis that "sparked a whole new journey for me."

Richard Ostling, "The Church Search"

so people circulate through churches, trying one and then another, with the result that the back doors are being used as much as the front. Knowing how to keep the "customer" becomes important knowledge.

The sudden fascination with Disney obviously goes beyond an interest in how to emulate a well-run, effective business. As Stephen Fjellman has pointed out, these amusement parks are pilgrimage sites, in which the memories of youth are rekindled in a context that is clean, civil, safe, and where fantasy abounds.[9] The Disney creations are, in

9. Stephen J. Fjellman, *Vinyl Leaves: Walt Disney World in America* (San Francisco: Westview Press, 1992), 9-10.

fact, a counterblast against life which is often not clean, civil, and safe. One cannot walk the streets of all of our cities at night in such a carefree way as people do in the Disney creations, nor do we commonly see parents and strangers making allowances for children who are tired and hot as they do here. Disney, the happiest place on earth, is, in fact, *utopian.* It is a compelling distillation of how the middle class wishes life looked in the United States or how they (mistakenly) remember it as having been. And the key to producing such a happy place is complete managerial control, considerable imagination, and technological wizardry. None of these points has been lost on emerging seeker churches. In them, one finds the same control beneath the apparent spontaneity, the same attempt at imagination, the same state-of-the-art technology, the same attempt at creating an atmosphere for the middle class which is safe, friendly, and fun, and one which offers an alternative kind of space. After all, how else is one to succeed in a context so deeply defined by consumer habits and preferences?

Disney is also about entertainment, and some churches have come to think that here, too, another page can be taken from its book. If the Church is to succeed in marketing itself in an age dominated as no other has been by entertainment, then going to church will have to be fun, and Disney knows how to do that well. Entertainment has therefore emerged as a very important factor in the new mix,[10] though of course it is the case that not every seeker church has walked down this road in the same way. Nevertheless, ministers who resemble comedians or other entertainers are beginning to show up on church teams. This, of course, is a concession to the fact, as Neil Postman argued in his *Amusing Ourselves to Death,* that all forms of public discourse are now in a format of entertainment because contemporaries, for probably many reasons, have a need for distraction which is bottomless and a matching inability to linger too long on anything too serious. We are haunted by boredom and, beneath all the layers of our accumulation, we are empty. We need to be amused.

It is true that figures in the past, like the born performer Billy Sunday, did employ eye-catching tactics to gain crowd attention and

---

10. See, for one expression of this, Walt Kallestad, *Entertainment Evangelism: Taking the Church Public* (Nashville: Abingdon Press, 1996).

did employ humor along the way. What we are seeing today, however, is different. It is a smoothly professional appropriation of what pervades our culture of entertainment. The question that is often left unpondered, however, is how the entertainment format affects what is being projected. How serious can Christian faith be in such a context? And how serious can it afford to be if it is to succeed? A faith serious enough to engage with the modern world as it really is with its loss of truth, meaning, and hope might very well become an impediment to spiritual seekers in the marketplace today. Theirs is a world of technique not of truth, a world where reality contracts into the self, and the self into feelings and intuitions, and evil is often just a bad day.

The New Social Environment

Fourth, these churches have been to the forefront in recognizing how the growth of our cities, the evolution in the ways people shop, and the ways in which they have adapted to large, impersonal structures in society have all changed what they expect from church, what they are and are not willing to tolerate. These churches therefore argue that it would be foolhardy for the Church to go on functioning as if it were still living in the benign suburbs of the 1950s, when life was less complicated, less competitive, slower, and relations were easier. That allowed for a different type of church experience from that which must now be part of a very different and changed world.

This changed social pattern has been clearly outlined by Lyle Schaller. When malls began to be built outside cities, he says, a "culture-changing concept" was under way. No longer would shoppers drive into the city but they would go to the malls. At the same time that this was happening, the importance of the neighborhood was diminishing. Those born before 1935, he says, value a sense of community which they found in the neighborhood but those who are part of the younger generations, those born after 1955, work off "a non-geographical basis for creating social networks."[11] So it was that the idea of a region, rather than a neighborhood or even city, became im-

11. Lyle E. Schaller, *Discontinuity and Hope: Practical Change and the Path to the Future* (Nashville: Abingdon Press, 1999), 81.

portant. And thus it is that we have the "emergence of the new regional megachurch as the successor to the old neighborhood parish."[12] But this is not all. The contemporary ethos is now quite different from what it used to be. As modernization has taken hold, much of what the earlier generation valued has been swept away: "familiarity, continuity with the past, kinship ties, small institutions, simplicity, predictability, longtime relationships, informality, and a slower pace of life."[13] Younger generations have only known a culture which is dominated by large institutions. They are used to having many choices, to experiencing much innovation, constant change, numerous surprises, and convenient parking lots. "One of the beneficiaries of this trend," he says, "has been that huge new discount store with the spacious parking lot. Another has been the new regional megachurch."[14] And the small church simply cannot survive the competition with the megachurches any more than Woolworth's could when Wal-Mart moved to the edge of town.[15]

This new world of competition has produced new ways of retailing. Pharmaceutical companies, for example, once advertised their products only in journals which doctors read but now they are marketing them on television directly to the consumer. What they are doing is bypassing the doctor through whom the drug must be obtained and going directly to the person with a need. It is a shift from the producer,

12. Schaller, *Discontinuity and Hope*, 77. A study undertaken in thirty-two countries and involving one thousand churches found evidence that contradicts Schaller's assertion. In terms of attraction to the Church, large size was the third strongest negative factor in people's minds, on a par with "liberal theology" and "traditionalism." In churches that are growing, the percentage of the growth in new people is far higher in smaller churches than in larger, although the base of the percentage is smaller in small churches, which does affect the picture. Measured over the prior five years, growth was 63% in churches of 1 to 100 worshippers, 23% in the 100-200 range, 17% in the 200-300 bracket, and 7% in churches 300-400. The churches in the smallest bracket, it turned out, were growing at 16 times the rate of megachurches with an average attendance of 2,856. See Christian Schwarz, *Natural Church Development: A Guide to Eight Essential Qualities of Healthy Churches* (St. Charles: ChurchSmart Resources, 1996), 46-48. In the United States, exactly 50% of churches have 100 or fewer worshippers. See Dudley and Roozen, 8.

13. Schaller, *Discontinuity and Hope*, 81.

14. Schaller, *Discontinuity and Hope*, 81.

15. Schaller, *Discontinuity and Hope*, 87.

who is the doctor, to the consumer, who is the patient. And this shift is reflected in the Church. Traditional churches have been "producer" churches; megachurches of the seeker-sensitive kind are succeeding because they are "consumer" churches.[16] The one is all about prescription; the other allows the "patients" to define their own needs and seek their own remedies. The one might advertise itself in the Yellow Pages in terms of its location, perhaps denomination, and the hours when worship is held; the other might begin its advertisement with a question in bold print: "Need Help in Raising Your Children?" The one has worshipped on Sunday in the same way for decades; the other offers four *different* worship experiences, each with a different music style. Preaching in the one might follow the lectionary; preaching in the other will arise from the daily conversations held during the week, for this is what people want to hear.[17] In short, in society and in the Church the consumer is now in the driver's seat.

If, then, society has been pushing us toward regional malls and megachurches, and if our postmodern culture has consumption at its heart, it is then rather natural to propose that the Church should now construe itself in terms of marketing. George Barna is blunt and to the point about this. The Church, he says, is a business and "must be run with the same wisdom and savvy that characterizes any for profit business."[18] It must be marketed. By this he has in mind all that has to be done to "direct the flow of goods and services from the producer to the consumer, to satisfy the needs and desires of the consumer *and* the goals and objectives of the producer."[19] There is here mutual benefit as the consumer's needs are satisfied and the producer's goals are met. This marketing, however, does not take place in a vacuum. It is taking place in the same world in which consumers ply the markets for their

16. What Schaller calls churches organized around consumption is what George Barna has in mind when he speaks about marketing the Church. See his *Church Marketing: Breaking Ground for the Harvest* (Ventura: Regal Books, 1992), 26-30.

17. Schaller, *Discontinuity and Hope*, 88-91.

18. George Barna, *Marketing the Church: What They Never Taught You About Church Growth* (Colorado Springs: Navpress, 1988), 26.

19. Barna, *Marketing the Church*, 41. See also Gustav Niebuhr, "The Gospels of Management: Religion Goes to Market to Expand Congregations," *New York Times*, 144 (April 18, 1995), A1, A10.

goods, hear innumerable pitches for products, and know how to resist the telemarketer.

McDonald's provides a good illustration of marketing success and may also provide insights into how the Church might market itself successfully. So how will the experience of being in church parallel being in a McDonald's? The answer is there will be efficiency in the delivery of the "product," control over the whole process from start to finish, and a completely predictable outcome — after all, no Big Mac ever tastes different from any other Big Mac. Buying a Big Mac is quick, convenient, and eating it is enjoyable. This is what might be learned from McDonald's.

Old Fears

Finally, at the root of this exuberant experimentation in how to "do church" differently is the fear that as society and culture change the Church, at least in its traditional configuration, is beginning to look like a relic, a bit of flotsam from the past. The experience of being in a church, especially one that is traditional, has become unlike any other experience in the contemporary world, it is asserted. Where else would one hear such music, sit on such benches, attend a ceremony so slow, so solemn (read: boring), and hear what is mostly, if not entirely, irrelevant to the issues and pains that roil the minds of those in attendance? What the Church is offering and what is needed, the argument goes, have become two entirely different things. And the reason is that the Church is now seriously out of step with the world. And this is also the explanation as to why it is not growing.

History has a curious way of repeating itself, though few in this current reprise of the past seem aware of what happened before. The argument made by those on the forefront of Protestant liberalism and Catholic modernism in the nineteenth century in Europe was that the modern world was passing Christian faith by, that it was becoming obsolete and outmoded, and that if significant changes were not made, it would be consigned to the dust heap of history. It was a line of thought which reached America a little later. The main difference is that the liberals and modernists worried that they were out of step with those on the high end of culture, those in the intellectual arena where Enlightenment dogmas had become unassailable "truths," whereas evangelicals worry that they are out of step with those on the popular end of culture whose wants and habits function no less authoritatively than did the Enlightenment dogmas though they are driven more by therapeutic and consumer desires.

In this earlier experiment, there was also a deep foreboding about the future of the Church — indeed, whether it would have a future at all — because Enlightenment forms of thought had triumphed and Christianity had been marginalized in the culture. Because of this dislocation, it had fallen back on a closed-minded, defensive strategy, some of its internal critics charged. George Tyrrell, a Jesuit and the leader of the English Catholic modernists, believed that if the Church did not adjust to the modern world it would be destroyed. She "seems like some little Alpine village," he once remarked, "doomed by the slow resistless progress of a grinding glacier. Can she change now, even at the eleventh hour, and plant herself elsewhere?"[20] How could the Church do this and avoid its demise? The answer, Tyrrell said, was that it had to adapt itself to the thought forms of the age, creating a synthesis out of "a careful criticism of Catholicism on the one hand and of modern culture on the other."[21] For in the nineteenth century, unlike the Middle Ages, the Church had become a cultural outsider and had "to ask to be heard."[22]

This was, in fact, the common thread that linked Catholic modernism and Protestant liberalism. This thread was the fear that Christian faith had been left behind, that it was no longer plausible, that it was not in tune with the modern outlook, that reasonable people could not do anything but abandon it, and that its survival therefore lay in finding ways of adjusting to the modern world by updating itself. In America, Shailer Mathews devoted a chapter in his *The Faith of Modernism* to the question: "Is Christianity Outgrown?" He went on to speak of modernism as the "projection of the Christian movement into modern conditions," as moving from the outside to the inside of cul-

20. Letter to von Hugel dated 9th November 1906, *von Hugel and Tyrrell Correspondence*, British Museum, Add. MSS 44929.

21. George Tyrrell, "Medievalism and Modernism," *Harvard Theological Review*, I (April, 1908), 304-05.

22. Maude Petre, *Life of George Tyrrell, 1884-1909* (London: Edward Arnold, 1912), 218.

ture.[23] But what was to be projected? It was certainly not the doctrines of historical orthodoxy but, as it turned out, only their afterglow. The language of Zion was still used but it had come to mean something quite different in the modern context than it had in its early years in the life of the Church. In fact, it was not uncommon, especially on the Protestant side, for all of this simply to contract into a set of moral beliefs, particularly those which were compatible with a scientifically dominated, naturalistic culture.

This was also clearly the intellectual strategy Friedrich Schleiermacher, the important pioneer of modern theology, adopted in his *On Religion: Speeches to Its Cultured Despisers* which came out at the height of the European Enlightenment in 1799. In his opening address, he remarked on the fact that this attempt to speak of religion was "an unexpected undertaking" because those whom he was addressing were so filled with the wisdom of the age and with its plenty that the subject of religion had been "completely neglected."[24] Here again was the fear that the modern world had happily left Christian faith behind. Part of his strategy, therefore, was to distance himself from traditional Christian faith, which he believed had been discredited, even as the megachurches are distancing themselves from the traditional church today. He redefined religion's essence as "neither thinking nor acting but intuition and feeling."[25] By the end of his little work he had made the argument that life opens up for us "vistas" into the eternal which create in us the feelings which are the raw material of religion, even if

23. Shailer Mathews, *The Faith of Modernism* (New York: The Macmillan Co., 1924), 15. For the larger picture in American Protestantism, see Leonard I. Sweet, "The Modernization of Protestant Religion in America," in *Altered Landscapes: Christianity in America, 1935-1985,* ed. David W. Lotz, Donald W. Shriver, and John F. Wilson (Grand Rapids: William B. Eerdmans, 1989), 1941.

24. Friedrich Schleiermacher, *On Religion: Speeches to Its Cultured Despisers,* trans. Richard Crouter (Cambridge: Cambridge University Press, 1988), 77.

25. Schleiermacher, *On Religion,* 102. A. N. Wilson argues that this kind of immanentism is, from a philosophical point of view, an "easy way out" because it dissolves the antagonism between belief and unbelief. "The easy way out, the easy way to explain the paradox of why intelligent people still practice their religion and still, presumably, believe in God, is to say that they and unbelievers see the same world, but religious people discern 'God' where sceptics see merely Nature or our sense of The Good." A. N. Wilson, *God's Funeral* (New York: W. W. Norton, 1999), 336.

the intellectuals he was addressing did not quite recognize these feelings for what they were.[26] The result, then, was that "religion" — or in the language of today, "spirituality," which is its substitute — could actually be found under many intellectual and artistic forms.

This same attempt to build a bridge across the intellectual divide which the Enlightenment had created, and by which Christianity was being rendered obsolete, was often put in a positive vein. What is modernism? It is, said H. D. A. Major in England, the attempt to find a synthesis between Christianity and modernity, the connection being Christians formulating their beliefs in light of what they saw as the new truth which was breaking out by means of the Enlightenment.[27] Much later, Bernard Reardon noted that although liberal Protestantism had come to mean many things, almost as many as the number of its proponents, yet it always resulted in "a piecemeal adjustment of the received theology to at least the more insistent demands of contemporary thought," and although this meant the erosion of orthodox doctrine, this effort had the virtue, he said, of "being more responsive to the needs of the present time."[28] The eventual outcome to this kind of project was a form of faith that, as Gresham Machen argued in his *Christianity and Liberalism,* was unrecognizable as Christian faith, yet the irony of it was that these liberals set out to *save* Christianity and not to destroy it, to preserve the possibility of some kind of belief when the Enlightenment was making traditional Christian believing quite impossible. The parallels between the liberal project and what is now being attempted in evangelical churches are quite striking in several ways, though there are differences, too.

It should be said immediately that, for the liberals, this was a deliberate, self-consciously accepted tradeoff between the necessary loss of historical, orthodox belief and acceptance within a culture dominated by Enlightenment humanism and rationalism. The loss of this orthodoxy was the price that liberals felt had to be paid for a seat at the table. For evangelicals today, this new strategy is also one of survival

26. Schleiermacher, *On Religion,* 150.

27. H. D. A. Major, *English Modernism: Its Origin, Methods, Aims* (Cambridge: Cambridge University Press, 1927), 8-12.

28. Bernard G. Reardon, *Liberal Protestantism* (London: Adam and Charles Black, 1968), 9.

but there is no sense at all that their orthodox views are in jeopardy. This effort to retail religion to a postmodern world, to bring about the "projection of the Christian movement into modern conditions," is, in fact, more intuitive than intellectual, more a matter of marketing savvy than of serious thought. For evangelicals, the tradeoffs seem nonexistent. Evangelical orthodoxy seems unscathed as faith is retailed.

While the routes taken by the earlier liberals and now by contemporary evangelicals may be a little different, there nevertheless is an important shared belief. It is that the only means to survival in the modern world is to adapt Christian faith in some way. The liberals did this by modifying its doctrinal content; seeker-sensitive evangelicals claim not to be doing this but, rather, modifying its form of delivery. This raises the issue as to whether traditional religion will be unaffected by its non-traditional delivery and practice, whether content is secure from the change which enters its form, how far and in what ways a traditional orthodoxy can be wrapped in contemporary consumer culture and still survive intact. In other words, the very way in which survival is being sought raises questions as to whether that strategy for survival may not itself bring on the demise of its orthodoxy just as it did in liberal Protestantism.

Seeker churches, then, represent a coalition bound together not by a theological vision of the world but by a common strategy for reaching particular segments of society and by a common methodology for accomplishing this. Interestingly, it is a methodology that can be hitched up equally as well to evangelical faith as to New Age belief, or to anything in between. Why is this so? The reason is that there is no theological truth upon which the methodology is predicated and upon which it insists, because theological truth, it is thought, is not what builds churches. What this approach is doing, Sargeant argues, is creating an institutional response "to today's consumerist ethos."[29] The objective, therefore, is "to reduce or minimize any cognitive distance between the religious realm and the working and shopping world of suburban middle-class Americans."[30] The rhythms of this consumption, however, happen almost entirely within the privatized realm of in-

29. Sargeant, *Seeker Churches*, 11.
30. Sargeant, *Seeker Churches*, 19.

terior spirituality. It is about offering choices for consumers to piece together for themselves some sort of meaning, a way to bring some sense
into, and establish some order within, their lives. It is this acutely privatized dimension that explains why so few of these churches have any
kind of social involvement. But it also explains why these churches are
appealing to so many people who are looking for a spiritual dimension
to life but who may want to distance themselves from religion. Here is
spirituality without theology, spirituality which is privatized and therefore, to some extent, freed from the external rhythms and authority of a
practiced faith. And that is producing many changes.

This is probably the first time, for example, that Christian people
anywhere in the West have thought that ecclesiastical architecture is,
in principle, offensive, that religious symbols, such as crosses, should
be banned from churches, that pulpits should be abandoned, that
hymns should be abolished, that pews should be sent to the garbage
dump, and that pianos and organs should be removed. All of this has
been happening on the forefront of this movement. This is probably
the first time, too, that churchgoers have wanted their buildings to be
mistaken for corporate headquarters or country clubs.

This, of course, is no small development, for church buildings, in
pedantic or grand ways, have always tried to express the fact visually
that these are places of *Christian* presence and places where God in all
his greatness is worshipped. Their architecture and their symbols have
pointed back to what happened at the Cross and in the Resurrection.
Churches are a reminder of the pilgrim status of the people of God as
they journey toward a different land. They are those who have wandered the earth for millennia, dispossessed by a fallen world, but
owned by God, by the God toward whom they journey. Churches have
therefore spoken of a Story far greater than any personal narrative.
They have pointed to a meaning far grander than what is seen in the
small compass of personal experience, one that comprehends all of the
worlds and stretches across all of time. This is why, in the past,
churches have wanted to be visually different from corporate headquarters and country clubs whose purposes are, by contrast, thoroughly this-worldly. They have wanted to reflect this other Story rather
than to disguise themselves as something else.

Now, the Church's nature is being visually removed from its buildings because it has become an impediment to success. Why is that? The answer, rather obviously, is that seekers are searching for spirituality but not for religion. Church buildings in the traditional mode may be about spirituality but they are undoubtedly also about religion. That is what now dooms them.

Business as Usual

Mention has already been made of the appearance of spirituality in the corporate world. It is the reverse side of this coin that has created the environment for the marketing of the faith: the appearance of the corporate world in religion. The line between faith and retailing, business and belief, the Church and the world has been under steady assault in evangelicalism for many years. Examples of the blurring of the line can be found not only in these seeker churches but on all sides — in Christian music, in Christian bookstores, and in those Christian churches which are not only marketing the faith but also facilitating the sale of life insurance, vacation packages, and hair styling, to name but a few. The marketing of the faith now seems so natural because the spiritual and the material markets have come to resemble one another.

It would be quite unfair to suggest that evangelicals have been the pioneers in blurring the line between faith and commerce. They have, however, become artful practitioners of it. This merging of the worlds of faith and commerce has gone on for a while in America. Liberal Protestants who today bemoan the success of religious television, as Laurence Moore has pointed out, were very happy to dominate the airwaves from the 1930s onwards when the FCC required that as part of their public service, radio and later television stations had to donate free time for such broadcasting. Indeed, the Federal Council of Churches, which represented the liberal Protestant denominations, actively thwarted conservatives who tried to purchase time for their religious programming.[31] However, in 1960, the FCC changed the rules, no longer requiring this kind of public service and that was the year that

31. R. Laurence Moore, *Selling God: American Religion in the Marketplace of Culture* (New York: Oxford University Press, 1994), 245-47.

Pat Robertson began his Christian Broadcasting Network, setting up the first television station to devote the majority of its time to religious broadcasting. However, Robertson also offered programming on his Family Cable Channel which one could see on any purely commercial network such as news, movies, and comedy.[32] The one came to seem no different from the other.

Televangelist Jim Bakker's ministry, which would end in 1987 in disgrace, initially was highly successful after he left his association with Robertson. In the 1980s he was boasting that he had "a better product than soap or automobiles." It was, of course, eternal life. Somehow, it did not seem to occur to him that as long as eternal life is only a product, even though it may be superior to soap and automobiles, it just might not be taken as seriously as it should. But never mind. He also had his Christian theme park, Heritage USA, advertised to Christians as "the ultimate in a pleasurable vacation." In an orgy of "reckless Pentecostal antinomianism," as Moore puts it, Bakker said that Christians did not have to prove the seriousness of their faith by turning the contemporary world into an enemy. "Only by enjoying in Christian form the full range of pleasures offered by commercial culture could they signal their control over modern technology."[33] Even the smallest trace of insight into what constitutes biblical worldliness would have set off the alarm bells but by the 1980s this kind of cultural accommodation had become so much a part of the evangelical world that the notion of worldliness had more or less fallen by the wayside. Actually, it had become quaint — and that is worse.

These excursions into entertainment by Robertson and Bakker — religion and leisure being the points of entry — were but the front end of a growing Christian penetration of the commercial market. Earlier rock bands such as Stryper, dressed and made up like other heavy metal bands of the 1980s, were now followed by many others like Audio Adrenaline and solo artists like Amy Grant and others who were among those in 2000 who helped the Christian music industry expand into a three-quarters-of-a-billion-dollar business when the rest of the music market retreated, though it was praise music in particular which

32. Moore, *Selling God,* 252.
33. Moore, *Selling God,* 251-52.

was responsible for this. Religious trinkets, videos, movies, and Bibles in every conceivable size and covering, Bibles for singles, for the depressed, for the young, for the old, for the divorced, for the recovering, for African Americans, Bibles fitted for every niche in the market, were all for sale.[34] Today there are Christian amusement parks and dance clubs, and sermons for sale for pastors who are too harried or too indolent to do the work themselves.[35]

It has not gone unnoticed in the secular world that there is gold in these religious hills. The result is that today there are evangelical publishing houses which are the religious arms of secular corporations, and *Songs 4 Worship,* a successful collection of Christian music, lavishly advertised on the TV networks, was launched by Time-Life. In 2002, General Motors unleashed sixteen Christian rock bands in a number of southern cities under the banner "Chevrolet Presents: Come Together and Worship." All of this, however, was only one end of a growing alliance between commerce and spirituality or, at least, the growing use of spirituality by commerce.

High fashion has often raided religion for its motifs, incorporating religious symbols like crosses and nuns' habits into new and compelling getups. And religious motifs and suggestions have spread else-

34. See "The Glorious Rise of Christian Pop," *Newsweek* (July 16, 2001), 38-48.

35. This interpenetration of commercial and religious concerns is more fully detailed by Charles Lippy. The key to it, he correctly believes, is that contemporary religion is now privately construed rather than being institutionally anchored and doctrinally shaped. He offers numerous instances of the crossover between religion and American commerce. He cites the studies showing the influence of Pentecostalism on the music of Elvis Presley, Jerry Lee Lewis, and Tammy Wynette. The more distinctly Christian pop music of Amy Grant, Sandi Patti, and Andrae Crouch builds "on the supposition that music itself becomes a means of gaining access to that realm of power that brings meaning out of disorder" (*Being Religious, American Style: A History of Popular Religiosity in the United States* [Westport: Greenwood Publishing, 1994], 226). Religious theme parks, he says, are places where attendance "can send a signal to others that they privately hold religious convictions, but they do not have to articulate them in any conceptually coherent fashion" (227). The boom in spectator sports has also seen this crossover between commerce and religion with teams overtly praying and players who score a touchdown or hit a home run publicly witnessing to God's help in a gesture that is without verbal or doctrinal explanation. It is a private experience of which the public is made the spectator.

where, too. Mitsubishi Montero "came to comfort earth," an advertisement solemnly informs us. Acura quotes unnamed philosophers as saying "the journey is the reward," thus connecting the very familiar spiritual image with driving an Acura. Gillette Venus, a razor for women, "will reveal the goddess in you." "True Redemption," it turns out, is the access which the accumulation of Starwood's points gains to "4,536 holes of championship golf." Campbell's soup is good, we learn, not only for the body, but also for the "soul." Quaker Oatmeal warms both the "*heart* and soul," a Ford Explorer will help you "recharge the batteries of your soul," and Pontiac is "fuel for the soul." The attention which the soul is now receiving originates, not in the board room, but in the marketing department. Until the 1990s, public space was kept free of religious terms and so the secular equivalent, *self,* or the simple pronoun *you* would have been used. Now there is some advantage to using the word *soul.* This word has the sense of something deep, mysterious, maybe even sacred. It therefore resonates with the new spiritual quest. And besides Ford's Explorer, which is ready to "recharge the batteries of your soul," other auto manufacturers have come up with names like Pathfinder, Odyssey, and Voyager, all suggestive of the spiritual quest. And Volvo seeks the high moral ground by linking itself with "that voice that tells you to do the right thing," conscience. Volvo has been "guided by conscience." The penetration by secular commercial interests into what is spiritual, not to mention evangelical, is now considerable.

Religion, of course, can strike back, too, as well as exploit commercial connections. In 2002, Jim Ball and his Evangelical Environmental Network launched a slogan campaign against gas guzzling SUV's that was carried on television. "What Would Jesus Drive?" was the slogan and the answer clearly was, not a gas guzzler!

Exploitation, however, has been far more common than confrontation in this relationship. Willow Creek Community Church's food court was, like its worship services, just the harbinger of things to come. Seeker churches often advertise themselves as serving Starbucks coffee. In Houston, there is a church that sells McDonald's hamburgers, in New York, a sidewalk bistro operated by a church which offers a full menu and a splash of Chardonnay to go with it. In Dallas, after feeding the soul, one can relax the body in a sauna in the church.[36] In Munster, Indiana, a church entered into a business relationship with a string of Burger King restaurants. The restaurants advertise the church's musical programs and plays and the church promotes Burger King on its radio program.[37] Others are luring the public with skating rinks and fully equipped fitness centers. In Florida, The Potter's House Christian Fellowship opened an entire mall in 1996 as part of its church operations. It purchased the former Southern Bell phone center and converted it into a mall with a bookstore, dry cleaners, a bus terminal, a café, a room for games, a hair salon called Angel's Hair, financial services, balloon shop, a school, law offices, and an art shop.[38] The fact is that across a broad spectrum of church life, enormous effort is now being invested in making the Church seem desirable for reasons that have nothing to do with worship, biblical knowledge, or service. Investment specialists, entertainers, and inspirational gurus make the rounds. There are dances and dinner theaters. There are music and voice lessons, karate, and travel excursions.

"You've got to get the 'do' done if you're gonna look good for the Lord."

Angel's Hair

There is, of course, nothing inherently wrong with many of these activities. There is no reason why Christians who need to do so should not seek financial advice or buy balloons, go to the theater or see a lawyer. My point is that these additions to what churches once used to offer illustrate the fact that buying and selling have entered into the Church's inner sanctum. They have become a natural part of its life. These are threads that now run through the evangelical fabric and therefore they are creating the condition in which the marketing of the faith to seekers also seems natural and commonsensical.

36. Elizabeth Bernstein, "Holy Frappuccino," *Wall Street Journal* (31 August, 2001), W1, 8.

37. Dale Buss, "Peddling God," *Sales and Marketing Management* (March, 2002), 44.

38. http://www.potters-house.org/vision.htm.

Growing the Church

Gated (Spiritual) Communities

The idea that there is a religious market is not new nor is the seeker churches' understanding about how the Church grows. This is really the updated version of Donald McGavran's theory from the mission field, now adapted to the home front. I have already touched upon some of the ideas which are in play here but we now need to think a little more precisely about them.

In 1955, McGavran wrote his *Bridges of God* and mourned the fact that on the mission field converts often became so alienated from their own ethnic or family contexts that they were unable to be witnesses at all. In fact, many often sought employment from the mission agency because, as Christians, they could find employment nowhere else. This obviously was a lamentable situation and it is one that still pertains today in some parts of the world. The solution, McGavran thought, was to construe conversion less individualistically and work more with whole social units or tribes. Then, if there were conversions in a tribe, perhaps following the lead of the chief, each convert would find acceptance and a place in which to live out his or her faith. In time, this led McGavran to formulate his theories about church growth.

In 1970, he wrote *Understanding Church Growth*, which soon became the foundational text of this movement, two of whose principles are now central to the current movement to market the Church. They are, first, the homogenous unit principle and, second, understanding the mechanism of conversion. On the first, he stated quite simply that "men like to become Christians without crossing racial, linguistic, or class barriers."[39] There are, in fact, other barriers which he also mentioned, such as economic and educational, and today we also have to add the generational divides. His is the very simple observation that birds of a feather like to flock together. This is our *preference;* it is not an inevitability.

The second principle was his belief that the chief barrier to con-

39. Donald McGavran, *Understanding Church Growth* (Grand Rapids: William B. Eerdmans, 1970), 198.

version is sociological and not theological.[40] This, actually, was the outworking of his homogenous unit principle because his argument was that once the barriers to conversion were removed, such as requiring a person to cross the lines of race, class, language, or education, then conversion would happen naturally.

The latest incarnation of these principles, then, is in this experiment in marketing the Church. The way that the first has been realized is that a number of these new churches have been started near relatively new housing developments or in suburbs which are growing. This is a deliberate strategy. Barna, Schaller, and others have argued that marketing today is marketing to a niche. And the niche most desired has been that of the Boomers. As Douglas Webster notes, this "numerically significant, financially powerful, high energy generation" is considered the "pivotal generation." For that reason, "Baby boomers and their children are the target audience, the market niche, that the innovative, trend-setting churches are shooting for."[41] In describing how he began his new church, Doug Murren says that "I simply concluded, after a lot of heart searching, that the Lord had called us to reach this age-group in their early 40s and younger. . . . Our music style, the decor of our building, everything about our church focused toward an age-group that our church very much needed — one that I personally felt comfortable about reaching."[42] He goes on to say that the age limit itself was not what was important. What his church was trying to do was to "reach a culture, a mentality that was considered 'illegitimate' in the 60s, that had become 'legitimized' in the 80s. It's the boomer worldview we're talking about."[43] These churches, as a consequence, are typically suburban, overwhelmingly white, middle class, and deliberately shaped for well-off, well-educated Boomers, though some churches are now moving on to the niche occupied by the Xers. These are the birds that are flocking together.

40. McGavran, *Understanding Church Growth*, 215.
41. Douglas D. Webster, *Selling Jesus: What's Wrong with Marketing the Church* (Downers Grove: InterVarsity Press, 1992), 59.
42. Doug Murren, *The Baby Boomerang: Catching Baby Boomers as They Return to Church* (Ventura: Regal Books, 1990), 21-22.
43. Murren, *The Baby Boomerang*, 22.

The young woman standing before us looks a lot like Morticia Addams. Like the classic TV character, her hair is long, black, and stringy. Her skin is typing-paper white, except for her lips, which are painted black, matching her floor length sheath. She is pierced. She is the worship leader.

In this incarnation, Morticia's warm contralto is replaced by an intense soprano that hugs a melody line of only three or four notes. Her tango is a rich, rhythmic amalgam of classical, grunge, and funk, produced by the band behind her: cello, bassoon, violins, flute, keyboard, bass, and drums. The sound is neo-classical funk, a little bit Celtic, a little bit rock-and-roll; Isaac Watts' hymns set to new tunes. To untuned ears, it is strange, stirring, not that singable, and in this setting, very right.

Eric Reed, "Ministering with My 'Generation'"

The way that the second principle is being worked out is by removing all supposed sociological barriers that stand in the way of faith, from the kind of building a person enters, to the symbols he or she sees, to the kind of nurseries where seekers deposit their children, the bathrooms they use, the program that is provided, and the language which is heard — the less overtly "religious" the better — the point of it all being to create a non-threatening, inviting, upbeat, and safe place for people to come.[44] What is truly remarkable about this development is that it is taking place at the very time when, as we have seen, America is becoming a genuinely multi-ethnic society. Churches that market themselves knowing that they will be attracting overwhelmingly white,

---

44. One such proposal argues that it is religious language that keeps men, in particular, away from church. The solution, then, is to eliminate the use of every word which is heard only in church. This may seem like a winning strategy but it does leave unanswered what we are to do with words like *sin, justification, propitiation,* and *faith* without which the gospel, at least in apostolic terms, is lost, for the gospel is not simply about a personal relationship with Christ. The New Testament explicates that relationship theologically and never speaks about it in any other way. See Stephen A. Bly, "Molding Ministry to Fit Men," *Leadership,* XII, No. 1 (Winter, 1991), 53.

well-to-do, middle class, suburban Boomers are churches which, to say the least, are quite out of step with their own world. Part of the reason for this, of course, is that this largely suburban-type faith is significantly cocooned from the much more complex world outside, for the suburbs tend to be far more monochromatic racially, socially, and economically than either the city or the workplace.

Not only so, but these mostly well-to-do, well-educated suburbanites are also well insulated against many of the harsh realities of life which are the common lot of some who live in America and of many who live in other parts of the world. The experience of affluent American suburbanites is so very different from that of people elsewhere. These Americans have not been on the receiving end of religious or ideological hostility, have not gone hungry, do not live in a world without antibiotics or with little medical care, do not know what it is like to be without access to retirement accounts, stocks and bonds, or even modest opportunities. The pressures in American life are more internal than external. They come from the ravaging of the spirit by anxiety, stress, broken marriages, market competition, loss of connections to place and people, the fear of failure, and the compulsive need for success or, at least, its appearance. American consumer religion reflects these needs but in doing so it reduces Christianity to something less than what it really is.

Robert Wuthnow argues that this is one of the main components in the "spiritual dilemma" of the middle class today. On the one hand, he says, "it enjoys enormous resources — education, job training, places to live, food on the table, longevity, relative freedom from fear and violence." On the other hand, "it feels overburdened with too much work and too many bills; it suffers from stress and anxiety; it wonders what its values should be and wishes it could cut back and get its life more under control; it even recognizes the need to think about spiritual concerns." Caught in this bind, many in the middle class have come to look to the church for help. Yet the churches, Wuthnow observes, "don't seem to be making much of a difference in middle-class lives."[45]

What Christian faith becomes in these contexts is often a way to satisfy the needs of affluent suburbanites who, in other ways, have ev-

---

45. Robert Wuthnow, *The Crisis in the Churches: Spiritual Malaise, Fiscal Woe* (New York: Oxford University Press, 1997), 68.

erything. Christian faith becomes virtually indistinguishable from the sounds, sights, and habits of white, consuming, affluent suburbanites who want the best, the most advanced technology, the most up-to-date nursery facilities, what amuses and entertains, and a great parking lot but who, for all of that, are often lonely, stressed, harried, and in debt. And the source of this internal distress is increasingly being read as the outside world, the world of fierce competition, ruthless business practice, drugs, morally eroded relationships, and empty, drifting teenagers.

So it is that some megachurches are responding to this disenchantment with the outside world by becoming almost like self-contained villages, combinations of mall and country club, with a full range of services and amenities that parallels much that can be had in the wider society. Some of them operate around the clock. They vary, of course, but they aim to enable people to be there for much of the day or, for those with hotels or housing complexes, for all of the day. Children will find water slides, amusement parks, gyms, climbing walls, and schools; parents may find employment at the McDonald's or other on-site fast-food restaurant, relief in the many recovering classes which are offered, and all will find a safe environment which is drug-free and where the ailments of a morally eroded society are kept outside. These complexes are secure, safe, "gated communities" for the spiritual which are secure from the harsh world outside.[46]

No Entry

Of the five factors which I have suggested lie behind this new experiment in "doing church," it is my judgment that only one has any legitimacy. It appears to be correct that evangelicalism is stagnant. Seeker-sensitive churches are picking up on only one aspect of this: the fact that conversions are not increasing, and even here the assumption seems to be that more conversions can be engineered by the right approach, which is really quite doubtful. It is, after all, in the hands of God to impart new life and not in our hands at all. Beyond this, however, the moti-

46. Patricia Leigh Brown, "Megachurches as Minitowns," *New York Times* (May 9, 2002), F1.

vating factors appear quite improper. This is undoubtedly a seeker culture, but seekers in this culture cannot come to Christ on their own terms and cannot have the gospel preached to them as if they could. It is true that the Church is in the marketplace of ideas, products, and experiences but to play by the rules of this marketplace is to invite disaster. It is true that society has reorganized itself into regions but why should this be the determining factor as to whether we move from neighborhood churches to megachurches? Should that not be decided by how best to meet the Scriptural objectives for the local church? And the fear about becoming obsolete is a fear that only those truly enculturated ever suffer and it is a telling indication of how deep and pervasive evangelical unbelief has become. So, where has this experiment gone wrong? The principal mistakes, I believe, arise, first, from the use of the homogenous unit principle and, second, from making the Church captive to the commercial motif. Let me now explore these two themes.

Birds of a Feather

Did the early church separate itself out into units of the like-minded in terms of ethnicity, class, and language as these megachurches have done following McGavran's principles? It did not. All of the evidence points the other way. Many of the problems which the early church faced arose from the fact that the first converts were *together* despite all of their diversity.[47]

From this point the gospel spread and its spread was both lateral and vertical, breaking down and leaping across the homogeneous units of race, class, and economic status of that world. It spread geographically from Palestine to Syria, and then on to Asia, Macedonia, Greece, Italy, and Spain. What was quite as significant is that it also spread vertically through all the layers of society. It touched slaves like Onesimus, those of rather ordinary birth like the pretentious Corinthians (I Cor. 1:26-29), those who were wealthy like John Mark's mother whose large house in Jerusalem was the first meeting place of Christians, and Lydia

---

47. René Padilla has developed this argument in his essay, "The Unity of the Church and the Homogenous Unit Principle," in *Exploring Church Growth*, ed. Wilbert R. Shenk (Grand Rapids: William B. Eerdmans, 1983), 285-303.

the trader. It spread to the well-connected like Manean, Herod the Tetrarch's foster brother; and to the powerful like the Ethiopian eunuch who served in a role comparable to the British Foreign Minister or the American Secretary of State. And in Paul's lifetime, the gospel entered Caesar's own household. What we see is the gospel traversing all socioeconomic, ethnic, linguistic, and class barriers to draw God's people not into subsets of the like-minded who could be comfortable with each other, but into the richly diversified people of God.

Peter, for one, was not ready for this. He was mentally unprepared to take the gospel to those who were not Jews, to take it beyond his own homogenous unit, until God gave him a vision that enabled him to see what he ought to do (Acts 10:9-48). Old attitudes, however, sometimes die hard, and so it was that later Peter reverted to his old ways and Paul "opposed him to his face" because he shrank back from his understanding of the whole people of God as composing all homogenous units and ate only with those with whom he was most comfortable, the Jews (Gal. 2:11-21). And what Paul said to Peter on this occasion was not that his action had been unkind, though it had been, and not that it was bigoted, though it might have been, but that Peter was not being "straightforward about the truth of the gospel."[48] In situations like this, it is the *gospel*, the gospel of justification by grace alone through faith alone which is at stake, a point largely lost on those pursuing success by the methodologies of seeker sensitivity.

Why was Paul concerned enough to risk division by confronting Peter? The answer is that the Church is not only to declare the gospel, but to model its truth, and if it does not model the truth it will undermine what it declares as truth. That was why Paul said Peter was not being "straightforward" about the gospel. And how is the church to model the gospel's truth?

---

48. To abstain from eating of meats proscribed by the Old Testament was not in itself wrong since what food is eaten is a matter of preference, after the gospel has come, and not of religious obedience. What was wrong was that Peter met the Jews on their own ground and participated with them in that Old Testament obedience. This gave the false impression that the keeping of this law was necessary for salvation and that overthrew the gospel and the work of Christ. (See Martin Luther, *Commentary on Saint Paul's Epistle to the Galatians* [Grand Rapids: William B. Eerdmans, 1930], 102-03.) Peter's theological blunder grew out of his ties to the Jews, which were still fresh and comfortable.

The gospel declares that there is no natural merit, no human standing, which advances a person toward God and his salvation, or makes one person more acceptable to God than another. All of the ways in life in which people seek importance and seek preeminence over one another are irrelevant to their standing before God. This is true of ethnicity, wealth, class, power, privileged birth, connections, profession, generation, and religion. If this is the truth upon which the gospel rests, then it is the truth which the Church is obliged to model. So it is that Paul declares that there "is neither Jew nor Greek, there is neither slave nor free, there is neither male nor female; for you are all one in Christ Jesus" (Gal. 3:28). And by extension, should we not also say that because we are all one in Jesus Christ, there is neither Builder nor Boomer, neither Xer nor child of the Millennium, city dweller or suburbanite, Westerner or Third Worlder? Exploiting generational distinctions in the pursuit of success, which is what is at the heart of the seeker church movement, should be as offensive as exploiting racial differences for personal advantage.

It is true that this unity of the Church of which the apostles speak is difficult to exhibit fully in the contexts in which people live in the West. Ethnic groups which have come to America, for example, have usually stayed together, at least initially. The result is that our cities and some towns have areas that are known to be dominated by one group or another. The same is true economically, too. The wealthy and the poor tend to live in different parts of the city, or the poor may live in the city and the wealthy outside it. Churches, therefore, will probably not be able to exhibit within themselves the full diversity of God's people, those who are rich side by side with those who are poor, those who are educated side by side with those who are not. Yet, when we set out with a methodology which we know will create churches that will be culturally, generationally, economically, and racially monolithic and monochromatic, something is amiss. The logic of the gospel as Paul understood it, and the logic of the marketing of the Church as we are practicing it today, are simply at loggerheads.

Racial, class, and generational differences are real but they are only a part of our human reality. Indeed, our world cannot be truly comprehended if it is viewed only through these prisms. Where this has happened, the Church has truly strained at a gnat while it has been busy swallowing a camel. Churches are successfully catering to the tastes of

Boomers and Xers, filling the seats, creating a show each Sunday, orchestrating warm feelings, but leaving entirely unattended the much larger world which exists outside the generational shelters. What does Christian faith have to say to a society that is losing its soul in consumption? What does it have to say about the way the meaning of life has been rewritten by the pervasive, ubiquitous, empty, trivializing, entertainment industry? What does it have to say about hope which transcends the narrow focus of privatized, personal experience? Indeed, does it have anything to say that Boomers and Xers do not want to hear?

The gospel calls for the Church to exhibit in itself the fact that what typically divides people has been overcome in Christ; marketing frequently leads the Church to capitalize on what divides people in order to exploit the niches of class and generation. What is at stake here, as Paul argued, is nothing less than the gospel. What is at stake is also nothing less than the work of the whole trinity. To the Ephesians, Paul argued that there "is one body and one Spirit, just as you were called to the one hope that belongs to your call, one Lord, one faith, one baptism, one God and Father of us all who is above all and through all and in all" (Eph. 4:4-6). Paul's argument is compelling for its simplicity. There is only one body because there is only one Spirit; there is only one faith because there is only one Lord; there is only one family because there is only one Father. The unity of the people of God is as secure as the unity of the trinity. The Church's responsibility, therefore, is not to create unity, as the ecumenical movement proposed, but to *preserve* the unity that God himself has already created in Christ. What militates against this unity is immaturity of doctrinal understanding (Eph. 4:14) and immaturity in moral behavior (Eph. 4:25-32). Can we say that the marketing of the Church is a methodology for growing the Church which will, at the same time, preserve its unity, that the birds of a feather which are flying together will want to exhibit among themselves the rich diversity of God's people? The apostolic vision and the marketing vision would appear to lead in different directions, and so we need to ask ourselves what fundamental assumptions the marketing of the Church has made which are taking it down a road that it should not be travelling.[49]

49. It is probably telling that Mark Mittelberg, of Willow Creek, devotes a long chapter to the theme "Owning and Modeling Evangelistic Values" but is oblivious to

Selling the Faith

The fact that this line between commerce and belief is eroding makes it easy for people to think that there may be a market for religion even as there is for goods and services and that these two markets work in similar ways. This is not an entirely aberrant observation. Yet the parallels are now being pressed so injudiciously, so unwisely, that the promotion of (imperishable) faith has come to be indistinguishable from the promotion of (perishable) products (I Pet. 1:4-5, 18-19) as if the dynamic of success in the one naturally duplicates itself in the other. Seekers become consumers, pastors become business tycoons, churches become marketing outlets, the gospel becomes a product, faith becomes its purchase, and increasingly the outcome in people's lives is no different than if they had made any other purchase.[50] So, do these parallels between faith and commerce really exist?

---

the corporate dimension of this in the Church and, instead, completely privatizes the notion. Modeling evangelistic values is about being personally committed to evangelism. See his *Building a Contagious Church: Revolutionizing the Way We View and Do Evangelism* (Grand Rapids: Zondervan, 2000), 87-111.

50. Although this is a homegrown effort at contextualizing the gospel, like almost everything else in America, it is being exported abroad to Europe, Australia, Africa, Latin America, and Asia. This is, on the face of it, quite extraordinary for it suggests that this method, which has arisen within the context of American consumerism, is not seen as being culture-specific by its originators. Those on the receiving end of this pragmatic, market-driven outlook, however, have not always welcomed it because of its serious theological deficiencies. In 1999, for example, participants from fifty-three countries met in Foz de Iguassu, Brazil, afterwards issuing the *Iguassu Affirmation,* which gave voice to the theological concerns behind their disaffection with this approach. See David Neff, "Market-driven Missions: Scholars Fault Western Approaches to Evangelism, Advocate a New Vision for Spreading the Gospel," *Christianity Today* (Dec. 6, 1999), 28. On another continent, *Christianity Today* offered an upbeat account of how "Willow Creek church-growth concepts are gaining ground among German Protestants" even, it claimed, among those in the state church whom it did not view as evangelical. "Willow Creek's Methods Gain German Following," *Christianity Today,* 43 (April, 1999), 24-25. However, a church planter in Europe perceptively noted that Willow Creek's approach may work in the American suburbs, where matters of economic and social status are more or less guaranteed to be similar, but it will be far more difficult in the city which is much more heterogeneous. Besides, he quotes a fellow worker as saying, "'The Willow Creek model is limited as so much of it is based on reaching the yuppies of the Midwest. The problem is, Paris doesn't really have yuppies. . . .'" Tom Zimmerman, "Willow Creek or Lima?" *Evangelical Missions Quarterly,* 27 (October, 1991), 398.

Rodney Stark and Roger Finke explored some of these parallels in their *The Churching of America, 1776-1990.* This book seeks to explain how it was that at the time of the Revolution only 17% belonged to a church, by the time of the Civil War it was 37%, and by 1980 it was 62%. What explains this steady conquest of the American soul? And what explains why some churches succeed and others do not, some gain ground and others lose it? Their answer was that in a free society there is a market for religion. It is one that works like that for goods and services. The religious market is made up of the potential customers for whom churches and religions compete, and consumers are as unforgiving of ineffective religion as they are of ineffective businesses in the commercial realm. If in the commercial market we have organization, sales representatives, products, and marketing technique, in the ecclesiastical sphere, they argued, are the counterparts of polity, clergy, doctrines, and evangelization techniques. With this in mind, they then set out to analyze why some churches and denominations had been more successful than others in this market.

It is the existence of this market that seeker churches have come to recognize but with one weighty difference. What Stark and Finke argued was that the content of the faith, its doctrine, has in the past been vital to the success of Christian churches and not, as the seeker-sensitive imagine, an impediment to success. Specifically, they argued that churches which flourish are those in which there is a high degree of distinction from the culture, where there is cognitive dissonance, and that failure often has followed the disappearance of this distinction and dissonance. The reason for this is that people in the past have been looking for something different, something which is other than and larger than life, something which cannot be had under a secular guise, and churches which have offered this have flourished. Churches which lose their distinction from the surrounding culture have failed and disappeared.

Seeker churches are assuming or arguing the reverse, that doctrine is really peripheral and that the level of tension that is felt over and against the culture should be minimized if churches are to succeed. This is what is being visually represented in those churches which are trying to look just like the buildings people enter during the work week and this is why seeker services have greatly de-emphasized the traditional religious dimension, removing pulpits, abandoning traditional sermons, hymns, offerings, or anything else that seems too religious. This is an important matter to which we will need to return shortly for what the marketers have done has been to read the needs of the consumer as being "spiritual" (in the contemporary sense) but not theological, as being psychological but as having little to do with truth, as being more about techniques of survival than about the need to understand that there is meaning in life that transcends the mere business of surviving. That, I believe, has been a fatal mistake, as fatal as the one which the liberal Protestants made earlier.

Given the kind of airy indifference to the place of biblical doctrine in the seeker methodologies, it is probably futile to suggest that there is, in fact, a doctrinal reason for this convergence between the seeker churches and the older liberalism. That explanation lies in the fact that there is a disconnect between the biblical orthodoxy which is professed and the assumptions off which seeker churches are building themselves. Seeker methodology rests upon the Pelagian view that human beings are not inherently sinful, despite credal affirmations to the contrary, that in their disposition to God and his Word postmoderns are neutral, that they can be seduced into making the purchase of faith even as they can into making any other kind of purchase. A majority of 52% of evangelicals, it was noted earlier, 52%, reject the idea of original sin. It would nevertheless be quite foolish to think that using what was once a dreaded word — Pelagian — to describe all of this would create dismay. It will not. The majority of evangelicals are deliberately undoctrinal. Their criterion of "truth" by which seeker habits of church building should be tested is simply the pragmatic one. Is this working?

In 1972, Dean Kelley's *Why Conservative Churches Are Growing* appeared and it could just as well have been entitled *Why Mainline Liberal Churches Are Declining*. His explanation at the time was quite shocking.[51] He proposed that the reason that conservative churches were

51. In 1994, however, his thesis was tested with respect to mainline Protestants and was corroborated. See Dean R. Hoge, Benton Johnson, and Donald A. Luidens, *Vanishing Boundaries: The Religion of Mainline Protestant Baby Boomers* (Louisville: Westminster/John Knox Press, 1994), 180-88. There is, of course, more to this story than simply the degree of seriousness with which faith was taken. The mainline denominations, for example, became engaged in the 1970s and 1980s in a series of un-

growing was that they were serious about their faith and liberal churches were not. He expressed this thought in the language of strictness. Conservative churches organized themselves around truth that was absolute, and expected believers to accept and to live in the light of that truth and practice the older virtues of self-denial and self-discipline.

However, there was a paradox at work here. Why would people pay such a high price to join churches like these when religion, on the other side of the theological aisle, could be had at very little cost, where it could be constructed in accordance with preference, truth could be tailored as desired, and dialogue was the name of the game? The answer, of course, is that people are willing to pay the price if that price can be justified by what one gets. Laurence Iannaccone argued that strict demands strengthen the church in three ways: "they raise overall levels of commitment, they increase average rates of participation, and they enhance the net benefits of membership."[52] This is true but the reason it is true is that the commitment, participation, and the enhanced value of membership are nurtured by the knowledge that what people are participating in is *true*. In other words, cost and value are closely related. It is because of the value of what is being obtained that people are willing to pay a high cost by way of repentance, commitment, self-denial, maybe even social ostracism or lost job promotions, for this truth is the pearl of very great price. And this understanding of its value needs constant reinforcement; otherwise entropy sets in. The fact is that as dazzling as the modern world has become, it has never outgrown its need for this kind of truth, never invalidates it, and therefore the liberal (and now seeker-sensitive) fear of becoming outdated is

---

wise political adventures which, it turned out, both went against what many in their congregations believed but also had little to do with Christian faith itself. See, for example, Thomas C. Reeves, *The Empty Church: The Suicide of Liberal Christianity* (New York: The Free Press, 1996), 133-65. On the evangelical side, Thom Rainer has argued that his research also sustains the Dean Kelley thesis. See his *High Expectations: The Remarkable Secret for Keeping People in Your Church* (Nashville: Broadman and Holman, 1999).

52. Laurence Iannaccone, "Why Strict Churches Are Strong," in *Sacred Companies: Organizational Aspects of Religion and Religious Aspects of Organizations*, ed. N. J. Demerath, Peter Dobkin Hall, Terry Schmitt, and Rhys H. Williams (New York: Oxford University Press, 1998), 271.

as groundless as the small child's nervousness about a monster in the closet.

The liberal mainline churches in the twentieth century in America found themselves walking a road that became ever lonelier, especially in the second half of that century, because they failed to understand the paradox which was at work. The paradox is that over the life of the Church in America, as Stark and Finke have shown, the churches which have grown are those in which a cognitive distinction and separation from the culture have been preserved. Whenever this spiritual antagonism has declined and then been lost, these churches go out of business. Stark and Finke then go on to suggest that often we ask the wrong question about the growth and decline of churches. When a denomination begins to lose members, the typical analysis has taken the line that demand for what those churches had to offer had fallen off. They suggest something different: that the problem lies on the side of supply, not demand. It is that churches begin to look for niches in the market to which they think they will be able to appeal, but this appeal soon takes the road of asking for low commitment and a casual relation to biblical truth.[53] As seeker churches mine this vein of spiritual yearning in society, without challenging its grounding in fallen human nature and postmodern individualism, they may be finding a marketing niche that will lead them into certain decline. The question they are going to have to ask themselves is whether the clientele they have assiduously courted have the kind of casual relationship to biblical truth, and the low commitment, to guarantee that their churches will go the way that many mainline churches have gone. If they cannot clarify for themselves who is sovereign — God or the religious consumer? — what is authoritative in practice — Scripture or culture? — and what is important — faithfulness or success? — they will find themselves walking the same road and facing the same fate as the churches that failed before because whatever seriousness now remains will dissolve into triviality.

Indeed, there are already signs that this is happening. In reviewing the research that had been done on church life between 1996 and 2002, Barna stumbled upon a most disconcerting fact. Why is it, he

---

53. Rodney Stark and Roger Finke, *Acts of Faith: Explaining the Human Side of Religion* (Berkeley: University of California Press, 2000), 193-96.

wondered, that Boomers were initially so opposed to institutional religion but now make up fully half of the born-again movement? The answer, he concluded, is that they are practiced consumers who were offered a deal that they simply could not turn down. For "a one-time admission of imperfection and weakness" they received in return "permanent peace with God." The result was that "millions of Boomers who said the prayer, asked for forgiveness and went on with their life, with virtually nothing changed." And Barna adds that they "saw it as a deal in which they could exploit God and get what they wanted without giving up anything of consequence."[54]

Here lies the principal false premise upon which this marketing of the Church is based. It is treating sinners as customers and that is bringing into the Church the insipid commitment and ignorance which has so alarmed Barna. In the marketplace, a customer's desires are all considered beyond reproach during the ritual of purchase. What salesperson is going to wonder aloud whether the Lexus someone is considering buying isn't, perhaps, just a little bit extravagant? The consumer defines his or her own wants and decides how those felt needs are going to be satisfied. In bringing this process into the Church, and pitching a "product" to the consumers in the pew (or its contemporary substitute), marketers have to assume the essential neutrality of felt needs. In the biblical world, however, consumers are not left to define their own needs because as sinners they always misunderstand themselves. That is why in our fallen condition we need God's revelation. And what we learn from it is that we are anything but neutral. Paul summons up the following phrases to describe people in sin: "None is righteous, no, not one; no one understands, no one seeks for God. All have turned aside . . . no one does good, not even one. . . . There is no fear of God before their eyes" (Rom. 3:10-12, 18). Removing crosses, pulpits, and pews, and creating a warm, uplifting, encouraging atmosphere, do not scratch the surface of the internal animosity toward God, Christ, and his Word that sin creates.

When the consumer is allowed to be sovereign in Church, the Church is abdicating from its responsibility because it is allowing truth

54. George Barna, "America's Religious Activity Has Increased since 1996, but Its Beliefs Remain Unchanged," http//www.barna.org.

Pelagianism is the natural heresy of zealous Christians who are not interested in theology.

J. I. Packer, "'Keswick' and the Reformed Doctrine of Sanctification"

to become displaced by spiritual and psychological desire. However, once the concession has been made, we then discover that satisfying needs becomes a frustrating undertaking. Needs, in a therapeutic society, multiply faster than fruit flies. No sooner is one need met than two take its place. Coopting the needy to church is not the same thing as seeing a sinner converted and brought into the Church.

Furthermore, needs that are identified, the ones that are felt, may in fact conceal far deeper and more real needs. The need to be amused and distracted, for example, though it may be very real and deeply felt, may conceal what lies beneath it, a gnawing, aching emptiness. And that emptiness itself would be misread as a need if it were not seen as an emptiness which has been unrelieved and unaddressed by God in Christ. Retailing help for felt needs is what the massive self-help industry is about. What distinguishes the Church from this industry is *truth*. It is truth about God and about ourselves that displaces the consumer from his or her current perch of sovereignty in the Church and places God in the place where he should be. There is much idolatry in the making in the current situation. "As sinful human beings," Os Guinness comments, "we have an instinctual, compulsive bias toward forms of religion that we ourselves can create and control"[55] and that is precisely what consumer-driven religion invites us to do.

What is going to happen to the Church when those from our postmodern culture bring into it, not simply their musical tastes, but the disposition, worked out in varying degrees of severity, for living as if there were no viable worldview and no absolute truth? This, indeed, is what Barna is already seeing. These notes of nihilism are not always

55. Os Guinness, *Dining with the Devil: The Megachurch Movement Flirts with Modernity* (Grand Rapids: Baker Book House, 1993), 37.

heard in blatant ways but, more commonly, in ways that are subtle and muted. Is it not the case that the radical individualism that inhabits most churches and which, in its therapeutic form, collapses all reality into the self, is also an expression of the collapse of any functioning, overarching meaning in life? Meaning, in the absence of such purpose, simply becomes privatized and internalized. Is it therefore surprising that the overwhelming majority of the American public do not believe that there are truths which are absolute? That disposition, as we have seen, is now reverberating around the churches. So is it surprising if preaching begins to cater to this disposition and reduces the meaning of Christian faith simply to what is "practical," to techniques for surviving in a baffling and painful world?

Producer churches, in Anderson's language, have offered prescription. That prescription has traditionally come through an understanding of the normative place of Scripture in the life of the Church and hence of the importance of attending to the preaching of the Word of God. Out of this have grown a set of doctrinal beliefs, ethical understanding, and, at its best, a way of looking at the world which is God-centered and God-honoring. How much this is transformed as churches move from being producer churches to being consumer churches depends, of course, on the degree to which the church rearranges itself around human needs and desires. There can be no question, though, that with the consumer in the driver's seat, be that consumer Christian or not, the nature and the place of the sermon are changed. Nor is there any question that this transition also signals the fact that the Church is surrendering the right, or has lost it, to tell God's Story on its own terms. To do so is being seen as irrelevant because for any valid, compelling story to emerge it must begin, not with God, but within the consumer. Thus begins a downward cycle. The question of truth degenerates into a question as to whether it works and that degenerates further into the question as to whether it even matters.[56]

56. In two national surveys in 2002, the Barna organization asked adults and teenagers if moral truth was unchanging or whether they thought it was determined by circumstances. At a national level, 64% of adults opted for the relativism of truth whereas only 22% thought it was absolute and unchanged by circumstances. Among teenagers, the figures were even more uneven with 83% aligning with the position of relativism and only 6% opposing it. Among those adults who claimed to be born again, only 32% asserted

In his analysis of seeker sermons, Sargeant notes that a distinction is often made between authentic Christianity and authoritative Christianity. The latter, of course, is that of the traditional church, that of producer churches. In the former, the sermon's topic, just as was the case in Protestant liberalism, now originates in the questions and psychological needs of the listeners. And while this is justified on the grounds that it is just good communication skill at work, the fact remains that there is much in Scripture that is not of much interest to many in these new churches, and much which does not seem to make any connection with their lives. These themes therefore fade away in much the same way as an unwanted product, sooner or later, will be taken off the store shelf. There is, therefore, a certain kind of poignant honesty at work in those seeker churches which have removed the pulpit and replaced it by a bar stool or a plexiglass stand.

In these churches, Christian orthodoxy is not jettisoned, but it is tailored for the new consumer audience, which is one much given to spirituality shorn of theology, one stripped of much of its cognitive structure. Messages are preached with civility and they are more user-friendly than they used to be. Their effectiveness is judged by their "market value" (that is, their practical usefulness). God is much friendlier, too. Gone are the notes of judgment, though these are more displaced than denied, and they are replaced by those of love and acceptance. God, in one such message, was presented as the one "who loves you, is proud of you, believes in you, and will give you strength to stand up to the forces of evil in the world."[57] Sin is preached but is presented

---

their belief in moral absolutes and only 9% of teenagers. Barna's conclusion was that when these lopsided majorities in the Church vote for relativism, the Church is in trouble. "Continuing to preach more sermons," he reasoned, "teach more Sunday school classes and enroll more people in Bible study groups won't solve the problem since most of these people don't accept the basis of the principles being taught in those venues" (George Barna, "Americans Are Most Likely to Base Truth on Feelings," February 12, 2002," http://www.barna.org). The failure to address this issue successfully, he said, is going to undermine the Church for at least the next generation. This is undoubtedly true; far from solving the problem, the seeker church formula which Barna helped devise, and now advocates, is the main offender today in this growing calamity because the practical and regulative function of truth has been surrendered in favor of practical technique and entertainment. That is simply a different way of capitulating to this pervasive relativism.

57. Sargeant, *Seeker Churches*, 86.

more in terms of how it "harms the individual, rather than how it of-fends a holy God. Sin, in short, prevents us from realizing *our* full po-tential."[58] Conversion is insisted upon but then, paradoxically, it is the this-worldly benefits that are accentuated, the practical benefits of knowing Christ receiving all the attention with scarcely a look at what happens if we turn away from him. To turn away from him, Hybels says, leaves that person not so much under God's judgment as unfulfilled. Thus the exclusive message of classical evangelicalism is maintained but parts of it are de-emphasized and parts are transformed to make the adjustment to this consumer-driven and therapeutically-defined culture. Evangelicalism is now presented "in the friendly guise of an egalitarian, fulfillment-enhancing, fun, religious encounter with God"[59] And is this not sailing dangerously close to adapting the gospel to the postmodern disposition for the sake of success, adapting it to those yearning for the sacred without addressing what stands in the way to knowing God? When Paul wrote to the Galatians, whom he had to rebuke, he was painfully aware of the temptation to soften the gos-pel. He firmly rejected the desire to "please men" because, he said, if "I were still pleasing men, I should not be a servant of Christ" (Gal. 1:10).

There is, of course, a spectrum of translation in this move to adapt the Christian message to postmodern horizons, ranging from the mild to the severe. But whether in blatant or understated ways, the logic is the same: servicing the customer means negotiating around his or her point of resistance and discomfort as much as possible. If seek-ers want to be comfortable, then statements about the moral grandeur of God are liable to be tamed. If they want to be at ease and enjoy them-selves, then the atmosphere must be light and entertaining and the costliness of Christian faith may be held in abeyance. Bring on the pop-corn but be careful about the Cross. If they find sin to be a dismal, dis-couraging matter, then the church may be loathe to speak of serious re-pentance. If they want to experience the sacred, in all likelihood on their own terms, then it would be unfriendly to stand in their way. And if they come wanting an upbeat, inspirational experience, then the church will feel considerable pressure to provide music, a message and,

58. Sargeant, *Seeker Churches*, 86.
59. Sargeant, *Seeker Churches*, 99.

indeed, a total program which focuses on the possibilities of personal conquest and self-improvement. The problem with this, as James Wall has suggested, is that its criteria for success are secular in nature. They are the measure of successful marketing and customer relations developed in the business world and now being applied to the Church. If this is done well, he says, people will come but then he goes to the heart of the question. The "larger question remains: will He come?"[60] What, one wonders, would John Wesley have done if on one of his preaching visits he had been preceded by some advance staff who surveyed the potential crowd to find out what they would be comfortable hearing and discovered that their desires were at odds with the gospel message? Or Martin Luther, George Whitefield, Jonathan Edwards, or Charles Spurgeon? What would they have done had they been told that their potential audience was not comfortable with discussions about God's moral grandeur or their sin, that they found justification by faith boring, and the substitutionary death of Christ dull and incomprehensible?

This new experiment in "doing church" is rooted, I am confident, in the desire, even the passion, to see the Church grow. What has not been grasped, however, is that in the modern world, the means that are available for this task are so effective that we need very little truth in order to have success. Marketing the faith works. At least, it works to the extent that churches can be filled very quickly if the mix between humor, fun, friendliness, music, entertainment, and inspiration is right. But Os Guinness is right to ask what the "decisive authority" is in each church. The Church is only the Church, he says, when it lives by God's truth, and if anything substitutes for this authority, "Christians risk living unauthorized lives of faith, exercising unauthorized ministries, and proclaiming an unauthorized gospel."[61]

Contextualization is not about exploiting a culture for the Church's own gain even as Christian faith is not about exploiting God for what we want. If there is a place for speaking of contextualization it

---

60. James Wall, "Between a Gush and a Smirk: Viewing the Megachurch," *Christian Century,* 112 (March 22-29. 1995), 315.

61. Guinness, *Dining with the Devil,* 35. See also his essay, "Sounding Out the Idols of Church Growth," in *No God But God,* ed. Os Guinness and John Seel (Chicago: Moody Press, 1992), 151-74.

Suppose a seeker came from a service of the kind I've been describing (let's say a heavy-duty service of that kind). Suppose she
came away and said to herself, *now* I understand what Christian
faith is all about: it's not about lament, or repentance, or hum-
bling oneself before God to receive God's favor. It's got nothing
to do with a lot of boring doctrines. It's not about the hard disciplined work of mortifying our old nature and learning to make
God's purposes our own. It's not about the inevitable failures in
this project, and the terrible grace of Jesus Christ that comes so
that we might begin again. Not at all! I had it all wrong! The
Christian faith is mainly about celebration and fun and personal
growth and five ways to boost my self-esteem!

Cornelius Plantinga, "The Seeker Service Dilemma"

is principally in the sense of speaking to the issues foremost in a culture and doing so in the language of *truth*. This means that the Church
cannot hide itself within a culture but must also speak to that culture
from outside itself. To the seeker-sensitive theorists, this kind of "authoritative" faith is what supposedly puts off the postmodern generations, but one must ask what is so "authentic" about Christians becoming cognitively indistinguishable from the postmodern unbelievers
they want to see join their churches? The paradox at work throughout
the past is still at work today. Churches which preserve their cognitive
identity and distinction from the culture will flourish; those who lose
them in the interests of seeking success will disappear.

In our churches we may have made a deal with postmodern consumers but the hard reality is that Christianity cannot be bought. Purchase, in the world of consumption, leads to ownership but in the
Church this cannot happen. It is never God who is owned. It is we who
are owned in Christ. Christianity is not up for sale. Its price has already
been fixed and that price is the complete and ongoing surrender to
Christ of those who embrace him by faith. It can only be had on his own
terms. It can be had only as a whole. It refuses to offer only selections of
its teachings. Furthermore, the Church is not its retailing outlet. Its

preachers are not its peddlers and those who are Christian are not its consumers. It cannot legitimately be had as a bargain though the marketplace is full of bargain hunters.

For we are not, like so many, peddlers of God's word. . . ."

II Corinthians 2:17

No. Let us think instead of the Church as its voice of *proclamation,* not its sales agent, its practitioner, not its marketing firm. And in that proclamation there is inevitable cultural confrontation. More precisely, there is the confrontation between Christ, in and through the biblical Word, and the rebellion of the human heart. This is confrontation of those whose face is that of a particular culture but whose heart is that of the fallen world. We cannot forget that.

CHAPTER VIII

The Day of New Beginnings

—◦◦◦—

What have been the eras of the Church's greatest influence? What have been the moments of its most powerful impact on the world? Not the epochs of its visible might and splendour; not the age succeeding Constantine, when Christianity became imperialistic, and all the kingdoms of the world and the glory of them seemed ready to bow beneath the sceptre of Christ; not the days of the great medieval pontiffs, when Christ's vicar in Rome wielded a sovereignty more absolute than that of any secular monarch on the earth; not the later nineteenth century, when the Church became infected with the prevailing humanistic optimism, which was quite sure that man was the architect of his own destinies, that a wonderful utopian kingdom of God was waiting him just round the corner, and that the very momentum of his progress was bound to carry him thither. Not in such times as these has the Church exercised its strongest leverage upon the soul and conscience of the world: but in days when it has been crucified with Christ, and has counted all things but loss for His sake; days when, smitten with a great contrition and repentance, it has cried out to God from the depths.

JAMES S. STEWART

Ours is a day of many superlatives. There is more affluence for more people than ever before, more knowledge, more information, more opportunities, more hope before life's intractable diseases, and more years to live life. And, in many ways, the Church, at least in America, shares in all of this largesse. It is wealthy, it is replete with religious books and Bibles, with churches and organizations, television programs and radio broadcasts, and with all of the other remarkable trappings of a remarkable time. This, of course, is a two-edged sword, for costs always attend benefits, dangers accompany opportunities. The question, therefore, is whether the Church can use the means and opportunities which it has without being corrupted by them. Specifically, this question comes into focus in what I believe are the two main defining marks of this time; our growing multi-ethnic and multi-cultural society, and its postmodern ethos. First, can the Church understand its own unique missionary context or will its entanglements in the largesse of the moment blind its eyes? Second, can the Church disentangle itself from postmodern culture sufficiently to exhibit in its own life, in stark contrast to that world, the realities of truth, beauty, and goodness? If the evangelical Church cannot answer these questions satisfactorily, it is fair to assume that it will continue to stagnate and contract despite all of its surface glitter and marketing savvy. It is not more marketing that is needed, not more marketing that is more effective, but more spiritual reality.

God's Open Door

The first question, then, concerns its missionary context. What we have seen is that the world seems as if it is beginning to empty itself into the West. East is moving West and South is moving North. What had once kept people apart, such things as oceans and national boundaries, are no longer so effective. The consequence of this immigration, whether legal or illegal, is that the West is more multi-ethnic and more religiously diverse than ever before. This is bringing in a flood of religions that were hardly known before and, with respect to America, merely stood on its doorstep. Today, they are inside the house. And this reality has played off against two others. First, there is the rise of the new spirituality. Second, there is the fact that America's soul is now much taken with the postmodern loss of absolutes, of what is true and right. The complex interactions between these realities is what is producing a missionary context as remote from Christian faith as are those in faraway places to which we send missionaries. This should be prodding the Church to think a little differently about its mission.

From one angle, this is now opening up doors of new opportunity. There are people coming to America to whom missionaries a generation or two ago would have been going. Indeed, some are coming from countries to which missionaries can go no longer. It is to America that the potential leadership of many countries in the world is coming to be educated and prepared for their roles in the future. The mission field, as missionaries used to think of it, is increasingly relocating, at least for short periods and sometimes much longer times, to the West and not least to America. This is true not *in toto,* of course, but nevertheless in significant numbers.

From a different angle, however, the countries to which these immigrants are coming throughout the West are those which are shedding their last remaining vestiges of Christian understanding. This is more true in European countries than in America and yet even in America the erosion of even the most minimal remnants of Christian orientation has been substantial. Even the civil religion which seemed to exercise some hold on the American soul midway through the last century when Will Herberg was writing is now much thinner. Or, perhaps, it is the case that the remnants of this civil religion have now been transformed by the emergence of the new spirituality. The result is that it is now a much privatized sense of what is believed about God and the sacred relative to the country. The parting of the ways is now becoming stark and unmistakable. The immediate consequence of this, it would seem, would be far less tolerance of Christian faith but that is true only in a limited way. In a postmodern culture, with its deep relativism and its pervasive individualism, any belief is tolerated up to a point. What is not tolerable, and what will not be tolerated, is the kind of faith which makes absolute claims, which recognizes the right of all religions and spiritualities to exist but does not accept as viable their claims to religious truth. Christianity practiced and believed in private is not in any jeopardy; Christianity which makes its beliefs public in the sense that it asserts its own beliefs as being normative is not wanted. This is seen as plain, unvarnished bigotry and, in this age of unrepentant relativism, it simply is not acceptable.

This is a situation, then, in which the issues are becoming clearer by the day. Civil religion could paper over religious differences but a robust biblical faith now stands out like an organ stop. Now the missionary context in which the Church finds itself becomes unmistakable.

Two developments have taken place, especially in the evangelical Church, which are obscuring this. First, in the scramble for success, many evangelical churches have adopted marketing strategies. Marketing being marketing, this has led them to concentrate on market niches. Almost inevitably, these are niches of class, economic status, generation, and often of race. The niche becomes a segment, almost a special interest, and certainly something less than the whole. It is the whole which is being lost in the scramble for success. It is precisely the opposite of what should be happening. This is a situation which is crying out for a large missionary vision that looks at and for the whole and not merely the segment; many evangelical churches are answering with a cramped, narrow vision, driven mostly by the desire for success in which there is a good slice of self-interest. Rarely has a missionary opportunity of such magnitude dropped into the lap of the Church; rarely has so large an opportunity been abandoned for other things.

What remains a matter of considerable curiosity, however, is that those most intent on finding success the marketing way appear to be those most unaware of their missionary context. The reason for this seems rather simple. Marketing works. Success can be had with very little truth. The missionary heartbeat of earlier generations is, as a result, slowly being extinguished today.

The second development which is obscuring the nature of our situation is rooted in the fact that the evangelical Church, for some time, has been slowly but inexorably stripping itself of its truth, doctrine, and discipline. In that process, it is stripping itself of the very things which would make it distinctive in this culture, those things that would give it a place from which to speak, and those things that would give it something to proclaim. So, while the cultural drift is one that is opening up a chasm between itself and Christian faith, Christians by their techniques for growth and their compromises with the spirit of the age are, in effect, trying to close that chasm in order to be successful! The more the culture abandons truth and goodness which are absolute, the less the evangelical Church speaks about truth and goodness which are absolute!

The Call to Authenticity

This evangelical version of spirituality, precisely because it has stripped itself of its doctrine — on the fallacious assumption that this doctrine won't "sell" in today's marketplace — is the kind of spirituality which has, then, been silenced in today's culture. It has been silenced in the sense that though its adherents and purveyors may congregate in churches, and though they may sell its benefits and attractions, it remains only one product among many others on the market. It can seduce but it cannot confront. It can lure but it cannot speak. It is because it has deliberately shed its doctrine, and its discipline, that it can only hold itself out to be taken by those who are in the market looking for something to take, but it has left itself devoid of the ability to proclaim. Thus it is that the evangelical churches have made their deal with the new generations. The deal, as Barna put it, is that for a one-time confession of weakness, God's eternal peace can be had. It is a deal in which God has come up in the short end because we get what we want and give up nothing of consequence. That is the inevitable outcome to the marketing of the gospel.

This, of course, cheapens our understanding of God, it demeans the nature of the gospel, and it works havoc in the Church. And what it also does is to leave behind a kind of faith whose central passion is no longer that of truth and goodness. If the Church is not in possession of truth, truth as an understanding that corresponds exactly to what is in reality, and corresponds exactly to what is in the will and character of God, then it has been left speechless. It has nothing to say. Without this truth, its private insights are no more believable, no more compelling, and no more desirable than anyone else's. Why, then, has the evangelical Church arranged itself around the marketing dynamic rather than around the truth which it is its birthright to proclaim?

Postmoderns are, of course, especially allergic to truth claims. In part this is a valuable corrective to the rationalistic truth claims of a humanistic kind which the Enlightenment spawned and which developed coercive status in the West. We do, indeed, need to be modest about ourselves as knowers, conscious of our propensities to rationalize reality in our favor. But more is at issue here than simply the reaction against the Enlightenment. What is also operating is a deep, pervasive relativism that now grips our society and it is to that that the evangelical Church has surrendered. In the evangelical Church, the belief in truth has substantially eroded. It is no wonder, if a majority no longer believes in absolutes of any kind, that the evangelical Church is finding itself without a voice in a culture which likewise does not believe in absolutes.

The postmodern reaction against Enlightenment dogma will not be met successfully simply by Christian proclamation. Of that we can be sure. That proclamation must arise within a context of *authenticity*. It is only as the evangelical Church begins to put its own house in order, its members begin to disentangle themselves from all of those cultural habits which militate against a belief in truth, and begin to embody that truth in the way that the Church actually lives, that postmodern skepticism might begin to be overcome. Postmoderns want to see as well as hear, to find authenticity in relationship as the precursor to hearing what is said. This is a valid and biblical demand. Faith, after all, is dead without works, and few sins are dealt with as harshly by Jesus as hypocrisy. What postmoderns want to see, and are entitled to see, is believing and being, talking and doing, all joined together in a seamless whole. This is the great challenge of the moment for the evangelical Church. Can it rise to this occasion?

The moments of the Church's greatest influence — and, in fact, its greatest moments — as James Stewart, the Scottish preacher noted, have not been those when the Church reached for worldly power, or when it adapted to its culture, but when it sought to be authentic. The Church has been most influential in those moments when its contrition reached down deeply into its soul, when in its known weakness it cried out to God from the depths, when it sought to live by his truth and on his terms, when it sought to proclaim that truth in its world, when it was willing to pay the price of having that kind of truth, when it was willing to demand of itself that it live by that truth, when it sought above all else God in his grace and glory. At such moments it has soared and out of its own inherent weakness found extraordinary strength and power. When all of these things have been present, then the Church has been the Church. Today, all too often, the Church is not being the Church. It has become a business for the retailing of spirituality, a spirituality in which truth is at best a peripheral consideration and sometimes not a consideration at all. Should we be surprised when we find out that those who are born again, or who say they are, live no differently, ethically speaking, from those who say they are secular? Of course not! This is the inevitable outcome to the massive defection from truth at a *practical* level which has happened in the evangelical Church.

This is a time of extraordinary opportunity and this time brings with it an extraordinary challenge. Can the evangelical church once again find its authenticity? Can it find its voice? There is no human perfection in this world and there are no golden ages in the life of the Church. There are simply moments when the Church is either less authentic or more authentic. We, today, are rapidly descending into serious inauthenticity. However, the people of God, across the ages, have also learned that they can, indeed, recover their lost authenticity when they are willing to cry to God from the depths and make good on what has gone badly. Today is just such a day, and God has always been, and always will be, the God of new beginnings.

Sober considerations such as these, however, need to be placed side by side with those that are joyous. Chief among these is the fact that Christ is ruling sovereignly in our world. The New Testament repeatedly states that "all things" have been put under his feet. It is this vision that mightily liberates us from the kind of anxiety and even panic which can set in when we consider the power of the postmodern world. So overawed have some become of this world of unbelief, so afraid are they of being taken as irrelevant, that they even imagine that Christian success cannot be had without taking on postmodern habits of thought and even unbelief. Since the postmodern world cannot be beaten, the Church must simply reckon on joining it if it is not to be put out of business! The postmodern world, however, is neither ours to join nor ours to overcome. Despite its glitter and brilliance it conceals in its workings its own fallenness and unbelief and so we must not join it. And we cannot overcome it by marketing, or any other kind of technique because these techniques do not scratch the surface of its real issues, which are those of sin. Indeed, it is entirely unnecessary to even think about overcoming the postmodern world because it has already been overcome in its sin. It is only ours to see the victory of Christ on the Cross being realized afresh in the actual circumstances of our time. That will happen when the Church humbles itself afresh, seeks the power and cleansing of God, and asks to have its vision renewed of the victory of Christ and to see, once again, his greatness. So may it be!

Bibliography

—◦◦◦—

Acquaviva, S. S. *The Decline of the Sacred in Industrial Society.* Translated by Patricia Lipscomb. Oxford: Blackwell, 1979.

Aichele, George, et al., eds. *The Postmodern Bible.* New Haven: Yale University Press, 1995.

Allen, Diogenes. *Christian Belief in a Postmodern World: The Full Wealth of Conviction.* Louisville: Westminster/John Knox Press, 1989.

Anderson, Leith. *A Church for the 21st Century: Bringing Change to Your Church to Meet the Challenges of a Changing Society.* Minneapolis: Bethany House, 1992.

———. *Dying for Change: An Arresting Look at the New Realities Confronting Churches and Para-Church Ministries.* Minneapolis: Bethany House, 1990.

Arnold, Matthew. *Culture and Anarchy.* Edited by Samuel Lipman. New Haven: Yale University Press, 1994.

Baillie, D. M. *God Was in Christ: An Essay on Incarnation and Atonement.* London: Faber and Faber, 1956.

Barak, Halim Isber. *The Arab World: Society, Culture, and State.* Berkeley: University of California Press, 1993.

Barna, George. *Church Marketing: Breaking Ground for the Harvest.* Ventura: Regal Books, 1992.

———. *Marketing the Church: What They Never Taught You About Church Growth.* Colorado Springs: NavPress, 1988.

———. *User Friendly Churches: What Christians Need to Know About the Churches People Love to Go To.* Ventura: Regal Books, 1992.

Barrett, David B., George T. Kurian, and Todd M. Johnson. *World Christian Ency-*

clopedia: A Comparative Survey of Churches and Religions in the Modern World. Oxford: Oxford University Press, 2001.

Barth, Karl. *Church Dogmatics*. Translated by G. T. Thomson. 5 volumes. Edinburgh: T&T Clark, 1936-77.

———. *The Epistle to the Romans*. Translated by Edwyn C. Hoskyns. New York: Oxford University Press, 1933.

———. *Evangelical Theology: An Introduction*. Translated by Grover Foley. London: Weidenfeld and Nicholson, 1963.

Baue, Frederick W. *The Spiritual Society: What Lurks Beyond Postmodernism?* Wheaton: Crossway Books, 2001.

Bauman, Zygmunt. *Globalization: The Human Consequences*. New York: Columbia University Press, 1998.

———. *Liquid Modernity*. Cambridge: Polity, 2000.

———. *Modernity and Ambivalence*. Ithaca: Cornell University Press, 1991.

———. *Postmodernity and Its Discontents*. New York: New York University Press, 1997.

Baumeister, Roy F. *Escaping the Self: Alcoholism, Spirituality, Masochism, and Flights from the Burden of Selfhood*. New York: Basic Books, 1991.

Baumer, Franklin L. *Modern European Thought: Continuity and Change in Ideas, 1600-1950*. New York: Macmillan, 1977.

Beckett, Samuel. *Waiting for Godot: Tragicomedy in 2 Acts*. New York: Grove Press, 1954.

Bellah, Robert N., et al. *Habits of the Heart: Individualism and Commitment in American Life*. New York: Harper and Row, 1985.

Berger, Peter L., ed. *The Desacralization of the World: Resurgent Religion and World Politics*. Washington: Ethics and Public Policy Center, 1999.

———. *The Heretical Imperative: Contemporary Possibilities of Religious Affirmation*. New York: Anchor Press, 1979.

———. *The Noise of Solemn Assemblies: Christian Commitment and the Religious Establishment in America*. Garden City: Doubleday, 1961.

———. *The Sacred Canopy: Elements of a Sociological Theory of Religion*. New York: Doubleday, 1969.

Berger, Peter L,. and Thomas Luckmann. *The Social Construction of Reality: A Treatise in the Sociology of Knowledge*. New York: Doubleday, 1966.

Berger, Peter L., Brigitte Berger, and Hansfried Kellner. *The Homeless Mind: Modernization and Consciousness*. New York: Random House, 1983.

Berman, Morris. *The Twilight of American Culture*. New York: W. W. Norton, 2000.

Black, C. E. *The Dynamics of Modernization: A Study in Comparative History*. New York: Harper and Row, 1963.

Bloom, Allan. *The Closing of the American Mind: How Higher Education Has Failed*

Democracy and Impoverished the Souls of Today's Students. New York: Simon and Schuster, 1987.

Bloom, Harold. *The American Religion: The Emergence of the Post-Christian Nation*. New York: Simon and Schuster, 1992.

———. *Omens of Millennium: The Gnosis of Angels, Dreams, and Resurrection*. New York: Riverhead Books, 1996.

Boorstin, Daniel J. *The Seekers: The Story of Man's Continuing Quest to Understand His World*. New York: Random House, 1998.

Brooke, A. E. *The Fragments of Heracleon*. Cambridge: Cambridge University Press, 1891.

Brooks, David. *Bobos in Paradise: The New Upper Class and How They Got There*. New York: Simon and Schuster, 2000.

Brower, Kent E., and Mark Elliott. *Eschatology in Bible and Theology: Evangelical Essays at the Dawn of a New Millennium*. Downers Grove: InterVarsity Press, 1997.

Brunner, Emil. *The Mediator: A Study of the Central Doctrine of the Christian Faith*. Translated by Olive Wyon. London: Lutterworth Press, 1952.

Brunner, Emil, and Karl Barth. *Natural Revelation: Comprising "Nature and Grace" by Professor Dr. Emil Brunner and the Reply "No!" by Dr. Karl Barth*. Translated by Peter Fraenkel. London: Geoffrey Bles, 1946.

Budde, Michael L., and Robert W. Brimlow. *Christianity Incorporated: How Big Business Is Buying the Church*. Grand Rapids: Brazos Press, 2002.

Bultmann, Rudolf. *The Presence of Eternity: History and Eschatology*. New York: Harper and Brothers, 1957.

———. *Theology of the New Testament*. Translated by Kendrick Grobel. 2 volumes. New York: Charles Scribner's Sons, 1952-55.

Busi, Frederick. *Transformation of Godot*. Lexington: University Press of Kentucky, 1980.

Butler, B. C. *The Theology of Vatican II*. London: Darton, Longman and Todd, 1967.

Butler, Jon. *Awash in a Sea of Faith: Christianizing the American People*. Cambridge, Mass.: Harvard University Press, 1990.

Cahoone, Lawrence E. *From Modernism to Postmodernism*. Oxford: Blackwell Publishers, 1996.

Cairns, David. *The Image of God*. London: SCM Press, 1953.

Campbell, Colin. *The Romantic Ethic and the Spirit of Modern Capitalism*. Oxford: Basil Blackwell, 1987.

Camus, Albert. *The Myth of Sisyphus and Other Essays*. Translated by Justin O'Brien. New York: Vintage Books, 1955.

———. *The Rebel: An Essay on Man in Revolt*. Translated by Anthony Bower. New York: Vintage, 1956.

Bibliography

Carr, Karen L. *The Banalization of Evil: Twentieth-Century Responses to Meaninglessness.* Albany: The State University of New York Press, 1992.

Carroll, Colleen. *The New Faithful: Why Young Adults Are Embracing Christian Orthodoxy.* Chicago: Loyola Press, 2002.

Carson, D. A. *The Gagging of God: Christianity Confronts Pluralism.* Grand Rapids: Zondervan, 1996.

————, ed. *Telling the Truth: Evangelizing Postmoderns.* Grand Rapids: Zondervan, 2000.

Carson, D. A., Peter T. O'Brien, and Mark A. Siefrid, eds. *Justification and Variegated Nomism.* Grand Rapids: Baker, 2001.

Chadwick, William. *Stealing Sheep: The Church's Hidden Problems with Transfer Growth.* Downers Grove: InterVarsity Press, 2001.

Charry, Ellen T. *By the Renewing of Your Minds: The Pastoral Function of Christian Doctrine.* New York: Oxford University Press, 1997.

Chesterton, Gilbert K. *Orthodoxy.* New York: John Lane Co., 1909.

Cimino, Richard, and Don Lattin. *Shopping for Faith: American Religion in the New Millennium.* San Francisco: Jossey-Bass, 1998.

Clark, Kelly James. *Return to Reason: A Critique of Enlightenment Evidentialism and a Defense of Reason and Belief in God.* Grand Rapids: William B. Eerdmans, 1990.

Cohn, Steven, ed. *Classics of Western Philosophy.* Indianapolis: Hackett, 1977.

Connor, Steven. *Postmodern Culture: An Introduction to Theories of the Contemporary.* Oxford: Blackwell, 1989.

Cooper, John, Ronald I. Nettles, and Mohamed Mahmoud. *Islam and Modernity: Muslim Intellectuals Respond.* London: St. Martin's Press, 1998.

Cotterell, Peter. *Mission and Meaninglessness: The Good News in a World of Suffering and Disorder.* London: S.P.C.K., 1990.

Crowell, John, and Stanford J. Searl, eds. *The Responsibility of Mind in a Civilization of Machines.* Amherst: The University of Massachusetts Press, 1979.

Cuddihy, John Murray. *No Offense: Civil Religion and Protestant Taste.* New York: The Seabury Press, 1978.

Cullmann, Oscar. *Christ and Time: The Primitive Christian Conception of Time and History.* Translated by Floyd V. Filson. Philadelphia: The Westminster Press, 1950.

Cushman, Philip. *Constructing the Self, Constructing America: A Cultural History of Psychotherapy.* Reading: Addison-Wesley, 1995.

Davies, W. D., and D. Daube, eds. *The Background of the New Testament and Its Eschatology.* Cambridge: Cambridge University Press, 1956.

Dawn, Marva J. *Powers, Weakness, and the Tabernacling of God.* Grand Rapids: William B. Eerdmans, 2001.

Delbanco, Andrew. *The Death of Satan: How Americans Have Lost the Sense of Evil.* New York: Farrar, Straus and Giroux, 1995.

DeLillo, Don. *White Noise.* New York: Penguin Books, 1985.

Desjardins, Michel R. *Sin in Valentinianism.* Atlanta: Scholars Press, 1990.

Dockery, David S., ed. *The Challenge of Postmodernism: An Evangelical Engagement.* Wheaton: BridgePoint Books, 1995.

Donfried, Karl P. *The Romans Debate.* Peabody: Hendrickson, 1977.

Donnelly, William J. *The Confetti Generation: How The New Communications Technology Is Fragmenting America.* New York: Henry Holt, 1986.

Dunn, James D. G., *The Theology of Paul the Apostle.* Grand Rapids: William B. Eerdmans, 1998.

Dunn, James D. G. and Alan M. Suggate. *The Justice of God: A Fresh Look at the Old Doctrine of Justification by Faith.* Grand Rapids: William B. Eerdmans, 1993.

Duthie, Charles S., ed. *Resurrection and Immortality: Aspects of Twentieth-Century Belief.* London: Samuel Bagster, 1979.

Eck, Diana L. *A New Religious America: How a "Christian Country" Has Now Become the World's Most Religiously Diverse Nation.* San Francisco: HarperSanFrancisco, 2001.

Edwards, James C. *The Plain Sense of Things: The Fate of Religion in an Age of Normal Nihilism.* University Park, Pa.: The Pennsylvania State University Press, 1997.

Elder, E. Rozanne, ed. *The Spirituality of Western Christendom.* Kalamazoo: Cistercian Publications, 1976.

Eliade, Mircea. *Myths, Dreams, and Mysteries.* Translated by Philip Mairet. New York: Harper and Row, 1960.

Ellingsen, Mark. *Blessed Are the Cynical: How Original Sin Can Make America a Better Place.* Grand Rapids: Brazos Press, 2003.

Emerson, Ralph Waldo. *Self-Reliance and Other Essays.* New York: Dover Publications, 1993.

Erickson, Millard. *Truth or Consequences: The Promise and Perils of Postmodernism.* Downers Grove: InterVarsity Press, 2001.

Ewen, Stuart. *All Consuming Images: The Politics of Style in Contemporary Culture.* New York: Basic Books, 1999.

Ewen, Stuart, and Elizabeth Ewen. *Channels of Desire: Mass Images and the Shaping of American Consciousness.* Minneapolis: University of Minnesota Press, 1992.

Fjellman, Stephen, J. *Vinyl Leaves: Walt Disney World in America.* San Francisco: Westview Press, 1992.

Ford, David F., ed. *The Modern Theologians: An Introduction to Christian Theology in the Twentieth Century.* Oxford: Blackwell, 1997.

Bibliography

Forsyth, P. T. *The Cruciality of the Cross.* Grand Rapids: William B. Eerdmans, 1909.

———. *The Person and Place of Jesus Christ.* London: The Pilgrim Press, 1909.

———. *The Work of Christ.* London: Independent Press, 1910.

Foucault, Michel. *The Archaeology of Knowledge and the Discourse on Language.* New York: Pantheon Books, 1972.

———. *The Order of Things: An Archeology of the Human Sciences.* New York: Vintage Books, 1973.

Foulkes, Francis. *The Acts of God: A Study of the Basis of Typology in the Old Testament.* London: Tyndale Press, 1958.

Frame, John M. *No Other God: A Response to Open Theism.* Phillipsburg: Presbyterian and Reformed, 2001.

Frankl, Viktor E. *Man's Search for Meaning: An Introduction to Logotherapy.* Translated by Ilse Lasch. New York: Simon and Schuster, 1959.

Frazee, Randy. *The Connecting Church: Beyond Small Groups to Authentic Community.* Grand Rapids: Zondervan, 2001.

Frum, David. *How We Got Here: The 70s: The Decade That Brought You Modern Life (for Better or for Worse).* New York: Basic Books, 2000.

Fuller, Robert C. *Spiritual, But Not Religious: Understanding Unchurched America.* New York: Oxford University Press, 2001.

Gaffin, Richard B. *The Centrality of Resurrection: A Study in Paul's Soteriology.* Grand Rapids: Baker, 1978.

Gallup, George, Jr., and Timothy Jones. *The Next American Spirituality.* Colorado Springs: Cook Communications, 2000.

Gasque, Ward W., and Ralph P. Martin. *Apostolic History and the Gospel.* Grand Rapids: William B. Eerdmans, 1970.

Gathercole, Simon J. *Where Is Boasting? Early Jewish Soteriology and Paul's Response in Romans 5–7.* Grand Rapids: William B. Eerdmans, 2002.

Gay, Craig M. *The Way of the (Modern) World: or, Why It's Tempting To Live As If God Doesn't Exist.* Grand Rapids: William B. Eerdmans, 1998.

Geddes, Jennifer L., ed. *Evil After Postmodernism: Histories, Narratives, Ethics.* New York: Routledge, 2001.

Gibbs, Eddie. *I Believe in Church Growth.* Grand Rapids: William B. Eerdmans, 1981.

Giddens, Anthony. *The Consequences of Modernity.* Stanford: Stanford University Press, 1990.

———. *Modernity and Self-Identity: Self and Society in the Late Modern Age.* Stanford: Stanford University Press, 1991.

———. *The Transformation of Intimacy: Sexuality, Love, Eroticism in Modern Societies.* Stanford: Stanford University Press, 1992.

Godfrey, W. Robert, and Jesse L. Boyd. *Through Christ's Word: A Festschrift for Dr.*

Philip E. Hughes. Phillipsburg: Presbyterian and Reformed Publishing Co., 1985.

Grant, Robert M. *Gnosticism and Early Christianity.* New York: Harper, 1959.

Green, Joel B., and Mark D. Baker. *Recovering the Scandal of the Cross: Atonement in New Testament & Contemporary Contexts.* Downers Grove: InterVarsity Press, 2000.

Grenz, Stanley J. *A Primer on Postmodernism.* Grand Rapids: William B. Eerdmans, 1996.

————. *Renewing the Center: Evangelical Theology in a Post-Theological Era.* Grand Rapids: Baker, 2000.

Grenz, Stanley J., and John R. Franke. *Beyond Foundationalism: Shaping Theology in a Postmodern Context.* Louisville: Westminster John Knox Press, 2001.

Groothuis, Douglas. *Truth Decay: Defending Christianity Against the Challenges of Postmodernism.* Downers Grove: InterVarsity Press, 2000.

Guder, Darrell L. *Be My Witnesses: The Church's Mission and Message.* Grand Rapids: William B. Eerdmans, 1985.

Guinness, Os. *Dining with the Devil: The Megachurch Movement Flirts with Modernity.* Grand Rapids: Baker Book House, 1993.

Guinness, Os, and John Seel. *No God but God: Breaking with the Idols of Our Age.* Chicago: Moody Press, 1992.

Gunton, Colin E. *Enlightenment and Alienation: An Essay Towards a Trinitarian Theology.* Grand Rapids: William B. Eerdmans, 1985.

————. *The One, the Three and the Many: God, Creation and the Culture of Modernity.* Cambridge: Cambridge University Press, 1993.

————. *Yesterday & Today: A Study of Continuities in Christology.* Grand Rapids: William B. Eerdmans, 1983.

Hackett, David G. *Religion and American Culture.* New York: Routledge, 1995.

Hahn, Todd, and David Verhaagen. *Helping a Generation Pursue Jesus: GenXers After God.* Grand Rapids: Baker Books, 1998.

Hardison, O. B., *Disappearing Through the Skylight: Culture and Technology in the Twentieth Century.* New York: Penguin Books, 1989.

Harris, Murray J. *Raised Immortal: Resurrection and Immortality in the New Testament.* Grand Rapids: William B. Eerdmans, 1983.

Harvey, David. *The Condition of Postmodernity: An Inquiry into the Origins of Cultural Change.* Oxford: Blackwell, 1992.

Hatch, Nathan O. *The Democratization of American Religion.* New Haven: Yale University Press, 1989.

Hawthorne, Gerald, ed. *Current Issues in Biblical and Patristic Interpretation.* Grand Rapids: William B. Eerdmans, 1975.

Hay, David, and Kate Hunt. *Understanding the Spirituality of People Who Don't Go to Church: A Report on the Findings of the Adults' Spirituality Project at the*

University of Nottingham. Nottingham: Center for the Study of Human Relations, 2000.

Helm, Paul. *The Providence of God: Contours of Christian Theology.* Downers Grove: InterVarsity Press, 1994.

Henry, Carl F. H. *God, Revelation and Authority.* 6 volumes. Waco: Word Publishing, 1976-1983.

Hibbs, Thomas S. *Shows About Nothing: Nihilism in Popular Culture from* The Exorcist *to* Seinfeld. Dallas: Spence Publishing Co., 1999.

Hill, Craig C. *In God's Time: The Bible and the Future.* Grand Rapids: William B. Eerdmans, 2002.

Himmelfarb, Gertrude. *On Looking into the Abyss: Untimely Thoughts on Culture and Society.* New York: Alfred A. Knopf, 1994.

Historical Statistics of the United States: Colonial Times to 1957, Prepared by the Bureau of the Census with the Cooperation of the Social Science Research Council. Washington: U.S. Department of Commerce, Bureau of the Census, 1960.

Hoekstra, Harvey T. *The World Council of Churches and the Demise of Evangelism.* Wheaton: Tyndale Publishers, 1979.

Hofstadter, Richard. *Anti-Intellectualism in American Life.* New York: Vintage Books, 1963.

Hoge, Dean R., Benton Johnson, and Donald A. Luidens. *Vanishing Boundaries: The Religion of Mainline Protestant Baby Boomers.* Louisville: Westminster/John Knox Press, 1994.

Hunsberger, George R., and Craig Van Gelder, eds. *The Church Between Gospel and Culture: The Emerging Mission in North America.* Grand Rapids: William B. Eerdmans, 1996.

Hunter, James Davison. *American Evangelicalism: Conservative Religion and the Quandary of Modernity.* New Brunswick: Rutgers University Press, 1983.

————. *Evangelicalism: The Coming Generation.* Chicago: University of Chicago Press, 1989.

Huntington, Samuel. *The Clash of Civilizations and the Remaking of World Order.* New York: Simon and Schuster, 1996.

Hybels, Bill. *Honest to God: Becoming an Authentic Christian.* Grand Rapids: Zondervan, 1990.

Hybels, Bill, and Lynne Hybels. *The Story and Vision of Willow Creek Community Church.* Grand Rapids: Zondervan, 1995.

Jameson, Fredric. *Postmodernism, or the Cultural Logic of Late Capitalism.* Durham: Duke University Press, 1991.

Jencks, Charles. *The Language of Post-Modern Architecture.* New York: Rizzoli, 1984.

Johnston, Arthur P. *The Battle for World Evangelism.* Wheaton: Tyndale Publishers, 1978.

Jonas, Hans. *The Gnostic Religion: The Message of the Alien God and the Beginnings of Christianity.* Boston: Beacon Press, 1958.

Jones, Cheslyn, Geoffrey Wainwright, and Edward Yarnold, eds. *The Study of Spirituality.* New York: Oxford University Press, 1986.

Jones, E. Michael. *Living Machines: Bauhaus Architecture as Sexual Ideology.* San Francisco: Ignatius Press, 1995.

Jones, Peter. *Spirit Wars: Pagan Revival in Christian America.* Mukilteo, Wash.: WinePress Publishing, 1998.

Kallestad, Walt. *Entertainment Evangelism.* Nashville: Abingdon Press, 1996.

Kaminer, Wendy. *I'm Dysfunctional, You're Dysfunctional: The Recovery Movement and Other Self-Help Fashions.* Reading: Addison-Wesley, 1992.

Keesmaat, Sylvia C. *Paul and His Story: (Re)Interpreting the Exodus Tradition.* Sheffield: Sheffield Academic Press, 1999.

Kelley, Dean M. *Why Conservative Churches Are Growing: A Study in Sociology of Religion.* New York: Harper and Row, 1972.

Kosmin, Barry A., and Seymour P. Lachman. *One Nation Under God: Religion in Contemporary American Society.* New York: Harmony Books, 1993.

Kyle, Richard. *The Religious Fringe: A History of Alternative Religions in America.* Downers Grove: InterVarsity Press, 1993.

Lacarriere, Jacques. *The Gnostics.* New York: Peter Owen, 1979.

Lakeland, Paul. *Postmodernity: Christian Identity in a Fragmented Age.* Minneapolis: Fortress Press, 1997.

Lasch, Christopher. *The Minimal Self: Psychic Survival in Troubled Times.* New York: W. W. Norton, 1984.

————. *Progress and Its Critics.* New York: W. W. Norton, 1991.

Lasch, Scott. *Sociology of Postmodernism.* New York: Routledge, 1994.

Lederer, William J., and Eugene Burdick. *The Ugly American.* New York: W. W. Norton, 1958.

Lewis, C. S. *The Abolition of Man: or, Reflections on Education with Special Reference to the Teaching of English in the Upper Forms of School.* New York: Macmillan, 1953.

Lippmann, Walter. *A Preface to Morals.* New York: Transaction Publishers, 1982.

Lippy, Charles H., and Peter W. Williams, eds. *Encyclopedia of the American Religious Experience: Studies of Traditions and Movements.* 3 volumes. New York: Charles Scribner's Sons, 1988.

Longenecker, Richard N., and Merrill C. Tenney, eds. *New Dimensions in New Testament Study.* Grand Rapids: Zondervan, 1974.

Lotz, David W., Donald W. Shriver, and John F. Wilson, eds. *Altered Landscapes:*

Christianity in America, 1935-1985. Grand Rapids: William B. Eerdmans, 1989.

Luckmann, Thomas. *The Invisible Religion: The Transformation of Symbols in Industrial Society*. New York: Macmillan Co., 1967.

Ludermann, Gerd. *Heretics: The Other Side of Early Christianity*. Trans. John Bowden. Louisville: Westminster/John Knox Press, 1995.

Lukacs, John. *Outgrowing Democracy: A History of the United States in the Twentieth Century*. New York: Doubleday, 1984.

———. *The End of the Twentieth Century and the End of the Modern Age*. New York: Ticker and Fields, 1993.

Lyon, David. *Jesus in Disneyland: Religion in Postmodern Times*. Cambridge: Polity Press, 2000.

———. *Postmodernity*. Minneapolis: University of Minnesota Press, 1999.

Lyotard, Jean-François. *The Postmodern Condition: A Report on Knowledge*. Translated by Geoff Bennington and Brian Massurri. Minneapolis: University of Minnesota Press, 1984.

Machen, J. Gresham. *Christianity and Liberalism*. New York: The Macmillan Co., 1923.

MacIntyre, Alisdair. *After Virtue: A Study in Moral Theory*. Notre Dame: University of Notre Dame Press, 1981.

Major, H. D. A. *English Modernism: Its Origin, Methods, Aims*. Cambridge: Cambridge University Press, 1927.

Malinine, Michel, Henri-Charles Puech, and Gilles Quispel, eds. *Evangelium Veritatis: Codex Jung*. Zurich: Rascher, 1956.

Mathews, Shailer. *The Faith of Modernism*. New York: The Macmillan Co., 1924.

McCracken, Grant. *Culture and Consumption: New Approaches to the Symbolic Character of Consumer Goods and Activities*. Bloomington: Indiana University Press, 1988.

McDermott, Gerald R. *Can Evangelicals Learn from World Religions? Jesus, Revelation and Religious Traditions*. Downers Grove: InterVarsity Press, 2001.

McGavran, Donald A. *Understanding Church Growth*. Grand Rapids: William B. Eerdmans, 1970.

McGrath, Alister E. *Christian Spirituality: An Introduction*. Oxford: Blackwell, 1999.

———. *A Scientific Theology*. 2 volumes. Grand Rapids: William B. Eerdmans, 2001.

———. *Glimpsing the Face of God: The Search for Meaning in the Universe*. Grand Rapids: William B. Eerdmans, 2002.

McGregor, R. K. *No Place for Sovereignty: What's Wrong with Freewill Theism*. Downers Grove: InterVarsity Press, 1996.

McLaren, Brian D. *A New Kind of Christian: A Tale of Two Friends on a Spiritual Journey.* San Francisco: Jossey-Bass, 2001.

Melton, J. Gordon. *A Directory of Religious Bodies in the United States.* New York: Garland Publishing, 1977.

———. *Encyclopedia of American Religions.* London: Gale Research, 1999.

Meynell, Hugo A. *Postmodernism and the New Enlightenment.* Washington: The Catholic University Press of America, 1999.

Meyrowitz, Joshua. *No Sense of Place: The Impact of Electronic Media on Social Behavior.* New York: Oxford University Press, 1985.

Middleton, J. Richard, and Brian J. Walsh. *Truth Is Stranger than It Used to Be.* Downers Grove: InterVarsity Press, 1995.

Milbank, John. *The Word Made Strange: Theology, Language, Culture.* Oxford: Blackwell, 1997.

Milbank, John, Catherine Pickstock, and Graham Ward. *Radical Orthodoxy: A New Theology.* London: Routledge, 1999.

Miller, Randall M., and Thomas D. Marzik, eds. *Immigrants and Religion in Urban America.* Philadelphia: Temple University Press, 1977.

Miller, Timothy, ed. *America's Alternative Religions.* New York: State University of New York Press, 1995.

Mittelberg, Mark. *Building a Contagious Church: Revolutionizing the Way We View and Do Evangelism.* Grand Rapids: Zondervan, 2000.

Molnar, Thomas. *The Pagan Temptation.* Grand Rapids: William B. Eerdmans, 1987.

Moo, Douglas J. *Encountering the Book of Romans: A Theological Survey.* Grand Rapids: Baker, 2002.

Moore, R. Laurence. *Religious Outsiders and the Making of Americans.* New York: Oxford University Press, 1986.

———. *Selling God: American Religion in the Marketplace of Culture.* New York: Oxford University Press, 1994.

Moore, Robert L., ed. *Sources of Vitality in American Church Life.* Chicago: Exploration Press, 1978.

Mouw, Richard J. *The Smell of Sawdust: What Evangelicals Can Learn from Their Fundamentalist Heritage.* Grand Rapids: William B. Eerdmans, 2000.

Muggeridge, Malcolm. *Christ and the Media.* Grand Rapids: William B. Eerdmans, 1977.

Murphy, Nancey. *Anglo-American Postmodernity: Philosophical Perspectives on Science, Religion, and Ethics.* Boulder: Westview Press, 1997.

Murren, Doug. *The Baby Boomerang: Catching Baby Boomers as They Return to Church.* Ventura: Regal Books, 1990.

Myers, David G. *The American Paradox: Spiritual Hunger in an Age of Plenty.* New Haven: Yale University Press, 2000.

Naugle, David K. *Worldview: The History of a Concept.* Grand Rapids: William B. Eerdmans, 2002.

Neuhaus, Richard John. *The Naked Public Square: Religion and Democracy in America.* Grand Rapids: William B. Eerdmans, 1988.

Newbigin, Lesslie. *Foolishness to the Greeks: The Gospel and Western Culture.* Grand Rapids: William B. Eerdmans, 1986.

Niebuhr, Reinhold. *Pious and Secular.* New York: Charles Scribner's Sons, 1958.

Nietzsche, Friedrich. *The Works of Friedrich Nietzsche.* New York: Tudor Publishing Co., 1931.

Noll, Mark A., and David F. Wells, eds. *Christian Faith and Practice in the Modern World.* Grand Rapids: William B. Eerdmans, 1988.

Nygren, Anders. *Agape and Eros.* Translated by Philip Watson. London: S.P.C.K., 1953.

Oden, Thomas C. *After Modernity . . . What? An Agenda for Theology.* Grand Rapids: Zondervan, 1990.

O'Donovan, Oliver. *Resurrection and Moral Order: An Outline for Evangelical Ethics.* Grand Rapids: William B. Eerdmans, 1986.

Olson, James S. *The Ethnic Dimension in American History.* New York: St. Martin's Press, 1994.

Orr, James. *The Christian View of God and the World.* Edinburgh: Andrew Elliot, 1897.

————. *Sin as a Problem Today.* London: Hodder and Stoughton, 1910.

Pagels, Elaine. *The Gnostic Gospels.* New York: Random House, 1979.

————. *The Johannine Gospel in Gnostic Exegesis: Heracleon's Commentary on John.* New York: Abingdon, 1973.

Paglia, Camille. *Sex, Art, and American Culture.* New York: Vintage Books, 1992.

Pannenberg, Wolfhart. *Christianity in a Secularized World.* Translated by John Bowden. New York: Crossroad, 1989.

————. *Jesus — God and Man.* Translated by Lewis L. Wilkins and Duane A. Priebe. Philadelphia: Westminster Press, 1977.

————. *Systematic Theology.* Translated by Geoffrey W. Bromiley. 3 volumes. Grand Rapids: William B. Eerdmans, 1993.

Patterson, James, and Peter Kim. *The Day America Told the Truth: What People Really Believe about What Really Matters.* New York: Prentice Hall, 1991.

Percy, Walker. *Lost in the Cosmos: The Last Self-Help Book.* New York: Farrar, Straus & Giroux, 1983.

Petre, Maude. *The Life of George Tyrrell, 1884-1909.* 2 vols. London: Edward Arnold, 1912.

Pinker, Steven. *The Blank Slate: The Modern Denial of Human Nature.* New York: Viking, 2002.

Pinnock, Clark H. *Most Moved Mover: A Theology of God's Openness.* Grand Rapids: Baker, 2001.

————, ed. *The Grace of God and the Will of Man.* Minneapolis: Bethany House, 1989.

————, ed. *The Openness of God: A Biblical Challenge to the Traditional Understanding of God.* Downers Grove: InterVarsity Press, 1994.

Pinnock, Clark H., and Robert Brow. *Unbounded Love: A Good News Theology for the 21st Century.* Downers Grove: InterVarsity Press, 1994.

Pinnock, Clark H,. and John B. Cobb, eds. *Searching for an Adequate God: A Dialogue Between Process and Free Will Theists.* Grand Rapids: William B. Eerdmans, 2000.

————. *Warrant and Proper Function.* New York: Oxford University Press, 1993.

Piper, John, Justin Taylor, and Paul Kjoss Helseth, eds. *Beyond the Bounds: Open Theism and the Undermining of Biblical Christianity.* Wheaton: Crossway Books, 2003.

Plantinga, Alvin. *Warrant: The Current Debate.* New York: Oxford University Press, 1993.

Plantinga, Alvin, and Nicholas Wolterstorff, eds. *Faith and Rationality: Reason and Belief in God.* Notre Dame: University of Notre Dame Press, 1983.

Polanyi, Michael. *Beyond Nihilism.* Cambridge: Cambridge University Press, 1960.

Polkinghorne, John. *The God of Hope and the End of the World.* New Haven: Yale University Press, 2002.

Porterfield, Amanda. *The Transformation of American Religion: The Story of a Late-Twentieth-Century Awakening.* New York: Oxford University Press, 2001.

Postman, Neil. *Amusing Ourselves to Death: Public Discourse in the Age of Show Business.* New York: Penguin Books, 1985.

————. *Technopoly: The Surrender of Culture to Technology.* New York: Vintage Books, 1993.

Pritchard, Gregory A. *Willow Creek Seeker Services: Evaluation of a New Way of Doing Church.* Grand Rapids: Baker Book House, 1996.

Ramm, Bernard. *The Pattern of Authority.* Grand Rapids: William B. Eerdmans, 1957.

Reardon, Bernard G. *Liberal Protestantism.* London: Adam and Charles Black, 1968.

Rainer, Thom S. *Effective Evangelistic Churches: Successful Churches Reveal What Works and What Does Not.* Nashville: Broadman and Holman, 1996.

————. *High Expectations: The Remarkable Secret for Keeping People in Your Church.* Nashville: Broadman and Holman, 1999.

Reeves, Thomas C. *The Empty Church: The Suicide of Liberal Christianity.* New York: The Free Press, 1996.

Bibliography

Rice, John Steadman. *A Disease of One's Own: Psychotherapy, Addiction, and the Emergence of Co-Dependency.* New Brunswick: Transaction Publishers, 1996.

Richardson, E. Allen. *East Comes to West: Asian Religions and Cultures in North America.* New York: The Pilgrim Press, 1988.

———. *Strangers in This Land: Pluralism and the Response to Diversity in the United States.* New York: Pilgrim Press, 1988.

Ridderbos, Herman. *The Coming of the Kingdom.* Trans. H. de Jongste. Philadelphia: The Presbyterian and Reformed Publishing Co., 1962.

———. *Paul: An Outline of His Theology.* Trans. John Richard de Witt. Grand Rapids: William B. Eerdmans, 1975.

———. *Paul and Jesus: Origin and General Character of Paul's Preaching of Christ.* Trans. David H. Freeman. Grand Rapids: Baker, 1958.

Rief, Philip. *The Triumph of the Therapeutic: Uses of Faith After Freud.* New York: Harper and Row, 1968.

Robinson, James M., ed. *The Nag Hammadi Library.* Trans. members of the Coptic Gnostic Library Project of the Institute for Antiquity and Christianity. New York: Harper and Row, 1977.

Roof, Wade Clark. *A Generation of Seekers: The Spiritual Journeys of the Baby Boom Generation.* San Francisco: Harper, 1993.

———. *Spiritual Market Place: Baby Boomers and the Remaking of American Religion.* Princeton: Princeton University Press, 1998.

Rorty, Richard. *Consequences of Pragmatism.* Minneapolis: University of Minnesota Press, 1982.

———. *Objectivity, Relativism, and Truth.* Cambridge: Cambridge University Press, 1991.

Russell, Bertrand. *The Basic Writings of Bertrand Russell, 1903-1959.* Edited by Robert E. Egner and Lester E. Denonn. London: George Allen and Unwin, 1962.

———. *A History of Western Philosophy.* New York: Simon and Schuster, 1945.

Sanders, John. *The God Who Risks: A Theology of Providence.* Downers Grove: InterVarsity Press, 1998.

Sargeant, Kimon Howard. *Seeker Churches: Promoting Traditional Religion in Nontraditional Ways.* New Brunswick: Rutgers University Press, 2000.

Saul, John Ralston. *The Unconscious Civilization.* New York: Free Press, 1997.

Schaller, Lyle E. *Discontinuity and Hope: Radical Change and the Path to the Future.* Nashville: Abingdon Press, 1999.

Schama, Simon. *The Embarrassment of Riches: An Interpretation of Dutch Culture in the Golden Age.* New York: Alfred A. Knopf, 1987.

Schleiermacher, Friedrich. *On Religion: Speeches to Its Cultured Despisers.* Trans. Richard Crouter. Cambridge: Cambridge University Press, 1988.

Schroeder, W. Widick, et al. *Suburban Religion: Churches and Synagogues in the American Experience.* Chicago: Center for the Scientific Study of Religion, 1974.

Schwarz, Christian. *Natural Church Development: A Guide to Eight Essential Qualities of Healthy Churches.* St. Charles: ChurchSmart Resources, 1996.

Seifrid, Mark A. *Justification by Faith: The Origin & Development of a Central Pauline Theme.* New York: E. J. Brill, 1992.

Shenk, Wilbert R. *Exploring Church Growth.* Grand Rapids: William B. Eerdmans, 1983.

Shepherd, Deborah, and Khoren Arisian. *Humanism and Postmodernism: Essays from the Humanist Institute.* New York: The Humanist Institute, 1994.

Shorris, Earl. *New American Blues: A Journey Through Poverty to Democracy.* New York: W. W. Norton, 1997.

Smith, Christian, et al. *American Evangelicalism: Embattled and Thriving.* Chicago: University of Chicago Press, 1998.

Stark, Rodney, and Roger Finke. *Acts of Faith: Explaining the Human Side of Religion.* Berkeley: University of California Press, 2000.

————. *The Churching of America: Winners and Losers in Our Religious Economy.* New Brunswick: Rutgers University Press, 1992.

Statistical Abstract of the United States: Prepared by the Bureau of the Census with the Cooperation of the Social Research Council. Washington: U.S. Department of Commerce, Bureau of the Census, 1965.

Statistical Abstract of the United States: Prepared by the Bureau of the Census with the Cooperation of the Social Research Council. Washington: U.S. Department of Commerce, Bureau of the Census, 1999.

Stendahl, Krister, ed. *Immortality and Resurrection: Death in the Western World: Two Conflicting Currents of Thought.* New York: Macmillan, 1979.

Stephens, W. P., ed. *The Bible, the Reformation and the Church.* Sheffield: Sheffield Academic Press, 1995.

Stuhlmacher, Peter. *Revisiting Paul's Doctrine of Justification: A Challenge to the New Perspective.* Downers Grove: InterVarsity Press, 2001.

Susman, Warren I. *Culture as History: The Transformation of American Society in the Twentieth Century.* New York: Pantheon Books, 1984.

Sweet, Leonard. *Post-Modern Pilgrims: First-Century Passion for the 21st Century World.* Nashville: Broadman and Holman, 2000.

Swete, H. B. *The Akhim Fragment of the Apocryphal Gospel of St. Peter.* London: Macmillan, 1893.

Sykes, Charles. *A Nation of Victims: The Decay of the American Character.* New York: St. Martin's Press, 1992.

Tarnas, Richard. *The Passion of the Western Mind: Understanding the Ideas That Have Shaped Our World View.* New York: Harmony Books, 1991.

Bibliography

Taylor, Barbara Brown. *Speaking of Sin: The Lost Language of Salvation.* Cambridge: Cowley Publications, 2000.

Taylor, Eugene. *Shadow Culture: Psychology and Spirituality in America.* Washington: Counterpoint, 1999.

Thielicke, Helmut. *Christ and the Meaning of Life: A Book of Sermons and Meditations.* Trans. and ed. John W. Doberstein. New York: Harper and Brothers, 1962.

————. *Nihilism: Its Origin and Nature — with a Christian Answer.* Trans. John W. Doberstein. New York: Schocken Books, 1969.

Thielman, Frank. *Paul and the Law: A Contextual Approach.* Downers Grove: InterVarsity Press, 1994.

Thornhill, John. *Modernity: Christianity's Estranged Child Reconstructed.* Grand Rapids: William B. Eerdmans, 2000.

Toynbee, Arnold. *A Study of History.* 12 vols. New York: Oxford University Press, 1934-61.

Turner, James. *Without God, Without Creed: The Origins of Unbelief in America.* Baltimore: The Johns Hopkins University Press, 1985.

Tweed, Thomas A., and Stephen Prothero, eds. *Asian Religions in America: A Documentary History.* New York: Oxford University Press, 1999.

Van Gelder, Craig, ed. *Confident Witness — Changing World: Rediscovering the Gospel in North America.* Grand Rapids: William B. Eerdmans, 1999.

Vanhoozer, Kevin J. *First Theology: God, Scripture & Hermeneutics.* Downers Grove: InterVarsity Press, 2002.

————. *Is There a Meaning in This Text? The Bible, the Reader, and the Morality of Literary Knowledge.* Grand Rapids: Zondervan, 1998.

Ware, Bruce A. *God's Lesser Glory: The Diminished God of Open Theism.* Wheaton: Crossway Books, 2000.

Wark, McKenzie. *Virtual Geography: Living with Global Media Events.* Bloomington: Indiana University Press, 1994.

Warner, Stephen R., and Judith G. Wittner, eds. *Gatherings in Diaspora: Religious Communities and the New Immigration.* Philadelphia: Temple University Press, 1998.

Warren, Rick. *The Purpose-Driven Church: Growth Without Compromising Your Message & Mission.* Grand Rapids: Zondervan, 1995.

Webber, Robert E. *The Younger Evangelicals: Facing the Challenges of the New World.* Grand Rapids: Baker, 2002.

Weber, Max. *The Protestant Ethic and the Spirit of Capitalism.* Trans. Talcott Parsons. London: George Allen and Unwin, 1976.

————. *The Sociology of Religion.* Trans. Ephraim Fischoff. Boston: Beacon Press, 1963.

Webster, Douglas. *Selling Jesus: What's Wrong with Marketing the Church.* Downers Grove: InterVarsity Press, 1992.

Wells, David F. *God in the Wasteland: The Reality of Truth in a World of Fading Dreams.* Grand Rapids: William B. Eerdmans, 1994.

———. *Losing Our Virtue: Why the Church Must Recover Its Moral Vision.* Grand Rapids: William B. Eerdmans, 1998.

———. *No Place for Truth; or, Whatever Happened to Evangelical Theology?* Grand Rapids: William B. Eerdmans, 1993.

———. *The Person of Christ: A Biblical and Historical Analysis of the Incarnation.* Westchester: Crossway Books, 1984.

Wilken, Robert L. *The Christians as the Romans Saw Them.* New Haven: Yale University Press, 1984.

Williams, C. J. F. *What Is Truth?* Cambridge: Cambridge University Press, 1976.

Wilson. A. N. *God's Funeral.* New York: W. W. Norton, 1999.

Wilson, James Q. *The Moral Sense.* New York: Free Press, 1993.

Wright, N. T. *Jesus and the Victory of God.* Minneapolis: Fortress Press, 1996.

———. *The New Testament and the People of God.* Minneapolis: Fortress Press, 1992.

———. *What Saint Paul Really Said: Was Paul of Tarsus the Real Founder of Christianity?* Grand Rapids: William B. Eerdmans, 1997.

Wuthnow, Robert. *After Heaven: Spirituality in America Since the 1950s.* Berkeley: University of California Press, 1998.

———. *The Crisis in the Churches: Spiritual Malaise, Fiscal Woe.* New York: Oxford University Press, 1997.

———. *Experimentation in American Religion: The New Mysticisms and Their Implications for the Churches.* Berkeley: University of California Press, 1978.

———. *Rediscovering the Sacred: Perspectives on Religion in Contemporary Society.* Grand Rapids: William B. Eerdmans, 1992.

———. *The Restructuring of American Religion: Society and Faith Since World War II.* Princeton: Princeton University Press, 1988.

———. *Sharing the Journey: Support Groups and America's New Quest for Community.* New York: The Free Press, 1994.

Yong, Amos. *Beyond the Impasse: Toward a Pneumatological Theology of Religions.* Grand Rapids: Baker Books, 2003.

Index

❦

Adams, John, 2
Anderson, Leith, 269, 304
Aquinas, Thomas, 229
Arminianism, 242-43n., 244-48
Arnold, Matthew, 17n.
Augustine, 229

Baillie, D. M., 9
Baker, Mark, 218, 219n.
Barna, George, 126, 128, 165, 166, 267,
    270n., 276, 301-2, 304-5n., 314
Barrett, C. K., 212
Barth, Karl, 7, 160, 171, 174, 200-201, 204,
    231, 260
Bauckham, Richard, 252, 254, 259
Bauerschmidt, Frederick, 67
Bauman, Zygmunt, 35, 44, 132
Baumeister, Roy, 51
Baumer, Franklin L., 25
Beale, G. K., 209, 230, 254
Beckett, Samuel, 179, 182-83
Bellah, Robert, 125n., 150, 153, 166
Berger, Peter L., 20n., 63, 89-90, 94-5n.,
    117, 148, 238, 240
Bloom, Allan, 85

Bloom, Harold, 134, 144, 145, 155
Bonhoeffer, Dietrich, 263
Boorstin, Daniel, 178
Brunner, Emil, 225
Bultmann, Rudolf, 136, 171, 208n., 210n.,
    213
Bunyan, John, 120-23
Butler, Jon, 101

Campbell, Colin, 40-41
Camus, Albert, 161, 177-78, 181-82
Carson, D. A., 86, 204n.
Cavanaugh, William, 56
Christo, 71
Christology: preexistence of Christ,
    128n., 215, 216, 217, 260; creator, 7, 256-
    57, 259; incarnation, 7, 143n., 170, 208,
    215, 217; above/below contrast, 128;
    this age/age to come, 206-9, 210, 212-
    16, 222, 229, 230, 257, 230, 261; baptism,
    143; kingdom of God, 209-11, 212-15,
    227, 261; divinity, 216-17; conquest on
    the Cross, 143, 172-73, 198, 207, 208,
    209, 211, 218, 222-23, 229, 230, 252, 257,
    259, 282, 310, 316; justification, 162,

335

206, 211, 218-22, 223-29; resurrection
and exaltation, 196-97, 282, 198, 210,
231; divine sovereignty, 254-55, 259,
261; authority, 255, 257; church, 258-
60; return, 207; judgment, 198, 207;
apologetics, 204n.
Church, 4, 5, 6, 8-9, 11, 78, 88, 90, 124, 137-
38, 143-44, 151, 152, 156, 158, 159, 162,
163, 164, 165, 168, 169, 175, 193, 208, 210,
232, 244, 251, 257, 258-60, 261, 262, 263-
310, 311, 312, 313, 314, 315-16
Connor, Steven, 71, 79
Contextualization, 6-8, 263-309
Coupland, Douglas, 13, 69, 89
Cuddihy, John Murray, 102n.
Cullmann, Oscar, 197n., 208
Culture, 4, 6, 7, 11, 17-24, 36, 42, 47, 56, 60,
104, 128, 131n., 148, 150, 163, 165, 234,
235, 242, 267, 268, 275, 293, 301, 308,
309, 313
Cupitt, Don, 73
Cushman, Philip, 50

Darwin, Charles, 240
Dawn, Marva J., 259
Delbanco, Andrew, 165, 240, 241, 242
DeLillo, Don, 45-46
Derrida, Jacques, 65, 72, 73, 75, 87
Descartes, René, 80, 89
Dillon, E. J., 196
Disney, Walt, 43, 271, 272-73
Donnelly, William, 234, 235
Dunn, James D. G., 210, 221, 255

Eck, Diana, 97, 100
Edwards, James C., 187
Edwards, Jonathan, 101, 307
Eliade, Mircea, 128
Ellul, Jacques, 36
Emerson, Ralph Waldo, 154
Enlightenment, 5, 16-17, 24, 25-59, 61, 62,
63, 64, 65, 67, 68, 70, 72, 73, 74, 78, 79,
80, 81, 82, 84, 86, 87, 88, 127, 128, 138,

146, 157, 165, 178, 203, 204, 229, 248, 278,
280, 314, 315
Ethnic diversity, 4, 5, 21-22, 45, 92-93, 95,
96-107, 293-96
Evangelicalism, 4, 11, 163-64, 262, 263-
309, 313, 315
Evil, 1-4, 6, 15, 48, 52, 68, 117-18, 119, 128,
142, 166, 167, 203, 206, 207, 209, 214,
218, 222, 261
Ewen, Stuart and Elizabeth, 18, 44, 46, 76

Finke, Roger, 298, 301
Finney, Charles, 101
Fish, Stanley, 65
Fjellman, Stephen J., 272
Forsyth, P. T., 226, 260
Foucault, Michel, 65, 66, 73, 75, 87
Foulkes, Francis, 172
Foundationalism, 79-84, 87
Franke, John, 83n.
Frankl, Viktor, 191-92
Freud, Sigmund, 83
Frum, David, 40-41, 52
Fuller, Robert C., 110-11

Gay, Craig, 24n., 37, 38, 56
Giddens, Anthony, 80, 238
Gilkey, Langdon, 29
Gnosticism, 134-45, 146, 159, 251
Grant, Robert M., 141
Green, Joel, 218, 219n.
Greene, Mark, 134
Grenz, Stanley, 73, 126n., 228-29n.
Groothuis, Douglas, 84-85, 169n.
Guinness, Os, 303, 307
Gunton, Colin E., 236, 237

Hagner, Donald A., 220
Hardison, O. B., 71
Harvey, David, 42, 66-67
Heidegger, Martin, 179, 190
Henry, Carl F. H., 171n.
Herberg, Will, 99-100, 102

Hibbs, Thomas S., 185, 188
Himmelfarb, Gertrude, 86
Hume, David, 33
Hunter, Archibald M., 216
Hunter, James Davison, 156n.

Iannaccone, Laurence, 300
Idolatry, 47, 130-36, 140-45, 149-52, 164-71, 303
Immigration, 91-107, 311, 312
Individualism, 11, 12, 42, 28n., 42, 68, 74, 95-96, 103, 115-16, 129-31, 132, 138-39, 141-42, 145, 149-55, 166, 168, 170, 175, 198n., 202, 208, 215, 238, 241, 248
Ionesco, Eugene, 179
Irenaeus, 136n., 142, 167
Islam, 4, 5, 28n.

Jameson, Frederick, 43
Jencks, Charles, 53-54

Jonas, Hans, 141
Jones, Michael, 54
Jones, Peter, 129

Kant, Immanuel, 29, 33, 53, 85
Kelley, Dean, 299-300
Kundera, Milan, 183-84
Kyle, Richard, 129

Lacarriere, Jacques, 140
Ladd, George Eldon, 213, 214
Lakeland, Paul, 72
Lasch, Christopher, 41, 57, 238
Lasch, Scott, 78
Lazarus, Emma, 91
Lewis, C. S., 16, 48
Lippmann, Walter, 40, 179
Luckman, Thomas, 125-26n.
Lukacs, John, 94, 97
Luther, Martin, 8-9, 204, 227, 294n., 307
Lyon, David, 31, 47, 61, 62
Lyotard, Jean-François, 61, 72, 79

Machen, Gresham, 280
MacIntyre, Alasdair, 88
Major, H. D. A., 280
Marketing, 4, 268-77, 277-92
Marx, Karl, 15, 24
Mathews, Shailer, 278, 279
McGavran, Donald, 288-89
McLennan, Scotty, 111
Melton, J. Gordon, 97, 108
Milbank, John, 73, 180
Milligan, William, 257
Modernity, 11, 29, 32, 41, 44, 45, 53, 79, 80n., 83, 119, 147, 156n., 179, 184, 193, 236, 238, 239, 241, 247, 250, 300
Modernization, 16, 27, 28n, 31, 32, 39-48, 69, 76-79, 89, 103, 117, 148, 149, 152, 194, 195, 237, 238, 241, 250
Molnar, Thomas, 139
Moore, Laurence R., 283-84
Moral absolutes, 3-4, 39, 40, 48, 49-50, 52, 118-19, 124, 154-55, 181, 193, 194, 195, 199, 203, 224, 233, 237, 304-5n., 312
Moral relativism, 4, 75, 81-82, 85, 132-33, 169, 175, 190-91, 199, 238, 249, 304-5n.
Murphy, Nancey, 72, 73
Murren, Doug, 289
Muslims, 4, 5

Nash, Laura, 111
Naugle, David, 74
Neuhaus, Richard John, 27
Newbigin, Lesslie, 34
Niebuhr, H. Richard, 17, 18, 19, 164
Niebuhr, Reinhold, 41
Nietzsche, Friedrich, 133, 181, 190
Nihilism, 67, 88-90, 177-99, 200n., 201, 203, 230-31, 233-38, 250, 303-4
Noel, Caroline, 233
Noll, Mark, 101, 102
Nygren, Anders, 135-36, 158, 159

Oden, Thomas, 63
Olson, James S., 99

Orr, James, 262
Ostling, Richard, 272

Packer, J. I., 224, 244, 303
Pagels, Elaine, 141, 142, 143, 144
Paglia, Camille, 135
Pannenberg, Wolfhart, 171, 207n.
Pascal, Blaise, 177
Peck, M. Scott, 115
Percy, Walker, 51, 147
Pinnock, Clark, 242-51
Plantinga, Alvin, 82-83
Plantinga, Cornelius, 308
Plato, 139
Polkinghorne, John, 211
Porterfield, Amanda, 115
Postman, Neil, 20-21n., 273
Postmodernity: description of
    postmodernity, 60-61, 67-73, 240-42,
    268-77; postmodernity and modernity,
    12, 26, 59, 88-90; postmodernity and
    the Enlightenment, 26, 59, 62-67, 79-
    83, 228-29, 315; postmodernity and
    consumerism, 76-79, 84-88; post-
    modern self, 170, 175, 202, 234-35, 248-
    52; postmodern spirituality, 5, 122, 123,
    126, 130n., 145-55, 157, 158, 162, 163;
    postmodernity and meaninglessness,
    5, 22, 177, 184, 193-94, 203-4; post-
    modern relativism, 5, 158n, 168, 169,
    233, 234-35, 303, 311, 312, 314-15;
    postmodernity and Evil, 167, 317;
    postmodern architecture, 53-54;
Powers, Eileen, 21

Ramm, Bernard, 174
Reed, Eric, 290
Reformation, 6, 120, 151, 152, 164, 174, 218,
    223, 243n., 247
Religion, 5, 11, 19, 34, 77, 89, 90, 93, 97, 98,
    99-115, 119, 126, 127, 128, 129, 144, 150,
    152, 158n., 160n., 161, 163, 165, 166n., 170,
    235, 286, 301

Rice, John Steadman, 57
Ridderbos, Herman, 209, 212, 255, 260
Rief, Philip, 51, 57
Riesman, David, 153
Roof, Wade Clark, 150-51
Rorty, Richard, 65, 81, 82
Rosen, Stanley, 31-32
Roszak, Theodore, 60
Russell, Bertrand, 180, 237

Sanders, John, 245n., 246
Sargeant, Kimon, 266n., 281, 305, 306
Sartre, Jean-Paul, 177-78, 190
Saul, John, 25
Schaller, Lyle, 23n, 274-75
Schama, Simon, 39
Schleiermacher, Friedrich, 279-80
Schlesinger, Arthur M., 92
Schroeder, W. Widdick, 100
Schuller, Robert, 166
Scotus, Duns, 229
Smith, Christian, 156n.
Spengler, Oswald, 18
Spirituality, 5, 12, 89, 90, 95-96, 109-24,
    125-76, 203, 238, 283, 299, 301, 311, 312,
    313
Spurgeon, Charles, 307
Stark, Rodney, 298, 301
Stewart, James, 310, 315
Stone, Samuel J., 262
Stuhlmacher, Peter, 225
Sunday, Billy, 273
Susman, Warren, 50
Sykes, Charles, 57

Tarnas, Richard, 29, 61, 81, 86
Taylor, Barbara Brown, 165
Taylor, Eugene, 110
Taylor, Mark C., 73
Tertullian, 142, 162
Thielicke, Helmut, 186
Thornhill, John, 63
Tindall, Matthew, 33

Toland, John, 33
Toplady, Augustus, 205
Toynbee, Arnold, 138n.
Tyrrell, George, 278

Vanhoozer, Kevin, 87, 174
Vos, Geerhardus, 210

Wall, James, 307
Walsh, Neale Donald, 116
Webber, Robert, 266
Weber, Max, 34-35, 38

Webster, Douglas D., 289
Wesley, John, 151, 157, 307
Whitefield, George, 151
Willow Creek Community Church, 265-
    66, 286, 296n., 297n.
Word of God, 7, 8, 9, 122, 128, 160, 161, 174,
    175, 176, 302, 304
Wright, G. Ernest, 169, 170, 207, 213, 221,
    222n.
Wuthnow, Robert, 36, 55, 112, 117, 119-20,
    130n., 131, 237, 291